FINDERS, KEEPERS

NICHOLAS ROYLE is the author of six short story collections – *Mortality*, *Ornithology*, *The Dummy and Other Uncanny Stories*, *London Gothic*, *Manchester Uncanny* and *Paris Fantastique* – and seven novels, most recently *First Novel*. He has edited more than two dozen anthologies and is series editor of *Best British Short Stories* for Salt, who also published his books-about-books, *White Spines: Confessions of a Book Collector* and *Shadow Lines: Searching For the Book Beyond the Shelf*. In 2009 he founded Nightjar Press, which continues to publish original short stories in the form of limited-edition chapbooks. He lives in Manchester and London.

IN THE SAME SERIES

White Spines: Confessions of a Book Collector
Shadow Lines: Searching For the Book Beyond the Shelf

FINDERS, KEEPERS

The Secret Life of Second-hand Books

NICHOLAS ROYLE

CROMER

PUBLISHED BY SALT PUBLISHING 2026

2 4 6 8 10 9 7 5 3 1

Copyright © Nicholas Royle 2026

Nicholas Royle has asserted his right under the Copyright, Designs and Patents Act 1988 to be identified as the author of this work.

This book is sold subject to the condition that it shall not, by way of trade or otherwise, be lent, resold, hired out, or otherwise circulated without the publisher's prior consent in any form of binding or cover other than that in which it is published and without a similar condition including this condition being imposed on the subsequent publisher.

First published in Great Britain in 2026 by
Salt Publishing Ltd
12 Norwich Road, Cromer, Norfolk NR27 0AX United Kingdom

GPSR representative
Matt Parsons matt.parsons@upi2mbooks.hr
UPI-2M PLUS d.o.o., Medulićeva 20, 10000 Zagreb, Croatia

www.saltpublishing.com

Salt Publishing Limited Reg. No. 5293401

A CIP catalogue record for this book is available from the British Library

ISBN 978 1 78463 341 7 (Paperback edition)
ISBN 978 1 78463 342 4 (Electronic edition)

Typeset in Granjon by Salt Publishing

Printed and bound in Great Britain by Clays Ltd, Elcograf S.p.A

For my mum

'My D. My darling, my love. And neither the angels in Heaven above/Nor the demons down under the sea . . . Valentine 2024. I love you with a love that's more than love, yours A.' Card found inside Ian McEwan's *On Chesil Beach* bought from Oxfam Books & Music Islington, London N1, 30 September 2024. A is quoting and paraphrasing Edgar Allan Poe. I believe A and D got married in 2025 and that this card was given away in error. If they see this and get in touch, I would be very happy to return it to them.

'Dearest Naughty, Please come as quick as you can – I can't wait. (I can actually wait but I'd prefer not to . . .) L. Mon 29 Aug 94.' Card found inside Julian Barnes's *The Porcupine* bought from Harington Charity Shop, Hornsey High Street, London N8, 12 September 2025. There's more to L's message, but this is a family show.

Contents

Introduction   1

Free books   14
Tickets, please! – outward   29
Library fines   46
London something   62
Tickets, please! – return   85
Side hustle   103
Doubles   117
Found maps   149
Christmas books   179

Acknowledgements   199

Introduction

Previously, in *Shadow Lines*, I wrote about returning a copy of Alan Sillitoe's *The Loneliness of the Long-Distance Runner* that I had found in a book sale at the University of Manchester students union to a house on Lees Road in Bramhall, Cheshire, where it used to live. The book had contained what I call an inclusion and most people probably call an insert. I like 'inclusion' because it's the word used to describe a foreign body caught in amber; 'insert', to me, perhaps because I am literal minded, suggests something very specific, something chosen and deliberately inserted, something that a bookseller, for example, wishes to place in the hands of a book's new owner, like a bookmark advertising their business, or, in the case of a newspaper or magazine, a leaflet that the publishers have been paid to insert and it's unlikely the reader will want to keep.

Incidentally, I would like to know who inserts all those Daunt Books bookmarks into second-hand books in charity shops. Does Daunt Books have some kind of arrangement with Oxfam? Two out of every ten 'shadow lines' – the term I use to describe a line on the top edge of the text block that reveals the presence within of an inclusion – are created by Daunt Books bookmarks. I like Daunt Books, but there are few things more disappointing than to flick through a second-hand book you can see contains a mysterious lost item, only to find it's a branded bookmark.

The Loneliness of the Long-Distance Runner contained, instead, a postcard from Kendals department store dated 28 December 1966 and addressed to Mr and Mrs N Kessel at an address on Lees Road. In addition, inside the front cover, had been written the name Valerie Kessel and the date, 1962. I delivered the Sillitoe book by Royle Mail to the address on Lees Road with a note explaining what I was up to, but received no response, which was not unusual. I always hope I'll hear back, but more often than not I do not.

Royle Mail involves my delivering a book – it's usually a book, or a Nightjar Press order – by hand, on foot as far as practically possible and using public transport where necessary. The car is a last resort and will be used only if there are other reasons for undertaking the journey by motor vehicle.

In January 2024, with *Shadow Lines* at the printers, I received a lovely hand-written letter from Joanne, writing, she said, on behalf of her boyfriend Simon, who lived at the address on Lees Road. He had saved the book and letter and given them to her, she wrote, because he recognised that it was more her thing than his. *The Loneliness of the Long-Distance Runner* is one of Joanne's dad's favourite films. (The book was a film tie-in edition, a Great Pan, with Tom Courtenay on the cover.) Joanne said that she was going to read it as soon as she had finished her current Jack Reacher novel. Then she would return it to Simon, who would keep it in the house where it had once lived. Also, she went on, 4 January, the date of the sale at Kendals, and the date at the top of the letter I had written to accompany the book, was the anniversary of her and Simon's first date. Joanne was kind enough to say that she thought it was 'a beautiful thing to return an old book to its former residence'.

I think it's a beautiful thing to go to the trouble to write back to the strange man who sticks a book through your door and asks you to look after it.

I wrote back to Joanne to thank her and to say that I would have to write a third book in the series so that I could publicly acknowledge receipt of her kind letter.

While I've just about managed to wean myself off buying multiple copies of the King Penguin edition of DM Thomas's novel *The White Hotel*, which I was doing for a chapter in *White Spines*, or copies of Paul Auster's *The New York Trilogy* containing distinguishing marks or inclusions for a project documented in *Shadow Lines*, I can't seem to stop myself buying books that contain old addresses and returning them to those addresses. In March 2024, in Oxfam Bookshop Chorlton, I bought George Orwell's *A Clergyman's Daughter* (Penguin) with an address on the flyleaf in Windsor Road, Levenshulme. Also a name: Ginia Bazley. My intention was to return it to Windsor Road at some point, but before I got around to it, in the intervening eighteen months or so, I found a number of other books with old addresses in, including a hardback edition of *Bring on the Girls* (Herbert Jenkins) by PG Wodehouse and Guy Bolton, with a lovely bit of blind embossing on the flyleaf giving the name of the book's former owner, Malcolm Parkes, and an address in Lime Grove in Denton. Embossing – forgive me if you know this – is the result of a process used to create raised 'print' on the page; 'blind' means no ink is used. I found *Bring on the Girls* in the delightful Towpath Bookshop, which I came across in Uppermill on a walk from Oldham to Diggle. Proprietor Martin

Byrom showed me the book after I had failed to find anything on his shelves that I wanted to buy. There was no hard sell, but he was glad to make a sale and was interested in my reason for buying the book. We both knew that if I did send or deliver it to Denton, I would likely have no knowledge of the book's eventual fate. A few days later, I walked from Didsbury to Denton and dropped the book, with a note, through the door of the two-up, two-down terraced house in which it once resided.

Throughout *this* book, there will be place names – Chorlton, Levenshulme, Denton – that you might not be familiar with if you haven't spent time in Manchester. Equivalent place names in London and elsewhere. I've been fretting a bit over whether I need to add 'in south Manchester' or 'in east London', but I've decided not to, for the most part. If you could try not to worry about that, I'll try to relax as well.

When I delivered Ginia Bazley's copy of Orwell's *A Clergyman's Daughter* to a Victorian semi in Windsor Road, Levenshulme, it was, similarly, more in hope than expectation, so I was very happy, a fortnight or so later, to receive an email from Andy Gardiner thanking me for the book. 'We've lived here since 2012 and the book definitely isn't one of ours,' he wrote, adding that he had emailed the previous owner of the house to ask if it had been hers. Researching the history of the house and its former residents had already been on his to-do list, he said. 'When we bought it, we were told that the house used to be a school. Indeed, the two main bedrooms on the first floor had been previously knocked through. An odd thing to do, unless they used that space as the classroom.'

I'm interested in, as Andy put it for me in his email, '[tracking] the journeys of the books, their previous owners and associated stories', in uncovering the secret lives of second-hand books, clues to which can often be found within their pages in the form of, say, old train tickets, or photocopied maps, artefacts themselves in the process of passing into history. The copy of Nicholson Baker's *Room Temperature* that I found in Sue Ryder in Didsbury that contained a seat reservation from London to Newcastle probably did make that very journey. Would recreating it allow me to attain some degree of ghostly proximity to the book's previous reader, about whom, otherwise, I know absolutely nothing? And if proximity is what I seek – perhaps partly inspired as a reaction against the isolation forced on us by the experience of the pandemic – why do I feel uncomfortable when someone gets too close in a bookshop, breathing down the back of my neck as they peer over my shoulder? Will reading Derren Brown's *Tricks of the Mind* while walking around Bolton help me feel any closer to the mystery reader who used his or her sheet of 'Local information for jurors at the Crown Court at Bolton' (including map) as a bookmark? Or would it just be an excuse to visit Bolton? Or to read Derren Brown?

If I start sending books in which I find business cards to the individuals named on the cards, what will happen?

If I take library books that look as if they might have become lost back to the libraries to which they used to belong, will they be welcomed back into the fold, or will librarians hand them back to me with withering looks?

There are as many ways to collect books as there are books to collect.

I didn't start collecting books that have the same titles as other books until I realised I had, if you see what I mean. I noticed that among my growing collection of Picador books – if *White Spines* was 'about' anything, it was about trying to collect all the Picadors published between 1972 and 2000, when they abandoned their signature white spine – were some 'doubles', such as *Tracks* by Louise Erdrich and *Tracks* by Robyn Davidson. In fact, that was it, as far as Picador went, although there was also Angela Carter's *Love* (Picador), doubled with Péter Nádas's novel with the same title published by Vintage, and Emma Tennant's *Hotel de Dream* (Picador) and its namesake by Edmund White with Bloomsbury's logo on its spine. Before you know it, you've started actively looking out for repeat titles and you find you've bought *Quilt* (Women's Educational Press) by Donna E Smyth, simply because you already own *Quilt* (Myriad Editions) by Nicholas Royle, a double of another kind, which reminds me that, once, a short story of mine was rejected by the two editors of an anthology to which I had submitted it. This was not unusual at the time, but the circumstances around it are, arguably, interesting. Editor A told me that editor B had ruled out my story, saying, 'I don't want that Nicholas Royle in this book.' I assumed until recently that 'that Nicholas Royle' had only one meaning, like 'that Nigel Farage' in the statement, 'I don't like that Nigel Farage,' but lately I've started to wonder if editor B was making a distinction between me and the other Nicholas Royle, as in 'I don't want *that* Nicholas Royle in this book, but I wouldn't mind the other one,' which wouldn't improve one's mood, unless one decided that it was possible that editor B thought the submission was from the other Nicholas Royle and that the possibility of this misunderstanding had not occurred to editor A, who did know which Nicholas Royle was which.

I remain fairly certain, however, that editor B also knew which Nicholas Royle was which.

Although it's also possible that editor A was just using editor B's objection as an excuse.

7

There are pros and cons to having the same name as another professional in the same field.

Another accidental collection: I probably had half a dozen or so books called *London Something* – *London Blues*, *London Bone*, *London Noir*, *London Orbital*, *London Particular*, *London Revenant* – before I became aware of the fact and so inaugurated a special shelf and started looking out for more titles to add to it, even writing one of my own, *London Gothic*.

One or two Amazon reviewers seemed to be generally in favour of *White Spines* and *Shadow Lines* but objected to one of the two bits of 'content' that I used in those books to break up long sections. I employed, for this purpose, transcriptions of conversations overheard in bookshops, and accounts of my own dreams about books. Some people will always object to anything to do with dreams, insisting that dreams are banal and that including reports of them in creative work is inevitably boring. I disagree, but there are books to sell and while one hates simply to break under pressure – like the so-called Shatterproof plastic rulers of my childhood that seem to have become Shatter Resistant – one also sees a certain virtue in being pragmatic, so I considered, this time, leaving out the dreams.

While I was considering it, the thought occurred to me that with the exception of lucid dreams, these nocturnal narratives cannot be controlled. Therefore, they are, to some extent, random, and randomness is a quality they have in common with the collecting of second-hand books. The moment we enter the second-hand bookshop is similar to the moment we fall asleep. Just as we don't know what we will find in the second-hand bookshop, we don't know what we will dream. So, where my dreams have to do with books, I may continue to include one or two.

An asterisk or other typographical symbol used to indicate a section break, if for some reason a line break is insufficient (or if the line break falls at the top or bottom of a page and might therefore not be noticed), is known as an ornament. Maybe, if they bore you, my dreams about books may be regarded as mere ornaments.

If you don't like them, don't read them, is what I'm advising.

I think it was writer and reviewer Harry Ritchie who described my book of writers' dreams, *The Tiger Garden*, as 'uniquely pointless and stupid', and he definitely referred to me in print as a 'specky guy' (factual, but calculated to cause offence) and dismissed my prize-winning novel *The Matter of the Heart* as 'remarkably unreadable', 'completely resistible' and 'utterly unseductive' (subjective, but also calculated to cause offence).

Prize-winning?

Yes, prize-winning.

What prize?

The *Literary Review*'s Bad Sex in Fiction Award.

Ah.

I wouldn't mind, but Harry Ritchie also wears glasses.

I came across one of Harry Ritchie's books, *Here We Go* (Penguin), an 'anti-travel book' about the Costa del Sol, in a Mind shop in Hackney.

I managed about thirty pages walking from Stoke Newington to Stratford. It was a slog, and I don't mean the walk across Queen Elizabeth Olympic Park.

Later, I spent more time with the book, not reading it exactly, more scanning the pages for certain words that would enable me to create a piece of blackout poetry, or erasure poetry. This is where you erase or cross out words in an existing text to create a new text made out of the words that remain. I found that the double-page spread 140–141 more than met my requirements, containing, as it does, the words 'I', 'tried', 'to', 'read', 'this' and 'nonsense'.

It would be a shame to let Harry Ritchie have the last word in this introduction. Short story writer, book-collecting essayist and publisher Mark Valentine is more deserving of that dubious honour.

'After (re)reading *Shadow Lines* in bed last night,' Valentine wrote to me in March 2025, 'I dreamt that in your next book you had a chapter on food found in books. This was not mere crumbs or grease ghosts, but included in various examples a pizza slice, some fresh salad leaves and some pineapple chunks. You explained it was perfectly possible for portions like this to be preserved between the pages unobserved, without damaging the book. I was impressed and convinced.'

The closest I can come to making Valentine's dream come true is to offer up a couple of paragraphs on serviettes – or napkins, as my wife calls them – found in books.

On Wednesday 13 November 2024, I lifted my self-imposed travel ban between Manchester and Sheffield. I like Sheffield – a lot – but there are a couple of people in Sheffield who I would really rather not bump into, in case I tell them what I think of them. So, I took a chance – the occasion was Salt's twenty-fifth anniversary party – and went to Sheffield and got away with it. In the afternoon, I went to the Oxfam shop on Fulwood Road where I found two love letters in a Penguin edition of Ernest Hemingway's *Men Without Women*. They were from A, who was away skiing in Austria, writing to a man – her husband? Her lover? – at an address in Brooksby Street, London N1. Less interesting, but more to the point, was Graham Greene's *The Third Man and the Fallen Idol* (Vintage) with a serviette at page 25. It made me want to go back to the Children's Society in Heaton Moor, Stockport, to see if a book I had seen there but decided against buying, containing a Virgin Atlantic napkin, was still there. (I did and it wasn't. By the way, when I say the serviette was 'at page 25', what I mean is it was between pages 24 and 25, but I shorten that to 'at page 25', for my convenience and yours.)

In May 2025, I went to Tesco in Burnage, where I helped myself to three books from the charity shelf, which didn't say which charity it was supporting, so I left a slightly mingy £2, in case it was going to the Tesco Shareholders Holiday Fund (I had previously left £5 for a single book, because I didn't have anything smaller, so I didn't feel too bad). The three books were: Michael Marshall's *Bad Things* (Harper), which I already had, but this copy was falling apart, meaning I could allow myself to read it in the rain, so making the most of my time while out walking in the rain, and in Manchester it does rain every now and then. Mike is one of my oldest friends and I had recently missed wishing him a happy birthday, and it was a big birthday, so I felt bad about that and buying this would make me feel a little bit better. Secondly, reminding me of seeing its author walking his dog in Hampstead, Tony Parsons' *Man and Wife* (HarperCollins), printed in the smallest point size I've ever seen in a commercially published book. The book comes in at 250 pages, but it would probably make 500 if printed in a legible point size. I didn't want to read it, just write about it, and my rule is that, if it's in a charity bookshop, or on a charity bookshelf, I have to buy it to write about it.

Finally, and here we get to the serviette, walking back from

Burnage, I opened Dave Pelzer's *The Lost Boy* (Orion), an ex-Withington Girls' School library book. At page 17, I found a folded-up bit of paper the quality of toilet tissue. Gingerly, I unfolded it to find – *ugh* – a brown stain. Actually, more of a mark than a stain. I'm not sure which is worse. A mark, in this case, I think. Even more gingerly, I unfolded it further to find, with some relief, that it was actually a serviette. Or napkin.

I slipped *The Lost Boy* back into my bag and allowed my mind to drift to happier associations with Withington Girls' School.

Janis Lamb, Pam Ford, Jane Threlfall . . .

An unexpected consequence of walking around with my nose in a book has been that it has led to more encounters with strangers. Like Zoë from Malvern, who was walking down Wilmslow Road in Didsbury. I can't remember what I was reading at the time, but when I look back at my Reading Diary for January 2025, I see that among the books I read that month was André Breton's semi-autobiographical novel *Nadja*, about the author's chance encounter with a woman with whom he became obsessed. I did not become obsessed with Zoë, although I liked her glasses (and she liked mine, which I told her had been my dad's) and she told me that she occasionally comes across a man in Malvern called Paul who reads as he walks. Six months later she bumped into him in the Co-op and sent me a picture of the two of them. (I noticed she said 'the Co-op', even though she was younger than me. My children and their generation say 'Co-op', although she wasn't that much younger than me.) I think Paul later sent me a message, but, although I'm sure I didn't delete it, I can't find it.

Or like Kate Hughes, who I saw coming towards me along

the Fallowfield Loop at St Werburgh's Road in August 2025. We were both reading and walking. I was reading Derek Marlowe's 1980 novel *The Rich Boy From Chicago* and she was reading a Fitzcarraldo book. I recognised the International Klein Blue cover instantly. This meant it was fiction. (Their fiction is blue, their non-fiction white.) As she got closer I could read the title and author. She was reading *Brian* by Jeremy Cooper, which I had read the previous March. 'That is a great book!' I blurted out, because it is. It's one of the best novels I've read in years. Kate told me she wrote a cancer memoir twenty years ago that sold six copies. The fact that she wrote her cancer memoir twenty years ago tells its own story, which is a happy one.

What I might do, if I'm going to include fewer dreams about books, is introduce another form of section break: brief reports of reader-walkers. When and where seen and what they were reading.

During the pandemic, when recreational exercise was allowed, I would go out walking for hours – often with a book, but not always – and somehow I fell into some superstitious habits. I already had a couple of these, if I'm honest. If I saw a rose in a garden, I had to stop and smell it. If I saw some rosemary growing, I had to go and touch it – I found I liked the feeling of the oil on my fingers – and smell it.

Soon, with the number of roses bushes in front gardens, it was taking longer to get to places, but during the pandemic that didn't seem to matter.

New superstitions took hold.

If I saw two posts holding up a sign, I had to walk between them. I didn't know if it was the walking between the posts that was important, or the walking under the sign. If I saw a single post that was close to the wall, I had to walk between it and the wall. If I passed some posts and I hadn't done what I was supposed to do, I had to go back.

Going back was annoying, but I had to do it – or something terrible would happen. Early in 2025 I decided that if my going back would be witnessed and I might be self-conscious about it, even embarrassed by it, should anyone be watching, then perhaps I didn't have to do it. As the year wore on, this gradually changed until, at some point in the summer, I decided that whatever the circumstances, I no longer had to go back.

If I see a rose now, I can go and smell it if I want to, but if I miss it, I don't have to go back. If two posts are holding up a sign and I don't have to deviate – or deviate far – then I'll go between them, but if I miss it or even choose not to do it, I don't have to go back.

I think I had to convince myself – or remind myself – that going forward is preferable to going back.

Onwards!

I

Free books

A few minutes' walk from my wife's flat in Stoke Newington, there's a neighbourhood book exchange. You've probably seen one of these. There are lots of them in London and Manchester, and I've seen them in other cities, and towns and villages. I see them in France and Belgium, where they're called *boîtes à livres* or book boxes. Some people call them little free libraries, or Little Free Libraries.

Little Free Library is a non-profit organisation based in St Paul, Minnesota. Their 'mission', according to their website, 'is to be a catalyst for building community, inspiring readers, and expanding book access for all through a global network of volunteer-led Little Free Library book-exchange boxes.'

Book exchanges you come across may or may not be part of this scheme. Near where I live, the book exchange in a front garden on Sandy Lane, Chorlton, is a Little Free Library. The 'Hutch', or 'Free Little Library', perched on a wall outside a house in Stephens Road, Withington, is not.

The idea is simple. If you take a book, you also leave a book, hence book exchange. I tend to think it's not imperative to always have a book in your pocket. I mean, I do always have a book in my pocket (or in my bag), but not necessarily one I want to leave in exchange for one you might take from a book exchange. You can always go back, even if it's some time later. Different people use book exchanges in different ways. Some people use them to dispose of unwanted crockery or children's clothes or VHS tapes labelled 'Naughty Films of the 40s'. I must admit I found that cassette irresistible. When I got it home, I found it contained two extended episodes of *EastEnders* and an England-Ireland rugby match from 2003.

That was in the book exchange on Nevill Road, Stoke Newington, in September 2018. Fast-forward six years, to Tuesday 21 May 2024: under a grey sky, I walked up Nevill Road and was beaten to the book exchange by a sweet older lady with white hair, who proceeded to virtually empty the pink wooden box, filling her bag without stopping to read titles or names of authors, or to check the condition of the books. She reminded me of the older gentleman who makes regular visits to the *boîte à livres* outside the home of my friends Brian and Cécile in Brussels to shovel its contents indiscriminately into his red shopping trolley.

Maybe every book exchange has one of these characters, just as they will have regular donors who fill them up again.

I walked on to Tottenham and then across to Walthamstow, where a quick visit to the bookshelves in Blackhorse Road tube station produced a white-spined Picador, Umberto Eco's *The Name of the Rose*. I already had the B-format – most Picador paperbacks are B-format – but this was A-format, a film tie-in edition. I've never fully committed to collecting the A-format Picadors, partly because often they were give-aways cover-mounted on glossy magazines, and those never feel like real books to me, although one probably would if it was my book, and partly because they just don't feel like Picadors. Sometimes, however, I think why not and pick them up. There weren't that many of them.

As I walked from Blackhorse Road to the High Street, it started to rain. Whenever this happens and I'm in London and I'm listening to music, I generally switch to Blossom Dearie singing 'I Like London in the Rain'. I do like London in the rain. Well, I don't mind London in the rain. But you hear Blossom Dearie and you can't help feeling lighter, even as the rain falls.

In Oxfam I bought Mary Roach's *Packing For Mars: The Curious Science of Life in Space* (Oneworld), because whoever donated it left a US dollar bill inside at page 179, and William Golding's *Rites of Passage* (Faber) for its former owner's address on Banbury Road, Oxford, the former owner named as Ruth Eynon.

I sent the Golding to the occupants of the address on Banbury Road and so far have not had a response, but you never know.

From the book box outside the Mill community centre on Coppermill Lane I took a copy of John Boyne's *The Boy in the Striped Pyjamas* (David Fickling Books) to read on the walk back to Stoke Newington and find out whether it deserves to have sold eleven million copies or whether I would agree with Mumsnet contributor CommunistLegoBloc, who described it as 'a terrible book littered with inaccuracies'.

I read it in four long walks over the next twenty-four hours. I will restrict my remarks to those from a pedantic linguistic perspective. Why does Bruno, the Kommandant's nine-year-old son, call Hitler the Fury, when the German word 'Führer' sounds nothing like any German word for 'fury'? The 'joke' only works in English. Same goes for calling Auschwitz 'Out-With'. The made-up name is supposed to sound like Auschwitz, but Bruno is German. Yes, 'aus' means 'out', but the German for 'with' is 'mit'.

A character called Pavel says, 'Before I came here, I practised as a doctor.' Bruno responds: 'Practised? Weren't you any good then?' Again, the joke only works in English. There's a similar joke about a spare tyre, but life's too short.

When Bruno puts on a pair of striped pyjamas to join Shmuel in the camp, I'm afraid it felt to me a little bit as if Boyne were pulling on a pair as well.

Maybe I should have followed the advice of Tanya Gold, who prefaced a brief synopsis of the novel in an opinion piece in the *Jewish Chronicle* of 13 October 2022 with the words, 'If you haven't read it – and you shouldn't . . .'

There are some book exchanges it's worth checking regularly, such as the one on Sotheby Road, Highbury, where the stock turns over quickly. I find proof copies here, signed and inscribed copies, unusual books, barely read books, very well read books. On a Sunday in August 2025, I walked over towards Holloway to deliver WB Gooderham's latest Nightjar order and on my way back stopped off at Sotheby Road. As usual, the book box there was bursting at the seams with interesting stuff, including *God's Englishman* (Pelican) by Christopher Hill, with a name on the flyleaf – Bruce Woodcock – at an address in Hull, probably Bruce Woodcock Jnr, the son of the former British Empire Heavyweight Boxing Champion. Also: *The Penguin Dictionary of Quotations* by JM and MJ Cohen, formerly belonging to writer and former chair of the Family Planning Association Jean Medawar in 1966, and Nicholas Rescher's *Scientific Progress: A Philosophical Essay on the Economies of Research in Natural Science* (Pittsburgh) inscribed by the author to biologist and author Sir Peter Medawar. Peter and Jean's grandson is the celebrated novelist, screenwriter and director Alex Garland. I wonder if Alex Garland put the books in the box.

Four months earlier, the box produced a battered US paperback edition of Norman Mailer's *The Executioner's Song* (Warner Books), with the name of a former owner – Bob Woffinden – and 'Charing X Road, May 89' written on the flyleaf in blue ballpoint.

November 2023: a 1976 edition of Aleister Crowley's *Tao Teh King* (Askin) with a ticket for the Aldwych Theatre acting as a bookmark at page 57 (seat B10, 2nd circle, £1.50), and Alan Hollinghurst's *The Folding Star* (Vintage) with a folded piece of paper at page 363 with a phone number on it ending in 0827. I tried calling the number. The call was answered and I explained what I was about, but the man on the other end said, 'I'm not interested. Thank you,' and hung up.

I tried reading *The Folding Star*, which I thought, given my deep affection for all things Belgian (it's set in Flanders), I would enjoy, but somehow it dangled just beyond my reach.

Bob Woffinden (1948–2018) was an investigative journalist and author. In 1989, when he bought *The Executioner's Song* from Henry Pordes, perhaps, or Any Amount of Books, on Charing Cross Road, Woffinden's own book, *Miscarriages of Justice*, came out from Coronet, followed a year later by his *Hanratty: The Final Verdict* (Pan).

Monday 17 November 2025
Oxfam Victoria Park, Hackney, London.
Two young women browsing.
Woman 1 [taking an Ian Rankin book off the shelf]: They've got a bit of Ian.

Woman 2: Mm?
Woman 1 [taking another book off the shelf]: Ah. *How to Keep a Boy as a Pet*.
Woman 2: No, thanks. I'd rather have a rattlesnake.
[. . .]
Woman 1: Short stories. That's more me.
Woman 2: *The Boy in the Striped Pyjamas*. That's a good book.

In March 2020, a ten-second video I made of myself running out of the front door of my block of flats in Manchester went viral on social media. In my dad's heavy-framed glasses, my head shaved, wearing a green jacket and carrying a rucksack, and generally trying to look as sneaky and furtive as possible, I achieved, if I say so myself, a striking resemblance to a certain senior adviser to the then Prime Minister.

When you impersonate someone and get inside their skin to the extent that you feel that anyone looking at you would see not you but the person you're impersonating, you can feel an uncanny sense of intimacy with the subject, even though you might never have met them and might despise everything they stand for. So when a little bird tells me that Dominic Cummings lives on a particular street in Islington that's just off my regular route from Euston to Stoke Newington, I don't hang about. I'm not told the number of the house, but it's easy enough to work out from videos online.

There's no sign of him, of course, but down that end of the road, rather neatly, there's a book exchange, a rather fancy one, actually, which seems only fitting given where we are. By that I don't mean in the vicinity of the home of the former government adviser who not only drove to Durham during coronavirus lockdown, but also took a spin out to Barnard Castle to check he was safe to drive back to London – you couldn't make it up, and we were assured he didn't.

I mean given the lovely Georgian terraced houses.

I find Dambisa Moyo's *Dead Aid: Why Aid is Not Working and How There is Another Way For Africa* (Penguin) with a foreword by Niall Ferguson. I can imagine Cummings approving of Ferguson. Also: *Push* (Vintage) by Sapphire and *What Do Women Want?* (CreateSpace) by Luise Eichenbaum and Susie Orbach. Can I picture Cummings tucking into either of these?

I also find a receipt in the name of an editor and author who in the 1990s took me out to lunch in South Kensington and told me she wanted to take on not one but two of my novels. It turns out she lives just up the road from Cummings, although, when I later do a bit more research, it seems Cummings might have taken his family up to Durham again and stayed there this time. That figures. I was told at primary school that I've got a good imagination, but I can't imagine Dominic Cummings having been very popular with his Islington neighbours.

I know what you're thinking. You're thinking, Hang on, this chapter is called 'Free Books' and these books in book exchange boxes are not really free if you're expected to leave one in exchange. We were promised free books. We want free books. Or, to be more accurate, some of your witty and charming writing about free books.

I can't tell if you're being sincere or sarcastic.

Free books, please.

OK, on the morning of Friday 19 July 2024, I was walking to the Blood Donor Centre on Plymouth Grove in Manchester, to give blood. Thank you for giving me an opportunity to get that in. I've been a blood donor since I worked at Time Out in the 1990s and one lunchtime I asked my colleague Sarah Guy where she was going and she said to give blood, and I thought, and maybe said, Oh, I couldn't possibly do that. You know, the needle, the pain. And off she went and later she came back and she looked fine. She didn't look like she had a pint less blood inside her than before, even though that was the case. So, I thought about it and a couple of weeks later I went along to Margaret Street and it was fine. They thanked me for my donation. It feels good to be thanked. And there were biscuits. Free biscuits.

I've given blood forty times now. It doesn't hurt – well, a small scratch – and I don't have to watch the needle going in and there are free biscuits. (There are even free books at Plymouth Grove.) There's an app as well. Ten more credits and I'll be on gold. I hope to make that and then keep going. It might seem like I'm saying all this to win approval or praise, but it doesn't matter, because the need for blood donors is greater than any embarrassment I might feel at appearing to need approval or praise. So, please consider giving blood, if you don't already.

On a wall on Amherst Road in Withington, on the way to Plymouth Grove were some books. Among them was *The Laboratory Detectives* (Arthur Baker) by Norman Lucas. On the flyleaf was written, 'Peter, best wishes, Vin.' I wondered about Peter and Vin, who they might have been and what might have been the relationship between them. I thought I'd see if the book was still there on my way back and it was, so I picked it up and while walking home read the first chapter, about Richard Brinkley, one of the first criminals to be convicted on scientific evidence. He was found to have murdered Richard and Elizabeth Beck and was hanged in Wandsworth jail on 10 August 1907. (An episode of BBC TV's *Murder, Mystery and My Family* in 2019 – unavailable on iPlayer – appears to have questioned the safety of the conviction.)

In the afternoon, I donated the book to a charity shop.

On Monday 12 April 2021, following an easing of Covid restrictions, non-essential shops were allowed to reopen, including charity shops. In Oxfam Books & Music Islington, I bought CH Rolph's *London Particulars* (Oxford), for my *London Something* collection (and corresponding chapter in this book), and Brian Flynn's *The Edge of Terror* (Dean Street Press) to give to another Brian Flynn, with whom I used to play football, before I did my knee in. It was a fine day and I walked from the Angel back up Essex Road. When I reached Annette Terrace, I came across a box of free books. I helped myself to a copy of Will Self's *Great Apes*, not in good condition, but signed.

I found another signed book in the street. Or should I say, *dans la rue*? On Monday 20 February 2023, on the boulevard des Batignolles, in Paris's seventeenth arrondissement, under a clear bright blue sky, I found a signed and dedicated copy of André Maurois's *La vie de Disraeli*. Maurois (1885–1967) was a biographer, historian and novelist, a member of the Académie Française. 'A Madame Grunberg,' went the inscription, 'en respectueux homage, André Maurois.' I *think* it says Grunberg. It's hard to make out.

In December 2023, Nightjar published a story by Cliff McNish called 'Snowdrops'. The month before, I was in Peckham, delivering Cliff's author copies, and just up the road were two houses with free books outside. One box was full of those magazines with single-word titles I don't understand, like *Anxy* and *Boat*. These magazines have thick matt paper and are heavily designed and packed with photographs of people looking gaunt and miserable. I don't know if they're art magazines or fashion magazines. Or neither. Hidden among them was a black hardback book by Russell Brand. I can't remember which one, and I don't – and didn't – care, but I could see it had an inclusion in it, which turned out to be a slip informing 'Annelise' she had an appointment with the University of the Arts student advice service on 26.3.12 at 11 a.m. I could have given Annelise some advice myself, on what not to read, long before Russell Brand's appearances in the news pages in 2023 – and subsequently.

In certain places, you can often come across books outside, on garden walls, on street-side window ledges, or in boxes on the pavement. Research – my research, which is not very scientific – has shown that it's common in London and not uncommon in Paris, whereas I don't often come across garden wall books in Manchester. (Amherst Road was an exception.) When I posted about it on social media, however, responses suggested that it's not uncommon outside London.

I'm interested in the impulse behind it. Generosity? Laziness? A bit of both?

One afternoon, in April 2023, I had just arrived in London and was walking up Essex Road in the rain listening to Blossom Dearie. I passed the Sue Ryder shop and turned right into Dibden Street and there on a wall were some books, among them Beatrix Potter's *The Tale of Peter Rabbit*, *The Guardian Book of English Language*, Heinen-Greubel's *Wesen und Anwendung duftender Essenzen*, Robert I Sutton's *Good Boss, Bad Boss: How to Be the Best . . . and Learn from the Worst*.

August 2023, I was in London again and it was raining again. I walked up to Crouch End. On a wall on the corner of Middle Lane and Palace Road, two streets away from at least half a dozen charity shops, were two books, Anne Michaels' *The*

Winter Vault and Jane Gardam's *The People on Privilege Hill*, the latter a hardback.

October 2023. Oxfam Bookshop Herne Hill tempted me with a couple of books containing inclusions. John Harwood's *The Séance* with a ticket for the Queen's Club tennis AEGON Championship, Sat 11 June 2011, in the name of David Sellman, who had a 'preferential seat'. In a copy of Ian McEwan's *The Innocent* previously owned by Valerie Daly, I found a sheet of stickers for a TDK SA audio cassette. A Proustian moment that perhaps only older readers will get. While I was in there, a hail storm raged outside. Well, it would be outside, wouldn't it? Once it had passed over, five minutes' walk away in Elmwood Road, I saw on a garden wall a copy of *Olive* by Emma Gannon – sopping wet, ruined.

I suppose what I'm trying to suggest is, whatever the impulse for putting books outside for people to help themselves, yes, fine, great, if it's not raining and is forecast to remain dry. But if, as Father Dougal once said, it *looks like rain, Ted*, then maybe it's not such a great idea. If you're lucky enough to live near a charity shop, maybe taken them down there.

On a dry day in March 2017, Gary Michael Perry, then assistant head of fiction at Foyle's, tweeted that he was culling his books and leaving some outside his place in the Stoke Newington/Dalston area. I DMed him to ask him where and he gave me the address, which happened to be directly across the street from my wife's place. The vibe, I discovered, was books from independent presses. I helped myself to a proof copy of Matías Celedón's *The Subsidiary* (Melville House), a series of fictional messages or announcements made via rubber stamp by a company employee during an office blackout, translated from the Spanish by Samuel Rutter. Two hundred pages, but it took me only seven minutes to read. It gets some great reviews online, so maybe I should go back and give it another chance. Among Gary's books I also found one of mine, *In Camera*, a collaboration with artist David Gledhill published by Negative Press London. I'd just about run out of copies, so that was a result.

I often walk past a building I used to work in at Manchester Metropolitan University, or as it used to like to be called, MMU. In August 2025, I popped back in to have a look at the free bookshelves in the atrium and spotted a copy of my 2004 novel *Antwerp* (Serpent's Tail). It was inscribed to a novelist, poet and short story writer, *not* a former colleague, whose name I'll shorten to J, and I'd written, 'Thank you for coming, lots of love, Nick, 09.06.04.' Slightly over-effusive, perhaps, given I didn't really know J all that well, but she is lovely and you can get like that at a launch party. It also had an inclusion. Readers might remember tax discs, which were abolished in 2014. When you renewed your road tax, you got a piece of paper from which you had to *release* your tax disc. Its perimeter was perforated and looked like you should be able to remove the tax disc with your hands, but it was fiddly and you could easily tear it, so you tended to use scissors and it was still not the easiest task. You would eventually stick your tax disc in your car (another oddly difficult manoeuvre involving a plastic cover and saliva – no wonder they did away with it) and then you'd be left with something you could only call a 'tax disc surround' to keep, as it had your name on it, in your file of papers relating to your vehicle, or throw away – or use as a bookmark, as in this case. The name was that of the partner of a former colleague, which allowed me to presume a connection between J and the named keeper of the vehicle, or between J and my former colleague.

Monday 1 September 2025
Oxfam Bookshop Muswell Hill, London.
Little boy: I hate books. I hate bookshops.
Manager: Oh dear.
Mother: Yes, he only likes toys.

The books in the Global Educational Bookshop in Sale are free – kind of. There's a box for donations, but you may take up to three books without making a donation if you wish. I imagine most people leave a donation, but I could be as wrong about this as I was about the 2025 Christmas special of *Amandaland*, which I thought might be worth watching.

    I visited the Global Educational Trust bookshop on 31 January 2024 and one of my three books – for which I did leave a donation, so they weren't technically free, but could have been – was Thomas Hardy's *Under the Greenwood Tree* (Penguin). A sticker suggested that the book had previously lived at an address in Broad Road, Sale, and either there or elsewhere had been the property of Lucy Wright, whose name had been written on the flyleaf. There was also a charming bookplate, embellished with blue ink, perhaps by Lucy. I dropped the book and a note through the door of the address on Broad Road in October 2025 and was WhatsApped the same day by Lisa, who, with her husband, purchased the property in 2012. The previous owner, Lisa told me, the late Michael Wright, was a university professor and avid book collector. Every room in the house had had at least one bookshelf. Lisa contacted Michael's son Matthew and received the sad news that Lucy had died in September 2023, having lived with a brain tumour for several years. 'She read widely and frequented charity shops, as we all did,' Matthew wrote.

In 2021 I walked an average of 6.4 miles a day. In 2022 this increased to 9.4, the average dropping slightly to 9.2 in 2023. Determined that this should not happen again in 2024, I achieved an average of 10.9 miles a day. So far in 2025, with three days to go until the end of the year (and my deadline for this book), I have walked an average of 11.4 miles a day.

The reasons for this perhaps slightly obsessive behaviour are many. Leaving my job at MMU in July 2022 gave me the opportunity. Retiring from five-a-side football in July 2024, through injury, was part of it, but far from the whole story. Health anxiety is also part of it – a big part. Also: superstition, magical thinking. Walking between posts or under signs. Smelling herbs and flowers, as discussed.

As a psychiatrist says of Basil in *Fawlty Towers*, 'There's enough material there for an entire conference.' Or a whole book. But I'll spare you that.

Some evenings, if I'm in London and it looks like rain, and especially if I haven't quite reached the magic number of ten miles, I might go out for a late walk looking for books left out on garden walls, to rescue them from the rain – or the dew. Then, the next day, or later, I'll take them to a charity shop. If A, of Queen's Drive, London N4, ever wonders where the hardback copy of Leslie Jamison's *Splinters* (Granta) containing various receipts and a letter from Sir Richard Branson that she left outside her house in the summer of 2025 ended up, I've got it and once this book is finished and I give away some of the materials obtained for research, it will end up in one of Stoke Newington's many charity shops. Although I generally like inclusions to be left inside the books in which they were discovered, I will remove the documents that identify A.

I'm not making any extravagant claim for this to be regarded as some kind of public service. I suspect the impulse behind it is closer to the need I feel to fold in wing mirrors on inconsiderately parked over-size cars, often straddling the pavement. Or my leaving a copy of JG Ballard's *Crash* under the windscreen wiper of a car that almost ploughed into mine one night when I was driving back from football. He – the car's driver is statistically more likely to have been a man; I was too busy looking at the number plate – ran a red light on Parrs Wood Road and missed me by inches. The number plate was familiar. I knew I would see it again sooner or later on one of my walks. Eventually I did and left a little present of the Ballard and an explanatory note, for once without a return address. Not the 1975 Panther edition of *Crash*, obviously, in orange with an illustration by Chris Foss, which I've had since the 1980s, but a less desirable Picador US edition that I bought in Oxfam Didsbury for £3.

2

Tickets, please! – outward

I went to Oxford.

I went to Oxford to visit my friend Geoff.

I'd wanted to go for some time, but the purchase of a second-hand book containing an old train ticket from London to Oxford seemed to give me permission. Strictly speaking, it wasn't a ticket, but a blank application form for an InterCity Rail Travel Account, with, on the reverse, timetables for services between London and Oxford. No date was specified, but its being InterCity means it was pre-1997.

The book was Luciano Canfora's *The Vanished Library* (Vintage), a work of non-fiction about the ancient library of Alexandria. When I picked it out of a box outside Collinge & Clark on Leigh Street, King's Cross, in March 2025, I was immediately drawn to the cover, by Andrew Hirniak, which reminded me of the cover of Christopher Burns's novel *In the Houses of the West* (Sceptre, uncredited on both hardback and paperback).

According to the quotes on the back from reviews by Allan Massie and Peter Levi, it was quite a book. 'I cannot imagine that anyone could read this book without receiving enlightenment and profound pleasure,' writes Massie. 'The atmosphere is that of an enthralling detective story,' adds Levi.

Hm.

I was reading, on page 28, about the learned grammarian Tyrannion, when I heard the train announcer say, probably while we were stopped at Reading, 'For the benefit of passengers with heavy luggage, please use the lifts provided.' Who was this announcement for, I wondered. For passengers with heavy luggage? In which case, why not just say, 'Passengers with heavy luggage, please use the lifts provided'? Doesn't starting with 'For the benefit of . . .' set up an expectation that the announcement is asking those of us *without* heavy luggage to do something to benefit those *with* heavy luggage? I mean, if necessary, I wouldn't mind helping someone with heavy luggage. I often offer; in fact, the last time I offered, at Paris's Gare du Nord, the reply came, 'Dieu vous bénisse.' *God bless you.*

I was finding the history in *The Vanished Library* the equivalent of heavy luggage. I never studied ancient history. I hardly studied history. After one year of history and one of geography, I had to choose between the two. I opted for drumlins, oxbow lakes and a field trip to Skelmersdale.

As we pulled out of Reading, I thought it would have been good to have spotted someone under the sign saying 'Reading' reading a book. I could have taken a picture. It would have been better to have had that idea while pulling *into* Reading. Never mind, I thought, there was always the way back.

When I realised that the main narrative of *The Vanished Library* ends half way through the book, I thanked the numerous gods of ancient Egypt and decided to stop when I got to that point and not bother with the 100 pages of 'sources'. But before I could get anywhere near page 100, we arrived in Oxford.

31

As you probably know, Oxford is one of those places where the station is some way from the centre, which suited me, as otherwise I was going to struggle to get my miles in. Geoff lives on Osney Island, near the station, but I had time to nip into town and visit Oxfam Bookshop St Giles, where I bought Jess Walter's *Beautiful Ruins* (Penguin) containing a Christmas card at page 75 and two photographs tucked in among the end matter showing a young woman playing sport. A little research reveals she's playing basketball for Queen's University at Kingston, Ontario, aka Queen's Gaels. I may return to this book in another chapter. Probably the chapter about books with Christmas inscriptions, because I'm not currently planning a chapter about university basketball.

When Geoff visited me one year at the Small Publishers Fair at Conway Hall, where I was selling Nightjars, people could not take their eyes off him. Tall, dark, handsome...

But, let's get back to Geoff.

No, Geoff is, actually, tall, dark and handsome, and when he came to the Small Publishers Fair he was wearing a long black coat of sleekest cashmere that somehow made him look even taller, darker and handsomer. There was a beautiful black brooch on his lapel. He even smelt exquisite.

More importantly, though, Geoff has a brilliant mind. If you've seen a film by the extraordinary French-Bosnian director Lucile Hadžihalilović, Geoff probably co-wrote it. He's exceptionally modest, though, so I'd known him for a while before I learnt this. And I only just found out, while checking the spelling of Hadžihalilović, that he also co-wrote Claire Denis's *High Life*.

After sitting chatting in his study for an hour, I had to leave, because the notebook in which I'd been writing down his recommendations of films, books and music was full. There's nothing that Geoff has recommended to me that I haven't liked. 'Liked' is an understatement. Whether it's director Giuseppe Patroni Griffi's *Il Mare* (1962), the novels of Swiss author Fleur Jaeggy, or the unsettling sound art of Baudouin Oosterlynck – I'm listening to 'Suite For a Bondage Room' as I write these words – you won't go far wrong following up on a recommendation from Geoff.

Plus, I had a train to catch.

However, when I got back to the station, it was to learn that there were no trains to Paddington due to an 'incident' at Didcot Parkway.

The incident was a fatality. A man in his thirties, according to a statement from the police two days later. They added that it was a 'non-suspicious incident' – which is code, as we all know; then came a further remark – 'there is unlikely to be a tribute' – which is not code, I'm assured by a friend who is a retired policeman, so what could it mean?

Three weeks before the fatality at Didcot Parkway, the suicide prevention charity the Samaritans had announced plans to close or merge many of its centres, moving to a model of regional hubs and remote-working. These plans were met with dismay by many volunteers.

I returned to London on the Chiltern line, entering London Marylebone by rail for the first time in my life.

Wednesday 6 November 2024
Shoreditch High Street, Shoreditch, London.
Young man, tall, black leather jacket, grey rucksack, striding north under railway bridge, past Boxpark, reading *If We Were Villains* (Titan Books) by ML Rio.

33

Another London station I had never used before: Cannon Street.

In January 2025, I found a couple of books containing train tickets in Oxfam in Dalston: Andrew Smith's *Moon Dust* (Bloomsbury), with a ticket from London terminals to Greenwich at page 119, and Jerry Della Femina's *From Those Wonderful Folks Who Gave You Pearl Harbor* (Canongate) with a ticket from Chichester to Penrith at page 265. That's some journey, I thought, fully intending to undertake it, but so far I haven't and with ten weeks to go till my deadline, it seems unlikely, as the journey would take about that length of time. (Is 'length' the right word here? I'm writing these words on a London Northwestern service from London to Stafford. At the start of that journey, as we waited to leave Euston, an announcement advised passengers for Atherstone to travel in the front four carriages because of the 'short nature' of the platform. Would not 'short length' have been better? Or 'shortness'?) The journey from London terminals to Greenwich was not only shorter than the one from Chichester to Penrith, but it would give me an opportunity to start a journey at Cannon Street. Also, the book looked more appealing.

Andrew Smith became interested in the fact that of the twelve men who had been to the Moon and looked back at Earth, between 1969 and 1972, only nine were still alive. His book was published in 2005; in the intervening twenty years five more have died, meaning that as this book goes to press, only four remain alive. One is Buzz Aldrin, part of the Apollo 11 crew, the first men to land on the Moon. The train ticket was inserted in the middle of a chapter devoted to Aldrin. Smith wanted to achieve a better understanding of the effect on the astronauts of their extraordinary experiences; Aldrin's history of depression and struggles with alcohol and drugs have been well documented and Smith asks some difficult questions.

Like Smith, I remember the first Moon landing. Born in 1963, I have no memory of the 1966 World Cup Final, but I do remember England's games at Mexico 70. Oddly, my 'memories' of that tournament are in colour, dominated by the yellow shirts of Brazil, despite the fact that our television set was black and white. I imagine my 'colorised' memories have something to do with the 'Squelchers' I collected later from Esso petrol stations. These tiny booklets – I have a full set of sixteen in their blue plastic wallet – were edited for Esso by Leslie Vernon and are gorgeous little things.

The first Moon landing was the year before, whatever Kim Kardashian might believe. *I* believe I was allowed to stay up, or perhaps was woken up especially just before 4 a.m., to watch Neil Armstrong and Buzz Aldrin set foot on the Moon. I text my mum to confirm this as she will be able to remember even if I can't. Her response: 'You very much wanted to watch it and bravely hung on for ages and then sleep won, I'm afraid.'

So, all the stories I tell about myself are false? Or just from the ages of six and under? Or just those about the Moon?

On leaving Cannon Street – the trip to Greenwich takes place on 15 September 2025 – the train comes out from under the station canopy and river views can be enjoyed up and downstream, but once on the South Bank, the view of the approaching Shard is breathtaking. I almost want to say Space Age. It takes barely seven minutes to reach Greenwich. Exiting the station, I scowl at Team Master across the road, where barbers cut hair in premises once occupied by Halcyon Books. Proleptic nominatave determinism, to be sure, although there is a surviving branch – with an espresso machine and a few tables, too – a mile or so away in Lee. I pass the Greenwich & Bexley Community Hospice shop on the left. In fact, I don't pass it, because it's open, so I go in. They have a Michael Morpurgo children's novel, *Listen to the Moon*, but my eye is drawn to shadow lines on the top edges of three or four older books. These, it turns out, are slips of paper on which staff have pencilled prices and notes along the lines of 'copy offered for sale online for £6'. Is anyone going to part with £6 for a battered US paperback edition of Aleksandr Solzhenitsyn's laugh-a-minute *Cancer Ward*? My dad, who feared cancer all his life and of course inevitably died of it, had a copy. (He also had two copies of Chairman Mao's *Little Red Book* and a complete set of Arthur Ransome's *Swallows and Amazons* books, in hardback. Those scrapbooky jackets were lovely, but I preferred and still prefer the paperbacks, with simple illustrations – blocks of colour, a sense of space and adventure – based on Ransome's own drawings.) I confidently predict *Cancer Ward* will still be here if I come back in a month's time.

In the Oxfam Bookshop, I'm disappointed by the removal of a wall of bookshelves, replaced by bars of chocolate. The young man on the till tells me the bookshelves caused constant traffic jams. 'Ours is the smallest Oxfam Bookshop in London,' he tells me. Sadly, too small to support the small but perfectly formed collection of foreign-language books that lived on those shelves and among which I once found three Agota Kristof novels, in smart red jackets: *Le grand cahier*, *La preuve* and *Le troisième mensonge* (Editions du Seuil).

Having noticed, on Instagram, in July 2023, that the tireless trawlerman of the Manchester second-hand book scene, Adrian

Slatcher, had netted some interesting stuff in Sue Ryder in Didsbury, I headed down there and found Richard Matheson's *What Dreams May Come* (Sphere) and Roald Dahl's *Over to You* (Penguin), which I already had, but this copy was in excellent condition and bore a former owner's name, 'JA Shuttleworth, Manchester July 78'. Other books on the shelf contained Mr Shuttleworth's first name – John – and I liked the idea that they had belonged not to a real person called John Shuttleworth, but to Graham Fellows' comic creation of that name, who I can easily imagine being a bit of a collector. Also: Nicholson Baker's *Room Temperature* (Granta) with an inclusion, a seat reservation label for an East Coast service from London to Newcastle, inside the back cover. East Coast ran the East Coast Main Line between 2009 and 2015, before it was taken over by Virgin.

As a return from London to Newcastle would take a sizable chunk out of my Nicholas Roylties for this book, I wrote to current franchise holder LNER, describing my project, and asked them if they might see an opportunity for some good PR in letting me travel for free. They very kindly offered me a complimentary pass for the return journey.

I had to make a seat reservation, so I chose carriage H, the 'quieter carriage'. As I put my dad's coat on the overhead rack, I noted that I could hear every word of the podcast the man in the seat in front was listening to. He was using AirPods. Back in the days when everyone was connected to their devices by wires, I used to fantasise about carrying scissors on rail journeys. No point now. Maybe someone will invent something that can interfere with Bluetooth. Actually, they already have. If I'm wearing cordless headphones at home and I put something in the microwave, the music cuts out. There are plug sockets on trains now. I'll bring my microwave in future. As a bonus I can heat up my lunch on the train.

I thought of retrieving my dad's coat and moving to a different seat, but stayed put.

London to Newcastle is a Great Train Journey – remember Michael Caine in *Get Carter* sitting in first class reading Raymond Chandler's *Farewell, My Lovely*? *Room Temperature* is about the thoughts that pass through the mind of a man called Mike while he feeds a bottle of milk to his baby daughter, Bug. Listening to his wife writing in a diary, he wonders if he might be able to work out what she is writing from the sound of the pen on the paper. For some years I imagined it might be possible to identify a PIN from the sound of particular buttons being pressed and I would listen to their beeps, believing they were subtly different from each other.

Mike remembers his father offering to pay him a dime a page to work through a Latin textbook and I'm reminded of the time my dad offered me sixpence to eat a small piece of Stilton. I put the vile, blue-veined supposed foodstuff in my mouth and my dad gave me the sixpence. I spat out the cheese and my dad took back his sixpence. Fair enough. Mouldy cheese has not passed my lips since. This, in turn, reminds me not to forget my dad's coat. It's a beige mac like the one Michael Caine wears in another great role, as Harry Palmer in *The Ipcress File*.

I left another of my dad's coats, a dark blue HM Customs gabardine, on an overhead rack on a train from Manchester to London. I haunted Lost Property for weeks but never got it back. I hope whoever took it has enjoyed wearing it as much as I did.

A man boards at Newark and sits in the seat behind me, sniffing.

As we leave Newark, I look out for a sign I saw from the train some years ago, a series of letters spelling out LONDON, but missing the first 'O', so it said L NDON. I became a bit obsessed by it, by the desire to find it in real life, as it were, seeing something through a train window being rather like seeing it on a screen, and when I mentioned it to someone who lives in Retford, he told me where to find it. I drove to the lonely spot he identified and walked around for hours, not finding it, and later writing a story about it instead.

The man behind me sniffs.

We pass the lonely spot I drove to. I don't see the sign that says L NDON.

Sniff.

Mike tells us that every two or three weeks his wife would ask him to tell her something about his past that he'd never told her before. I wonder if my wife and I should try this.

After York, the sniffing stops. The man in the seat behind has got off.

I wonder if anyone has mentioned the mentions of the *Times Literary Supplement* in *Room Temperature* – there are two – to Michael Caines of the *TLS*, who records *TLS* mentions in his column when readers send them in. The *TLS* is mentioned at the start of chapter two and in the penultimate line of the novel, which I close with a sense of great satisfaction. (The *TLS* is also mentioned in this paragraph in this chapter in this book. If one of you would be kind enough to drop a line to Michael Caines at the *TLS* and let him know, he might mention it.)

As we cross the Tyne, I stand up and reach for my dad's coat.

I get the Metro to Whitley Bay, where I was living when those men walked on the Moon. I look for the bus shelter behind which my mum used to hide the pushchair, in the days when you couldn't take a pushchair on the bus. There's still a shelter there, but it's facing the North Sea, which doesn't seem like a very good idea. I remember the wind off the North Sea. I stand outside our old house on Granada Place. I remember the central heating vent and the face in the curtains. I remember the room divider with spider plants between the lounge and the dining room, the pull-down light over the dining table, Blossom Dearie's *That's Just the Way I Want to Be* on the stereo.

Whatever happened to Spanish City? It's still there, kind of, but the amusements have gone, replaced by restaurants. What became of the funfair it used to be?

To lift the spirits again, I visit the gorgeous Keel Row Books. I don't find anything but just browsing in such beautiful surroundings is a deep and sensual pleasure. I get off the Metro at Jesmond so I can call in at Oxfam Books & Music. I don't find anything there either. My bag is empty, but my heart is full. I catch the lovely LNER train back to London.

Tuesday 12 March 2024
Global Educational Trust Bookshop, Sale.
Youngish woman with male friend.
Woman: There's loads of fucking diet books.
Man: [. . .]
Woman: All the books I need are all bulky. Like I've got a body-building book and it's fucking huge.
Man: [. . .]

On the penultimate day of October 2024, in Oxfam Bookshop Chorlton, I bought Sebastian Barry's novel *The Secret Scripture* (Faber), for the London to Manchester train ticket I found inside it at page 149. I know how ridiculous this will seem, but I find that if an author is particularly good looking, not just normally attractive – handsome or beautiful – but startlingly pulchritudinous, and I see their author photo plastered all over their books before I read their work, it can make me feel slightly suspicious about their writing and level of success. I have examined my feelings in this regard to see if what I'm talking about is something as base and banal as envy and I'm confident it's not. I'm as certain as I can be that I wouldn't want to be as arrestingly handsome as Sebastian Barry. I swear to you that I would feel uncomfortable owning his flowing silver locks – or even my own.

I wrote to Avanti West Coast and asked nicely if they might want to follow LNER's example and give me a comp. The Scrooge of UK rail operators, they didn't even reply. So I bought a ticket and boarded a train at Euston on Monday 23 December 2024. I had *Monsieur* by Jean-Philippe Toussaint to finish first. Toussaint is one of my favourite writers, a tough act for Barry to follow, but the moment came. First I looked at the old ticket again. It was dated 3 November 2009, when the route was operated by Virgin Trains. It was a single, costing £84.50 (in fairness, dearer than a single from London to Manchester at the time of writing – £68 or £79.80, depending on time of departure). It's faint, but a name is printed on the ticket: the initials are MY. I find MY's address online, a five-minute walk from where I bought the book, and think about dropping *The Secret Scripture* through his door, with a note. Then I think that he might not see the funny side. *I've already given this away once. Do I really have to give it away a second time?*

Switching imperceptibly to the present tense, I manage to nab my favourite seat, A48, in the so-called Quiet Zone, one of two seats reserved for cyclists, but in my experience, cyclists rarely get on this service. Cyclists with a bicycle booked on to the train, I mean, or had you worked that out?

Across the aisle, a man in seat 45 is droning on to a younger man in seat 46. (By coincidence, I am sitting in carriage A, seat 45, as I write these words, in October 2025.) 'Canada . . . Los Angeles . . . little winding streets . . . Heathrow, Paddington . . . reverse out . . . when you're younger you're happy to live in a shared house, partying all night, but when you get older, relationships, you need more space . . . Finland, Russia . . . frozen solid, you can even walk across . . . they change cars all the time . . .'

He's Ted Striker in *Airplane*. I imagine the young man unbuckling his belt, looking for somewhere to loop it through. Annoyingly, my AirPods have packed in. I promise myself I will not only replace them, but buy a spare pair. (If you're wondering about my using AirPods in the Quiet Zone, I find that drone or ambient or piano music – jazz or classical – tend not to leak.) I turn to *The Secret Scripture*. The narrator, Roseanne, tells us about her father and how he met her mother. 'A more beautiful girl Sligo never saw, she had skin as soft as feathers, and a warm, generous breast all new-baked bread and delight.' If my wife's breast resembled new-baked bread in any way, I think I'd be quite alarmed. (I see in my notes here, I've written 'Baps?', in the hope that I would come up with a good line about baps later on. Reader, I'm sorry, but I have failed to do so.)

The young man in seat 46, when the older man in seat 45 is drawing breath, says: 'Me and my friend Joe used to jump these trains all the time. The seats used to be back to back and you could slide under and hide between them.'

Which reminds me that I have a friend called Joe, who is a writer and is easily as handsome as Sebastian Barry, in fact handsomer, but I could read his work all day long and not tire of it, so I have to question my earlier remark about good-looking writers. In fact, when I find a copy of Karl Ove Knausgaard's *Boyhood Island* in the RSPCA shop in Manchester's Northern Quarter, with a train ticket from Manchester to Stoke tucked in at page 111, in August 2025, I ask Joe if it was his, since there was a time when he did that journey regularly and I know he likes his Knausgaard.

It wasn't.

I quite enjoy the bit of the Knausgaard I read, but not enough to read 490 pages of it and then all the other volumes.

As for Sebastian Barry, I manage sixty pages of *The Secret Scripture*, but it's just not my cup of Irish breakfast tea.

Ten a.m., Thursday, 18 September 2025. I'm at Paddington Station, half an hour early for the 10.36 to Exeter St David's. I walk up and down the long, wide, polished platforms, which are a bit like kitchen worktops in the homes of friends who have proper jobs. I'm reading the magazines I've brought with me, so I can drop them in the recycling bin. There's a book in my bag the size and weight of a gravestone, so dumping a few copies of the *TLS* and *New Statesman* won't make much difference. The train is delayed. No platform has been announced. Departure time comes around. Still we wait. Finally, the platform pops up. It's like a Le Mans start, and, if you don't know what a Le Mans start is, imagine a crowd of people waiting at Paddington Station for a platform to be announced. And then it is.

And how is it that when you finally board a delayed train or, worse, plane, you recognise everyone around you from the crowd who had been in your immediate vicinity on the concourse, or at the gate? How come they're all in your carriage, or in your doomed section of the fuselage? (Because of my early exposure to *Alive: The Story of the Andes Survivors*, Piers Paul Read's account of the fate of Uruguayan Air Force Flight 571, that thing you call the cabin, I think of as the fuselage, and every time I take off in a plane, I fully expect it to crash. In the Andes.)

The train accelerates surprisingly quickly as it leaves Paddington. We are running eight minutes late. Of course, I want those eight minutes to become fifteen, so I can claw back a pathetic fraction of the £76.55 I paid for my ticket, Great Western Railway having chosen, like Avanti, not to respond to my request for a free ride.

From my bag, I take out the gravestone: a hefty paperback edition of *Surreal Lives: The Surrealists 1917–1945* (Black Cat) by Ruth Brandon, a biographical study of key figures André Breton, Guillaume Apollinaire, Tristan Tzara, Marcel Duchamp, Louis Aragon and Salvador Dalí.

I bought it from Oxfam Bookshop Victoria in July 2023. Buried within its pages was a train ticket, from London terminals to Tiverton Parkway. It also had a name written on the flyleaf: E Croxford. The date on the ticket: 12 April 2001.

On the train to Exeter, which will call at Tiverton Parkway, I settle down to read about Breton, the so-called 'pape du Surréalisme'. I wonder why it is I'm not really drawn to biography, even if I am greatly interested in the subject, or subjects, or their work, which is true of the Surrealists. If what I am writing in these books is partly memoir, a form of biography, then I'm as bad as those novelists who don't read novels, like Belle and Sebastian's Stuart Murdoch, who said in an interview in the *Observer*, around the publication of his first novel, 'I'm a poor reader, especially of fiction. I gave that up a long time ago.'

I'm interested in the revelation that Breton occasionally wore glasses, with 'clear glass'. We know what Brandon means, though I like the implication that prescription lenses are perhaps sprinkled with magic optical crystals rather than just ground and polished. Why did he sometimes wear glasses, asks someone. He confesses that it's in memory of a 'grammatical example': '"noses were made to hold glasses".'

At Reading, I tear my eyes away from *Surreal Lives*. There are lots of people on the opposite platform, under, alongside and in front of signs saying, 'Reading.' Unfortunately, they're all looking at their phones. They might be reading, but it's not the same.

On arrival at Exeter, I visit Oxfam Books & Music, where staff confirm they are happy to accept a donation of a single book. I like *Surreal Lives* and if I were ten miles from home, I would hang on to it, but I'm ten miles from the start of a six-mile walk along the South West Coast Path to Budleigh Salterton. As I find it unthinkable to leave Oxfam without having a scout about, I do so and find a local Ordnance Survey map.

An hour later, I'm dodging paragliders on the red cliffs of the Jurassic Coast. My hosts in Budleigh Salterton are my old friend Ian and his wife Catriona. I've known Ian since I was chief sub at Reader's Digest in the early 1990s and he was a researcher. I would write headlines, standfirsts and captions for articles and he would check the facts, then all our work would be undone, first by an issue editor, then by a senior editor and then we'd start all over again. I timed this trip to coincide with an invitation to do something at the Budleigh Salterton Literary Festival, but as the date approached and no further details appeared, it got to the point where I felt that if I were to contact the person who had invited me, he would feel obliged to insert me into the programme at the last minute, which would probably not go well. My route takes me right past the festival marquee. From beyond the rippling canvas walls can be heard a guitar and a male voice, singing.

Ian gladly accepts my gift of *OS Landranger Exeter & Sidmouth*.

3

Library fines

If you can imagine this book as a large aeroplane, perhaps an Airbus 380, with me as the captain and my deadline as the runway lights, half way through December 2025, those lights were growing bigger and brighter in my windscreen – and a treacherous crosswind was picking up. But instead of sitting at home knocking out another thousand words, I opted to meet my good friend Gareth Evans at Bread & Butter in Haggerston for a coffee and a pastry. He arrived even later than usual, having stopped to check out the contents of the book exchange shelves in Haggerston Overground station on the way.

Knowing that they would be of interest to me, Gareth mentioned three books from the Royal London Hospital Patients' Library. I didn't want to curtail our coffee and chat, but I knew if I didn't act quickly, the Phantom Bookshelf Clearer of Haggerston Station, who Gareth has watched in action – this individual can empty those shelves in a matter of seconds – would beat me to these precious library books.

Precious library books?

The title of this chapter was originally going to be the title of the whole book – it rhymed with *White Spines* and *Shadow Lines*

– but when we focus-grouped it, two out of the three people we casually asked for their opinion said they thought *Library Fines* was a bit of a downer. Hence *Finders, Keepers*, which I've been a little uneasy about since we settled on it, partly because of the lack of alliteration and partly because of that comma. The comma may differentiate it from the 2015 Stephen King novel, *Finders Keepers*, and it may be required in the original phrase, 'finders, keepers', but how many people will even notice the comma and use it if they do – and does it even matter?

Precious library books because this chapter is all about library books, specifically finding library books that look as if they have gone missing from libraries, rather than been discarded, and about returning them where they belong.

Go on, skip, if you want, but then you'll never find out what that low wooden fencing is called, you know, the nasty stuff you can't sit on without making a dent in your backside – the wrong way. You may never know what New Mills smells like, how MMU is like footballer Andy Cole, or where Bark Psychosis recorded their first album.

Gareth and I did not curtail our meeting. We exchanged the usual despairing observations about the increasingly challenging landscape facing small presses and we talked about the recent initiative by Prototype publisher Jess Chandler and others to improve the situation, with an open letter in the *Bookseller* and various exciting plans, and then who should pop up at Gareth's shoulder but Jess Chandler. Bread & Butter is that kind of place. The last time I was there, I held the door open for Lemn Sissay.

In Haggerston station, the library books were still there. Resisting the lure of a paperback biography of Ray Charles, I took the two others, two big hardbacks – Wil Haygood's *In Black and White: The Life of Sammy Davis, Jr* (Aurum Press) and

Roy Hattersley's *The Edwardians* (Little, Brown) – and headed straight down Kingsland Road in the direction of Whitechapel, because on the spine and cover of each book was a sticky label saying, 'Please return to: The Patients' Library, The Royal London Hospital, Whitechapel, London E1 1BB.' It was my intention to do exactly that. There was even a phone number: 020 7377 x 3495. The Hattersley had entered stock in October 2004 and last been borrowed on 9 May 2005. In fact, that appeared to be the only time it had been borrowed. There was no indication the Sammy Davis biog had ever been borrowed, but nor was there any evidence on either book to suggest that they had been withdrawn/discarded/deleted from stock, so every reason to suspect the Patients' Library at the Royal London Hospital would be glad to get them back.

The first thing that happened on arrival at the Royal London Hospital was I got clobbered by volunteers to sign up for regular charitable donations to the London Air Ambulance. As an avid viewer of *Ambulance* and *24 Hours in A&E*, I felt I couldn't refuse. I then wandered about for a while, generally preferring to find my way around than ask for help, but when I soon found myself at the back of the hospital, I asked at the reception desk there. Over the road, came the answer, Near Sainsbury's.

Hm, OK, I thought, returning to the front of the building and exiting. Over the road and not too far from Sainsbury's was the local Tower Hamlets Library or 'Idea Store'.

Hm, I thought, but crossed the road anyway and had a little look down Brady Street, towards Sainsbury's. No sign of a Patients' Library or any outlying buildings belonging to the Royal London Hospital. I sat down for a minute on a stretch of timber knee rail fencing, also known as birdsmouth or diamond rail fencing, designed to discourage anyone from sitting on it – you know the sort of thing, hostile architecture, often used to demarcate a car park – and called the Royal London Hospital using the number on the stickers. An automated system prompted me to key in the five-digit extension number if I knew it. My extension number had four digits, so I hung on for the operator, who, when I said I wanted the Patients' Library, asked me to hang on. After a moment she told me it wasn't going very well, that the number she had tried didn't seem to exist. She asked me to hang on again and I did, but after about five minutes two short beeps indicated that the call had failed or been terminated, so I crossed the road and reentered the hospital and asked at the reception desk at the front of the building.

Second floor, said the man there.

OK, thanks, I said, heading off to look for the stairs and settling instead for a lift. I mooched around the second floor for a bit before picking up signs to the Staff Library.

Hm, OK, I thought. I found the Staff Library and went in and asked the librarian if there was a Patients' Library. No, she said. Is there one at Bart's, I asked. No, she said. There's no patients' library at any of the hospitals that belong to Barts Health NHS Trust, I asked, slowly getting the picture. No, she said. OK, thanks, I said.

As I trailed around the second floor looking for the stairs, I noticed, in a waiting area for 'Outpatient Therapies: Lung Function/Foot Clinic', not a bookcase exactly, more of a magazine rack, or leaflet rack, but there were no magazines or leaflets on it, only some unused plastic cups and a face-out copy of American televangelist Joel Osteen's book, *Your Best Life Now: 7 Steps to Living at Your Full Potential*. I placed my two books face out on the shelf below Osteen's and declared the Royal London Hospital Patients' Library reopened.

The Haygood and Hattersley titles were not the first library books I took from the book shelves at Haggerston. Towards the end of November 2025, I found a copy of Chelene Knight's *Dear Current Occupant* (Book*hug Press), a memoir in hybrid form combining prose, poetry and photography, and winner of the City of Vancouver Book Award. The book belonged to Whistler Public Library and did not appear to have been withdrawn from stock, so I packaged it up and sent it to Whistler in British Columbia. Less than two weeks later, an email popped into my inbox from Maz Esnouf, Technology and Support Services Librarian at Whistler Public Library. Maz explained that Knight's book had been deleted from their catalogue having been considered 'lost', ie 'borrowed by a patron and not returned', for more than twelve months, but whereas they normally score through the bar code with a marker pen to indicate a deleted book, in this case they hadn't. They had another copy of the book and so the copy I had sent them had now had its bar code scored through and would be placed on their free cart to 'live another life in someone else's collection'.

Haggerston is not the only station in which I've found library books waiting as if for the right train to get home. On a Sunday in October 2025, I walked to Levenshulme to deliver George Orwell's *A Clergyman's Daughter* to an address in Windsor Road. You may have read about that in the introduction to this volume. Having made my delivery, I thought Levenshulme station might be worth checking out. Levenshulme is the new Chorlton, you see. (As Chorlton is the new Didsbury, or the new West Didsbury, at least, although where that leaves Didsbury, or West Didsbury, I'm not sure.) A book exchange at the station would be either something they would have needed in order to become the new Chorlton, or something that would somehow inevitably follow, *having become* the new Chorlton.

Levenshulme station does indeed have a book exchange and among the books on the shelves that Sunday was a library book, *How to Be a Space Scientist in Your Own Home* (Lippincott) by Seymour Simon, illustrated by Bill Morrison. It was from the DC Public Library in Washington, DC, and had not obviously been withdrawn from stock. It would cost a bit to send it, but the following day I wrote an accompanying letter and packaged up the book and took it to the Post Office and sent it off.

Nothing yet – by mid December – but that's OK.

Nothing either from the school librarians at two schools in Highbury who would have returned to school after their summer holidays in 2025 to find some school library books waiting for them that had somehow ended up in the book exchange on Sotheby Road that I wrote about in the 'Free Books' chapter.

Nor from the secondary school in Hove to which I sent the copy of John Steinbeck's *Of Mice and Men* that I found in Cancer Research UK in Cheadle in May 2025.

That's OK as well.

My first return to a school library had gone well. The source, again, was the book exchange on Sotheby Road, the date a Sunday in October 2024 and the book Mal Peet's *Life: An Exploded Diagram* (Walker Books), which Daisy May Johnson says, on her blog, is 'a book that should not be shelved under YA fiction' and Meg Rosoff in the *Guardian* acclaimed as 'a rare treat for thoughtful readers of any age'. What attracted me to it was the fact that it had belonged to Cardinal Vaughan Memorial School library, where it had been due back on 26 September 2018. I dropped it off at CVMS, close to Holland Park in west

London, two days later, with a letter in which I mentioned that CVMS rang bells for me because it had been where my favourite writer, Derek Marlowe, had gone to school.

School librarian Katie Davies wrote me a kind email thanking me for helping her to accomplish one of her tasks. *Life: An Exploded Diagram* had been officially lost and Katie, who had only just joined the school staff, was chasing down a number of lost books. 'The book is now safely back on the shelves where it belongs as it had not been withdrawn,' she wrote. She was interested to hear about Old Vaughanian Derek Marlowe and said she would order in some of his titles. To get her started, I sent her a copy of *The Disappearance*, Penguin's reissue of Marlowe's 1970 novel *Echoes of Celandine*, the title changed to that of Stuart Cooper's chilly 1977 film adaptation.

Wednesday 17 April 1996

William Styron took me to one side and said he/she was determined he/she would not contribute to the book of writers' dreams I was putting together. I say 'he/she' because although I knew he was William Styron, he looked like Meryl Streep. It seemed there was the potential for talking him/her into it – all he/she wanted was to be asked to do it. I said, 'I very much want you in the book,' and he/she said, 'I'm in.' Pleased, I walked up the road with him/her and one other (unknown). Then I was leaving a building by a white-painted stairwell. Every time I went through the door at the bottom, it appeared to lead outside, but then I was back inside again. There were always two ways I could go and they both led back the same way. The place I was trying to leave was a library I'd been in earlier in the dream. The library was surprisingly noisy. I complained to the librarian (my former colleague Chloë Bryan-Brown, although she didn't look like Chloë) who said silence was not mandatory.

New Mills is a small town in Derbyshire on the edge of the Peak District. The excellent High Street Books, of New Mills, had posted on social media about having to close if they couldn't raise some cash, which they intended to do by having a half-price sale on books and records.

It was a bright, clear day in September and the time was 11 a.m. I walked by the Mersey to Stockport, then up the A6, through Hazel Grove, to High Lane, then bore left up Carr Brow and Jacksons Edge Road. Lovely, but a bit of a climb. Through Disley, then up Hollinwood Road on to the Peak Forest Canal. You know you've reached New Mills when you smell the Swizzells sweet factory.

Adam Morris at High Street Books reported that it had been busy since the weekend. 'Queues out the door. No one asking for the 50 per cent discount, apart from one bloke buying a record priced at 80 quid. People behind him in the queue tutting.'

I bought two old Penguins: one with an orange spine, Evelyn Waugh's *Unconditional Surrender*, with an inclusion at page 61, a photograph of a governess with her three charges, a boy in a pram, a girl standing by the pram and an older boy playing near two parked cars from the 1930s or 1940s; and one in the green and white livery of Penguin's crime list, a 1949 edition of Kenneth Fearing's brilliant noir thriller *The Big Clock*, which someone had recommended to me. (It was the last time I would write down a recommendation in my notebook without also keeping a record of who had made the recommendation.) A previous owner, Jean Bilby, has written her name and the date, 1959, on the flyleaf, and on the title page she has copied out the title, matching its use of italics. I read several chapters on the walk back along the Peak Forest Canal, which I stayed on until Marple, where there was a book box containing a Stockport Libraries book, Faye Kellerman's *The Hunt* (HarperCollins). Stockport Central Library was closed when I passed it on my way home. (I delivered it in the following days; it was received with thanks.) I got home at 10pm, having walked 34.3 miles, the most I'd ever walked in a day.

The shortest distance I've walked to return a lost library book is from Manchester's Northern Quarter to MMU. In Oxfam on Oldham Street, on a Friday afternoon in November 2024, they had just put out a large donation of Agatha Christie paperbacks, including an edition of *The Murder at the Vicarage* with a different Tom Adams cover than the one I already had. So, obviously, I had to buy that. Also: a copy of Rachel Cusk's *Outline* (Faber) purporting to be the property of MMU Library, so I popped it round there and spoke to a librarian who happily took it back into stock. It had been missing presumed lost, or lost presumed missing. It wouldn't actually go back on the shelf, though, because the library was in temporary accommodation and would remain so for four years. The floors of the John Dalton Building are non-load bearing, apparently. Nice one, MMU. A library without books. MMU, by the way, had always been known as MMU until a certain point when I was working there, when my colleagues and I were encouraged to start calling it Manchester Met. This reminded me of when Manchester United footballer Andy Cole let it be known that he wished to be referred to henceforth as Andrew Cole. It had felt somewhat vainglorious.

MMU staff would refer to the University of Manchester as 'the place down the road'. In February 2025, in Oxfam in

Withington, I found Ian Fleming's *From Russia With Love* (Penguin Modern Classics). It was a John Rylands Library copy, so the next day I walked up to the University of Manchester Library. I spoke to a man with a shaved head, crystal-framed glasses and a soul patch and asked him if this was the John Rylands Library or if the John Rylands Library was the famous library in town, on Deansgate. He said this library – the building we were in – was the University Library, which had previously been called the John Rylands University Library, but now they just called it the University Library to make it less confusing, but it didn't seem to have worked. We both smiled at that. I explained about the book, which he confirmed was theirs and when he looked it up he found that it was still on loan, until 25 June. He could see who it was on loan to, but obviously was not going to say. Of course, I said, but in fact I would have been very interested to find out. Still, I said I didn't want to get anyone into trouble – that wasn't the point – and he said he wouldn't contact them, but would just return the book to the stock and maybe they would see on their account that it had been returned. Maybe they would wonder how. We both wondered how the book could have ended up in Oxfam. He suggested there might have been a break-in, which we agreed seemed unlikely. I said I hoped the student was OK. He said it was nice to know I'd be writing about it, then added, as long as I was going to write about them in positive terms.

A couple of weeks later, I was walking into town again, via the university district, reading Shane O'Mara's *In Praise of Walking* (Bodley Head). I don't normally write in books, preferring to make notes on small pages torn from hotel memo pads, but in this case, because the jacket was in such poor condition and because I found myself agreeing so often with what O'Mara has to say about the benefits of walking, I drew lines in the margin beside whole paragraphs, even whole pages, almost entire chapters, such as the one devoted to 'Creative Walking'. I found Professor O'Mara's academic email online and wrote to thank him for his research and his book. I imagined him writing back and us becoming great pals and going out for walks together, but I didn't hear back. He was probably too busy getting his miles in. 'Lots of regular walking, especially if conducted at high tempo, with an appropriate rhythm, forestalls many of the bad things that come with ageing,' he writes in his book.

In July 2024, I tore the meniscus in my right knee playing football. A scan revealed osteoarthritis, a bigger problem than the torn meniscus and one about which not much could be done, according to the two orthopaedic surgeons I would see in the fracture clinic over the coming months, who I will call Good Cop and Bad Cop. What are you doing playing football, Bad Cop would mutter, at your age? What are you doing walking ten miles a day, at your age? Good Cop, meanwhile, when I was lucky enough to see him instead, would go, You want to play football? Play football. You want to walk ten miles a day? Walk ten miles a day. Do what makes you happy.

Good Cop still didn't seem any keener than Bad Cop when it came to the subject of keyhole surgery for the torn meniscus, however.

I thought about quoting lines from *In Praise of Walking* to Bad Cop, or better still, giving him the book. Maybe it would be seen as a bit too passive-aggressive. Or just aggressive. 'The cure is right in front of us: to get up and walk,' writes O'Mara, as he extols the benefits of walking, to the heart, the gut, even the brain.

In the book and record sale at the University of Manchester

students union, I found *A Safety Match* (Penguin) by Ian Hay, which I bought to give to another Ian Hay, he of the Saul Hay Gallery (it would not be his first copy), and another book from the John Rylands Library, the 'First Annual Hopkins Sermon', as in poet Gerard Manley Hopkins, by the Rt Rev Dr Trevor Huddlestone, Bishop of Stepney. It was dated 1969 and stamped by the library in 1976, stickered with BASEMENT and NOT TO BE REMOVED FROM THE LIBRARY. The sermon was preached at St John's Parish Church, Stratford, in east London. I decided to walk over there when in London at the weekend and read it in situ. I saw from the internet that Bark Psychosis had recorded their debut album, *Hex*, in St John's Church in the early 1990s.

That Sunday I walked from Stoke Newington to Stratford reading some more of *In Praise of Walking*. On the way, I bobbed into Mind on Chatsworth Road and bought Harry Ritchie's *Out There* (Penguin), which I wrote about in the introduction to this book. Once at St John's Church, I put on the final track from *Hex*, a ten-minute instrumental called 'Pendulum Man', and read Trevor Huddleston's sermon about Gerard Manley Hopkins. It didn't turn me on to Hopkins, whose work I had struggled with at A-level – or on to religion.

The church looked a bit unloved. Temporary barriers fenced off most entrances. A sign declared that any non-church cars parked in the car park would be locked in. It didn't sound very Christian to me. I've always had a rather simplistic expectation of Christianity, that its adherents should be kind and unselfish. When I was acquiring and editing fiction for Salt Publishing, one of my authors suggested I ask a certain Christian novelist for a quote. A university colleague asked him for me and obtained no response. I asked again and the colleague asked again – I was told – and still no response. I tried a third time with the same result.

I hated asking writers for quotes. You're asking them for that most valuable commodity, their time, and there's nothing in it for them, apart from the warm feeling of helping someone in a less privileged position. I believe that if quotes are required, and I tend to think we should wean ourselves off our dependence on them, it's the editor's job to get them, not the author's. It's fairer on those being asked as it's easier to say no to an editor. The least you have a right to expect, as an editor asking for a quote, is a response, even if it's a no.

In the car park at St John's Church, a single black car was parked. I was walking in circles around an obelisk in the churchyard and had reached the last page of the Huddleston sermon when I realised the car had turned around and was being driven out of the gate. Fearing I would be locked in, I exited the orbit of the obelisk. A gentleman then got out of the car and started preparing to lock the gates. I approached him and showed him the sermon, thinking he might be interested. He said the church would be open at 11 a.m. the following day. I asked him if he was the vicar. He said he was a member of the church.

The following Wednesday, I took the Huddleston pamphlet to the University of Manchester Library. The librarian who accepted it said she would pass it on to 'collections management'. I asked if she wouldn't mind looking it up. She could find Hopkins lectures but no sermons. I asked her to drop me a line should she have any joy. Didn't Hopkins write about joy, in 'Spring'? 'What is all this juice and all this joy?'

I'm not exaggerating when I say that joy is what I felt when I found, in a book exchange on rue Guillaume Stocq in Ixelles, Brussels, in December 2024, a book in perfect condition that gave every indication, not only that it still belonged to the Bibliotheek Tweebronnen in Leuven, but that it was actually due back there. The book was a novel, *Thriller* – great title! – by Iegor Gran, and the publisher was one of my favourite French publishers, P.O.L. I would have liked to read it, but time was short, and the following day, I boarded a bus to Leuven.

Take care around the Town Hall in Leuven. One's first glimpse of this Gothic masterpiece can cause the jaw to drop so violently, it may become dislocated. Mandible back in place, I found the library and nipped up to the first floor, where I approached a young librarian. Do you speak English, I asked him. (Don't try to show off your French in Flanders. It's all Flemish/Dutch or English.) Of course! he said. He accepted the book and my story of its recovery and return with the same level of pleasure as evinced by the librarian at Stretford Library when I turned up in May 2025 with a copy of *The Handmade Marketplace* (Storey Publishing) by Kari Chapin that I'd found in Barnardos Vintage in Cheadle. It had been deleted on 21 March, she told me, 'believed lost'. With one click of her mouse, she returned it to the system and she told me she would send it to Coppice Avenue, the branch where it had lived. Win win.

The only time I returned a book to a library only to have it returned to me was on Monday 12 May 2025. The previous day, I had been walking back from watching my son's football team, Limehouse Tigres, entertain East London Spartans at Hackney Marshes. It was a cup game and, unusually, Limehouse Tigres were not victorious, but in Mind on Chatsworth Road I found a Hackney Libraries copy of Robert Louis Stevenson's *Dr Jekyll & Mr Hyde* (Vintage), which did feel like a small victory. Its last due-back date was 29 June 2011, but I knew that stamped due-back dates were ghosts from the past. The next day, I took it to the CLR James Library in Dalston. The man there said it had been removed from the catalogue and promptly ripped out the flyleaf in front of me. I felt something tear inside me. I asked would it have been removed from the catalogue after being reported missing and he said it could have been removed and someone simply forgot to tear out the flyleaf. He said after fifteen years or so a book would often be removed. Even if it was still being borrowed, I asked. Yes, he said. Lose lose.

He handed the remains back to me and I donated what was left of the book to the Dalston branch of Mind.

July 2025. Tram into town, then train to Liverpool. Off at Broad Green and on foot to the Dead Ink shop, which I'd been meaning to visit since it opened in 2022. On the way, called in at the Roy Castle Lung Cancer Foundation, where I bought a signed copy of Ramsey Campbell's *Somebody's Voice* (Flame Tree Press), inscribed to Carol. (I would later send it to short story writer Carol Farrelly.) At the Dead Ink shop, I delivered the fifty Nightjars that bookseller Michael Lacey had ordered.

In Oxfam on Bold Street, I bought Clare Wigfall's collection, *The Loudest Sound and Nothing* (Faber), because it looked like a lost Liverpool John Moores University Library book, so I took it straight up there and talked to a nice man called Jonathan who checked and found that they had had two copies, so this one had probably been weeded out. He asked if I would like to keep it or donate it to their free bookshelf. I opted for the latter. He was keen to hear about the book I told him I was writing – the one you are reading now – and said the library would be interested in putting on an event.

When I return lost library books, I'm not looking to obtain anything, so this was a bonus, and it reminded me of my first time. In September 2024, in Oxfam in Richmond, Surrey, I found a Lambeth Libraries copy, in excellent condition, of Giorgio Bassani's *The Heron* (Penguin Modern Classics). I bought it and took it, two days later, to Waterloo Library in the Oasis Centre. The librarian was pleasantly surprised by my explanation of how I came by the book and when he looked it up he said it had been reported lost. He was delighted to get it back and asked me if I'd paid for it. I said yes, but that I didn't need the money. He gently insisted and asked what I'd paid for it. I said a couple of quid, which he gave me from the photocopier. He preferred not to be mentioned by name, but said I could say the librarian had been very grateful for the book's safe return.

I gave the £2 to a young man sleeping rough in the doorway of my local library in Manchester.

4

London something

The St Giles Book Fair in St Giles' Cripplegate Church had been trailing its latest seasonal opening and I was pleased to be in London for its first weekend. I have found good stuff there in the past, and even if I leave empty handed, I still have an opportunity to wander off afterwards and get lost in the tiled walkways of the beautiful, bewildering Barbican.

I walk down there from Stoke Newington listening to Yes's *Close to the Edge*, having read on the book fair's Instagram that Rick Wakeman's organ solo on the album's title track was recorded on the St Giles pipe organ. As I enter the church, the first thing I hear is that very instrument. Whether it's Rick Wakeman on *Close to the Edge* or the church's organist practising for an upcoming service, the sound of the organ in St Giles' Cripplegate causes one's heart to beat faster.

It raises an interesting question. While browsing, is background music welcome or unwelcome? Does it depend on the music? I'm not a big fan of disco or power ballads or Simply Red, but I think Wendy Elliott née Royle (no relation), the otherwise utterly irreproachable manager of my local Oxfam, might be. Certainly of disco and power ballads, anyway. In the spirit of helpfulness, I made her a mix tape CD of ambient music, but she wasn't keen. I wonder if browsing, since it generally involves some reading, might be incompatible with listening to – or even hearing in the background – music with words. Having said that, the first time I heard American singer-songwriter Bill Callahan – his 2009 album *Sometimes I Wish We Were an Eagle* – I was browsing in Brussels' gorgeous Librairie Nijinski, and I found I was able to appreciate the music and make good choices in terms of what to buy (books by Alain Robbe-Grillet, Roland Topor, Hélène Lenoir and Pierre Bourgeade). The free espresso may have helped.

Back in St Giles' Cripplegate, between arpeggios on the organ, I overhear a customer asking a volunteer how they get so many interesting art books and the answer comes back that the books are mostly donated by people who live near by and that the local population includes a lot of artists. Indeed, I know an artist who lives in the Barbican and two authors and one writer who used to live here before he moved to Earl's Court, where he died, which just goes to show, you shouldn't move out of the Barbican, or not to Earl's Court. Actually, that suggests I knew Robert Aickman, which I did not, and that I know Olivia Laing, which I do not, or not beyond us having read some of each other's books and liked the odd Instagram post. But I know Sarah Guy, who writes about food, London and travel, and painter and printmaker Julia Hamilton.

I leave St Giles' Church with a Penguin Modern Classics edition of Len Deighton's 1985 novel *London Match* in my bag. *London Match* followed *Berlin Game* and *Mexico Set*, concluding Deighton's *Game, Set and Match* trilogy. In the 1980s, I wrote a story set in the Barbican that, mercifully, remains unpublished. 'Picnic at the Barbican' was my rather juvenile response to two great works of art that I encountered around the same time. One of these was Peter Weir's 1975 adaptation of Joan Lindsay's 1967 novel *Picnic at Hanging Rock*. The other was the Barbican itself. If you don't know the Barbican, it's a residential estate of just over 2000 flats and a masterpiece of Brutalist architecture, built between 1965 and 1976, with a prestigious arts centre at its heart. The Barbican has a well-earned reputation for being impossible to find your way around. I've been visiting it for more than forty years and still get lost, like the schoolgirls who go missing at Hanging Rock. I am currently thinking about a ghost story I have to write set in the Barbican, for an anthology of Brutalist ghost stories. I stand at the bottom of Cromwell Tower and wonder how I'm going to get in there. A problem for another day.

I ask Sarah Guy, who has lived in the Barbican for twenty years, if she struggles with the geography. 'No,' she tells me, 'these days I don't ever get lost. Sometimes I have to stop and think about certain routes eg rain-free, scenic, fastest etc, or if I want to get to an area I haven't been to for years (eg the tennis courts).'

As I walk back up towards Angel, I enjoy reading the opening chapter of Len Deighton's *London Match*, but the question I'm asking myself more urgently than 'Do I want to read 400 pages of this, enjoyable as it is?' is 'Why has Derek Marlowe, whose first book, like Deighton's, was a best-selling spy novel, and who, in my opinion, is as good a writer as anyone on the Penguin Modern Classics list, never been picked up by PMC?' I always used to think it was because Marlowe was a butterfly of an author flitting from genre to genre, a spy novel here, a detective story there, even one or two that didn't fit in anywhere, while Deighton, say, had the good sense to stick to espionage, except he didn't. There was variety in his output — a dystopian alternative history, military histories, even cookery books — but he was known and celebrated as a spy writer. Maybe if you do one thing well enough and become known for it, you're allowed to try on a few different hats, whereas if you hop restlessly from pillar to post, no one knows what to call you and so you don't get called anything. You suffer the indignity, instead, of forever being confused with another writer with a similar name. Oh yes, the Factory novels, people say when I mention Derek Marlowe's name. No, I say, that's Derek Raymond, and of course that wasn't even his real name. Still, at least they're mixing Marlowe up with another good writer and — I met Raymond, real name Robin Cook, on two occasions — a charming man, whereas I never met Marlowe, but I told that story in *Shadow Lines*.

The best of Marlowe's novels — *A Dandy in Aspic*, *Echoes of Celandine*, *Do You Remember England?*, *Somebody's Sister* and *Nightshade* — deserve to be in print on a good list, as they were in 1977 when Penguin reissued them in uniform white-spined editions with photographic covers by Paul Wakefield.

The Barbican pops up in chapter two of *London Consequences*, a chain novel or group novel written by twenty authors and edited by Margaret Drabble and BS Johnson. Published in 1972 by the Greater London Arts Association, *London Consequences* was also a competition. The first and last chapters were written by Drabble and Johnson together, but while the names of the other eighteen authors appeared on the back cover in alphabetical order, who had written which chapter was left up to readers to guess. The GLAA offered £100 to any reader who could match authors to chapters.

Newspaper editor Raoul Twomey, the novel's antagonist, has a flat in the Barbican: 'He picked up his glass of lemon juice and walked over to the window. His move to the Barbican had coincided with the board's decision to make his editorship . . . a permanent appointment.' This struck a chord with me, since in 1992, I accepted a job on the colour supplement of an obnoxious Sunday newspaper and put in an offer on a flat on the eleventh floor of Great Arthur House, on the Golden Lane Estate, close enough to the Barbican that you could fly a paper aeroplane from one to the other. The flat had a balcony – something I had always dreamed of – facing west. I pictured myself sitting there watching the sun go down and decided there were compensations to selling your soul.

The magazine was the worst working environment I ever experienced (if I forget a couple of weeks' caddying at Dunham Forest Golf Club in the 1970s – if only I could), dominated by bullying, misogyny and terror. I was chief sub on the magazine, which was edited by a short man called Nick, whose appearance on the floor of the editorial department would strike fear into the heart of everyone present, as he stalked from desk to desk picking up a proof here, a galley there, criticising, humiliating. Sharing a name and physical stature with the editor did not grant me any special status.

After a few weeks, he called me into his office and indicated the seat across the desk from his. I remembered sitting there a few weeks earlier, at my interview, when he had told me the salary on offer. Perched on the edge of the seat, I heard the amount, which was twice what I was on at the time, as chief sub at Reader's Digest, and almost fell off the chair. I must have been aware of the salary in advance, but hearing it spoken out loud, I struggled to keep a straight face. It was life changing, but was it worth it? I hated the newspaper the magazine was attached to, and everything it stood for, so how could I work for it? Maybe I wasn't selling my soul. Maybe I was just letting it. It didn't have to be for ever. Or even for very long. (It wasn't.)

Back on the edge of the same chair, I heard Nick ask me how I was getting on. OK, I said. What about the subs? he asked. Emerson and Simon have been showing me the ropes, I said. What about the cunts? he asked. What could he mean? Mentally I went around the rest of the subs' desk. I find that now I can remember the name of only one of them, the one who wasn't constantly shooting me icy glares, because we had a friend in common. The truth was they all associated my having been hired with the sacking of my predecessor, their friend, the former chief sub. She had been well liked. Apart from Emerson, Simon and myself, the subs desk was entirely composed of women. I felt a cold weight drop into my stomach as I realised who Nick meant by 'the cunts'.

After six months, Nick was fired and a new editor installed. I sat on the edge of the same seat once more, facing a different person behind the editor's desk. 'As you know, Nick,' she said, 'I'm making a few changes. Unfortunately, you don't figure in those changes.' I was tempted to sub that, because from where I was sitting, losing my job definitely meant figuring in her changes, but I knew what she meant, and I could not have been happier, although a moment later when she mentioned the amount of money they would have to pay me to get rid of me, I suddenly found I did feel even happier. The cash wouldn't last long, however, if I was using it to pay the mortgage on the flat in Great Arthur House, so I withdrew my offer. The vendors were not happy and neither was I. Sitting on that balcony watching the sun go down over west London is a moment-that-got-away to rival having my novel *The Director's Cut* almost made into a film by Jeremy Thomas (he had it under option for five years, paid me to write a script, even got as far as talking about casting Cillian Murphy in the lead role).

Mrs Twomey, the newspaper editor's wife in *London Consequences*, still lives in Kensington and calls the Barbican an 'elephant's grave yard', but Raoul likes the view, 'the river lying down there like flexible steel, the gold cross on the dome of St Paul's catching the light, the dawn haze lifting so that the concrete and glass monoliths in Threadneedle Street suddenly came into focus.'

As you might expect of a novel with twenty authors, *London Consequences* is rather bitty. 'I don't know what it is about novels these days, [Judith] thought,' we read in chapter 15, Judith being the wife of protagonist Anthony Sheridan, a political journalist. 'I just can't seem able to get interested in them. I can't relate to the weird characters they write about nowadays, the way the narrative jumps about, I suppose it's meant to be frightfully modern but half the time I haven't the faintest idea what is supposed to be going on. She threw the book across the room.' I was never tempted to throw *London Consequences* across the room; at the time of writing, there are only ten copies on AbeBooks, priced between £50 and £175. I don't know where I found my copy as it was more than ten years ago, before I started keeping records, but I paid only £2 for it. I think it likely the author of chapter 15 was writing, perhaps with her tongue lodged in her cheek, about the book she was helping to write. She? Who knows? The eighteen authors whose names were not attached to the chapters they wrote were all 'well-known novelists living in London', namely Paul Ableman, John Bowen, Melvyn Bragg, Vincent Brome, Peter Buckman, Alan Burns, Barry Cole, Eva Figes, Gillian Freeman, Jane Gaskell, Wilson Harris, Rayner Heppenstall, Olivia Manning, Adrian Mitchell, Julian Mitchell,

Andrea Newman, Piers Paul Read and Stefan Themerson. The GLAA commissioned the book to mark the 1972 Festivals of London. The closing date for receipt of entries to the competition was 11 August 1972 and entries would only be accepted if they used the form provided on the last page of the book. The last page of my copy is intact and bears no markings, suggesting that the original owner was not up to the challenge.

Margaret Drabble does not have a very high opinion of *London Consequences*. In an essay published in the *TLS* on 16 February 2024 she describes the book as 'more or less unreadable', but she is right to say it gives readers 'a sense of the zeitgeist'. It's notable that the editors of *London Consequences* allowed the anonymous author of chapter nine to get away with saying that painter and poet Adrian Henri had 'a thing about school girls': it was a different time.

I have a degree of familiarity with the work of half of the writers involved, yet my own efforts, as I read the novel, to assign chapters to authors, never really got beyond the simplistic assumption that the chapters focusing on Judith were mostly written by women and that the men wrote mainly about the male characters. Drabble's essay made me feel a little better about this, as she confessed, as co-editor, to not being able to remember who had written which chapter.

In 2022, novelist and *A Personal Anthology* curator Jonathan Gibbs announced that he, David Collard and Michael Hughes were planning to produce a follow-up volume, *London Consequences 2*. Hughes and Gibbs would co-write the first and last chapters and Gibbs would team up with Collard to be joint editors or, in the modern parlance, show-runners. A line-up of able seamen and women was chosen – Kevin Boniface, Marie-Elsa Bragg, Ruby Cowling, Wendy Erskine, Tim Etchells, Shelley

Hastings, David Hayden, Vlatka Horvat, Heidi James, Toby Litt, Linda Mannheim, Melissa McCarthy, Sam Mills, Simon Okotie, Ben Pester, Devika Ponnambalam, Eley Williams – but the ship ran aground for mysterious reasons. A little bird – a stormy petrel, perhaps, to stretch the analogy – told me that one unnamed contributor had objected to something or other and the whole thing had had to be dropped.

In 2023, guest-editing an issue of *Confingo Magazine*, I approached Simon Okotie for a story and he sent me 'Chapter From an Abandoned Collaborative Novel', which I read and accepted. I told Okotie I liked the title, finding it of a piece with his experimental approach and either not knowing or having forgotten that he had been one of the prospective contributors to *London Consequences 2*. He explained where it came from and we decided to keep it. I asked him to spill the beans on what led to the abandonment and he demurred, claiming not to know what had happened. And so, the guessing game around *London Consequences 2* ended up having less to do with who wrote what than with who jumped ship.

You can't keep a good masterpiece of Brutalist architecture down. The Barbican pops up again in Mick Herron's *London Rules* (John Murray), which I bought (from Mind in Didsbury in 2018) but didn't read before *Slow Horses* aired on Apple TV in 2022 with Gary Oldman as the hilariously revolting Jackson Lamb. *London Rules* became season five of *Slow Horses* in September 2025. I haven't seen it yet, though I have seen the first four seasons, and it's weird how reading the novel feels a lot like watching the adaptation that I haven't yet seen. The dialogue is sharp and funny, and Herron is especially good at steadily increasing the tension in dramatic scenes by switching between points of view. He gives us two different points of view on the

Barbican as well: first, Roddy Ho's – 'the ugly concrete towers of the Barbican' – and a few pages later we get this, filtered through the POV of JK Coe: 'Coe stopped mid-sentence and stared through the window at the Barbican opposite. It was an Orwellian nightmare of a complex, a concrete monstrosity, but credit where it was due: like Ronnie and Reggie Kray before it, the Barbican had overcome the drawback of being a brutal piece of shit to achieve iconic status. But that was London Rules for you: force others to take you on your own terms. And if they didn't like it, stay in their face until they did.'

Towards the end of the novel, MI5 Deputy Director-General Diana Taverner turns on the TV. 'Aerial images of London filled the screen. Just ten years ago, it had looked so different: no Heron Tower, no Needle. Fold back twenty years, and you lost the Gherkin, the Eye, half the skyline. And twenty years from now, who knew; there might be monorails stretched between hundred-storey towers. But it would still be London because that was the rule. Under the glitter and glad rags, the same heart beat.'

It seems a long time now since we were promised monorails – and jet-packs and lives of leisure. Did those visions of the future include leaf blowers, complicated 'meal deals' and 'See it, Say it, Sorted' alongside dwindling savings and pensions, not to mention Brexit and a possible descent into government by the far right in a suit and tie?

Saturday 25 October 2025
Upper Street, Islington, London.
Man, forties, glasses, walking north, towards Islington Green, reading *City of Miracles* (Arcadia) by Robert Jackson Bennett.

Nicola Upson's *London Rain* (Faber) offers us a vision of the past – May 1937 to be precise. It's the sixth in her series of novels featuring a fictional version of acclaimed crime writer Josephine Tey. Another historical novel, *London Dust* (Arrow) was university support worker Lee Jackson's debut. Set in the 1850s, it opens with a leap from Blackfriars Bridge. I bought my copy a few miles downstream at Oxfam Bookshop Greenwich. On the same visit, I bought a duplicate Picador edition of Josef Skvorecky's *The Bass Saxophone*, the name Bonnie VandeSteeg written in blue ballpoint on the flyleaf. Bonnie VandeSteeg is the author of *Land For What? Land For Whom? Senses of Place and Conflict in the Scottish Highlands*, published in 2021 by Stormy Petrel Books, unless there are two Bonnie VandeSteegs.

Two more first novels – *London Triptych* (Myriad Editions) by Jonathan Kemp and *London Blues* (No Exit Press) by Anthony Frewin – prompt me to wonder if *London Something* is a title formula that is attractive to the first-time novelist. *London Triptych* was shortlisted for the Green Carnation Award and won the Authors' Club Best First Novel Award. I bought it from St Vincent charity shop in Hackney and read it not long after reading another first novel, *Isaac*, by Curtis Garner, a former student of mine living half a mile up the road from St Vincent. Both novels owe something to another debut, *A Matter of Life and Sex*, by Oscar Moore, a novel I fell for before it was published in that form. Moore's debut was drip-fed into readers' imaginations via chapters excerpted in 1980s magazine *The Fred*, before it was published in book form by Paper Drum and later reprinted by Penguin. When I look back at my copies of *The Fred*, I see that Jonathan Kemp appeared in those pages also, alongside the likes of Kathy Acker, Sue Tilly, Gilbert & George and a callow youth by the name of Nicholas Royle. *A Matter of Life and Sex* was my first exposure to explicit gay content, although probably no one called it content in the 1980s. (As I typed those words, a link to the London Book Fair 2026 pinged into my inbox with a line across the screen – 'Defining the future of creative content.') I found it as startling as it was fascinating and not unexciting.

Kemp's novel is a triptych in respect of its timeline. There are three stories, dated 1894, 1954 and 1998, with male prostitution a common thread. Oscar Wilde appears as himself and I was intrigued by Dominic, who the narrator of the 1998 strand encounters when he moves to a squat in King's Cross. 'In his soft, serious voice, Dominic told us he was working on a long poem about the place and its history . . .' I'd bet my gorgeous Goldmark first edition of Aidan Andrew Dun's epic poem *Vale Royal* that Dominic is Dun. Dominic recites part of his poem and the narrator quotes a line: 'He was mad by every measure of a standard man.' I listen to Dun's recording of *Vale Royal*, supplied on two CDs tucked into the back of my copy. I listen all the way through, which takes over two hours, and don't hear the line, but then open the book at random and there, two-thirds of the way down page 62, we read:

> Thomas, Thomas. He believes too much.
> He has drunk too deeply from the River of Wells.
> He is mad by every measure of a standard man.

The tense is different. Either Kemp misquoted it or Dun changed it in his redrafting, or Kemp deliberately altered it to fictionalise it.

Still, the character I feel most drawn to in *London Triptych* is

Colin, the frustrated narrator of the 1954 strand about an artist who falls in love with his life model.

Anthony Frewin's *London Blues* (No Exit Press), which I acquired in 1997, the year it was published, took me a couple of goes to get into. On my second attempt, I read it in three days walking around London. Its strength is its portrayal of Bayswater and the East End, of Soho and – OK, so it's half way to Cambridge, but it's only just beyond Luton, where you'll find what is supposedly one of London's airports – Hitchin. Although it takes a while to get going, I did eventually find it compelling. When I wasn't reading, I was looking forward to getting back to reading, although there were long sections that could have been shorter and perhaps a few too many blow-by-blow descriptions of blue films.

The cover is a liability – a photograph, credited to Rapho, of a woman in what I call complicated underwear. I was reading the novel while walking down Essex Road and an older lady coming towards me looked at it and then looked at me and I wished I was reading Conrad Williams's *London Revenant* (The Do-Not Press) instead, with its harmless palimpsest design by Zaz Kee. In Conrad Williams's second novel, a dark urban fantasy, someone is pushing people under tube trains. Narrator Adam Buckley thinks he knows who's doing it. *London Revenant* is set in, on and under the streets of the capital, which Williams names on every page with relish, for our pleasure. 'Adam's feeling for the city is pretty much how I feel,' said Williams in an online interview with Jeff VanderMeer at SF Site in January 2006. 'Very much love-hate. I've lived in London since 1994, give or take the odd six months here and there, and whenever I leave I feel happy and when I come back I feel bad, but once I've been here for a while, I love the place. I love its second-hand bookshops, its cafés, its parks, its history. No city I've ever been to lifts the hair on the back of my neck as much as London when I see it from Waterloo Bridge. It's a stunning place, but it's also incredibly insular. The novel was my Valentine and Dear John to the city at the same time.'

If in the course of his research Williams has ingested an *A–Z* – I mean this is a good way – then Iain Sinclair has made short work also of the *Nicholson London Streetfinder*, the *Times Atlas of London*, and Harry Beck's tube map. I read most of Sinclair's *London Overground* (Penguin) on a Sunday in April 2023, walking from Dalston to Notting Hill and back via the Regent's Canal. As I passed within earshot of London Zoo, I read that Angela Carter 'took off with her man, whenever they could, to a narrowboat. I think she said it was parked in Camden, somewhere near London Zoo. Did she lie in her tight bed listening to the lions and the shrieking birds?'

I called in at the Oxfam Bookshop on Portobello Road – it would have been rude not to – and was disappointed to find Simon Kinch's excellent novel, *Two Sketches of Disjointed Happiness* (Salt), still on the shelf after I had, on my previous visit, recommended it to a young woman who had been perusing its pages.

The London Overground might have been orange, before its transformation into a network of many colours, but *London Overground*, subtitled 'A Day's Walk Around the Ginger Line', turns mysteriously yellow as it nears its end: 'yellow twilight', we read, and 'yellow hoists', not to mention 'yellow-nosed trains'. Then: 'The characters who truly understood film, yellow from cheap cigars and years chasing festivals . . .' There is also a line I will try to remember for Bad Cop: 'Walking inhibits reflex systems of censorship.'

Sinclair is the only author who features twice in my collection of *London Something* titles. On a Tuesday in September 2020, I staggered away from Oxfam Books & Music Berkhamsted – one of the best Oxfam bookshops, if not the best – with twelve books, among them Sinclair's *London Orbital*. In *The Verbals* (Worple Press), Kevin Jackson asks Sinclair to elaborate on the origins of *London Orbital*. The Hackney bookman answers: 'Everything I did was always based on walking, so having decided that the M25 more or less described this perimeter fence of London, then the only way to deal with it from my point of view was to walk it.'

A publisher that features twice in my collection is Jim Driver's The Do-Not Press. Ken Bruen's *London Boulevard* is pitch-black noir. Mitch, a voracious reader of crime fiction, leaves prison after a three stretch for GBH and moves into temporary accommodation that's full of good clothes and crime novels, among the threads a raincoat from London Fog and among the authors Elmore Leonard, James Sallis, Charles Willeford, John Harvey, Jim Thompson and Andrew Vachss. Mitch lucks into a job as a handyman for a faded actress living in a Holland Park mansion. Is it good luck or bad, though? She may be sixty, but he's strongly attracted to her, and why the hell not? Her butler, Jordan, might have the answer to that. Jordan looks after Mitch, preparing a studio flat for him over the garage, where a Rolls Royce Silver Ghost sits waiting. Over the course of an engrossing narrative, Mitch drops more names, Bruen paying his dues: Derek Raymond, Lawrence Block, Dennis Lehane, John Sandford, Edward Bunker, George Pelecanos, Fred Willard, James Ellroy, Mickey Spillane, Harry Crews and Thomas Boyle. In among the crime writers are mentions for Albert Camus, Laurie Lee and 'some poet' (page 70), which made me laugh, but not as much as a line on page 188, when Jordan makes a brew for him and Mitch and pours in a drop of Scotch. 'It tasted like tea with whisky added.' It reminds me of a line from a short story, 'The Blue Goose', by Boris Vian: 'Little clouds gave the sky the appearance of a sky dotted with little clouds, which was the case.' (My translation.)

Friday 12 September 2025
Nevill Road, Stoke Newington, London.
Young woman, twenties, wearing hoody with hood up, walking north reading *Where Sleeping Girls Lie* (Usborne Publishing) by Faridah Àbíké-Íyímídé.

It was Elmore Leonard who said, 'Never open a book with weather.' Indeed, it was the first of his ten 'Rules For Good Writing'. Given its title, maybe he would give *London Particular*, a 1952 crime novel by Christianna Brand, a pass. It begins: 'The dank grey fog was like an army blanket, held pressed against the windows of the car.' Further down the same page, we read, 'A bus crept by, a ghost bus, a-glimmer with eerie lights, with more lights making pin-points in the leaden dark where a line of lesser vehicles crawled in its broad wake.' But after that, once we meet the extended cast of characters, most of whom become murder suspects, the dialogue is jolly this and frightfully that and I find myself longing, not for the grey fog of early 1950s London, but the deep-shadow noir of Chandler's LA in more or less the same period.

London Noir is such a good title for an anthology of crime stories set in the capital, it's been used twice, by the same publisher. In 1994, Maxim Jakubowski assembled a forbidding crew for Serpent's Tail featuring Liza Cody, Derek Raymond,

Ian Rankin, Christopher Fowler and several more, and twelve years later Cathi Unsworth put together a line-up that included Ken Bruen, Barry Adamson, Stewart Home and Joolz Denby for Brooklyn-based Akashic Books' Noir series. Serpent's Tail reissued this in the UK.

The same cover illustration – John O'Connor's *Ludgate, Evening, 1887* – was used on paperback editions of CH Rolph's *London Particulars* (Oxford University Press) and VS Pritchett's *London Perceived* (Hogarth Press). I like Dennis Leigh's cover for the Flamingo paperback of Doris Lessing's *London Observed* so much I bought it twice. Leigh is also a musician, known as John Foxx, originally the lead singer in Ultravox before going solo in 1980. Collaborating with him in 2025 on a contribution to the *Sleeve Notes* project curated by David Gaffney and Adrian Slatcher was a pinch-me-and-wake-me-up moment for a sixty-two-year-old man who can remember being a sixteen-year-old boy hearing 'Underpass' for the first time like it was yesterday.

Some titles tell you with admirable straightforwardness what you're getting. *London Style* (Taschen) is, as you'd expect, a superb collection of photographs of streets and exteriors and interiors. In *London Under* (Vintage), Peter Ackroyd takes you by the hand and leads you *under* the streets of London. It's hard to imagine a better informed or more entertaining guide. I bought my copy a long way from Euston, in the beautiful Beckside Books in Penrith. Merlin Coverley's *London Writing* is an insightful 2005 study of fiction set in the capital, from Dickens' *Bleak House* to – well, can I just say I've always found Merlin Coverley to be a brilliant and perceptive critic with excellent taste – my novel *The Director's Cut*.

Perhaps you'll forgive me if I segue to another book of mine. *London Gothic* (2020) was the first of my trilogy of short story collections inspired by the cities in which I have lived. I say 'was' because it's out of print and Confingo will reprint it – and *Manchester Uncanny* – if *Paris Fantastique*, published towards the end of 2025, sells like hot *gateaux*.

London Gothic joined three other short story collections on my *London Something* shelf: Michael Moorcock's *London Bone* (Scribner), Gary Budden's *London Incognita* (Dead Ink) and David Edward's *London Tales* (Gadfly). David Edward was born in south-east London, but divides his time – or did in 2008 – between London and Florida, which puts my dividing mine between London and Manchester somewhat in the shade.

Moorcock, whose *Mother London* has been my favourite London novel since my then girlfriend gave me a copy at the start of the 1990s, moved from London to Texas in that decade. At the time of writing, Gary Budden, whose fictional compendium of London lore is fuelled by its author's deep affection for folk horror and earlier metropolitan stories, is doing a PhD in Australia.

We may have become tired of Samuel Johnson's line about when a man is tired of London, but maybe, with all these London writers leaving London or dividing their time between London and somewhere else, we should bear it in mind. My wife, a Londoner who has lived in London most of her life, gets wound up by people who tell her, having occasionally been to London, that London is all right, but they wouldn't want to live there.

There's only one book of poetry on my *London Something* shelf; *London Undercurrents* (Holland Park Press), by Joolz Sparkes and Hilaire (who inscribed my copy before she gave it to me), tells 'the hidden histories of London's unsung heroines, north and south of the river'. Only one children's book: Barbara

Whelpton's *London Majestic* (Burke), part of a 1960s series that also included *Paris Triumphant* and *Rome Resplendent*. And only one play: Dion Boucicault's *London Assurance* (New Mermaids), which opened at Covent Garden in 1841.

The only book on the shelf that was signed by its author, but neither in my presence nor to me, is James Craig's *London Calling* (Robinson), the first in his Inspector Carlyle series of crime novels. It's a proof copy, which I bought in Oxfam Dalston in May 2022, and it's inscribed, 'Aideen, I apologise in advance. Craig.' It's the only novel I've ever come across that opens with a detailed description of the preparation of beans on toast. It begins: 'Shuffling into the tiny kitchen of his one-bedroom flat in Tufnell Park, north London, George opened a cupboard above his head and pulled out an economy tin of baked beans.'

That's your first mistake right there, George. Some things may be worth economising on – tins of chopped tomatoes, for example, since you're going to add various ingredients with their own flavours to create your pasta sauce, perhaps – but beans are not. They've got to be Heinz. Other brands are available, sure, but they're not as good.

'After opening it, he poured about half of the contents into a small pan resting on the stove.'

Interesting that he goes for half a tin. I sometimes do, but usually I empty in the whole tin, making sure to get the last bean, the one that's trying to hide, with my wooden spoon. Invariably I'll feel too full after a whole tin, and there are other considerations to bear in mind for later on in the day, but half a tin is never enough, and with half a tin, if you pour it in, you inevitably get too much sauce and not enough beans, meaning that your second helping, tomorrow or the day after, will have too many beans and not enough sauce. But something makes me think that George doesn't have to worry about his second helping.

'What was left in the tin went into a small fridge that was otherwise almost empty, containing only a pint of milk and a couple of bottles of Red Stripe beer that had been on special offer in the local minimart.'

Oh, the poignancy of an almost-empty fridge. I'm saving this for a future essay on the contents of fridges in fiction.

George should know that it's highly advisable to transfer leftover beans to a jar or container rather than leaving them in the tin if he wants to avoid a metallic taste or even rust or oxidation. Still, again, we sense that's the least of George's problems.

'When he estimated that the beans were on their way to being hot, he fished his last two slices of white bread out of their wrapper, and carefully dropped them into an ancient toaster.'

White bread? Not very healthy, George, but, as discussed . . .

'Though bubbling away nicely, they were still quite cold. He then decided to pop the toast; the bread was barely coloured, but that was, he always thought, better than waiting too long and incinerating it.'

Well, I'm not sure, George. What you've prepared there is what I call hotel toast, barely coloured, as you say. I think you have to at least flirt with incineration. Obviously don't let it happen and cut those bits off if it does, because we all know what happens if you eat too much burnt toast, even if Cancer Research UK insists that 'eating acrylamide in burnt food in unlikely to increase the risk of cancer'. Acrylamide is a chemical that's produced when you incinerate your toast, but it's also present in biscuits, cereal and coffee, apparently.

'After a few moments, his ears picked out the sound of footsteps coming up the stairs. He heard them stop outside his front door. After a couple more seconds, the buzzer sounded, harsh, flat and insistent.'

Oh, George.

'The buzzer sounded again: another short, authoritative burst.'

Don't answer the door, George. Switch off the heat and climb out of the window.

'Dropping the toast on a nearly clean plate, he wondered if he should have any butter.'

I appreciate that Craig is wielding the wooden spoon of narrative to get the last bean of dramatic irony out of the tin of the opening scene, but 'he wondered if he should have any butter'? Unbuttered *bread* with soup, fine, but unbuttered *toast* with anything – or on its own, for that matter – is like a bath without bubbles. Still, at least there's been no mention of margarine or low-fat spread.

'Turning off the gas, he decided against the butter and poured the beans directly over the toast. Sticking the pan under the tap, he half filled it with water and dropped it in the sink.'

A number of things here, George. You've gone without butter. We've talked about that. But then you pour your beans directly over your toast. I know it's called beans on toast, but let's not take it too literally. The beans should be on the side so that your toast does not become soggy. But then your toast is unbuttered, therefore inedible. I don't know what to say, except that the pan needs not only to be filled completely with water – hot soapy water – but also submerged in the sink, otherwise there will be drip encrustation. Still, George, as we know and you still haven't quite worked out, you're about to face a much bigger problem than washing up.

I miss Twitter, before it became X, when it was still fun and a few of us – Dan Norcott, Kevin Sommerville, and the two nice young men who made up the Woodford Can Appreciation Society – would post pictures of our beans on toast and discuss the merits of adding cheese, and if so what kind, or Worcestershire sauce or Henderson's Relish. However, as Harold Macmillan said, presciently, in 1960, 'The wind of change is blowing through this continent . . . whether we like it or not . . .'

On Saturday 25 January 2020, I walked from Stoke Newington across Finsbury Park and up the Parkland Walk to Archway Road where I bumped into Patricia Myers waiting for a bus. Patricia was head of research at Reader's Digest when I worked there, and I hadn't seen her for almost thirty years. She was going to the East Finchley Phoenix, where she would meet her husband David Moller, to see *The Personal History of David Copperfield*. It was a pleasure to see her and to see her looking so well.

I walked on to East Finchley and visited the Mind shop where I bought Geoffrey Household's *A Rough Shoot* (Penguin) which I thought I would send to my friend Ian Cunningham, who had worked under Patricia at Reader's Digest. I felt sure he would like it. (I have just checked with Ian. I did send it to him. He did read it and he did like it, although not as much as *Rogue Male*.) Then I walked on to Black Gull Books, where I bought two Picadors – *Passion of Youth: An Autobiography 1897–1922* by Wilhelm Reich and Clive Sinclair's *Bood Libels*, which I already had, but this copy had an inclusion, a visa for a visit to Israel in the name of Anne Yardley, at page 185 – and a Penguin, Graham Greene's *The Lawless Roads* (1976 edition, Paul Hogarth cover illustration – I would later find the 1947 Penguin edition outside EJ Morten in Didsbury with Greene's name misspelt on the spine). I walked back down to the bottom of the High Road and turned right into Bishops Avenue and walked along it in the direction of Hampstead Heath. I gawped at the empty mansions and plots. Houses that are clearly not visited for months or even years at a time. In Hampstead I visited the Oxfam Bookshop, where I didn't find anything, although on a later visit I found a first edition of Martin Amis's *Money* for £3, and then my friend Dave Mundy's stall in the Hampstead Community Centre. I bought Muriel Spark's *The Go-Away Bird* (Penguin) off him. He asked me if I'd been to Keith Fawkes in Flask Walk. I asked if he was really still there. Yes, said Dave, so over the road I went and bought Amis's *London Fields* (Penguin) for my *London Something* collection, because I had had a copy years ago and let it go, having tried to read it and found the names thing a bit too distracting. Guy Clinch, Keith Talent, Nicola Six. But I had in the meantime met Amis, firstly in a snooker club under the Westway and later in Manchester after he had taken up his post at the University of Manchester and I found him completely charming, so I thought I should get over the names thing.

Then I walked down Haverstock Hill, turned left into Pond Street, Constantine Road. Gospel Oak, Dartmouth Park, Finsbury Park, then Clissold Park and back to Stoke Newington. Had I kept going in a straight line, after the last leg, I would have ended up in London Fields.

5

Tickets, please! – return

If you enjoyed 'Tickets, please! – Outward', this chapter offers more of the same. If you didn't, then 'Tickets, please! – Return' is completely different.

In any case, research has shown that a return journey is more than just an outward journey in reverse.

Fenchurch Street Station: easier to find on the Monopoly board than in real life.

I know I've used this station before, because I remember going to Southend, but what I remember most clearly from that day was the wonderful Bookshop Experience, which isn't there any more. I have no memory of Fenchurch Street Station. Walking through the City of London is a strange experience. Views are occluded and partial. There are too many buildings for the space, and they are over-sized, increasingly incongruous edifices, almost carbuncles.

I wonder if King Charles has ever been inside a second-hand bookshop. Maggs Bros maybe, somewhere like that.

In March 2025, I attended the London Book Fair with the Salt team. On the walk back, I popped into the Oxfam

Bookshop on Portobello Road and came across a copy of Helen Fielding's *Bridget Jones: The Edge of Reason* (Picador) concealing a train ticket at page 41. Approaching the till, I glanced out of the window. The Electric Cinema was showing the new Bridget Jones film. The stars were aligning.

I had neither read a Bridget Jones book nor seen any of the films, though I may have read the odd column in the *Independent* in the 1990s. I liked the *Independent*. I liked its Saturday magazine. I liked the paper's books pages (and was lucky enough to write for them, and the magazine). But I also liked to exchange snide remarks with a friend about one or two of the paper's columnists. One in particular, one of whose big, fat books sits on a shelf in a restaurant I often go to with my wife. Every time we go, I turn the book spine in, so as not to have to sit looking at its author's name while enjoying the best chilli and pepper squid in London, and often when we go back, someone has turned it spine out again.

I suspect the Bridget Jones books are Not For Me. This does not mean I think they are no good. It means they are Not For Me. Just as some readers will have decided that my books are Not For Them. Like Neil Wishart, who, when the *Herald* ran an extract from *White Spines*, posted a comment: 'Ridiculous glasses, black polo, left wing tw*t. I'd rather let Fred West teach my grandson yoga.' (His asterisk. Or the *Herald*'s. Not mine, anyway.) I reported his comment and remarked, 'While mostly factually accurate, this comment is personally abusive and perhaps, therefore, should be removed.'

The Bridget Jones train ticket was from Laindon to Upminster, dated 31 October 2000.

Although my survey of UK train operators is ongoing, I can report that, so far, c2c trains, which run between Fenchurch

Street and Shoeburyness – and maybe to other destinations, but I doubt I'll find out – offer the meanest amount of legroom, and my legs are not the longest. There are no seat-back pull-down tables, because if there were and you pulled one down, it would break two ribs. Jammed into a regular seat, you can forget about using a laptop unless you're a praying mantis. There are a number of single seats, marked 'Priority seating', but obviously these are all taken by the time I board.

I message my friend John and tell him I'm on a train from Fenchurch Street to somewhere this side of Basildon so that I can get the train back the other way and read a bit of Bridget Jones between Laindon and Upminster and write about the experience. Proper writers don't do this, I say. He says, It's more of a performance piece than writing, though, isn't it?

A couple of weeks before the Laindon trip, I went to Brentwood, having found, in Oxfam Books & Music Islington, a copy of Julio Cortazar's *Blow-up and Other Stories* containing at page 75 a ticket from Brentwood to London. The ticket was dated 18.12.11, when you could still travel between Brentwood and London on what we can perhaps call a normal train. In 2025, you go on the Elizabeth line and if you say to staff at Liverpool Street that you want to go on a normal train, they give you a funny look. I love Cortazar's stories, and it was a pleasure to reread some on the Elizabeth line to and from Brentwood. But let me not get ahead of myself. While I was in Brentwood, in an unnamed charity shop for the homeless, I found a copy of Jonathan Carroll's *After Silence* (Abacus) containing a train ticket from London to Manchester and in Oxfam I bought a Penguin Modern Classics edition of Richard Hughes's *A High Wind in Jamaica* with a gold sticker on the flyleaf bearing the name Hilary Ruth Robinson, to give to a poet I know called Hilary Robinson. Maybe her middle name is Ruth.

It isn't.

I romp through *After Silence* on one of my journeys from London to Manchester. Sometimes I read a book that I believe I've read before and find I have no memory of it. It's like I'm reading it for the first time. It's interesting but a little unsettling not knowing if I *have* read it before and have forgotten it, or if my memory of having read it before is a false memory. Either way, my memory could do with an upgrade. I know I've read *The Land of Laughs* and *Voice of Our Shadow* (and that they're works of genius) and at least the first four novels of the Answered Prayers Sextet. After that, it starts to get a little hazy.

Meanwhile, back on the train to Laindon, I work out that on my trip to Brentwood, I could have taken a single to Brentwood, reading Cortazar, then walked the seven miles to Laindon and read my bit of Bridget Jones on the way back from Laindon.

I check the times of the trains back from Laindon and I see there's one due three minutes after we arrive there, so, seeing as how my wife and I are going out for a drink tonight and time's getting on, I might just head straight back to Fenchurch Street (like when I headed straight back to St Pancras from Elstree, reading Armando Iannucci's entertaining *The Audacity of Hype* with its 2009 London to Elstree train ticket at page 23). At Laindon, I'm half way across the bridge when I hear the London train enter the station. (Is it right to say a train enters a station if there's no roof?) I'm half way across the bridge when I hear the London train start to come alongside platform one. I descend to platform level as the doors are opening. I jump on, regret doing so, but then rejoice when I see the unoccupied 'Priority' single seats. I sit down, take out Bridget Jones and start reading the entry for Wednesday 29 January, in which there's some business about biological clocks and a joke about the phrase 'the N-word in the woodpile' that I suspect Helen Fielding would not attempt in 2025.

I flick forward to see if there's an entry for 1 September, the day I'm doing this journey. There is and it's a Monday, as it is today, so that's nice. 'Bridge' seems to have been released from a Thai jail, which reminds me my wife said I should read the bit in the Thai jail. I read the 1 September entry and think maybe I'll just leave it there. I look outside. It starts to rain. We stop at West Something and there's an announcement I don't hear, because I've got my headphones on. We don't stop at Upminster. I don't know why. Or at Barking. Maybe that's what the announcement at West Something was about. Next stop West Ham. At Fenchurch Street, I exit the station into a street some distance away from where I entered it. I start walking and look back. The station has already disappeared from view.

In the pub, I ask my wife to tell me something about her past that she has never told me before. She tells me about the time she worked in an office near Old Street. She had to get there very early in the morning, before the start of the *Today* programme, which she had to listen to, via headphones, and while listening produce a log of its contents. 'They told me my logs were very good,' she says, 'but after a few weeks some freelance work came up at Time Out...'

Friday 8 April 2022
Whiteladies Road, Clifton, Bristol.
Man, fifties, shaved head, glasses, leather jacket, Adidas tracksuit bottoms, tan hoody, walking north reading CL Taylor's *Sleep* (Avon).

FINDERS, KEEPERS: *The Secret Life of Second-hand Books*

At the end of May 2025, I drove from Manchester to East Kilbride, where I had booked into the Premier Inn. The following day I would drive the short distance to Clarkston, from where I would get the train into Glasgow and then get the train back to Clarkston, and on that train I would start reading Guillermo Martínez's *The Oxford Murders* (Abacus), translated by Sonia Soto, which I had found on the crime fiction shelves of Oxfam Bookshop Chorlton the previous September. A shadow line had revealed, at page 153, a train ticket from Glasgow to Clarkston, but I liked the look of the book anyway. The author is Argentinian; one of the reviews (*Observer*, no name) quoted in the prelims links him, and his novel, to Borges.

Arriving back in Clarkston, I would get back on the road and hope to reach Moniack Mhor, Scotland's National Writing Centre, by 4 p.m. Ideally, I would travel to Moniack Mhor by train, but I have an aversion to taxis and there are few other ways to get from Inverness to Moniack Mhor. I walked it once, along the Great Glen Way, but thirteen miles is a long way carrying a laptop, assorted workshop materials and a week's supply of Belgian beer.

East Kilbride is a new town made mostly out of roundabouts, underpasses and two pubs, both heaving. I got a seat, but could barely uncross my legs, never mind do the crossword. I returned to the Premier Inn to bang the door of my room against my head repeatedly for half an hour, which was much more relaxing.

On the Monday, I took a train to Glasgow, where there wasn't time to visit Voltaire & Rousseau Bookshop, Thistle Books or Caledonia Books, which are all out of town, then boarded a train back to Clarkston and started reading *The Oxford Murders*. Although I started off enjoying it, I became a little tired of the interminable speeches. It felt a bit like an episode of the rebooted *Dr Who*, which had always felt to me to have been dominated by characters explaining things to each other, Robert Shearman's *Dalek* being an exception.

A mathematician arrives in Oxford from Argentina to do a PhD. (This is *The Oxford Murders*, not *Dalek*.) He meets one of his heroes, another mathematician, Arthur Seldom, who appears to be related to the granddaughter of the woman in whose house the hero is lodging. When the granddaughter speaks to Seldom, she calls him 'Uncle Arthur'. No British readers of a certain age will read that without hearing it spoken plaintively by Ian Lavender as Private Pike in *Dad's Army*. Young female characters are evaluated in terms of their sexual attractiveness (in *The Oxford Murders*, not *Dad's Army*) in a way that seems surprising even for 2005. Puzzling over this and wondering if cultural differences could have something to do with it, I was reminded of how football pundit Graeme Souness lost his job for describing Tottenham's Argentine midfielder Erik Lamela's collapse to the turf clutching his face, after a 'tickle across [his] chops' from Manchester United's Anthony Martial, as 'very Latin'.

I decided that even if I thought cultural differences might have something to do with it, I would refrain from saying so. After all, I couldn't quite imagine Borges coming up with a line like, 'Her apron, of a very fine fabric, was stretched pleasingly tight over her bust.'

I'm on a train to Hull. It's not yet 10 a.m. and I want to unwrap my sandwiches in their silver foil. (Every time I find myself on a train with sandwiches wrapped in silver foil, I remember *The*

Lighthouse author Alison Moore's observation that this is something you don't see any more.) I've got a non-fiction book with me: *In it Together: The Inside Story of the Coalition Government* (Penguin) by Matthew D'Ancona. I found it in Oxfam Books & Music Crouch End on a Sunday in January 2025. I could see a couple of shadow lines. The first, at page 319, revealed a strip of unused vouchers for Subway issued by WH Smith. For only £1.99 you were invited to get either a six-inch Chicken Teriyaki Sub, a six-inch Meatball Marinara Sub or a six-inch Italian BMT Sub. I don't know what BMT stands for, but it's trademarked. I think I'd rather have a strip of vouchers for WH Smith (and homemade butties in silver foil).

I am due to arrive in Hull at 10.30 a.m. and I note that JE Books opens at 10.30, but this train is traveling very slowly. The cause of the delay is a Northern stopping service ahead of us, delaying our arrival into Brough.

The other inclusion in the D'Ancona book is a ticket, at page 421, from Hull to Seamer, dated 30 December 2014. It cost £15.90 (return). Seamer is one stop from Scarborough.

I'm hungry and as I want to save my sandwich I'm wondering if I can get something like a croissant in Hull. Has anybody ever – before me, just now – wondered if they can get a croissant in Hull? The last time I came to Hull was for a reading for a little book published by PS Publishing to which I had contributed a story. My story was later made into a short film, but, outside of a single screening at a film festival in Argentina, it has never been seen. I mean, I've seen it. I've probably seen it more times than anybody else, including its director, but almost nobody else has, which I suppose makes it a lost short film.

We're through Brough and we're not going any faster than before Brough. Brough, by the way, is pronounced Bruff. We've just gone through Ferriby, which is pronounced Ferriby. Soon I should be able to see the Humber Bridge on my right.

I see the Humber Bridge on my right.

In Hull I just have time to buy a ticket to Seamer that will let me break my journey twice, at Beverley and Driffield, and then dash to JE Books in the lovely old Hepworth Arcade. Entering a shop that looked bigger in photographs online, I ask the cheerful woman tucked into a space beneath a steep staircase where I might find her second-hand section. 'Second hand?' she says. 'Behind you, outside and upstairs.' The stairs look fun, although I wish I'd brought my crampons. I perform an obligatory stumble on my way up, and find a shelf of Miss Read titles in Penguin. I scan the top edges. Nothing. Downstairs, I tell the bookseller it's a lovely shop and I'll come back when I've got more time. I wonder how many times I've said this – and really meant it every time.

I leg it back to the Paragon Interchange and just make the 11.20 to Scarborough. I get the last unoccupied double seat on the train and soon find myself on my feet again to put a suitcase on the rack for a woman whose son claims he is not tall enough to do it himself. He's sitting down, but he's easily taller than me, and it is easy to be taller than me.

The second stop on the line from Hull to Seamer is Beverley. I've been here once before, more than thirty years ago, when my sister Julie lived near by. I soon realise something's up. A huddle of sharp-faced young men, clipboards and sheaths of glossy literature clutched to quilted jerkins. Light blue stickers with white type. Conservatives? Worse. I walk on past small groups of well-heeled locals who might vote Conservative, but never Reform, surely. I've picked the wrong day to visit Beverley. I see the reassuring green sign of Oxfam and duck in. I select a Picador I don't think I've got, yet even as I flick through it, I decide I probably have, but I'll buy it anyway, so I don't leave empty handed. It's Amit Chaudhuri's *Freedom Song*. The talk behind the till changes from the difficulty of the new system and I hear his name. Farage. Someone has spotted Farage. Here. In Beverley. They want to see him, to see how different he looks in real life. He'll be on *Look North* tonight, one says. Do they still have *Look North*? *Look North* is my early childhood in Whitley Bay, before we returned to the north-west. Surely *Look North* is *Newsroom North-east* or the 'News Where You Are'. I take a chance, express my opinion of Farage, buy my unwanted book and leave. I make my way back to the station, careful not to step in anything.

I arrive at Driffield and walk into town. Not as posh as Beverley. Bakers and charity shops. Vape shop. I'm almost at the end of the main street when I see the Emporium. Promising, although new and second-hand books are mixed in together. They have price stickers on the spines, which worries me slightly (they rarely come off without causing damage), although not as much as the whispered mention, by a customer, of Farage. I spot the white spine of a Picador book I don't believe I have ever seen and therefore do not have in my collection: *On the Nature of Things Erotic* by F Gonzalez-Crussi. I ask the proprietor about *Drif's Guide*. Does she have a copy? She looks puzzled and asks if I mean a guide to the town. I explain about Drif Field and his *Drif's Guide to the Secondhand Bookshops of the British Isles* and she shakes her head.

On the way back to the station I pop into one of the bakers and buy a large apple pie for £3 and as soon as I leave and take a bite, I wish I'd asked for a little fork. Apple pie everywhere.

Back at the station, I can't put off reading D'Ancona's book any longer. I dip in but a train pulls up and a man in tight trousers steps off, Reform paraphernalia under his arm, and I wish that, instead of an apple pie, I had bought a custard pie.

I have a go at the book on the rest of the journey to Seamer. I read the introduction and then, since the ticket was among the notes at the back, the chapter where the Subway vouchers are. Entitled 'Trouble and Strife', it's about gay marriage and how Cameron managed the unlikely feat of making it seem attractive to Tory MPs and voters. It would strengthen the institution of marriage, seemed to be his approach. Also, reading between the lines, it was becoming inevitable, so maybe he wanted to tick it off on a to-do list. I wonder if tearing the UK apart by having a Brexit referendum was on the same list. I was all for same-sex marriage, but I can't say that the story of how it was achieved makes for great reading. Things pick up when D'Ancona writes about the spectacular collapse of the different-sex marriage between Chris Huhne and Vicky Pryce, but a book about David Cameron and Nick Clegg written by a former editor of the *Spectator* was never really going to be a book for me.

At Seamer I walk over the top to Scarborough. As soon as I enter Mrs Lofthouse's Emporium on Queen Street, I start finding shadow lines – a Skipton solicitors business card here, a folded piece of kitchen roll there – but I have to be picky. An excellent wall devoted to 'literature' (I like that there is a copy of Iain Banks's *The Bridge* in among the Bölls and the Becketts), a huge crime section, with some lovely old Agatha Christie Fontana paperbacks with Tom Adams covers, lots of SF, fantasy and horror. A brilliant shop, superbly run by owner Daniel and his colleague Ian, who I can hear dealing with customers on the phone and in the shop in a manner that is fair, respectful and friendly. I only buy one book – *Kurt Singer's Second Ghost*

Omnibus (Four Square Horror). It's £10, but it's scarce and I want to buy something, and when I take it to the till, Daniel knocks a couple of quid off – truly the mark of a decent second-hand bookseller.

Horror is good to Daniel, as it has been to me. I first visited Scarborough in the 1990s, to attend Fantasycon at the Grand Hotel. I had broken my scaphoid bone playing football and had my arm in a cast, but it didn't stop me playing the slots with Michael Marshall Smith and probably Conrad Williams and Mark Morris as well. That weekend was somewhat coloured by an unspeakably revolting story told to us by a small press magazine editor about a relative and involving either a glass-topped table or a wicker basket, or possibly both. Far, far worse than the story we've all heard now – true or otherwise, it doesn't really matter – which D'Ancona *doesn't* tell in his book, about Cameron and a pig's head.

Sunday 2 May 2021
Mount Pleasant Hill, Clapton, London.
Man, twenties/thirties, black baseball cap, black jeans, green hooded jacket, pink plimsolls, walking past the Co-op reading Madeline Miller's *The Song of Achilles* (Bloomsbury).

I found a Manchester to Sheffield ticket in one book (Alice Sebold's *The Lovely Bones*) and a Sheffield to London ticket in another (Paul Golding's *Senseless*), but, as discussed in the introduction, I'm avoiding Sheffield these days. Some journeys strike me as doable without being particularly enticing, like Birmingham to London return. Or London to Birmingham return. Neither *The Circle Way: A Leader in Every Chair* (Birmingham to London), by Christina Baldwin and Ann Linnea, nor

Fatland: How Americans Became the Fattest People in the World (London to Birmingham), by Greg Critser, tempts me to buy a ticket.

Manchester to Warrington, on the other hand – excuse me while I put on a recent charity shop find, Lewis Gill's *Parochial Chamber Works: Music Inspired by Warrington*. Although, wait a minute, I've been to Warrington and I remember thinking I probably didn't need to go back. (That's quite enough of 'The Ackers Pit Concerto'. Skip to 'Bridgewater Dream'.) But what book was the Warrington-bound reader in the middle of? Samuel Beckett's *Trilogy* (Calder). Beckett begged his English-language publisher (the novels – *Molloy*, *Malone Dies* and *The Unnamable* – were written in French and published in France and later translated into English) not to use the word 'Trilogy', but that didn't stop Calder. (It didn't stop Picador either, who reprinted it in 1979, and then again in 1980 with a set of photographs from Deirdre Bair's biography of Beckett erroneously included.) The edition I found in my local Oxfam was a heavy, unattractive volume, first published in 1959 and most recently reprinted in 2003, but it had the train ticket and, having only read Beckett's stories and novellas, I knew I needed to embark on *Molloy* at some point.

This took place on the train from Manchester Oxford Road to Warrington Central. As you may know, there are only two paragraphs in the first 90 pages and I didn't get very far into the second one. On arrival at Warrington, I got off, stepped out of the station, had a quick look around to make sure I hadn't been unfair to Warrington after my last visit, and returned to the station to get the train back to Manchester.

As for *Parochial Chamber Works: Music Inspired by Warrington*, I prefer *The Nation's Most Central Location* by

Warrington-Runcorn New Town Development Plan, aka minimal ambient electronic composer Gordon Chapman-Fox.

I did, however, go to Warrington again, or through it, to get to Liverpool, so that I could travel from there to Formby.

Wise people in little interviews in the Sunday papers always say they don't have any regrets. Don't waste your energy on regrets, they say. But how can I not regret those 28 minutes on the train from Liverpool Central to Formby reading Russell Brand's *Revolution*? Just a couple of chapters. I bought it from Oxfam in Withington because I saw it had a shadow line. When I investigated, I found, at page 225, a train ticket from Liverpool stations to Formby dated 29 December 2014 and costing £3.30 (with a 16–25 railcard). For £11.65, I could obtain a return ticket from Manchester stations to Formby via Liverpool (with a senior railcard). Yes, I know, you can't believe I qualify for a senior railcard. Neither can I. Until I try to stand up.

Everyone in the north-west, unless they were either home-educated or not educated at all, has been to Formby. Like Skelmersdale, it's a favourite destination of school trips; unlike Skelly, it's home to sand dunes, red squirrels and footballers from Merseyside clubs.

At Liverpool Central I head for the Northern line. Merseyrail trains remind me of the times I used to get invited by Professors Robert Sheppard and Ailsa Cox to talk to creative writing students at Edge Hill University. I enjoyed my visits to Ormskirk, apart from one time when I was getting the train back to Liverpool with Robert Sheppard and there was a member of non-academic Edge Hill staff on the train who had taken a drink and, for some reason, didn't like the look of me. 'Molloy!' he growled. 'Molloy!' Did I look like someone he knew called Molloy? Did he know that I hadn't read Beckett's *Molloy*? Was he actually saying something else that just sounded like Molloy? I was glad of the presence of Robert Sheppard.

What concerns me about the train to Formby is not that I might bump into the man from Edge Hill, but that someone might see what I'm reading. I think about strategies, like switching the jacket (it's a hardback). But if I was going to do that, I needed to have done it sooner. And anyway, someone might look over my shoulder. Was it Tibor Fischer who said he was reading Martin Amis's *Yellow Dog* on the tube and was terrified of anyone looking over his shoulder in case they thought he was enjoying it?

I wonder about hiding *Revolution* in my *Observer New Review*, which I always keep in my bag until I've finished the crossword, but when I look, I see this is the one time I haven't got it, and anyway I remember what happened to Woody Allen in *Bananas* when he grabbed a dirty magazine, as we used to call them, and took it to the till along with a bunch of innocent publications. 'Hey Ralph,' the guy at the till shouts across the store to his colleague, 'how much is a copy of *Orgasm*?' Allen pleads, 'Just put 'em in a bag, will you?' The man continues: '*Orgasm*. This man wants to buy a copy. How much is it?'

Luckily it was not busy and in terms of other people seeing what I was reading, I got away with it. The book seems to have been inspired by Brand's appearance on *Newsnight*, when he was interviewed by Jeremy Paxman. I remember being disappointed when Paxman left *Newsnight* in 2014 and outed himself as a 'one-nation Tory', but I also remember him giving Brand a hard time for not voting in elections and encouraging others to follow suit. I'm not very keen on people not voting. When Brand adopted the idea of not-voting as a rallying cry, it was just another reason, like I needed one, to distrust him. I always had done. I couldn't understand how anyone could take him seriously, and yet so many people did, including Century publishers.

I don't know whether Century stood by Russell Brand after the allegations of sexual misconduct (he was later charged with rape and sexual assault).

Russell Brand hit with allegations of sexual misconduct? You could have knocked me down with the quill I imagined him using to write *My Booky Wook*. That title. Brand says it was inspired by Anthony Burgess's *A Clockwork Orange*, a short and brilliant novel in which a self-aggrandising young man commits various crimes including rape.

In chapter twenty-one of *Revolution*, which I read because it was the last one before the position of the train ticket bookmark, and because it's only two pages long, Brand is watching England go out of the World Cup, in a pub, 'shoulder to shoulder with strangers with shared intentions'. More hopes than intentions, surely? But let's leave the editing to Century.

Century Publishing was launched in 1982 by Anthony Cheetham with Gail Rebuck, later joined by Rosie de Courcy and Peter Roche (although Roche isn't mentioned in the chapter on Century in Cheetham's memoir, *A Life in Fifty Books*, published by Head of Zeus, a publishing start-up founded by Cheetham in 2012). *Revolution* is a far cry from Flora Thompson's *The Illustrated Lark Rise to Candleford*, an early success for Century, but within five years Century had swallowed up the much bigger Hutchinson and published Donald Trump's *The Art of the Deal*, so maybe it isn't too far downhill from there to *Revolution*.

In January 2025, in the Children's Society in Heaton Moor, I bought *Bleak House* (Penguin Classics) with a Manchester to

Burnage train ticket at page 21. Two days later, at Piccadilly, I paid £1.65 to undertake the same journey. Walking through the train, I spotted Jack from football. He didn't see me and for a moment I wasn't sure it was him, as he was wearing a tie.

No offence, Jack, but I didn't want to spend the ten minutes the journey would last explaining what I was doing. We would have been at Burnage before I'd managed to read even Dickens's preface, never mind Terry Eagleton's introduction, which – forgive me, Professor – I'd decided not to read. I walked on, found a seat and almost gave up on the first chapter, which was littered with so many footnotes it was like reading Velcro. I persevered, but there wasn't enough time to get to the end of the chapter. Maybe I shouldn't have spent so long looking out of the window at Longsight depot, where I'd misspent a good part of my youth. In the distance I spotted an 08 shunter that could easily have been one whose number I'd underlined in my *Locoshed Directory*.

I finished chapter one of *Bleak House* walking home through Fog Lane Park and I can tell you that, because of its size, *Bleak House* is very hard to read while walking. It wasn't until the last page (of the first chapter) that I became aware of the fact that the narrative is in the present tense, so those unforgiving critics the Two Philips – Hensher and Pullman – are presumably not fans. When I finished the chapter, I turned to the two pages of footnotes. That's two pages for chapter one and it wasn't just explanations of arcane and archaic words or expressions that the modern reader might need explaining, but included definitions of words like 'rigging', 'gunwales' and 'players', and described streets and explained jokes. One feels as if one is being condescended to. This from the publisher who, in 2013, accepted Morrissey's terms regarding his *Autobiography*, that it be published straight into Penguin Classics. '[It] could be published as a Penguin Classic because it is a classic in the making,' said a mealy-mouthed Penguin representative.

A month after my first visit to the Greenwich & Bexley Community Hospice shop, I return, to see if I was right about overpricing. I am looking in particular for Solzhenitsyn's *Cancer Ward*, the opposite of a steal at £6. It's not here. Some other rather modest paperbacks are, with notes inserted, as before, about copies on sale online for however many pounds, but I don't remember these titles from before, and I didn't make a note, apart from about *Cancer Ward*. It could have been removed from sale, or marked down and subsequently sold. But it's not here and I predicted it would be, so I was wrong.

I spot Natasha Brown's *Universality* (Faber), the hardback, at £5. I loved Brown's first novel, *Assembly*.

But haven't you stopped buying hardbacks?

More or less, yes, but this second novel isn't out in paperback yet.

I suppose it is a hospice charity.

Exactly.

Sold.

6

Side hustle

Parts of this book – and of *White Spines* and *Shadow Lines* – were written in Lapwing Deli, near to where I live in Manchester. Before it became Lapwing Deli, it was called Fusion Deli, but even as I write that, it sounds wrong. What is the 'it' in that sentence? Lapwing Deli? Am I really saying that Lapwing Deli used to be called Fusion Deli, as if Fusion Deli were a person who changed their name, to become Lapwing Deli? To be accurate, I should say that the premises at 109 Lapwing Lane were once home to a business called Fusion Deli, whose owner sold it to new owners, who changed the name of the business to Lapwing Deli.

Anyway, before you tire of this literal-minded writing-in-circles, let me tell you that in February 2019, in the Sue Ryder shop in Chorlton, I found a heavily battered and equally heavily annotated copy of Ann Charters' biography of Kerouac entitled, simply, *Kerouac*. I bought it even though I already owned a copy (part of my Picador collection), because this new copy also contained an inclusion, a business card from Fusion Deli. I hung on to it for some time, thinking it should become part of a new research project, in which I would buy second-hand books containing business cards – actually, I need to interrupt myself again, because I had been buying second-hand books containing business cards for some years already, but the difference now would be, I would buy them and then send – or otherwise deliver – the book to the individual named on the card. But in the case of the Kerouac biography, although the owner of Fusion Deli, Peter Davies, was named on the business card, and I knew him a little bit to say hello to, did I not have a stronger attachment to Lapwing Deli, where I had started going as a regular thing, for coffee, in the morning, if I was in Manchester? Should I give the book – and business card – to Peter Davies or to the new owners of the business, who, if you remember, had changed its name to Lapwing Deli?

To cut what has started to feel like a long story short, I decided to give it to Peter Davies, who I had seen working behind the counter in another deli, Barbakan, in Chorlton. I was intrigued by his having closed his own deli and then started working for the owner or owners of another deli a couple of miles away. The next time I saw Peter at Barbakan, where I would sometimes go for their excellent bread and pastries, I gave him the Kerouac biography, babbled incomprehensibly about the business card that he would find within, and heard myself asking why he was working for another deli, having sold his own. He said he had missed the contact with people and was very much enjoying working at Barbakan. Or something like that. He thanked me for the book. I insisted that I didn't expect him to read it, or even keep it. It was just something I was doing – although I didn't really know why.

On a Thursday morning in June 2024, I had breakfast at Barbakan – I can't remember if Peter was working that day, or Mark Kureishy, another acquaintance and very nice man

– before visiting Oxfam Bookshop Chorlton where I found another book containing a business card. This one was *Beyond Possible: One Soldier, Fourteen Peaks – My Life in the Death Zone* (Hodder & Stoughton) by Nimsdai Purja. The business card, at page 159, was in the name of Martin Ellerby, founder of Yoga Republic.

I wrote to Martin Ellerby and delivered the book to his address in town, as we call it, ie Manchester city centre, that afternoon.

A few days later, Martin Ellerby emailed me, apologising for the delay and explaining that he had wanted to read the book before getting in touch. 'I was familiar with the book, having watched the Netflix documentary, but thoroughly enjoyed it, so thanks for sharing.' Also, he went on, his dog had eaten my letter, leaving just my contact details intact.

I hadn't anticipated such a good start to the business cards project. I had thought I would be mainly sending books off and never hearing anything. Or not even getting as far as sending books off, as some business cards lack addresses. Isabel Bolton's compendium of three novels *New York Mosaic* (Virago), which I found in Oxfam Books & Music Islington in March 2024, contained a business card at page 177 in the name of a creative consultant and former editor of *Elle Decoration*. It was a larger-than-usual business card, giving only name, mobile and email, printed on top of a serene photograph of sky and ocean.

The French cellist and music teacher whose unusually small business card I found at page 97 of Stephen Fry's *The Ode Less Travelled: Unlocking the Poet Within* (Arrow) in Oxfam in Withington in August 2024 contained the same categories of contact details, or *coordonnées*, as the French call them, and no address.

In both cases I emailed and texted, but no replies were

forthcoming. Who's this weirdo, they no doubt thought, or *c'est qui ce barjo?*

(Anyway, do we really want to unlock the poet within? I tend to think more poets should be locked up, starting with those who read, at live literature events, in the 'poet voice'.)

Sometimes, there's an address, but there's no point sending the book.

At the end of September 2023, in the wonderful Westwood Books in Sedbergh, England's book town, I found a Penguin edition of Ruth Prawer Jhabvala's *In Search of Love and Beauty* containing, at page 185, a business card in the name of Jean Carroll, Principal, Dunfermline College of Physical Education, Edinburgh. Jean Carroll, who died in November 2021 in Grange-over-Sands, Cumbria, made a 'significant contribution to the evolution of Human Movement as a field of study and to the teaching of Physical Education in Scotland', according to her obituary in the *Scotsman*. Having taken up the post of Principal Lecturer at Dunfermline College of Physical Education in 1973, she later became Assistant Principal, Vice Principal and, ultimately, Principal, retiring in 1987 and settling with her civil partner Mollie Abbott in Kirkcudbright. They later moved to Grange-over-Sands, where they built their own house.

In another Penguin, Evelyn Waugh's *Black Mischief*, which I bought at a book sale at the University of Manchester students union, I found the business card of a painter, José Benet Espuny, with a phone number and address in Rome. 'Peintre,' it says on the card. 'Prix de Rome.' Benet Espuny, a Spanish artist born in 1910, who had exhibitions of his work in many countries, was based in Rome from 1949 to 1953 and travelled from there to museums throughout Europe to study the work of other artists and to paint. Among the countries he visited during that time was Great Britain. The Penguin edition of *Black Mischief* was published in 1951. Benet Espuny died in 2010.

Sometimes, the address on the card will be overseas and I think about the cost of sending a book to Abu Dhabi or the Maldives, or the cost and Trumpian hassle of sending one to the US, balanced against the likelihood of obtaining a reply, and I don't head straight to the Post Office. In April 2024, in Oxfam Dalston, I bought Marlon James's *A Brief History of Seven Killings* (Oneworld) for its business card inclusion at page 103 in the name of Steven Stimmel, concierge of Omni Hotels & Resorts in Austin, Texas. I mull over the extra form-filling, the mandatory tracking, the tedious questions. In Jambala Buddhist charity bookshop in Bethnal Green, in January 2025, I bought Clare Wigfall's *The Loudest Sound and Nothing* (Faber) with its business card for Mohamed Ali Mamoun at Lux* Resorts in the Maldives at page 173. In October 2025, back at the book sale at the University of Manchester students union, I bought Roger Martin de Gard's *Jean Barois* (Folio) for its business card inclusion – Paul Bugden of Bugden's Bookshop – at page 197. Paul Bugden founded Bugden's Bookshop in Victoria Street in Sydney in the late 1990s; since 2013, it has been owned and operated by Tamara and Tom, who introduced vintage clothing, Bugden having already added records to the mix when moving to the present premises on William Street, King's Cross.

If I were to send *Jean Barois*, which also contains a name and phone number written on the flyleaf – M Cain 446-6273 – and a pencilled price of $5.50, would I send it to Tamara and Tom at Grand Days, their new name for the business, or would I try to track down Paul Bugden, author of *Tales of an Accidental Bookseller*?

I do neither.

Maybe if I sent Clare Wigfall's *The Loudest Sound and Nothing* to Mohamed Ali Mamoun in the Maldives, he would invite me for an all-expenses stay at Lux* Resorts. He is the general manager, after all, but I look at the sea plane skimming across the waves on the promotional video and I think (a) it's unlikely and (b) it's not really me. I'm interested to see, though, that the business card nestles at the start of 'Slow Billows the Smoke', my favourite story in this excellent collection when I reviewed it for *Time Out* in 2007.

Asim Dar is – or was – a Food and Beverage Manager with Etihad Airways based at Khalifa City, Abu Dhabi. His business card was hiding at the start of the chapter devoted to North Yorkshire's Forbidden Corner in *Far From the Sodding Crowd*, a humour/travel book by Robin Halstead, Jason Hazeley, Alex Morris and Joel Morris that I think I'm just going to give back to Oxfam on Oldham Street in Manchester.

Before this descends into a list of things I'm not going to do, I should do something.

In June 2025, I bought Dr Rangan Chatterjee's *Feel Great Lose Weight* (Penguin) from Mind in Dalston. I didn't need to lose weight; lurking within, at page 43, was a business card for Tayo Aluko, a baritone and writer based in Liverpool.

I fully intended to send *Feel Great Lose Weight* off to Tayo Aluko. I wrote the accompanying letter and printed it off. I took the letter to London, where the book, which was too heavy to carry to Manchester if I didn't have to, sat waiting. But for some reason I didn't put the letter inside the book and parcel it up and head off to the Post Office. I pictured this Liverpudlian baritone opening his mysterious package and reading the title and thinking, Someone thinks I need to lose weight. Maybe he has a little paunch. I look him up. He looks in great shape. Or he did in 2023. No paunch. I don't know what to do.

On the same day, still in Dalston, I found two more books containing business cards. These were in Oxfam. Ali Smith's *Hotel World* (Penguin) and Marilyn Mufson's *Neon Dreams* (no publisher named). The card in the former, at page 83, was in the name of Julia Ratcliffe, Director of Expedition, at an address on Regent Street in the West End, while the latter had, at page 31, a card that had once belonged to Charlotte Ilet, sales negotiator at Douglas and Gordon, Kensington Gate. This was the second estate agent's card I'd found in a second-hand book. On Wednesday 5 November 2020, the day after the US election, with the results still unclear, but looking like Trump could hang on, I walked down to Angel to visit Oxfam Books & Music Islington for the last time for at least a month. In case you thought the news from America meant things couldn't get any worse, we were about to enter, the following day, the second national coronavirus lockdown. In Oxfam, I found Françoise Sagan's *Bonjour Tristesse* (Penguin), not the nice edition with photographic cover by Steve Campbell but it had an inclusion, a business card at page 25, for Allesandro Furno from Knight Frank estate agents of Chelsea.

For some reason, I didn't send *Bonjour Tristesse* off to Allesandro. Maybe because I knew he wouldn't be at work for at least a month. But nor, some years later, did I send *Neon Dreams* to Charlotte Ilet at Douglas and Gordon. Is there a word for a fear – or mild aversion – of estate agents?

Before sending *Hotel World* off to Julia Ratcliffe, I Googled her, because you never know. It turned out she'd left Expedition and was now running a new business. Since there was no address on the website, I emailed and asked if I could send her the book. Structural engineer, designer and founder of Scale Consulting Julia Ratcliffe replied the next day. She thanked me for my email and added, kindly, 'Sounds like an interesting project.' Thank you, Julia. She went on to say, 'I believe that the book you found is one I donated fairly recently. I must have used an old business card as a bookmark and put it back in the book when finished – so no need to return it.'

Similarly, London-based soul/R&B/jazz singer-songwriter Kianja used an old business card as a bookmark when she was reading Thomas Hardy's *The Woodlanders* (Penguin), which she then donated to Jambala in Bethnal Green and I subsequently bought. When I emailed her, she replied, 'Isn't life such a beautiful thing, everything happens as it's meant to.' Kianja has a beautiful soul – and a beautiful voice. Check it out.

Thursday 15 January 2026
Highway Hope, Stockport.
Young man in baseball cap: Look at that. *The Book of Knowledge*. Is that all knowledge, ever, in the world?
Young man in beanie: Wow. Must have a pretty small font.
Young man in baseball cap [taking book down from shelf]: It is quite small actually.

On 24 September 2024, the thirtieth anniversary of my dad's death, I place flowers on his grave then drive to Prestwich to pick up Matthew Adamson and together we drive to Yorkshire to do an event at the Richmond Walking & Book Festival. On the way, we stop outside Skipton. Matthew is like me, happy to park some distance from his destination and walk the rest of the way. Our partners agree with each other but not with us in this matter. In the Oxfam Bookshop I buy Annie Ernaux's *Journal du dehors* (Folio) to read and Toby Litt's *Ghost Story* (Penguin), for the chapter in this book on books that have the same titles as other books. In Harrogate we visit the wonderful Books For All, where I buy two Michael Innes green Penguins, *A Family Affair* and *Lament For a Maker*, with striking covers by Crosby/Fletcher/Forbes and Pentagram respectively (Crosby/Fletcher/Forbes expanded and changed their name to Pentagram), and two books containing artists' business cards – Tibor Fischer's *The Thought Gang* (Polygon) and Knut Hamsun's *The Women at the Pump* (Souvenir Press). One of these artists, a stained-glass artist, didn't get back to me. Potter Rupert Belfrage did and we had a lively exchange. He recommended the Old Pier Bookshop in Morecambe, Carnforth Books, and Halewood's in Preston, excellent bookshops that I've visited many times, and advised that I look out for books by Belfrage family members Cedric, Sally, Bruce and Nicolas.

I found another business card in another Tibor Fischer book.

In June 2019, in the big Barnardos at Birchfields Road, in between Fallowfield, Longsight and Rusholme, in Manchester, where the books were four for a pound, I found – alongside Ian McEwan's *The Comfort of Strangers* (Picador) with a Russell Mills cover and containing a cinema ticket for HOME, for a film called *Free Fire*, booked in the name of Sarah Cotterill, and a book that I was able to deduce had been donated by Levenshulme resident, author Paul Magrs – Tibor Fischer's short story collection *Don't Read This Book If You Are Stupid* (Secker & Warburg), with, at page 127, Tibor Fischer's business card, with an 0181 number and an address in Brixton.

It was October 2024 before I stuck Tibor Fischer's book containing his own business card through his front door in Brixton. I'd just come from hand-delivering a copy of Nicholas Cook's

Music: A Short Introduction (Oxford) containing the business card of a line producer at TV production company Glasshead to their offices in Haymarket. I didn't get a response from Glasshead, but I did get one from Tibor Fischer: 'Interesting side hustle,' he wrote. 'I don't have anything especially amusing or poignant to offer. I read at the Deansgate Waterstones a couple of times, so it may be a copy I forgot there with my bookmark. As for the business card, if I did give it to someone, I've always found that giving your card to someone is practically a guarantee you'll never hear from them again. But as the Latin tag has it "habent sua fata libelli", books have their own destinies, you never know where your progeny will end up. It is a rather worn copy so I'll probably return it to its natural habitat, Barnardos, but minus the business card.'

Some more books with business cards in that went off without word ever coming back: Charles Cumming's *Box 88* (Harper-Collins) to a Westhoughton physiotherapist. Ernest Hemingway's *For Whom the Bell Tolls* (Penguin Modern Classics) to a Customer Care Executive at Johnsons Apparel Master Textile Rental Services in Hull. Another copy of Ian McEwan's *The Comfort of Strangers* (Picador) to the managers of a restaurant in Wakefield.

On the same trip to the book sale at the University of Manchester students union that produced Paul Bugden's business card inside Roger Martin de Gard's *Jean Barois*, I also found Steven Waling's poetry collection *Travelator* with the poet's own business card inserted at page 5. He'd signed the book to Mike and Eva. I wrote to Waling and with fingers crossed delivered his book by Royle Mail to the address on the business card.

Fingers crossed not only that he would still be at the same address – *Travelator* was published in 2007 and the inscription was the kind you might dash off at a launch event – but also that Waling would not take offence. One hesitates to offer a book (back) to an author that he has previously inscribed to another, in case his feelings might be hurt that his signed book has been given away or sold, but a lot can happen in eighteen years and maybe Mike and Eva were not close friends, or maybe not friends at all. Maybe, strangers, they bought it at an event and asked him to sign it. Or maybe they were – and are – friends. A friend of mine picked up a book of mine second-hand and shared with me the fact that it had been inscribed by me to another friend, but that friend had moved overseas. You don't take all your books with you when you move overseas. Maybe you sell some, or give them away.

Luckily, Waling, who I see around occasionally at Peter Barlow's Cigarette and other live literature events in Manchester, was still at the same address and replied: 'I only had one copy of *Travelator* left so it's good to have another. The guy who owned it I think now lives mostly in America, and is an expert on British folk music. That was the second of my collections. I was largely satisfied. I'd started to cut and paste and use found material as a technique.'

I confessed to Waling that I struggle with poetry and mainly read – and I acknowledged how pretentious this would sound – the French Surrealist poets, in French. But I liked the title of the poem on page 5, where I found the business card – 'Harold Wilson' – so I read that. I used to 'do' Harold Wilson, but I suppose really I was doing Mike Yarwood doing Harold Wilson. My dad liked Harold Wilson; my mum preferred *my* Harold Wilson. I also liked 'Poem (Abandoned)', in *Travelator*, which made me think of forlorn bookshelves in railway stations and other transitory places.

'Harold Wilson's statue outside Huddersfield Railway station reminded me of my own dad,' Waling wrote. 'I'm glad you liked it. By the way, I find the best way to read poetry is to stop trying to make sense of them right from the off, but to start by just going along on a linguistic ride. Then read it again.'

The business cards project draws to a close with a lot of unanswered questions. Did the itinerant charity worker whose business card I found inside Manuel Rivas' *The Carpenter's Pencil* ever get the book and letter I delivered to her latest work address in Euston, or had she moved on again?

Is Daniel Morris still planning kitchens for Skanska and did Brandon Sanderson write any more books in the Mistborn series after *The Final Empire: Book One*? (Yes, another six novels, plus a novella.)

Did I ever send the copy of Will Wiles's novel *The Way Inn* I found containing a business card for a London literary agent to the agent or did it simply get lost?

How did Umberto Eco, author of *The Name of the Rose*, end up writing a novel as bad as *Numero Zero*?

Will I ever find out the missing details from the partial business card in the name of Glassford that I found inside Garrison Keiller's *Lake Wobegon Days*?

Was the hour I spent exploring empty offices in Exchange Quay looking for an ERM hydrogeology consultant so that I might give her Tim Bradford's *The Groundwater Diaries* wasted or did the fact that I enjoyed roaming those abandoned carpet-tiled premises – PLEASE LEAVE YOUR FOB WITH A MEMBER OF THE PEOPLE TEAM TODAY! – make it worthwhile?

Is the David R Clarke who is the inaugural Extended Tarr

Family Professor of Materials in the Harvard School of Engineering and Applied Sciences the same David R Clarke who once worked for consulting engineers Large & Associates at an address in Fleet Street and whose business card I found inside PG Wodehouse's *Pearls, Girls and Monty Bodkin* in Lyalls in Todmorden?

Did Elliot Gill stay in printing after Momento Print in Crouch End closed down and would he, if I had been able to track him down, have enjoyed Matt Haig's *The Humans*?

Was Ulla Ward, whose business card with an address in Covent Garden I found in an American paperback edition of Bernard Malamud's *The Fixer* in the Shakespeare Hospice in Stratford on Avon, an individual or a business – or both? It's a beautiful business card, the name in red foil (styled as handwriting), the address, at 26 Wellington Street, and 01 phone number, in a sans serif font in green foil. For me, there's a strong 1960s or 1970s fashion boutique vibe about it.

I've decided the card bearing the name Thomas Naylor – with blots and splashes of an unidentified rusty brown liquid that could be jus, wine or blood – that I found inside John Yorke's *Into the Woods: How Stories Work and Why We Tell Them* from Oxfam Bookshop Chiswick is a place-setting card rather than a business card. And the two identical cards bearing only the name, in italic print, Mrs RH Kelly, that I found inside a damaged hardback edition of Alan Bennett's *Untold Stories* in Oxfam Dalston may be what were once known as visiting cards.

In Mind in Stoke Newington on Sunday 3 December 2023, I found a copy of art historian and antiques expert Janet Gleeson's 1998 book *The Arcanum*, which tells the story of the invention of European porcelain. It contained not only a business card, in the name of artist Alexandra Mckenzie, but also a photograph of a young woman and two tiny children, with a caption, on the back, naming the children. The young woman was identified only as 'Me'.

I sent the book, with inclusions, to Alexandra Mckenzie at the north London offices of *Digital Energy Journal*, the address on the card.

A few days later, Alexandra Mckenzie emailed me. An ex-colleague had called her to let her know about the package that had arrived with her name on it. Alexandra had worked for *Digital Energy Journal* as an illustrator making oil and gas images for magazine covers and conference holding screens. She had just finished an archaeology degree and was about to embark on a forensic and archaeological anthropology MSc, but she still accepts commissions as a sculptor and scenic painter. The book had been hers and she was glad to get back not only the photograph, but also the book itself, which she had given away in error during a cull. Alexandra's son Rio, one of the two little ones in the photograph, she told me as our exchange progressed, is now at university.

'I love the serendipity of life,' she wrote.

7

Doubles

Tracks by Robyn Davidson is a work of non-fiction first published in 1980. It won the Thomas Cook Travel Book Award. I have two copies of the 1998 paperback edition in my Picador collection, one obtained from second-hand bookdealer Dave Mundy and the other I bought from Oxfam Bookshop Coventry because it contained the name of a previous owner, Louise McCance-Price, an 'international voiceover artist' and, I see from her website, keen traveller. The back cover features a rather peculiar quote from a *Daily Telegraph* review: 'As eccentric, undisciplined, flashily brilliant and pig-headed as its author.' Also rather peculiar is the claim, in the book's blurb, that Davidson's journey covered 'seventeen thousand miles of Australian desert'. Australia is only two thousand five hundred miles across at its widest and the journey from Alice Springs to the Indian Ocean is more like one thousand seven hundred miles. The blurb writer found another o from somewhere.

I read the opening chapter on a trek of about one mile to the Post Office in Withington and was hooked. Davidson writes entertainingly about her arrival in Alice Springs and her attempts to get on with locals whose attitudes towards members of the

Aboriginal community could at best be described as obnoxious. Somehow, without making herself beholden to racists, she has to find – in Alice Springs – work, accommodation and camels. I like chapter one and I'll be reading on.

Tracks by Louise Erdrich – another Picador – is the third in a tetralogy of novels exploring the lives of four Anishinaabe famlies on a Native American reservation in North Dakota. The action of *Tracks* takes place earlier than the time periods of the two previous novels. I wonder if, in tetralogies, there might be a pattern in which the second part takes place after the first part, which you'd expect, but then the third part goes back in time to a point before the first part, and then the fourth picks up where we were at the end of the second part.

No?

Oh, OK.

It might bear a little research. The thing to know about Louise Erdrich, apart from the fact that she writes beautiful prose and has rightly been showered with prizes and awards, is that her novels often use more than one first-person narrator. Not everyone likes that sort of thing. Mind you, not everyone likes Sparks, which I find utterly baffling.

I read the first chapter of *Tracks* while walking back from the Post Office in Withington, and I may or may not read on.

'It was going to be the happiest of times.'

The opening sentence of Derek Marlowe's 1975 novel *Nightshade* leaves little doubt about how happy those times are going to be.

When you've read a novel as many times as I've read *Nightshade*, you wonder if there's anything left to discover.

But then you see this on page 28 (of the 1977 Penguin edition),

'... pushing a cedilla of hair from her eyes', and you remember that some pages earlier (you find it eventually on page 17) you noticed this: '... a shallow frown appearing between her eyes. That finely etched *W*.' And then you're on alert, for similar typographical imagery, and it's not too long before we get this, on page 48: 'an italic *c* of hair that has stubbornly remained on the base of the tub to bother the aesthete'. Then there's a longer gap until page 106, but it's worth the wait: 'He was aware of the moon in a clear sky, though not a full moon. That would be too artificial. Instead, a moon in parenthesis.'

We enjoy these images as we come across them. It's perhaps not too much of a stretch to say that we start *collecting* them, like you might collect a particular series of books – maybe it's this 1977 series of Marlowe titles (*A Dandy in Aspic, The Disappearance, Somebody's Sister, Do You Remember England?, Nightshade*) in white-spined Penguins, or white-spined Panther paperbacks from 1968–70, or those lovely non-standard-format Jupiter Books with author photographs on the front cover from John Calder in the mid 1960s (also with white spines). Once you decide you're going to collect this or that author or series or imprint, you start noticing them on bookshelves in a way that you wouldn't before. They pop out at you, like those similes in *Nightshade*.

Nightshade is the story of a British couple, Edward and Amy, on holiday in the Caribbean. Although they are a long way from home, they have not left England – specifically Tewkesbury – very far behind. Tewkesbury is mentioned numerous times. Something terrible happened there, but we don't know what. Marlowe creates and builds tension and suspense like the master thriller writer he is – or was. His first novel, a best-seller, was the spy thriller *A Dandy in Aspic*, made into a fascinating British film with Laurence Harvey in the main role and taking over the helm after director Anthony Mann died during the making of the film.

'I have made a mistake,' says Edward, towards the end of part one of *Nightshade*. He's supposedly talking about having thought he could smell cigarettes, but Marlowe is up to something. Towards the end of the novel, knocking on the door of a hotel room and finding it opened by a particular character, Edward says, again, 'I've made a mistake.' About the room, he means, but, whether he realises it or not, Edward may have made a bigger mistake.

Nightshade is out of print and has been for a long time. If you spotted a copy in a second-hand bookshop and bought it, you would not, I suggest, be making a mistake.

You're more likely to come across a copy of *Nightshade* by Annalena McAfee, published in 2020 by Harvill Secker and in print from Vintage. McAfee was the founder-editor of the *Guardian Review*, then Arts & Literary Editor of the *Financial Times*.

Nightshade, her third novel, about an artist facing a crisis in her life and career, got enthusiastic reviews in the *Guardian* and the *Financial Times*. I liked this line: 'The train rattles past, each window a bright frame of film reel with its own starring cast and complicated back story...' There's quite a lot of complicated back story.

Alberto Moravia's 1985 novel *The Voyeur* is a book I thought I would like more than I did. I've read a few of those.

The novel, translated from the Italian by Tim Parks, is packed with explicit sex and lengthy discourse on voyeurism, as a married professor watches his wife and his father perform intimate acts. It's not that I object to the subject matter. If I had the self-discipline to compile a top twenty favourite novels and actually restrict it to twenty, David Knowles's *The Third Eye*, in which a New Yorker rents out his apartment so he can watch and photograph his tenants, would be on that list. It's more that I find Moravia's *The Voyeur*, which the *Los Angeles Times* described as a 'tale of enervation and ennui', really rather boring.

Alain Robbe-Grillet's 1955 novel, *Le Voyeur*, is similar to his earlier *Les Gommes* with its obsessive male loner character endlessly walking (and in this case cycling) around an environment that is both familiar and unfamiliar to him. In *Les Gommes* the setting was an unnamed city; in *Le Voyeur*, Mathias, a watch seller, returns to the island where he was born.

A young girl has met with an accident, falling off a cliff while tending sheep. Could Mathias be to blame? The motif of a figure of eight (on its side, suggesting infinity) acquires a fetishistic regularity, reflected in Mathias's penchant for collecting bits of rope. Tension, absent in the Italian's novel, grows and grows as the watch seller continues to circle the island, like a minute hand crawling around a clock face, or a noose tightening around a neck.

My copy of the Moravia, an Abacus edition with a cover illustration by Mark Harrison, came from Manchester's Empire Exchange on Newton Street, a treasure trove of collectables and probably the last shop of its kind in Manchester. I found a copy of the original French Minuit edition of the Robbe-Grillet in one of my favourite second-hand bookshops in Brussels (now closed – 'J'ai un concert,' I heard the owner say to me, in explanation, and I pictured him attending a performance at Flagey, and I couldn't quite understand why this meant he had to close, permanently. 'Ah,' I said, finally, 'un cancer') and a copy of the

Richard Howard translation published by John Calder in Astley Book Farm, Warwickshire.

A few years ago at Moniack Mhor, I was talking to writer and translator Sonya Moor, who is bilingual. We were talking in French – I can't remember what about, only what she said to me, out of the blue: *Ton accent est terrible.*

Oh, I think I said. I looked at her, but she was looking at her drink, or at the book we were talking about, or just at the floor. I can't remember. I just remember how I felt.

Ton accent est terrible.
(Your accent is terrible.)

I was surprised by the depth of hurt I felt. Not only was it dismaying that my accent, which I had thought was not bad verging on pretty good, was actually terrible, but I was also puzzled by Sonya's directness. It wasn't like her. But the upside was I worked hard to improve my accent. From then on, when reading French books, I would read out loud and it seemed to me that my accent was getting better.

It was at least a year before I heard someone say, of a film that they hadn't liked, *C'est pas terrible*. It turns out that *terrible*, in French, can mean the opposite of itself, so to speak. It can mean *great*.

C'est pas terrible.
(It's not great.)
Ton accent est terrible.
(Your accent is great.)

The first two crime novels in Derek Raymond's Factory series, *He Died With His Eyes Open* and *The Devil's Home on Leave*, were translated into French (by Jean-Bernard Piat) and published in French before they appeared in English. By the time of the third novel in the series, *How the Dead Live*, the British publishers had caught up with the French. It was published, in France and the UK, in 1986. One key difference between the two editions was the name of the author. Derek Raymond was a pseudonym adopted by the novelist previously known as Robin Cook, to prevent confusion with the American thriller writer Robin Cook; in France, Robin Cook remained Robin Cook.

In 2007, Serpent's Tail published a new edition of *How the Dead Live* with an introduction by Will Self, whose own third novel, published in 2000, had been given a familiar title. 'I ripped off Robin Cook's title *How the Dead Live* quite shamelessly, and gave it to one of my own novels,' wrote Self in his introduction to Cook/Raymond's novel. 'He was dead, so he couldn't do anything about it. Some Raymond acolyte thought this was *a bit much* and wrote me an irate letter. Big deal. Besides, I don't think Cook would have given a toss – he was enough of a Wildean to know flattery when it was staring him in the face.'

When I found Olivier Pauvert's 2005 novel *Noir* in Jambala Buddhist charity bookshop in Bethnal Green in February 2019, I thought it was a French novel, and it is, but I'd found the English translation, by Adriana Hunter. Publishers Atlantic Books had done a number on it. It's a modish black and white design, credited to Mr & Mrs Smith, even a funky format, as wide as a B-format and shorter than an A-format, and it has an enticing blurb: 'A man wanders the streets of Paris haunted by the memory of a young woman's bloodied corpse and tormented by the possibility that he was her murderer. He rushes home, but his wife recoils from him, the neighbourhood he loves is violently hostile and when he looks in the mirror, he sees nothing. Terrified by the world in which he finds himself and pursued by the secret police, he has no choice but to flee. Chilling and uncomfortably timely, *Noir* is an electrifying novel about political responsibility and moral choice.'

Well, I thought it sounded good.

C'est pas terrible.

I was going to say that Pauvert's *Noir* does Robert Coover's extraordinary postmodern spoof-homage second-person-narrative private-eye novel *Noir* a disservice by using the same title, but it turns out Coover's novel came later, in 2010. I recommend it.

In Emma Tennant's 1976 novel *Hotel de Dream*, Mrs Routledge runs the Westringham Hotel, a boarding house with a pervading stench rising from the back basement where her servant Cridge lives and defecates in a collection of antique jars and vases, which he empties once a week, in the Gentlemen's Cloaks behind the reception. Guest Mrs Houghton is a romantic novelist wrestling with characters who don't like being told what to do, raising interesting questions about the difference between novels and dreams. Cridge appears in Mrs Houghton's book – or in her dreams – but is also writing a book of his own. 'If there was one thing he had picked up from the novelist in the dreary days of his incarceration in her work, it was that real places must be shown, in order to give a solid background to the actions and emotions of the characters.'

Hotel de Dream was one of the first Picadors I bought and I started reading it many years ago, but didn't get very far. This time I was more determined. I enjoyed the vivid imagery of the dreams. 'The drawing room . . . was littered with the forms of huge, sated and sleeping women. Their sandy buttocks made an undulating mound of pale flesh . . . and their brown eyes were lazily open, lying like puddles of forgotten water when the tide has left the beach.'

I tried to get into Edmund White's 2007 novel *Hotel de Dream*, inspired by nineteenth-century American writer Stephen Crane's abandoned novel about an encounter with a teenage male New York prostitute. Maybe next time.

Sunday 5 October 2025
I dreamt I was back at work at the university and I was asked to do something and I said I couldn't do it because I was invigilating and then I realised that the two things were the same thing and so I had to do it. Someone took me to a room where I had to climb over a load of typewriters. It was very dangerous and I got cross and said, This is the kind of thing I'm talking about. It's dangerous and nobody cares. It was horrible being back at work.

I was glad to be invited to join my wife and her cousins for Sunday lunch at a pub by the Brunswick Centre in Bloomsbury in March 2022, because it meant I could drop into the Skoob Books pop-up shop in the Brunswick Centre. I was even gladder when I spotted a copy of *The Search* by Naguib Mahfouz, translated by Mohamed Islam, because it meant I could include it and Geoff Dyer's novel with the same title – it feels weird writing 'of the same name' – in this project.

In Mahfouz's 1987 novel, a young man is told by his dying mother to find his father. His search takes him from Alexandria to Cairo, where he falls in love with two women. Violence follows. Has he fallen into a trap? Has he been duped? I found myself *rooting for* the killer.

In James Lasdun's 2006 novel *Seven Lies*, an East German dissident turned informer moves to the US in the hope of bagging a film deal, but Hollywood producers drop the project because 'they couldn't see a way to present someone who betrays all his friends as a "sympathetic" character; someone audiences can "root for", whatever that means . . .' The irony is not lost on the reader, who may realise they have been *rooting for* the narrator of the novel despite his hardly being a sympathetic character himself. One of the many things I like about *Seven Lies* is that I only counted, when I reread it for this project, three actual lies, whereas James Buchan, in his review in the *Guardian*, finds nine. (I'm no doubt taking 'lies' too literally. When I look back at my *Independent* review of the novel, I see I settled rather too easily on 'tissues of lies'.)

Elizabeth Kay's 2020 novel *Seven Lies* sets out its stall more straightforwardly. The novel is divided into seven parts, 'The First Lie', 'The Second Lie', 'The Third Lie' and so on until 'The Seventh Lie'. It feels surprisingly ingenuous for a novel about lies.

Who do we *root for* in Geoff Dyer's *The Search*? Perhaps for the novel's protagonist, Walker, who passes through various cities (Iberia, Meridian, Horizon) that remind me of the Neighbourhoods in Michael Marshall Smith's *Only Forward* and the lands at the top of the Faraway Tree in Enid Blyton's *The Enchanted Wood* and related books. (I suspect they should remind me more of Calvino's *Invisible Cities*. If they don't, that's down to me, not Dyer.) Or maybe we *root for* Dyer, whose prose is studded with what feel to me like aspiring and often successful Chandlerisms – 'the freeway roar of the ocean', 'His reflection posed the question it was supposed to answer', 'On the writing desk was a phone that looked like it had never rung'. Dyer may or may not be paying homage to Chandler, but his own original phrase-making ensures *The Search* avoids pastiche (if pastiche is something that needs to be avoided). I'm thinking of phrases such as 'a guy in a red-faced blazer' and '[a] cigarette-faced woman', which maybe we can call Dyerisms.

The copy of the first Penguin edition I read on this occasion contained an inclusion, a paper wallet from a hotel, the Nijmegen Centre, that would have been given to a guest with a key card. There's a name, Gada, and a room, 303, an arrival date of 9/10 and departure date two days later. If I had more time – and money – I'd get the Eurostar over to Amsterdam and a local train down to Nijmegen and ask for room 303. I'd expect to open the wardrobe door to the jangle of metal hangers, like Walker in Meridian.

I'm always a little perplexed when I read that a defendant has asked for more offences to be taken into consideration. Do they do it to clear the slate or in the hope that the judge will show leniency? At this point I'd like to ask that several more offences, briefly summarised, be taken into consideration. (I know 'offences' is the wrong word.)

I bought a copy of *Bella* by Jilly Cooper to Blu tack to my daughter's bedroom door, but it kept falling off, and I couldn't bring myself to tear the cover off the book, and then my daughter moved to London and got her own place, so the next time it fell off I didn't try to stick it on again. Then RM Francis very kindly sent me a copy of his Black Country folklore-inspired novel *Bella*, which I added to one of the many to-be-read stalagmites that have turned my flat into something resembling an outlying Peak District cavern, and now of course I can't find it. But I know it's there somewhere and it will let me find it when it wants to be found.

When I reread DM Thomas's *The White Hotel* in 2021, on the fortieth anniversary of its publication, I found it slow going in the middle, after the still-surprising verse section, but then the section about the massacre of Ukrainian Jews is still incredibly powerful. I was reading it while walking in London, on my way to the Barbican to visit the St Giles Book Fair, and it started raining, but I took shelter, and the water-damaged pages are not due to the rain.

I've not reread Thomas's *Ararat* since reading it thirty-odd years ago, partly in case I find I like it less than I liked it then, but when I saw Christopher Golden's *Ararat* in Oxfam Bookshop Chorlton, I bought it, just in case.

On the last Wednesday of July 2017 in Barnardo's in Didsbury I bought Val McDermid's *Northanger Abbey*. The following Tuesday, two hundred miles away in Oxfam Bookshop Balham, I found Jane Austen's *Northanger Abbey*. I still haven't read either of them.

Similar story with Marthe Blau's *Submission* and Michel Houellebecq's *Submission*. I found the former in Age Concern in Chorlton in January 2017 and the latter eight months later in St John's Hospice shop on Finchley Road, north London. I tell myself I haven't read them because I want to read the Houellebecq in French, but what I've found with Houellebecq is I prefer his short novels, *Whatever* and *Lanzarote*. When he starts going on, I find my enthusiasm wanes. I think I prefer narcissistic self-loathing in short bursts. Does love – as distinct from self-love – exist in Houellebecq's universe? I found *Love* by Péter Nádas in the basement of Burley Fisher in Hackney to read alongside Angela Carter's *Love* that I'd had in my Picador collection for ever. I enjoyed both.

It makes me disproportionately happy that of the three different editions I have of Paul Auster's *The Red Notebook*, none of them is red. It's not that, as a lifelong supporter of Manchester City Football Club, I object to the colour, as I know some City fans do. I like red in certain contexts, such as the frequent splashes of scarlet in Nicolas Roeg's *Don't Look Now*, but it's true that I almost never wear red, with the exception of a pair of red shoes that I wore till they wore out when I was 18. I remember wearing them on a family holiday to London, when we stayed on a caravan site at Crystal Palace and I travelled into the West End on my own to see Alain Resnais's *Providence* at the Minema on Knightsbridge. And, in the late 1990s, a red Chevignon bomber jacket belonging to Time Out colleague Chris Hemblade. 'Hem of your trouser and then blade,' I must have heard him say a hundred times on the phone, at the next desk, while his red Chevignon jacket hung off the back of his chair, and I would covet it shamelessly, repeatedly, telling him it had gone out of fashion, in the hope that he would give it to me, and one day he did. I wore it for years, over a denim jacket, because it was too big for me, but it was a good fit for my daughter when she came to be the age I was when I went to London in my red shoes. It suited her better than it had ever suited me, but when she grew less fond of it and her mum gave it to the Francis House Children's Hospice charity shop in Withington, I *ran* up there, and I don't run anywhere, unless it's in pursuit of a ball, and I don't even do that any more, and the man there remembered it, but said it had been sold and, no, he didn't know who to, and obviously even if he did ... To this day, I am drawn to any glimpse of red on the streets of Withington, not unlike Donald Sutherland in Venice in *Don't Look Now*.

It had been a shock hearing that Chris Hemblade had died, at the age of 42, in 2013.

I must admit, I thought not of Lao Tzu, but of the line Dr

Eldon Tyrell says to replicant Roy Batty in *Blade Runner*: 'The light that burns twice as bright burns half as long, and you have burned so very, very brightly, Roy.'

All of which was a bit of a diversion – unplanned – from the cover of *The Red Notebook* and its not being red or featuring an illustration of a red notebook, because that would be just too easy. The hardback goes with a moody black and white portrait of the author by The Douglas Brothers against a dark green background, and the first Faber paperback has a different portrait of Auster, by Arturo Patten, and a black background, and a later paperback edition reproduces the hardback cover.

But I wrote about *The Red Notebook* in the chapter about Auster's *The New York Trilogy* in *Shadow Lines*. I'll just pick up on the last line from the piece about high-wire walker Philippe Petit, who performed a walk between the Twin Towers, 400 metres above the ground, in 1974. 'May he live to be a hundred,' wrote Auster in 1982, when Petit was 33. At the time of writing, Petit is 76, Auster having died at the age of 77 in 2024. Fingers crossed for the Frenchman.

In terms of what it reveals about its author's interests and writing practice, *The Red Notebook* shares some common ground with AL Kennedy's *On Writing*, which reminds me, in turn, of Stephen King's *On Writing*, but Auster's non-fiction collection has a connection to another book, Antoine Laurain's 2014 novel *La femme au carnet rouge*, which was translated (by Emily Boyce and Jane Aitken) and published in English by Gallic Books as *The Red Notebook*.

There's lots to like in Laurain's novel about bookseller Laurent, who finds a lady's handbag and wants to return it to its owner. When Laurent eventually looks inside the handbag, he finds a copy of Patrick Modiano's *Accident nocturne*, one of my favourite Modianos (basically, I like everything from 1981 onwards; before that, not so much). Not only that, but the copy is inscribed by Modiano to Laure, 'in memory of our meeting in the rain'. Later, Laurent tracks down Modiano in person. I love that kind of thing – real people in novels – if it's well done, and it's well done here. Perhaps less well done is the plot.

I don't believe Laurent would hide the handbag from his girlfriend.

I don't believe she would leave him over it.

I don't believe how many adverbs the author uses. People say things coldly, soberly, gloomily, wonderingly, laconically, enthusiastically, sardonically. Maybe *how* they deliver those lines could be implied by the context and by the content of the lines themselves, rather than by using adverbs. Aren't adverbs a bit too easy, for writer and reader alike?

But I like the fact that another character successfully reads a letter in a sealed envelope by holding it up to the light. I did this myself with a sealed thank-you letter from 'Carla' to 'Auntie Voula' that I found inside a copy of John Updike's *Couples* bought from Oxfam Bookshop Chiswick in November 2023. (By coincidence, it was only days later that I read *The Red Notebook* – the novel.)

As Auster's *The Red Notebook* is non-fiction and Laurain's is a novel, I think that lets both Laurain, whose original title was different anyway, and his translators off the hook.

When I read Mazarine Pingeot's *Premier roman*, I wondered if the author was deliberately making all the mistakes people talk about being exhibited in first novels – overwriting, verbosity, prioritising autobiography over the art of fiction (the author's mother is art historian Anne Pingeot and her father was French president François Mitterrand) – and then I wondered if it would turn out to be the book being written by one of the characters, but, no, it seems this was Pingeot's own stab at a first novel and she simply used that title, *Premier roman*. At least, it hadn't been translated and published in English, I told myself, but it raised an interesting question. If a French novel, entitled *Premier roman*, remains untranslated, and someone – me, for instance – writes a novel in English and gives it the title *First Novel*, should these two novels be considered to have the same title or would they only have the same title once *Premier roman* is translated and published in English? Of course, when I did a little more research, some years after my *First Novel* was published, I found that was precisely what had happened. *Premier roman* was translated by Ros Schwartz and published in 1999 by Maclehose Press with the title *First Novel*.

If I had checked earlier, would I have used a different title? I had originally been going to use a different title anyway. The working title was *Either Or*. After I had given a reading from the novel-in-progress at an event at which he and I were both speaking, Professor Nicholas Royle, author of *Telepathy and Literature* and *The Uncanny*, said to me, 'You've read the Kierkegaard, of course?'

'Of course,' I said, and quickly changed the subject.

I bought a copy and started reading it.

Either I finished it or threw it across the room after a couple of chapters.

When Nicholas Royle published his first novel, *Quilt*, in 2010, I should have said to him, 'You've read the Donna E Smyth, of course?' But I only learned of the existence of Smyth's *Quilt*, the Canadian playwright's first novel, published in 1982, when I came across a copy in Oxfam Dalston in September 2020.

Monday 12 April 1999

In or near Doncaster to visit the other Nicholas Royle – or his wife. I realise I've left it too late to get back to the station to catch the InterCity back to London. I catch a bus. On the top deck are two Mrs Royles. I talk to one. The other is shy. In a desperate bid still to get my train I jump off the bus and look for a cab. I end up in a village walking down a road next to a golf course. I'm looking for a way in over a high fence. Later I'm with another Nicholas Royle. He's a magician and he's perfected a trick in which he can make two facsimilies of himself appear in the same room as himself. One is hitting a tennis ball with a racquet, keeping it up. Another is sitting watching him. Dressed as a baby, he has a grown man's legs sticking out of the bottom of his baby-style leggings. A third Nicholas Royle adopts a pose a few yards away. I talk to the one with the tennis racquet. He has thick fair hair.

I enjoyed David Szalay's 2018 work *Turbulence*, but was distracted by the question of whether it's a novel or a series of linked short stories. I also enjoyed Chico Buarque's 1992 novel *Turbulence*, translated from the Portuguese by Peter Bush (the original title, *Estorvo*, means trouble or hindrance. *Turbulence* was chosen by Bush after discussion with Buarque), although when I was reading it while walking in Manchester, a woman with holes in the knees of her trousers came towards me and said, to herself but in an angry voice and for me to hear, 'That print'll be too small.'

The only times I'd been in the unstaffed Book Nook in the Great Northern shopping and leisure complex on Deansgate in Manchester, I'd been the only person there. I still don't know if you're meant to take books, borrow them, or just treat it as a reference library. When I popped in on 1 May 2024, a homeless guy came in to charge his mobile phone. He very politely asked me if I minded if he sat in the armchair right by where I was standing on tiptoe trying to see if books on the high shelves had shadow lines. I said, Go ahead, of course, and gradually moved along to give him space. I left with a copy of Giles Foden's *Turbulence*, which, seeing as it's longer than both Szalay's and Buarque's books put together, I'm not going to read, or not for this project. It was published in 2009, between Buarque and Szalay.

I think I'll shuffle the chapters of BS Johnson's 1969 book-in-a-box *The Unfortunates* and give it another read before I get to Laurie Graham's 2002 novel *The Unfortunates*, partly because, like RM Francis's *Bella*, my copy has gone missing.

The narrator of Christopher Petit's debut 1993 novel *Robinson* never introduces himself, although Robinson calls him Christo. 'When Robinson wasn't in the George, he was usually to be found in the Blue Posts soon after five-thirty, sitting upstairs in a lounge bar left over from the Fifties . . .' The Blue Posts in *Robinson* could be one of two of the four pubs that went by that name in Soho – indeed, they marked the four corners of the district – in the early 1990s. I, too, used to hang out in them. I came to pubs late. As an adolescent, I didn't go to pubs. Not even as a student. 'I'm not thirsty,' I used to say, missing the point. Mostly I arranged to meet people outside cinemas. In pubs, there was nothing I wanted. When I looked after the bar in my hall of residence, I developed a taste for gin and lime. I made sure to add enough lime to mask the taste of the gin. I didn't feel I could do that in a pub. Then I discovered the Tufnell Park Tavern. Dry cider. Jazz nights. Every Thursday and Friday night in the late 1980s would find me at the Tufnell Park Tavern in north London listening to the John Richardson Trio and their guests, Alan Barnes, Eddie Dove, Theo Travis, David Newton, Dave O'Higgins, Philip Caramazza and many others. And then the Tufnell Park Tavern closed for a refurb and reopened and the jazz was over. I can't remember what took its place, but it wasn't as good. The pub wasn't as good. Nothing is ever as good. Everything should always remain the same. I mean the good things. The good things should always remain the same. But they never do.

In the early 1990s, I started going to the Blue Posts on Rupert Street. Upstairs. I can't quite remember if it looked like a lounge bar left over from the 1950s. I was too busy gazing into the eyes of my date. One of those occasions was a blind date, although it was not supposed to be. I had arranged to meet X, who I remembered from workplace Y, but when X arrived, she was not the X I remembered, but another X. That was fine and we had a good time, and lots more good times, but I knew that at some point her boyfriend would reappear, which he eventually did, by which time, with great good fortune, I had been introduced to the woman who would become my first wife and the mother of our children.

Petit's *Robinson* is not only a London novel; it's a Soho novel. 'Soho: a state of mind, that crumbling time zone built up of absenteeism, dereliction, vagrancy and atheism.' Muriel Spark's 1958 novel *Robinson*, her second, is a desert island novel. The narrator, January Marlow, is one of three passengers who survive a plane crash on an island in the North Atlantic. The survivors are nursed back to physical health by a mysterious loner called Robinson. I judge all Muriel Spark novels by the first one I read, *The Driver's Seat*, and *Robinson* is not up there with *The Driver's Seat*.

In March 2024, my wife – my second wife, or my current wife, as the joke goes – took me to Paris for my birthday so I could do research for some new stories I was writing set in the French capital. We took the metro to Bir-Hakeim and then walked across the Seine to rue Beethoven, where we split up. My wife got back on the metro to Belleville and I mooched around rue Beethoven for a bit, thinking about the story I wanted to write, before walking back across the river to avenue de la Motte-Picquet and the apartment block where Michael Haneke filmed a scene from *Code Unknown*. I needed to get inside. If you approach the entrance to a secure building with the correct amount of confidence just as a resident is coming out, chances are they'll hold the door open for you.

Walking from avenue de la Motte-Picquet back to the 20th, I came across a second-hand bookshop I had not been in before, Megacomik, run by self-published writer Phil Marso. He writes crime novels, or *polars*. I didn't buy one of those but I did buy a 1972 Série Noire edition of *Scoop* by Jean-Gérard Imbar, as it would give me an excuse to reread a book I had last read in school and which people had been urging me to reread. 'It's really funny,' they assured me. Hm, I think I replied.

As I read Evelyn Waugh's 1933 novel *Scoop*, for the first time in four and a half decades, I laughed once, at the bit about the mix-up of the beaver and the great crested grebe. Thereafter I found it less funny and a bit racist. The telegrams Boot sends to his employer, not understanding that he's supposed to keep them short, are quite funny. But the racism is not.

Jean-Gérard Imbar's *Scoop* is an action-heavy crime novel about a photo-journalist who takes on a trio of former US

Marines now working as heavies in Paris. There's lots of violence that's not particularly interesting to read about, but at least it isn't racist.

Monday 18 March 2024
Avenue d'Italie, Paris, 13ème.
Man, sixties, thin steel-rimmed glasses, green coat and scarf, blue jeans, grey Merrell trainers, walking south reading Laurent Binet's *La septième fonction du langage* (Livre de Poche).

On the opening page of *Staring at the Sun*, Julian Barnes's fourth novel, published in 1986, we read, 'Inside the cockpit, red light from the instrument panel fell softly on Prosser's hands and face; he glowed like an avenger.' On the second page: 'But the black smoke had stopped, and there seemed nothing wrong; probably she had just been stoking up.' Two impeccable examples of how to use the semi-colon in the first two pages. I once did an event with a much-fêted young novelist in which I praised his use of the semi-colon, and afterwards a friend came up to me and said it had been really funny. What, I asked, what was funny? The semi-colon thing, said my friend. But I meant it, I said, and I did. That young writer knew how to use the semi-colon – which a lot of writers seem to think is nothing more than a comma on steroids, or worse, is interchangeable with the colon – and so does Julian Barnes. In the examples quoted above, each half of the sentence, either side of the semi-colon, is grammatically independent, while the clauses are related in terms of content; in addition, in each case, the subject of the second clause is different from the subject of the first clause. Textbook.

I admire Julian Barnes's short stories and asked Jonathan Cape if I could reprint the title story of his 2011 collection *Pulse* in *Best British Short Stories 2011* (Salt). Cape said they would normally ask for £900; I wrote back saying, How about £75? There was a flat rate, I explained. They wrote back saying that, in any case, Julian didn't want the story extracted. I left it at that, although I wondered why, when more than half the stories in the collection had already been published elsewhere.

Cynan Jones was happy with the flat rate when I reprinted his story, 'Stock', in the Salt series, the same story later reappearing in Jones's 2025 collection, *Pulse*.

I was very happy when I came across Irvin D Yalom's 2008 work of 'popular psychology' *Staring at the Sun* in Sue Ryder in Didsbury in August 2024, partly because it added another pair of titles to this project and partly because I hoped it might be of practical use. Its subtitle is 'Overcoming the Dread of Death' and there are chapters headed 'Recognising Death Anxiety', 'Overcoming Death Terror Through Connection' and 'Addressing Death Anxiety: Advice For Therapists'. I'm not a therapist, but I have an overactive fear of death and wondered if I might just be able to cut out the middleman by reading Yalom's book. Actually, I've always thought it's not really a *fear* of death, as such; it's more that I just really don't want it to happen, and given that it's going to, I'd like to put it off for as long as possible. I'm about a quarter of the way through (Yalom's book, not life – I wish) and finding it slow going. Hopefully I'll finish it before something else finishes me.

William Sutcliffe's 1996 debut novel *New Boy* is – like Christopher Petit's *Robinson* and Alain-Fournier's *Le Grand Meaulnes* before it – one of those novels in which a shy narrator puts the charismatic main character centre stage, in this case the new boy of the title, Barry. The narrator, Mark, is a pupil at a minor public school in north London, next door to which is a girls' school with which Mark's school is partnered, but so discouraged are relations between the two sets of pupils that the dividing line between the two schools is known as the Berlin Wall. Physical contact is forbidden. 'The most famous infringement of this rule was when the daughter of Alvin Stardust's drummer was caught in the cricket pavilion giving a blow job to the son of Golders Green's best optician.' While the identification of Golders Green's best optician might be subjective, the identity of Alvin Stardust's drummer should be a matter of record. Alarmed for Sutcliffe, I have a word with Mr Google and find that 'Alvin Stardust was known for working with various drummers throughout his career'. Well, blow me down. It's almost like Sutcliffe did his research. Doing mine, I find, to my disbelief, that Alvin Stardust didn't actually sing 'My Coo Ca Choo'. Younger readers, please note: 'My Coo Ca Choo' was a hit single for Alvin Stardust in 1973. But hang on, I watched Alvin Stardust, his gloved hand curled around the mic, sing 'My Coo Ca Choo' on *Top of the Pops*, along with millions of others. Well, didn't I? It turns out Alvin Stardust was a character created by Peter Shelley (not Pete Shelley of Buzzcocks, before you ask), co-founder (with Michael Levy) of Magnet Records, and it was Shelley who wrote, recorded and sang 'My Coo Ca Choo'. Technically, I learn, Shelley was Stardust at the time, although surely the man we saw on *Top of the Pops* with the sideburns and leather glove was Stardust, even if, as we all knew, but never quite understood, he wasn't actually singing. The real name of the public face of Stardust, Bernard William Jewry, makes me wonder if Sutcliffe picked him for his surname rather than the convenience of his having worked with various drummers. Jewish identity is very much at the heart of *New Boy*. Most of the pupils at the school in the novel, it seems, are either Jewish or Asian. The blow job incident apart, 'little interest was shown by the boys in the girls', we read. 'The general consensus was that they were all ugly.'

There were enough Jewish boys at my school in Manchester for there to be a separate Jewish assembly. Although I never attended it, I doubt it was as entertaining as the Jewish assemblies Mark describes. There was more contact in Manchester between my school and the neighbouring girls' school. Indeed, I formed some fond attachments to a number of Jewish girls; some of them were even aware of these attachments.

In chapter sixteen, pupil Joel Schneider organises a riverboat disco on the Thames. Schneider showed 'admirable business acumen by single-handedly operating the ticket selling, for which he also generously offered to do the accounting. Somewhere along the line a few hundred pounds vanished'. I would like to reassure anyone who attended the Hughes Parry Hall riverboat disco I organised for my University of London hall of residence in June 1984 that I was too unambitious – not to mention financially inept – to even think about embezzlement.

After Barry is expelled from school for having an affair with a teacher, Mark finds himself feeling sorry for Mrs Mumford, who had left her husband and children to shack up with Barry in Notting Hill. 'After all,' Mark reflects, 'the only thing worse than having a mid-life crisis is not having one . . .' He then adds, 'As I was having these thoughts, it occurred to me what a perceptive chap I was, and for the first time it dawned on me that my future career should be as a psychotherapist.' Fast-forward three decades and William Sutcliffe, describing himself as an ex-novelist, is now a registered psychotherapist.

Mark eventually makes it to his A-levels: 'French was a piece of piss as long as you read the texts in translation' – my strategy with regard to German A-level – and then he adds, 'my A-level book was *Le Grand Meaulnes*, which is without doubt the crappest, most juvenile book ever written.'

Ah.

If you are into modern-day retellings of Shakespeare, you might enjoy Tracy Chevalier's 2017 novel *New Boy* as much as I enjoyed William Sutcliffe's *New Boy*.

Tuesday 21 May 1996
I'm fishing in a river with a short rod and on my right are a bunch of guys with very long, whippy-looking rods. They are casting and striking with great elan and fluidity. One of them reels in and has what looks like a three-foot eel on the end. I realise it's his bait. I see movement on my rod tip, so I strike. I play it but it's only small. It swings out of the water, a washed-out, anaemic-looking perch. Suddenly the river is in a library. I see someone looking at *Time Out* which has a thing about Dennis Etchison's new film. I see a girl with bright pink hair, her eyes olive green. I touch her on the shoulder and she flinches and says, Don't you know who I am?

There are some short stories I return to with a degree of regularity – William Sansom's 'Murder', Jamaica Kincaid's 'Blackness', Giles Gordon's 'In Spite of Himself', Alison Moore's 'When the Door Closed, it Was Dark', M John Harrison's 'Black Houses', Shelley Jackson's 'Cancer', 'Dennis Etchison's 'The Dog Park', Lawrence Durrell's 'The Cherries' – because there's something about them that I forget, almost as soon as I've read them. I might forget what happens in them, or how they work, but what I remember is how they make me feel. When I reread them, it's like lighting a candle, and when I've finished reading, the draught created by the closing book blows out the candle and I'm left with a curl of smoke, my memory of the story, which slowly dissipates.

I know where to find all these stories in my home apart from 'The Cherries', because my copy of Peter Haining's *Detours into the Macabre* anthology has disappeared.

Not to worry, I thought. I can read Lawrence Durrell's novel *Justine*, the opening novel in his Alexandria Quartet.

The blurb describes the novel as 'the tragic story of the mysterious and fascinating Justine', but I'm not sure I'd agree that 'story' is the right word. Isn't it more a series of descriptions of place and character sketches? The narrator is in love with two women – Melissa and Justine. At the same time? Is there some crossover? I think so, but I couldn't swear to it. At least one other man is in love with either or both of them. 'When I thought of Justine I thought of some great freehand composition, a cartoon of a woman representing someone released from bondage in the male.' Then: 'But Melissa was a sad painting from a winter landscape contained by dark sky; a window-box with a few flowering geraniums lying forgotten on the windowsill of a cement-factory.' A rather lovely image and one that actually draws me more to Melissa than to Justine. Part II begins: 'To have written so much and to have said nothing about . . .' I'm expecting him to say 'the story', 'the great mystery', or whatever, but no, be goes on: '. . . Balthazar is indeed an omission.' Part III starts with the account of the discovery of a headless corpse, but the anecdote goes nowhere.

The narrator is offered a job with the secret service. Could this be the start of something? Sadly not. Then there's a set piece, a duck shoot, which is great. At the close, there are 'workpoints' that prefigure the annoying questions-for-book-groups in certain publishers' 'book group books', but, weirdly, they're inserted here by the author.

Beautifully written, with lots of lovely descriptions of Alexandria, *Justine* makes me long for the brevity and suggestion and mystery of 'The Cherries'.

Alice Thompson's *Justine*, like Durrell's, is narrated by a man who becomes obsessed with Justine, but also with Juliette, Justine's twin sister, who perhaps represents Durrell's Melissa. Another echo of the earlier novel sees the narrator, as a boy, diving into a lake. In it were starfish, 'as if they are stars fallen straight from the sky', like a passage in Durrell where the narrator swims in the sea late at night and describes the stars caught in the waves.

I've read all of Thompson's novels and count myself a fan. *Justine* may not be her very best, but reading it after Durrell's *Justine*, you appreciate her commitment to narrative.

Toby Litt's 2004 novel *Ghost Story* starts with what appears to be an alarming fifty-page mostly-memoir that sits somewhat uncomfortably – deliberately so, I think – with the not-particularly-scary haunted-house fiction that makes up the bulk of the book. Among those fifty pages is a passage in which the narrator – Litt himself, we can only assume – believing that he is to become a father, thinks, 'I'm going to be a God,' which leads on to the thought that 'Our father' would be a good title for something, 'a story or a book', and then he remembers that Andrew O'Hagan has already written a book called *Our Fathers* – 'it was a great title, it was his. Good luck to him. Bastard.' It *was* a good title, but an even better title is *Ghost Story*, and Peter Straub had already written a book – a novel, indeed – in 1979 called *Ghost Story*. Why is Peter Straub not a bastard for nabbing that title? It's inconceivable that Litt didn't know of Straub's 500-page doorstop. Is he deliberately ignoring its existence? If so, I can't work out why. In her review of Litt's novel in the *Guardian*, Joanna Briscoe writes, '*Ghost Story* seemingly pays homage to *The Turn of the Screw* . . .' and maybe that's true, but, just as lots of boys born in Kosovo after 1999 were called Tonibler or Toni or Bler, in recognition of the impact of Tony Blair's role in the 1999 NATO intervention in the region, there can surely be no greater homage than to name something after something, or someone after someone.

My Futura paperback of Straub's *Ghost Story* – £1.50 from Popular Book Centre in Lavender Hill, Battersea, a lifetime ago, a duplicate spotted more recently in a very smart second-hand bookshop in Edinburgh, as we'll see in the next chapter, for nine quid – contains a boarding pass, in my name, from Tokyo's Narita Airport to London Heathrow. It's a big book for me to have carried to the other side of the world. The date given is 31 July and of course there's no year – I've never understood why they don't put the year on boarding passes – but it was 2003. Maybe I thought I needed a big book for a long flight. It was optimistic. I didn't read it at the time. More recently, I read the novel's twenty-page prologue in which a writer called Don Wanderley drives south – West Virginia, South Carolina, Georgia – with a young girl the reader is encouraged to think he has abducted. I was more than happy to go along for the ride and will read on.

In June 2024, in the book exchange outside novelist Naomi Hamill's home in Chorlton, I found a copy of *Rain* by VC Andrews, which I started reading on the walk back to Didsbury. It wasn't raining, but I wouldn't have had any compunction about reading *Rain* in the rain. On the imprint page we read, 'Following the death of Virginia Andrews, the Andrews family worked with a carefully selected writer to organise and complete Virginia Andrews' stories and to create additional novels, of which this is one, inspired by her storytelling genius.' That 'carefully selected writer' worked very hard, in the prologue to *Rain*, which I read while walking through Southern Cemetery, to avoid using 'said', which is always a bit of a giveaway. Instead, we are treated to 'gasped', 'roared', 'chanted', 'threatened', 'assured', 'challenged', 'warned', 'muttered', 'cried', 'asked', 'snapped', 'fired back', 'retorted', 'protested', 'declared', 'whispered', 'promised', 'agreed', 'mimicked', 'followed', several of these used more than once, and eighteen 'saids', but these mostly come in the last three or four pages, when the author has clearly given up.

To consider alongside VC Andrews' *Rain*, I can't choose between Conrad Williams's 2007 novella, *Rain*, which was actually written by him, and Stephen Gallagher's 1990 novel, *Rain*, which was actually written by him. I've read both, long ago, I like both, and both authors are friends of mine. I can't get into discussing both of them, because then we'd have a three, rather than a two, which could fatally undermine the integrity of this chapter.

While I'm at it, some more titles I'm going to mention in brief. The eponymous character in *Stitch*, Richard Stern's 1965 novel, is Thaddeus Stitch, a world-famous sculptor, while the antagonist of Mark Morris's 1991 novel *Stitch* is cult leader Peregrine Stitch. Albert Camus's 1942 classic *The Outsider* (sometimes translated as *The Stranger*) and Colin Wilson's 1956 study of alienation and creativity, *The Outsider*. *Signs of Life* – a 2012 first novel by Anna Raverat, and M John Harrison's eighth novel published in 1997. Brian's Moore's 1976 *The Doctor's Wife* and Elizabeth

Brundage's 2004 *The Doctor's Wife*. My copy of the latter, which I bought from Open Book in Chicago in the summer of 2025, contains an extremely personal letter from K to S. Both parties are suffering from depression and at least one, probably both, have attempted suicide. I hope both are now enjoying better mental health.

Author and lecturer in creative writing Joe Stretch once told me that the key to good dialogue is that if one character asks a question, the other character should not answer it. Or that each line of dialogue should not follow on neatly from the previous one. Or something like that. He would deny it now, I'm sure, possibly because he never said it and I've misremembered what he actually said, but it made me think and I got an exercise out of it for a workshop, and I was reminded of it when reading Richard Ford's 1990 novel *Wildlife*. Ford's fourth novel is a short, absorbing and strangely thrilling novel about a marriage break-up as witnessed by sixteen-year-old Joe, who is a bit thrown when his father, unjustly sacked from the golf club, goes off to fight a wildfire, and bewildered when his mother, given the opportunity, has a fling and, she says, falls in love. (I don't think she falls in love at all.) Ford is far too smart a writer to tell us that Joe is 'thrown' or 'bewildered', but he allows us to infer the boy's feelings as we share his perspective on unfolding events. There's something mesmerising about the dialogue, which is never predictable, but always feels absolutely right. It's not quite that characters don't answer other characters' questions, nor that lines don't follow on from those before, but there's something off-kilter about a lot of what characters say that feels real. These same characters come alive like figures that you've paused on TV and then you press play. Each character – Joe, his father Jerry and mother Jean, even unlikely lover Warren Miller – has depth and feels real. The novel pulls off a feat I would have thought impossible, to make me care about a guy who plays golf.

Writing in the *Chicago Tribune*, Joseph Coates gets my goat. 'Especially when it came to the excruciating pain of childhood emotional trauma, [Hemingway] never went beyond short-story length in confronting it,' he wrote, in his review of *Wildlife*. 'What Ford has done in *Wildlife* is fashion a beautifully modulated full-length novel.'

What the heck, I ask myself whenever I read this phrase, which is surprisingly often, is a full-length novel?

Actually, what I say is slightly different, but my mum is going to be reading this, I hope, and she doesn't need language like that.

I mean, I understand, in this context, Coates is contrasting Ford's novel with a Hemingway short story, but the implication that a short story is not full length, simply because it is short, is, frankly, silly.

Joe Stretch tells me that when he wrote his own 'full-length' novel also called *Wildlife*, published in 2009, he had no idea that the title had already been used by Richard Ford, so maybe I need to think again about *Ghost Story* and my conviction that Toby Litt could not possibly not have known about Peter Straub's novel. Joe Stretch bought Ford's novel and couldn't get into it, but he 'imagine[s] it's great'. It really is, but so is Stretch's *Wildlife*. His second novel, it followed *Friction* and was in due course followed by *The Adult*.

I read *Wildlife* before it was published, having had a degree of involvement in Joe Stretch's path to publication, and I loved it, about the same amount as I'd loved *Friction*, while *The Adult*, in whose publication I played no part, was clearly a more grown-up book. Rereading *Wildlife*, immediately after finishing *Wildlife*, while walking through Manchester's university district in mid December 2025, I was surprised by the amount of – sorry, Mum – shit in the opening couple of chapters. I wouldn't have not been aware of it when I first read it, but I suppose I'd forgotten about it and with a colonoscopy in the diary for the new year, maybe I was being over-sensitive. Aware that a tall and distinguished-looking rake with greying hair had entered my peripheral vision, I looked up. It wasn't Joe Stretch, but our mutual friend, poet, novelist and short story writer Adam O'Riordan. I showed him what I was reading and we had a laugh about it and I guessed that Adam would tell Joe he'd seen me and that I was reading *Wildlife*, so I felt that meant I didn't have to finish it. I mean, I'd have liked to, but I was running out of time and it's quite long and I'm a slow reader. I asked Adam if he'd read Ford's novel and he said he had and he'd liked it too.

Finally, I wonder if it might be the case that when Roberto Bolaño said, 'The only novel that doesn't embarrass me is *Antwerp*,' he was talking not about his own novel, *Antwerp*, written in 1980 and published in 2002, a year before his death, and not published in English translation (by Natasha Wimmer) until 2010, but about my fifth novel, *Antwerp*, published in 2004. The timings would suggest not, but with Bolaño, you never know.

8

Found maps

On the last day of January 2019, in Oxfam Books & Music Kentish Town, I fill my bag. Marlon James's *A Brief History of Seven Killings* (Oneworld), because my wife wants to read it, Will Self's *How the Dead Live* (Penguin), for an ongoing project (see chapter, 'Doubles'), Philip Hensher's *The Bedroom of the Mister's Wife* (Vintage), so that I might check whether he acknowledges where his own stories were first published (yes, he does, which makes the fact that he doesn't bother when reprinting other writers' stories in anthologies he's editing, making do with a credit to wherever he came across the story, often not where it was first published, all the more puzzling), and Salman Rushdie's *Midnight's Children* (Picador) with an inclusion, a street map of Dorking, or Woking, at page 117. Prior to finding this map, and ever since, Dorking and Woking, in my mind, have always been indistinguishable. Similarly, Margate and Ramsgate are unlikely ever to become Kentish seaside towns that I can tell apart. As I write these words, I've never been to Woking or Dorking, or Margate or Ramsgate.

Even though I *have* been to both Burnley and Barnsley, I still have to stop and think about which is which.

Still, the discovery of this map of Dorking, or Woking, marks the start of another project: I will collect books that I find containing maps. Not maps bound in as part of a book, but maps popped in and left by a previous owner. Hand-drawn, printed, photocopied – however they come. I'll make up the rules as I go along. Where practical, I will visit the location portrayed on the map. I will take the book with me and read it, all of it or part of it, while walking the streets on the map. Assuming there are streets.

I allow this newly acquired copy of *Midnight's Children* to displace the copy I already had in my Picador collection, the old copy slipping quietly into the shadow collection. I won't go to Dorking, or Woking, yet. I still haven't been to the unidentified town represented on the hand-drawn map I found at page 77 of Keri Hulme's *The Bone People*, another Picador, which I found in Oxfam on Marylebone High Street in September 2017. It's a simple map, hand drawn in blue ballpoint on peach-coloured writing paper with a satin finish. There's one long street, Dublin Street, with a post office and a sports shop called Eddie's, although this same location is also marked 'Long Johns'. On another street, curiously filled in, as if it were a river, is a police station and a place to get 'latte', and then we have Dublin Street again, oddly at right angles to the earlier Dublin Street. Overleaf, this part of the map is redrawn, with 'latte' marked again and Dublin Street has become Dublin Street Bridge.

I thought at first, not unreasonably, it was a map of a neighbourhood in Dublin, but now wonder if it might not be any Irish town or city. More research is needed.

In the meantime, on Saturday 15 October 2022, I walk from Stoke Newington to Hammersmith, where I visit La Librairie, a second-hand French bookshop, or French second-hand bookshop, on King Street, days before it's due to *fermer* and go online only. My friend and agent John Saddler joins me there and we chat to owner Marine. She gives me three photographs she's found in books – two captioned on the back 'Ondine Burckhardt, 1959' – and I buy Didier Daeninckx's *La mort n'oublie personne* (Folio), Patrick Modiano's *La ronde de nuit* (Folio) and Jean-Philippe Toussaint's *Made in China* (Minuit). After John and I leave La Librairie, we pop into the Amnesty shop, where I'm thrilled – yes, thrilled – to find Edmund White's *States of Desire: Travels in Gay America* (Picador) with a photocopied map of part of south London tucked within, at page 103.

Winter comes and goes before I find myself in this particular corner of south London, with the book and the map. The date is Saturday 22 April 2023. I take the London Overground down to Crystal Palace, obeying the instruction in red ballpoint on the map – 'OFF AT CRYSTAL PALACE' – and walk the length of Auckland Road, outlined in red, reading chapter four of *States of Desire*, 'Santa Fe, Salt Lake City and Denver', which is beautifully written – 'One evening, stoned on grass, I walked with a Mormon friend through the city. Though it was late, past dinner, the summer light persisted. There was a sense that the city had inhaled a sharp intake of breath and refused to release it' – but it all feels quite remote from my experience, unless, having always felt like an outsider looking through a series of windows into the literary world, I might have something in common with the gay man or woman trying to reconcile their sexuality with the teachings of the Mormon faith.

A couple of years later, my wife and I take a train from Chicago to New Mexico and spend a weekend in (gay-friendly) Santa Fe, where I'm reminded of White's descriptions of the architecture. 'The adobe shades from faded brown to burnt siena to geranium pink. Everything is low and horizontal and few masonry corners are sharp...' I visit Big Star Books and Music, which looks and feels very much like a book lover has put a sign outside their house and left their front door open. I dither over a copy of Francis Ponge's *Le parti pris des choses* in the lovely Gallimard Poésie series that I collect in spite of not understanding what the hell most poets are going on about, unsure if I already have it or not. I leave it and discover later that I bought a copy four years ago in Gosford Books in Coventry. Usually I buy such books *before* finding out I already have them.

I don't like long novels, and hospitals give me the heebie-jeebies, so you can imagine how excited I was to find, in Cancer Research UK in Withington, in August 2025, a copy of Sarah Perry's 418-page novel *The Essex Serpent* containing, at page 413, a map of Stockport NHS Foundation Trust, specifically Stepping Hill Hospital. But a project is a project, even if I'm the one who devised it.

I walk by the Mersey, heading for Edgeley, and Hardcastle Road, a minor detour. In January 2024, in the Global Educational Bookshop, in Sale, I found two books that had once belonged to a Mr D MacDonald at an address in Hardcastle Road, Stockport. One was Philip K Dick's *The Variable Man* (Ace), which I kept despite its sorry state (falling apart), and the other was *New Writings in SF-3* (Corgi), edited by John Carnell, which I knew I already had, because I've got the full set – all thirty volumes. I'm not a big fan of science fiction, but I make an exception for Philip K Dick, and I understand how annoying it must be for science fiction writers when people say they are not big fans of science fiction, but they make an exception for Philip K Dick, which I imagine a lot of people say. But then I also make exceptions for JG Ballard and M John Harrison and certain other writers who zhuzh up their names with initials. None of these is included in *New Writings in SF–3*.

In his Nightjar story, 'This Area Only', Joe Stretch writes about the regeneration of Stockport, with a particular focus on Edgeley. I wonder, how is regeneration different from gentrification? Regeneration is widely held to be a good thing, whereas gentrification is not. Out with the old, in with the new. But for every net curtain that's replaced by wooden shutters, for every PVC frame usurped by a wooden sash, for every front door painted a nice bright colour, there's perhaps one less lower-income household in the community. The front door I'm looking for on Hardcastle Road looks to have been newly painted and I hope this might mean I get some kind of response to my returning *New Writings in SF–3* to the house in which it used to live, though why middle-class residents should be more likely than working-class householders to drop me a line to say 'Thanks for the book', I don't know.

As I walk away from Hardcastle Road, rain falls in steel rods, and I take cover. Ten minutes later, wet through, I think I might abandon the hospital visit and go straight to Stockport station and the train to London, my ultimate destination today. I get half way down the ramp when the sun comes out and I stop and I think, regarding the matter of the hospital visit, if not now, when? I realise I just don't really want to go to the hospital, but I also realise I'm not going to want to go there on my way back from London, and the sun has come out, but it's a long walk and I've already had a long walk.

On the bus – I don't like buses; have I mentioned that? – I stand in the area reserved for pushchairs and wheelchairs.

Somehow this makes me feel less like a prisoner on the bus, the fact that I can choose to stand and lean against the rail, like someone who still has some agency, which I feel I lose the moment I step on a bus. (I liked the old Routemaster, when you could hop on and, crucially, hop off. The new Routemaster, with its rear door, is to the old Routemaster like 2009's *Reggie Perrin*, starring Martin Clunes, is to *The Fall and Rise of Reginald Perrin*, produced in the 1970s with Leonard Rossiter as Reggie.) But someone presses the bell – and keeps pressing it. Several things wind me up about being on a bus. The speed of travel – generally slower than walking. The intermittent tinny, sibilant noise from the speakers of people's phones as they scroll. The lurching, the sudden braking. The alarming proximity of endangered cyclists. Even the images of buses' top decks ripped off by low bridges. But nothing winds me up more than the fact that people press the bell when they don't need to, because it's already been pressed. And here is someone doing it constantly. I wriggle around to see if I can see who it is. As I twist, my lower back parts from the rail behind me and the bell stops. I turn and look at the rail. Halfway along it is a bell push, which I was leaning against. We are already slowing down for the next stop. I look out. No one is waiting at the stop and no one is preparing to get off. I can either own up and apologise and stay on, or get off. The bus stops and I thank the driver and get off.

Some roads seem endless. The A6 out of Stockport towards Hazel Grove is one. Its straightness and width, its relentless uphill gradient. Low buildings, big skies.

I've been to Stepping Hill twice before. Once when Joe Stretch's daughter was born and on a second occasion after I crashed my car in High Lane. No one was hurt but an ambulance brought me to A&E to be checked out. I remember how kind everyone was. Police, paramedics, even a fire engine – and an angel called Charlie, who invited me into her home to wait for all of the above to arrive on scene. She made a lovely cup of tea.

On this third occasion, carrying *The Essex Serpent*, I avoid A&E. Highlighted in pink on the map is block 14, identified in the key as 'Lilac Suite', located, ominously, opposite the mortuary. For a few minutes, I wander and start reading. In 2014, I read Sarah Perry's debut novel, *After Me Comes the Flood* and liked it very much. The late John Burnside made a perceptive remark in his review in the *Guardian*. 'It is as if some doleful figure from a Kafka story, a Josef K, perhaps, had wandered into the magical otherworld that Alain-Fournier created in *Le Grand Meaulnes*.' That would have made me want to read it, if I hadn't already made up my mind. *The Essex Serpent*, over 400 pages and set in 1893, was a big success for Perry, but appeals to me less than her earlier, shorter novel. I read the prologue and opening chapter as I dodge doctors, visitors, porters wheeling beds. In *The Essex Serpent*, a young man walks by the River Blackwater on New Year's Eve, unwisely contemplating a dip. The first chapter finds us in London: Greenwich Observatory, Royal Exchange, Charing Cross Road. The roaming camera eventually settles on a Dr Luke Garrett, sitting on a westbound Circle Line train out of Paddington – 'the scent of rain on raincoats' – reciting the names of the chambers of the human heart. It feels like a *bigger* book than *After Me Comes the Flood*, more ambitious, more conventional. Beautifully written, but not as much my kind of thing.

I see a sign. 'Welcome to Ward A1. Every Patient Matters.' It reminds me of the Transport for London slogan, 'Every Journey Matters.' If they decided one journey didn't matter, which one would they choose? The journey to a certain destination? Or the journey undertaken by a particular passenger? As for 'Every Patient Matters', well, gosh, really?

Just before I reach block 14, I read another sign attached to the ceiling of the corridor and with an arrow pointing to the left. 'Stockport Eye Discharge Lounge.' *Shudder.* The sign over the door is less alarming: 'Stockport Eye Centre Discharge Lounge.' What a difference a word makes. Just beyond the Stockport Eye Centre Discharge Lounge is the Lilac Suite, corresponding to block 14 on my map. Again: 'Every Patient Matters.' Also: 'Welcome to the Urology Treatment Unit (UTU) Lilac Suite.' The door is painted lilac. When I look out of the window on the other side of the corridor, I see the mortuary. Weirdly, the doorway under the sign that says 'Mortuary' is bricked up. Maybe that's meant to be encouraging. No one dies here. Everyone gets out alive.

I get out alive and get a bus back to Stockport and a train to London. It is only twenty minutes late. Not bad going for Avanti West Coast. Looking forward to Delay Repay.

Thursday 15 January 2026
Children's Society, Heaton Moor, Stockport.
Middle-aged couple browsing.
Her [taking Dr Richard Shepherd's *Unnatural Causes: The Life and Many Deaths of Britain's Top Forensic Pathologist* off the shelf]: The thing is, I'll buy this and then I won't read it.
Him: What about this?
Her: I've got all the Narnia books.

I find three books with loose tube maps in: *The Penguin Guide to London* by FR Banks, tube map at page 241, found in House of

Grace charity shop, Hackney, August 2023; *The Maisky Diaries* (Yale University Press) edited by Gabriel Gorodetsky, tube map at page 103, found in Oxfam Bookshop Chorlton, April 2024; Max Pemberton's *Trust Me, I'm a (Junior) Doctor* (Hodder), tube map also at page 103, obtained from Oxfam Whitworth Park, June 2024. In the case of Paul Morley's *Earthbound* (Penguin), which I picked up off a table at Abney Books, Stoke Newington, in September 2025, the tube map was not *in* the book, but *underneath* a copy of Paul Auster's *The New York Trilogy* lying *next to* it. Because it was underneath rather than inside the Auster, I couldn't rely on its having been inside *that* book either. It could just as easily have been inside the Morley, and seeing as how I have numerous copies of *The New York Trilogy*, and seeing as how the Morley looks interesting, I go for it. *Earthbound* has a great cover – a photograph of an audio cassette, the brown tape matching the colour of the Bakerloo line, the line Morley writes about in this Penguin series in which different writers take on different tube lines.

I read *Earthbound* not travelling underground between north-west London and the Southbank, but walking around Stockport, where Morley grew up. The Bakerloo line, writes Morley, is 'dated and forlorn', 'meat-and-potatoes', 'a floppy brown slipper'. Thanks to his girlfriend bringing him back a new bit of kit from Japan, he believes he might have been the first person to travel on the tube listening to a Sony Walkman, which allows him to write a great chapter in which he tries to work out what he might have listened to first. The world above ground is represented by the likes of 'the Village People, the Bee Gees, Art Garfunkel, Cliff Richard, Dr Hook, Pink Floyd', while underground is the post-punk music that he suspects he might have been the first rock writer to label as such, and connecting these two worlds, like 'the escalators, the stairs, between one level and another', were what he calls the 'new-wave novelty songs' of 'Ian Dury, Blondie, the Boomtown Rats, the Police, Gary Numan and the Buggles'. Gary Numan? Not Tubeway Army?

On Saturday 18 November 2023, at St Giles Book Fair, at the Barbican in London, I found Nicholas Shakespeare's *The Vision of Elena Silves* (Picador). I already had the same edition, but this copy has a map at page 19, in fact a photograph of a map of the rivers of London in the style of a tube map, a rather lovely thing.

On 15 February 2023, in Oxfam Books & Music Kentish Town, I bought Raymond Carver's *Elephant* (Vintage), a not very attractive edition, but with an inclusion, at page 97, a press release for an exhibition at Bearspace (in 2008) of work by Japanese artist Toshie Takeuchi. On the back of the press release is a sort of map showing which works are hanging where. The Deptford gallery still exists, but the exhibition will have finished, turning the map into a historical artefact. Like all maps, perhaps, the moment they're published.

Printed on the back of a business card for Japanese restaurant Ikkyu, in the basement of 67 Tottenham Court Road, which I found in Milan Kundera's *The Unbearable Lightness of Being* (Faber) in Mind in Stoke Newington, was a little map. On the flyleaf, a name: Susie F Walker, London. September 87 (or is it 89?). At 68 Tottenham Court Road was, and still is, the Scientology shop, or, to give it its proper name, Dianetics & Scientology Life Improvement Centre. (Tottenham Court Road uses consecutive address numbering.) When I worked across the road at Time Out Guides in the 1990s, I used to walk past the Scientology shop on the way to and from the tube deliberately slowly, giving them every opportunity to invite me to enter, so that I could share with them my opinion of their work. I do the same thing with street-corner Jehovah's Witnesses. I keep meaning to print my own leaflets to hand to Jehovah's Witnesses in exchange for theirs. Mine would be about how I've tried very hard to see things from their point of view, but I'm sorry, I just can't bring myself to condone allowing children to die for the sake of religious beliefs.

Early one evening in November 2025, I walk past the Scientology shop very slowly. A woman is bobbing about outside trying to entice people in. I make myself as available as I possibly can without actually saying to her 'Please induct me into your high-control group', but she doesn't take the bait. I must be giving off the wrong vibes. Next door, the ground-floor premises of No.67 are now occupied by mayonnaise-based sandwich chain Prêt à Manger, while of the basement there's no sign. It's like the episode of *Fawlty Towers* where Basil goes to open the door to the dining room and can't because O'Reilly's men have covered up the doorway.

Inside the Kundera, at page 87, a note written in that bubble handwriting not uncommon to girls educated in England in the 1970s says: 'Susie. Have said to Catherine that we will meet her at the Chelsea Pasta Bar (opposite ABC Cinema) in the Fulham Road at 7.30 p.m. Hope this is alright with you. If not, give me a ring at the office 01-351 5775 ext 28. Trust you slept well. Love Jane.' Another note to younger readers: this is an example of how we made arrangements to meet in the 1980s.

I'm not especially taken with *The Unbearable Lightness of Being*, but to be fair to Kundera, it's a small map, so I'm not giving it much of a chance.

Some maps of distant places: a home-printed map of the

Bosphorus with notes on the back in a French-language guide to Istanbul by Celik Gülersoy, from a book box in Lewisham. My job at Time Out involved editing city guides and books of short stories. I wanted to do a guide book to an imaginary city. I suggested it to my managing editor, but he didn't go for it. Probably very wisely. We did produce guides to Dubai and Las Vegas, however, neither of which particularly strikes me as being a real place.

A commercially printed map of Paris fell out of a slim Penguin edition of DH Lawrence's *The Virgin and the Gipsy*, from Crisis in Dalston, and, staying in Dalston, in Oxfam I bought a film tie-in edition of Piers Paul Reid's *Alive!* (Mandarin), for its road map of Malta and Gozo. Malta is tempting, but Piers Paul Reid's *Alive!* is why I don't like getting on a plane.

In Oxfam on Bold Street in Liverpool I got a Liverpool *A–Z* for its postcard map of Lake Como lodging at page 3, but I'm no more likely to get there before the deadline for this book than I am to find my way to Biarritz and Bayonne to make use of the map I found at page 71 in Shamim Sarif's *Despite the Falling Snow* (Review) in Oxfam in Dalston. And I have to be realistic and admit I'm unlikely *ever* to find my way to Hamilton Island, the largest of the Whitsunday Islands, a short distance off the coast of Queensland. Nothing against Australia – I loved exploring the WA coastline in 1994 – but Hamilton Island, pop. 1759, looks less to my taste than the book in which I found a map advertising its resort opportunities and activities, in Oxfam Books & Music Islington, and that book was Jonathan Coe's *The Rotters' Club* (Penguin). The map was at page 295.

Back in Manchester, in January 2025, in Oxfam Withington, I found Sean Slater's *The Survivor* (Simon & Schuster). The name is a pseudonym employed by a Vancouver police officer.

The novel is his first. Cover line: 'Dying is easy. Living is the hard part.' The hard part of what? At page 403 lurked two bookmarks promoting Manchester Little Library Trail and Manchester City Council, and a map of the Little Library Trail around Didsbury and Withington – a walk, it claimed, of 7.2 miles. It would take two hours ten minutes, it said, but I felt it might take longer because of the map, which was not likely to win Top Map in the National Map Awards. I suspected I might search in vain for some of the little libraries, but a few days later I set out, starting in Didsbury Park and aiming to finish in Fog Lane Park. From the book exchange in the Pavilion Café in Didsbury Park I picked up *Harold Pinter: Plays 1* (Faber); it contained a photograph at page 175 of two little girls walking by the pond in Fog Lane Park, which felt like a good omen.

I walked 8.3 miles, most of them *after* falling on the ice in Fletcher Moss Gardens, causing my knee to bend in a way it hadn't bent in six months. The pain brought on nausea and it was convenient I was on the deck, because I felt a pressing need to sit down for a few minutes.

The walk probably did take over two hours, mainly because of my knee. And the map.

Most of the libraries were either no longer in existence or the books were wet through. No blame for this could be laid at the door of whoever produced the map, which was a nice idea badly executed. Like the first eighteen months of Sir Keir Starmer's time in Number Ten. A few of the libraries were still OK: Brunswick Road and Stephens Road, and the ones in the parks. Well done to locals for keeping them going.

On the walk, I read 100 pages of *The Survivor*, but, before you say anything, I wasn't reading when I fell on the ice.

FINDERS, KEEPERS: *The Secret Life of Second-hand Books*

Tuesday 3 June 2025
Berners Road, Islington, London.
Man, twenties/thirties, bleached-blond hair, sunglasses, headphones, black hoody, cross-body bag, short shorts and Converse, walking past Tanning Shop reading Dr Benji Waterhouse's *You Don't Have to Be Mad to Work Here: A Psychiatrist's Life* (Jonathan Cape).

On a Thursday in May 2024, I'm in the library at MMU, having negotiated continued access to the library after leaving my job in the Manchester Writing School two years earlier. I am trying to do some writing – a new story for my next collection, *Paris Fantastique* – but it's not going very well, so I walk to Oxfam Bookshop Chorlton and buy Derren Brown's *Tricks of the Mind* (Channel 4 Books) containing, at page 7, an information sheet for jurors at Bolton Crown Court. A map is incorporated.

That morning, I'd been to the GP, who referred me to haematology for a lump under my left arm.

I could do with my own personal Derren Brown to hypnotise me into stopping thinking that every time I get a new ache or pain, there has to be a sinister reason behind it. I tried seeing a man in Levenshulme. That went quite well for a while before he said he was switching from hypnotherapy to tapping and (as if in case I might be tempted to try tapping) moving to Liverpool. I tried a woman in Didsbury, but I wasn't feeling it. Maybe it was too close to home. Another woman in Prestwich, but that was a long way to go to sit in a garage extension and be told to relax.

But a lump under the arm – no one would say of that, It's nothing, forget it, would they? Would they?

My dad had lymphoma, I told the GP.

It's probably nothing, the GP said, but I'll refer you to haematology.

Eighteen months later, the lump gone (blocked hair follicles eventually become unblocked), I'm waiting on platform two at Manchester Oxford Road for the delayed train to Bolton, but first there's the delayed train to Redcar to come through. I was knocking on the door of my sixties before I realised how best to cope with long waits on station platforms for delayed trains, having spent several decades switching between sitting down and standing up. My enthusiasm for walking long distances having turned into something verging on the obsessional, I realised a year or two ago that I was wasting those seconds, minutes, even hours spent waiting for trains. Walking up and down the platform would not only keep me warm, but also add to my mileage.

On my third pass, I noticed a visually impaired man on a bench. Moments later, the Redcar train arrived and I saw the visually impaired man rise and reach out – as if for the train itself – and appear to over-balance. Normally, when witnessing something awful about to happen, I find that I lose the power of movement and watch in horrified fascination as a scene plays out. On this occasion, I acted, offering help and taking the man's arm. The platform was busy and the train was full. I heard myself asking people to move down inside the carriage. My companion heard me too and suggested we try another carriage. Good idea, I thought, although would we make it before they closed the doors? I spotted a Northern employee and asked for his assistance, which he provided, escorting my new friend to the rear of the train and the first class section. A simple, pragmatic solution that sent Northern shooting up my personal rail operator chart.

What a difference one person can make.

I start reading Derren Brown on the train to Bolton. Generally, I don't like funny author biogs, but this one, unusually, is funny.

In his preface to the paperback edition (also funny), he remembers a visit to an aquarium, where he paid some attention to signs that said what fish were in which tanks, and he noticed there was a version in Braille. He wondered why. If I'd read that before my encounter at Oxford Road, I could have asked the visually impaired rail passenger. He might have made the point that a lot of visually impaired people are not completely blind. Derren Brown goes on to discuss signs in Braille in toilets on trains. He wonders how easy they will be to locate. 'This sounds like an unpleasant and even unhygienic search to be undertaking while bumping around somewhere near Didcot Parkway.' I understand this is *meant to be* funny – and you will have noted the second appearance in this book of Didcot Parkway – but would the man at Oxford Road have found it funny? If not, does that matter?

I'm soon laughing again, however, when Derren Brown refers to his 'desire to make the contents of the book as worthwhile and unpatronizing as possible ("patronizing", of course, means "to talk down to people").'

I've heard the joke before, but it's a good one and he tells it well.

Plus, I like Derren Brown.

I don't like what I see when I get off the train at Bolton, however, and walk out of the station on to Newport Street.

Flags.

Flags of St George. Union flags. Flags, flags, flags.

Flapping in the wind and bright sunshine, over the passing

heads of the ethnically diverse crowds ambling up and down the pedestrianised shopping street.

I walk past the law courts. I walk past the so-called University of Greater Manchester, or as most people think of it, the University of Bolton, before a name change in December 2024 put noses out of joint at the University of Manchester and Manchester Metropolitan University. I stop for a moment outside the University of Bolton – sorry, Greater Manchester – to gaze at the union jack flying from the top of what looks like it's the university's own flag pole. Later, I email the university to ask what message it thinks this sends, in the current climate, to its diverse student body and the wider population. The university does not respond.

At Emmaus, a 'charity shopping destination' at Derby Barracks on Fletcher Street, I find the heart of Bolton. Various different units – café, bookshop, scrap store, furniture outlet et cetera – grouped around a courtyard, Emmaus Bolton feels like a counterbalance to those in the town who spread hate and create division.

Wednesday 21 August 2024
Greenhouse Books, Stockport.
Three female customers representing three generations.
Granny [holding up book by Alexander McCall Smith]: It's
    inane, but it's enough to hold your attention.
Mum: OK.
Little girl: [. . .]

After a week at Moniack Mhor, at the end of May 2025, I drop Megan Taylor and Giselle Leeb at Waverley, then drive out of Edinburgh towards the south and walk back in. I enter Tills on

Hope Park Crescent, a gorgeous second-hand bookshop opened in 1985, under new ownership since 2019. But the prices! Three Philip K Dick non-SF titles in Paladin paperback, in good condition and admittedly you don't see these often, but they do pop up – £20, £20 and £18.50. Peter Straub's *Ghost Story*, the same Futura paperback edition I have at home – £9.

I leave empty handed and head for South Bridge. In my pocket is a Penguin edition of Osbert Sitwell's short story collection *Triple Fugue* sold to me for a couple of quid the previous October by Roland Bates at the excellent Kirkdale Bookshop in Sydenham. I bought it for the flyer from the Edinburgh Bookshop inside the back cover with a little map showing the locations of three bookshops: James Thin, James Thin's Penguin Bookshop and the Edinburgh Bookshop. As I go, I read the shortest story in the book, 'The Machine Breaks Down', which makes me want to reread EM Forster's 'The Machine Stops'. James Thin and James Thin's Penguin Bookshop have gone and the Edinburgh Bookshop is not where it was. It's not *what* it was, either, which doesn't really make sense. There is a bookshop called the Edinburgh Bookshop, but it is a different bookshop from the Edinburgh Bookshop that used to be on George Street.

I walk on to Stockbridge, where, in the Shelter Bookshop, I buy Elizabeth Taylor's *The Sleeping Beauty* (Virago Modern Classics), simply because Elizabeth Taylor is really good and I love those dark green covers with their well-chosen illustrations. Elizabeth Taylor is like the Edinburgh Bookshop in that she is not to be confused with another Elizabeth Taylor, but probably often is.

The spring and summer months of 2025 were the warmest and sunniest on record. But, with a wide-brimmed hat, lots of factor fifty and a preference for the shaded side of the street, I was still able to walk three different maps of London that I found in three different books.

The Bloomsbury Theatre ticket stamped 'GUEST' and costing £0.50 for an unnamed show or event at 6.15 p.m. on 15 January 1986 that I found inside Borges's *The Book of Sand* (Penguin) had a little map on the back. I knew where the Bloomsbury Theatre was, having been there more than once when I was younger to see John Hegley perform. When I go on about not liking poetry, I'm not being entirely honest, because I like John Hegley's poetry, and his songs. I've probably seen John Hegley perform more times than any other act. When possible, I would sit in the front row, and because I was – and remain – a glasses-wearer, I would occasionally be picked as Section C in 'Eddie Don't Like Furniture'. If you wanted to be picked to be Section C, all you had to do was be a man sitting in the front row wearing glasses. 'For this song,' Hegley would say, 'I am going to divide the audience. This side is Section A and this side is Section B . . . and you, sir, are Section C.' Section A was given the job of singing 'Ner ner, ner ner' after the first line of the chorus and Section B was asked to sing 'Ner ner ner ner ner ner ner' after the second line. Section C was then required to sing scat style for a good thirty seconds or so, improvising wildly on the 'Ner ner' theme. Sometimes, Hegley would write out the 'Ner's on a bit of paper and give it to Section C. I still have one of those somewhere.

I contacted the Bloomsbury Theatre to see if they had a record of what had been going on at 6.15 p.m. on 15 January 1986. They didn't have any archives at all, they told me. I tried the British Library: no luck. Then I did what I should have done in the first place and emailed Time Out and received a very helpful response from receptionist Anne Gerrish, who looked up the listings for the Bloomsbury Theatre that week. Children's show *The Gingerbread Man* was on at 11 a.m. and 2.30 p.m. and musical comedy *Cover Girls* at 8pm, but only until Saturday 11, so it seems they were between shows. Anne's colleague Rosie Hewitson, Time Out's Things to Do editor, said the ticket was giving off 'student show vibes', the Bloomsbury Theatre being part of University College London. Vibes are always welcome. I was getting good vibes off Anne and Rosie. Time Out had been the heart and soul of London for decades. Working there had been a dream. Even after the print magazine had folded, that heart was still beating.

I walked the streets of the map on the reverse of the ticket stub while reading *The Book of Sand*. Borges's stories are always a source of pleasure, especially when accompanied by a latte and a caramel slice in the Bloomsbury Theatre café, located in the UCL students' union, where I found myself surrounded by earnest young people putting up posters for SU candidates. 'Vote for Ben Francis as Arts Officer.' He was promising more collaboration, more transparency and more support. Sounds good. I would have voted for you, Ben, if I could have done.

In July I walked down through Hackney towards Broadway Market carrying Laurie Gilmore's *The Pumpkin Spice Café* (One More Chapter), which had contained, at page 255, when I bought it from British Heart Foundation, Dalston, a map of a corner of E8 printed on an invitation to a Well Church discussion group that took place on 18 September 2024 in Yeast Bakery on Sheep Lane. On pedestrianised Martello Street, my glasses fell apart, an arm landing on the tarmac. I crouched in search of the tiny screw that had fallen out. A couple of passersby joined the search, but it was not to be found. It had made bids for freedom before, in enclosed spaces. This time, I sensed, it was gone for good.

I walked on with my one-armed glasses, but they tilted alarmingly. I folded them into my top pocket, but felt naked – and the world was a blur. I had received a lot of compliments for those glasses. The frame was thick, black plastic, the lenses photochromatic. As I told everyone who commented on them, they were my dad's glasses, from the 1970s, although I'd had them glazed with my prescription by Natalie Edwards of the Worshipful Shop of Spectacles in Netil Market, only a few minutes' walk from where they fell apart. Natalie had since closed the shop to open a workshop, the House of Spectacles, with Matthew Lambert, making new frames.

On Broadway Market, I called in at Jimmy Fairly and they very kindly put a replacement screw in, turning down my offer of payment. Glasses people are good people. I walked on – Ada Street, Sheep Lane – reading *The Pumpkin Spice Café*. In this 'small-town romance' novel a woman inherits a café and meets a farmer. It has been a 'viral TikTok sensation', but is perhaps not for me, just as the Well Church's Alpha Course – 'a series of interactive sessions that freely explore the basics of the Christian faith' – is not for me either.

I walked on to Bethnal Green Road and in Oxfam bought Natasha Brown's debut novel *Assembly* (Penguin), which I started reading immediately, then had to put to one side when I reached Commercial Street and got out the copy of Miss Read's *Storm in the Village* (Penguin) that I had bought in Abney Books, Stoke Newington, back in February, for its flyer advertising the opening of a patisserie, Nice Croissant, on 18 March 1991, in Beaufort House, Middlesex Street, with a map of the East End on the back. 'We are here,' it said, with an arrow pointing to the corner of St Botolph Street and Middlesex Street. They're not there any more, Beaufort House having been replaced by Aldgate House, but there is a café in almost the same spot. I read a chapter or two of *Storm in the Village*, but, as my wife pointed out, I'm not really its target readership. I switched back to *Assembly*, which is brilliant, and read all 100 pages on the rest of my walk to Old Kent Road and later Oval to meet my daughter and her boyfriend. *Assembly* makes you believe that because of their experience of systemic racism, a person might consider refusing treatment for cancer.

Friday 25 April 2025
Butcher Row, Beverley, East Riding of Yorkshire.
Man, fifties, blue baseball cap, jumper and quilted jerkin, chunky brown leather shoes, walking grey lurcher and reading Alan Bennett's *Rolling Home* (Faber).

Rowfant House, a grade II* listed Elizabethan manor house, can, in theory, be found in the West Sussex countryside. Arriving at Three Bridges by train on a warm summer's day in 2025, I found my way to the Worth Way, a seven-mile shared-use path linking Crawley with East Grinstead. I was enjoying reading Henning Mankell's *The Dogs of Riga* (Vintage), his second Wallander novel, bought from Sense in Peckham on Saturday 8 March 2025. Tucked inside Mankell's 340-page thriller at page 157 was a home-printed leaflet with on one side an extract from the 1:50,000 Ordnance Survey map of the area and on the other an invitation, in Latvian, to an unnamed individual, from the United Latvian Evangelical Lutheran and Peace Congregation of London to celebrate Easter at Rowfant House. The date given was Sunday 24 April, meaning, if the issue of the invitation was made after the publication of that edition of Mankell's novel, it would have been either 2005, 2011 or 2016. The Latvian church, having acquired the house in 1962, sold it in 2020.

After a great opening at sea, *The Dogs of Riga* gets a bit bogged down in police procedure, and then picks up once the action shifts to Latvia and the atmosphere changes to that of a spy novel, with the possibility of a romantic subplot. Reviews of translated novels invariably include a brief adverbial comment on the translation – in the *TLS* of 28 November 2025, I found 'carefully translated', 'meticulously translated', 'sparklingly translated' and 'deftly translated' – and I always wonder how they know. Do they have the original edition and can they read the language it's written in? All I feel qualified to say about Laurie Thompson's translation of *The Dogs of Riga* is that the prose is clean and flowing and easy to read, but I was surprised when a character dialled 999. They would have dialled 112 in the Swedish original. If you're going to change 112 to 999, why not change Stockholm to London and Ystad to Scarborough?

Late on in the novel, Wallander receives a letter from a Joseph Lippman that is similar, in a way, to the communication I found in my copy. Lippman is a Latvian living in exile, like whoever was the recipient of the invitation to Rowfant House. I wonder if they went along and if they did, if they found it more easily than I did. Blundering around in a patch of woodland I had convinced myself concealed the remains of the house, I finally started to question whether I could still read a map that didn't have a blue blob to show me where I was. Tumbling out of the wood on to the road, I came upon a turning on the other side that I realised must lead to the house, but then saw a big sign with a picture of a guard dog on it. Although, in recent years, I have become a dog person, I still retain a healthy respect for/absolute terror of guard dogs, even if they are only theoretical.

FINDERS, KEEPERS: *The Secret Life of Second-hand Books*

❦

I find a copy of Kate Ellis's *Seeking the Dead* (Piatkus) containing a bookmark from the House of Books and Friends, a bookshop in Manchester. The bookmark is at page 13 and has a map on the back.

On a Thursday in August 2025, I walk into town – and around town, or the part of town depicted on the map, the streets surrounding House of Books and Friends – reading *Seeking the Dead*. It's a crime novel set in Eborby. Yes, Eborby. Clues in the first chapter allow us to locate this improbably named city in the north of England on the east side of the Pennines. A bit of online research allows me to narrow it down to York. Ellis writes on her website about the fact that she sets her novels in real places – kind of – but then changes their names. 'This approach allows me a good deal of freedom to use my imagination and to change things around to suit the story I want to tell,' she writes. So, there's a series of novels, for example, set in Dartmouth, or should I say Tradmouth. In some of these novels, I gather, the action might shift to Morbay, Ellis's version of Torbay. Or is it Torquay?

Then there's Eborby.

You have to admire a writer so wedded to their vision they will invent a place name no reader would know for certain how to pronounce. I'm reminded of Brichester, setting for a number of Ramsey Campbell's early horror stories. I never knew if it was Bry-chester, like *dry* white wine, or Bri-chester, like *Chi*-chester, but it never spoilt my enjoyment of 'Potential' or 'Reply Guaranteed' or other stories in *Demons By Daylight* and *The Height of the Scream*.

On a grey day in October 2025, I finally set out for Dorking. Or Woking. I'm carrying a Picador edition of Salman Rushdie's *Midnight's Children* containing an estate agent's map of Dorking, or Woking, at page 117. Well, as I write, the map is at page 11, functioning as a bookmark, but I will return it to page 117 before I'm done, as that was where it was when I bought the book from Oxfam Bookshop Kentish Town on 31 January 2019. Really, though, I should be carrying a copy of *The Trial* or *The Castle*, because I feel more like a Kafka character, than Rushdie's Saleem Sinai, who, he tells us on the opening page of *Midnight's Children*, was born on the stroke of midnight on the day India gained independence.

But my journey to get to Dorking – and by now I suppose I should admit I know I'm trying to get to Dorking, even if Woking would be easier – bears closer resemblance to that of Josef K as he negotiates the maze of the law, or that of K as he tries to get to the castle.

Maybe starting my journey at Clapham Junction was a mistake, but I had a delivery to make in Battersea. Spotting the pink chimneys of Battersea Power Station I thought about the Northern line extension to Battersea, comprising stations at Nine Elms and Battersea Power Station. If you approach Nine Elms, on foot, at street level, you see it says, adopting the format used for other stations not just on the Northern line but across the network, Nine Elms Station, yet when you get to Battersea Power Station, it says just that, Battersea Power Station. Shouldn't it say Battersea Power Station Station?

After I have banned leaf-blowers and meal deals and people casually scrolling through reels and videos in public places with sound on, and made quiet carriage rules enforceable by law, my next act will be to rename Battersea Power Station – at its entrance at street level – Battersea Power Station Station.

The ticket machine at Clapham Junction will not let me buy a ticket to Dorking, or to Dorking Deepdene, only to Dorking West. As you use the keypad to input your destination, the options narrow. It removes keys as you go. This is probably meant to be helpful, but when you think you should be able to travel to a particular station and the machine will not let you type in its name, you start to wonder who's in charge.

Once I've finally got a ticket, the gate won't open. I ask a man to open it for me. When I ask him how to get to Dorking, he gets out a smartphone. I'm always dismayed when this happens, as I think, I could get my smartphone out and look it up. I expect them to have access to systems I don't even know exist.

Go to East Croydon, he says. *Five minutes. Platform fifteen.*

With a strong sense that East Croydon is in the opposite direction to where I want to go, I head for platform fifteen.

Having changed at East Croydon, I'm now on a train bound for Redhill.

I could have walked from Clapham Junction to Dorking faster than this.

I start reading *Midnight's Children*. Everything about it communicates the sense that this is a Big Book. You're in for a roller coaster ride. Epic sweep. Great themes. Is it bad to prefer small books?

At Redhill, I change to the Reading train. *We are now approaching Redhill*, says the digital readout, confusingly, as we sit at Redhill waiting to depart. *The next station is Reigate*, it says as we do depart. I am tempted to sack off Dorking and visit the Oxfam Bookshop in Reigate. As we stop at Reigate, the sun pops out for the first time today. I am still tempted. The train pulls out of Reigate and I'm still on it. There's a level crossing. Reigate looks nice. The GWR wifi is not working. Another level crossing. Approaching Betchworth. Green fields, little cottages. Last chance to avoid Dorking. Turns out I'm now in the Surrey Hills, an 'Area of Outstanding Natural Beauty'. The next station is one that was not available to me at Clapham Junction. Dorking Deepdene. I get off.

My map – undated, produced by Patrick Gardner & Co Estate Agents – has been marked with red ballpoint pen. Four crosses and two blobs. They're all central apart from one, and that's the one I'm going to first. I start walking south down the A24 and take a left fork up Deepdene Drive. Big houses, gravel drives, terraced gardens. I go left again along a footpath to tree-shaded Punchbowl Lane. The Surrey Hills roll away to my left. A robin sings from the woods to my right. I try to concentrate on *Midnight's Children*, which is a forest of dashes, brackets and exclamation marks. I'm not entirely sure what's going on, only that I've only just met the narrator and already he's skipped back a generation or two. I find that sort of thing hard to follow, whereas the map of Dorking is straightforward. If I keep going to the bottom of Punchbowl Lane, then go right and left, I'll find myself at the location of the first red cross.

I enter Chart Downs and there's another Robin, but this one is parked in front of a modest semi. Reliant Robin, same shade of yellow as Del Boy's Reliant Regal. Houses on four sides of a square with a big green space and children's playpark in the middle, couple of union jacks. Low-rise pebble dash pub. Sky Sports. I cross the A24 and dive into Devil's Den, a thickly wooded area with paths that run into undergrowth or fallen trees and just seem to give up. The high-pitched *seep* of a goldcrest in the tree canopy.

To reach the second red cross – Nower Road – I take my chances on a stretch of road without pavement. Nower Road is a long cul-de-sac of semis. Welcome absence of flags. The first of the two red blobs is on the south side of the A25. There's nothing there.

The next cross is another cul-de-sac, only three houses. Then I cross the A25 again and duck into a warren of little paths between mews houses. No flags here either. Heartfelt sign on fence. *Please please please! Do not throw dog waste bags or litter over this fence. This is a Nursery School where children play. Thank you.*

Hanging used dog waste bags from railings or tree branches or throwing them over fences. Add that to the list.

When I emerge on to South Street, in search of the other red blob, again, nothing, unless the red blob was marking the location of a 'smile clinic', whatever one of those is, or a Michelin-starred restaurant called Sorrel. When I was little, on holiday in Cornwall, I swallowed sorrel seeds and thought they were poisonous and I was going to die. I didn't. I turn left into Rose Hill. Rose Hill, like Deepdene Drive, is the sort of area people who write books about collecting second-hand books can only dream of moving to. Unless lots more people buy this book than bought the last two. Well, you never know. I feel it's precisely this kind of deep dive into the social topology of Dorking that could turn things around.

Just beyond Rose Hill is the fourth and final X. It's nice enough, but if you walk over Rose Hill to get here, you've going to have a bad case of us and them.

I head to Dorking West instead of Dorking Deepdene. The

station is as quiet as the grave. The next train anywhere is not for 45 minutes, so I set out to walk to Dorking Deepdene. On the leafy avenue between the two stations, a sole St George's flag dangles flaccidly from a window. Reaching the end of the road, I see that here, yards away from Dorking Deepdene, is Dorking station, which was not available from Clapham Junction, and yet here, with a minute to spare, I board a train to Victoria, via Clapham Junction.

On the train I have another look at Rushdie's novel and after a while I realise I'm probably more likely to return to Dorking than go back to *Midnight's Children*.

The map I found inside Keri Hulme's *The Bone People* corresponds to a type described in Kris Harzinski's endlessly fascinating resource *From Here to There: A Curious Collection From the Hand Drawn Map Association* (Princeton Architectural Press) as a 'direction map', but also as a 'found map'. I suppose it was once a direction map, drawn for its intended user, and later became a found map, after I found it. I had assumed, because of the street name – Dublin Street – that the map showed a town in Ireland. When I Googled 'Dublin Street' and 'Post Office', I came up with Dundalk, Co Louth. When I put in 'Dublin Street Bridge', I got Dublin. But when I typed 'Dublin Street Bridge' and 'latte', the results took me somewhere a long way from Ireland.

What a difference a latte makes.

I should have paid more attention to the name of the author. Keri Hulme was the first New Zealand author to win the Booker Prize, for *The Bone People*, in 1985. Dublin Street Bridge crosses the Whanganui River in Whanganui, a city on the west coast of New Zealand's North Island. You'd be able to get a latte at the Yellow House Café on the corner of Pitt Street and Dublin

Street, more or less where X marks the spot on the map. The police station is still where it was, on Bell Street, but the post office on Dublin Street appears to have gone. Of Eddie's sports shop, where maybe you could buy long johns, there is no trace.

9

Christmas books

I don't know how she does it.

I wouldn't put it past Allison Pearson to have attempted to trademark that phrase.

I did once buy that book, but only because it had a boarding pass in it, in name of Joan Gale, flying from Edinburgh to Norwich. Reach Out to the Community charity shop in Chorlton, three books for a pound. I gave it away as part of an exercise at Moniack Mhor.

But I'm talking about my mum.

I don't know how she does it.

Every year, at Christmas, her presents arrive bearing the same gift tags that I saw on my presents each year as a child. I don't mean the same ones endlessly recycled. I mean unused gift tags from the same batches. One is mainly orange, with a small child marching through the snow carrying the end of a ribbon attached to a huge, gift-wrapped present. The other one is mostly blue, the blue of the night sky, flecked with snow. Mother and child singing carols by the light of a lantern. The figures are stylised, cartoonish. These gift tags transport me back to the magical Christmases of my childhood with more immediacy and power than watching YouTube clips of Eric Morecambe grabbing 'Andrew Preview' by the lapels and saying, 'I'm playing all the right notes, but not necessarily in the right order.'

I don't understand how my mum can possibly have an inexhaustible supply of the same gift tags that she used more than fifty years ago. How many must she have had back then? How – why – did she have so many? I could ask her, but I don't want to in case she tells me they're nearly gone. I'd rather believe they're going to go on for ever. The magic of Christmas.

In spite of its heading, this chapter is not about Christmas books in the sense of *Beano* annuals or *The Snowman* or *A Christmas Carol*, but about second-hand books that I've found that were – or might have been – given as Christmas presents.

I say 'might have been' because in some cases it's hard to be sure.

In the case of the Penguin edition of EM Forster's *A Passage to India* that I found in the book exchange on Nevill Road, Stoke Newington, on Monday 23 December 2024, I've got a gut feeling. There's nothing written in the book, which is a 1954 reprint, but there is an inclusion, the non-business part of a book token, at page 289. On the front is a beautiful painting of a tree in winter, maybe a silver birch, by Adrian Hill; it bears his signature and he is credited on the back. The colour illustration has some qualities that I associate with illustrations in Ladybird books – a softness in the light and restrained colour palette – and has a 1950s feel about it. On the reverse, using a fountain pen, Barbara has written, 'With best wishes for Christmas and New Year, and with very many thanks for making me so happy.'

I think the recipient, who made Barbara happy, went out and spent the token on this copy of *A Passage to India* and then used the retained part of the token as a bookmark when he – or she – read it.

Jess Walter's *Beautiful Ruins* (Penguin), which came from Oxfam Bookshop St Giles, as previously mentioned in another chapter, 'Tickets, please! – outward', contains a miniature Christmas card made from a larger Christmas card. Who hasn't done that? It's good recycling and saves money. The original version of this card would have been addressed to Thurston. This one says, 'To Robert, Love Thurston.' I found it at page 75.

Arthur has done the same. 'Dear Howard,' goes his Christmas message on the back of a woodcut of trees in snow, 'Sorry about this gift, but your main pressie hasn't arrived yet (at the time of writing this). Have a lovely Christmas, Lots of love, Arthur xxx.'

Arthur, you need never apologise for giving someone – anyone – a copy of Geoffrey Household's *Rogue Male*. OK, maybe this Orion edition is not a patch on the 1971 green Penguin, on which only the spine is green, back and front covers shiny black, the title in big, fat pink type – brilliant design by Peter Gill in a set with *A Time to Kill*, *A Rough Shoot* and *Watcher in the Shadows*.

The day I found that copy of *Rogue Male*, in Oxfam Bookshop Herne Hill, on Monday 14 October 2024, two other interesting things happened. A contemporary of mine from school who is now a professor of curating at a prestigious university got in touch, which was nice, because it always feels to me like there's a strict pecking order and that people above you in the pecking order do not 'reach out' to you, meaning that you have to 'reach out' to them if you're to have any kind of relationship. Then, in Crisis in Dalston, I bought *Cities: A Scientific American Book* (Pelican), formerly owned by Laurence Marks, meaning I've now found two of Laurence Marks's books three years and 200 miles apart. The other one was a Picador, Louis Begley's *Wartime Lies*, which I found on Tuesday 18 May 2021 in George Street Books community bookshop in Glossop. Of course, these books might not have belonged to Laurence Marks the screenwriter and one half of comedy writing duo Marks and Gran, but I like to think they did.

I bought Günter Grass's *From the Diary of a Snail* from Oxfam Walthamstow on Friday 4 October 2019. It's a Picador from 1989 that I already had in my collection, but I bought this copy for the homemade card tucked inside at page 149, a single piece of lightweight card, similar in size and weight to the book token in *A Passage to India*, with a picture of Santa and a reindeer cut out and stuck to the front. On the back is written, in black ink, 'I wish you a merry Christmas & a Happy New Year. (I do hope I've chosen well.)' The signature is a single initial that could be an N or a P. Then: 'Christmas 1993.' The card is tanned, not quite to the same degree as the inside covers of the book, but getting there. Published in 1989, the title would quite possibly have still been in print four years later, maybe lodged in one of Picador's elegant spinners that you still see in second-hand bookshops here and there, like in Halewood & Sons in Preston and Abacus Books in Altrincham.

On Wednesday 23 August 2023, in Oxfam Bookshop Chorlton, I bought two books that used to belong to Charmaine Findlow Brook, who wrote her name on the flyleaf of Alexander Solzhenitsyn's *For the Good of the Cause* (Sphere), and the date, 29/9/71. She didn't write in Günter Grass's *Cat and Mouse*, but she did use a gift tag – 'To Charmaine, love and best wishes from Graham' – as a bookmark (page 79).

I found *F/32: The Second Coming* (Virago) by Eurudice in

Oxfam Dalston on Thursday 1 December 2016. I picked it out because I could see it was hiding something inside. At page 61 is a homemade card with a playing card glued to the front, a three of spades, and inside we read, 'No.3 Triple Goddess,' and 'A card for Chrimbo Moo, Much love Haze & Ali X.' For avoidance of doubt, there's an inscription on the inside front cover: 'From me to you at Winter Solstice Moo, Dec '97, with much love to ya X.' If I knew how to do it, I'd add a plus sign to the bottom of the 'o' in 'love', just like either Haze or Ali did.

On a single visit – Tuesday 21 May 2024 – to Oxfam Dalston, I found three books with Christmas messages in. I think you'll agree, that's a bit odd. Richard P Feynman's *Surely You're Joking, Mr Feynman* (Vintage) had a handwritten note torn from a spiral-bound notebook at page 273. It reads: 'Dan, Merry Christmas! Awesome catching up these past few days. Let's make oven dinners a regular thing. Here is some banana bread for your arduous journey home. Beth xoxo.'

I love bananas, but always politely refuse banana bread, the reason being I've seen too many fruit bowls groaning with black bananas and heard a voice, usually my daughter's or her mum's, saying, Oh I must make some banana bread.

Bananas must be eaten while still slightly underripe. As soon as black spots appear on the skin, they belong in the food waste. I'm sorry, that's just the way it is.

James Nestor's *Deep: Freediving, Renegade Science and What the Ocean Tells Us About Ourselves* (Profile) contains, at the flyleaf, a Naked Wines £60-off voucher that needed to be used within thirty days, a crumpled gift tag reading, 'Dear Tim, Merry Christmas, Love Ermine & Chris' and, on the inside front cover, an inscription: 'Dear Tim, Seems very interesting. Enjoy your read. Merry Xmas 2015. Ermine & Chris.' Lovely name

– Ermine. Oxfam's shop in Dalston sits on Kingsland Road, once a Roman road called Ermine Street.

Lastly, on this visit to Oxfam Dalston: Jorge Luis Borges's *The Book of Sand* (Penguin), with an inclusion, two obituaries of the author, at page 115, where we find Borges's poem 'You', and, on the flyleaf, a Christmas inscription: 'Happy Christmas, Owen. Love Helen x.'

Borges died in 1986, at the age of 86.

On Friday 7 October 1983, Borges took part, with Mario Vargas Llosa and Bruce Chatwin, in a live recording of the *Frank Delaney* show for BBC2. I can't remember how I came to know about it, but I was in the audience at the Greenwood Theatre, in the grounds of Guy's Hospital, with two friends, Par Kumaraswami and Steven Rayner. I had come across Borges's name in *Time Out* film reviews, of Nicolas Roeg and Donald Cammell's *Performance* and no doubt numerous other films as well. I had bought the Jupiter Books edition of *Fictions* – 50p, it says, inside my copy – most likely from Camden Market. I'd even read it and decided that 'Funes, the Memorious' was my favourite story. To be in the presence of Borges, although several rows of seats away in that steeply raked theatre, was a thrill and a formative experience. I had started writing short stories just three months earlier. Sitting behind the bar in the hall of residence where I was staying over the summer holiday, I was writing a letter to my friend Dell about what it felt like to be running a bar with no customers. 'This is starting to feel like a short story,' I think I wrote, in the letter. 'I'll carry on as if it were.' Something like that. 'The Barman' later appeared in *Jennings Magazine*.

The assistant producer on the *Frank Delaney* show was Nicholas Shakespeare. I emailed him when I started thinking about Borges for this and the previous chapter.

'Greetings from Tasmania,' Shakespeare replied the same day. 'I am actually rereading Borges right now, so the memory is reasonably fresh. I had known him in Buenos Aires already (where my dad was in the embassy) – reading to him a couple of times, as everyone did (Kipling, *Hamlet*, Chesterton, Anglo-Saxon verse), and even asking him for a poem for my school magazine. I did an interview with him for the *Spectator* at the precocious age of 16, which was my first piece of journalism, and then a larger profile in the *Times* when he came to the UK in 1983.'

Because of their previous encounters, Shakespeare was able to persuade Borges to come on to the *Frank Delaney* show – 'Delaney was momentarily furious; not having heard of him, he thought I had invited Victor Borge.' Shakespeare also invited Chatwin ('his first TV appearance') and Vargas Llosa ('my father had by then moved to Peru') onto the show.

'As I prepared to lead Borges on stage at the Greenwood Theatre, we both watched the monitor in which Chatwin was ululating about how you can't travel anywhere without taking a collection of Borges, "It's like taking a toothbrush" – to which Borges murmured to me, "How unhygienic." I later learned that Edwin Williamson, Borges's future biographer, was in the audience. He told me that the sight of Borges with his walking stick being escorted on stage affected him profoundly and it was in that moment he decided to write his life. Last year, 50 years after I first climbed the stairs to his dark flat in Avenida Maipu (where I remember waiting in vain for his mother to come out of the bathroom so he could introduce us), I finally made it to Borges's grave in Geneva and I stood before it feeling a similar powerful emotion.'

Shakespeare added: 'I remember we then had a battle

with Alan Yentob, then head of music and arts, who had an *Arena* going out shortly on Borges (with Norman Thomas de Giovanni). Incredible to relate (or not so incredible if you met him), Yentob wanted us to bin or delay our programme, which was scheduled to go out before his. We stood fast and it went out first.'

The entry in my diary for Friday 7 October 1983 reads, 'Borges is a star.'

The show was broadcast a couple of weeks later, at 10.15 p.m. on Monday 24 October 1983.

Some books get given more than others.

I've got four inscribed copies of David Eagleman's *Sum: Tales From the Afterlives* (Canongate), but only one was a Christmas present. It came from the Mind shop in Didsbury in January 2022. On the flyleaf, we read, 'Jane, with much appreciation for all the hard work in 2011. Happy Holidays, Marc.' Does that count as a Christmas present?

There's no question about the Christmas-present status of the two copies I have of the Livre de Poche edition of Alain-Fournier's *Le Grand Meaulnes*, the edition with green-sprayed edges, or 'spredges'. One came from Bookcycle in Exeter in July 2024, where the manager was being grumpy and irritable with a young volunteer and a customer with a tattooed head and face was repeatedly clearing his throat. It was '3 Books per Person: You decide the price', so I picked out Alan Lightman's *Einstein's Dreams* (Sceptre) and Georeges Pérec's *Les choses* (J'ai lu) to go with *Le Grand Meaulnes*. The Pérec had been owned by a Chris Pearson in February 1974, so I sent it to artist Chris Pearson in France, who I wrote about in *Shadow Lines*, to ask if it had been his. It hadn't. *Le Grand Meaulnes* contained a Christmas card inside the front cover. All it says, apart from the printed greeting, is 'FROM G ELKINS'.

The other copy of *Le Grand Meaulnes* came from Oxfam Bookshop Bloomsbury Street, in September 2024. The young woman on the till said she loved the green sprayed edges and I asked her if she knew the book. She said she didn't. I recommended it, because, I'm sure we can agree, it's a masterpiece. The man who wrote in this copy, on the flyleaf, would agree, *sans aucun doute*. Any man who gives this book to a woman is casting himself in the role of Augustin Meaulnes and the recipient as Yvonne de Galais, the love of his life. 'À ma précieuse Minou,' writes the gift-giver above the printed title on the flyleaf, after which he correctly adds a handwritten comma before continuing, 'un petit cadeau de Noël (77), son lapin qui l'adore.' I've added another comma after the date, just for sense. Maybe you get the gist, because it doesn't translate very well. Well, it translates, but – trust me – it sounds better in French. 'To my precious Kitty, *Le Grand Meaulnes*, a little Christmas present (77), her rabbit who adores her.' See, I told you.

Which reminds me of the copy of Sartre's *Nausea* I bought from the Cancer Research shop in Didsbury Village in April 2025. It was the lovely Penguin Modern Classics edition featuring Dalí's *The Triangular Hour* and inside there was an inscription: 'To Martin from Kitty, Christmas 1977.'

I have two copies of Paul Auster's *The New York Trilogy* that were Christmas presents. One from Crisis in Dalston in August 2022 – 'Merry Christmas! Love Kate' on the title page – and one from Abney Books, Stoke Newington, which I'll come back to in a moment. It's a Penguin edition published in 1990 and the Christmas greeting takes the form of a handwritten quote added at the end of two pages of quotes from reviews: 'Have a nice Christmas, Daphne! (Read and rest . . .) – Lisa Volbracht, Germany.' Top marks to Lisa Volbracht for originality.

Sunday 13 October 2024
Waterstone's Islington, Islington Green, London.
This isn't a dream, or an overheard conversation, or a report of a person reading and walking, but I wanted to squeeze it in. I went into Waterstone's and there in front of me, facing customers as they entered, was a table stacked high with copies of Boris Johnson's *Unleashed* (William Collins). A little way off to the right was a trolley with various rejected books on it and a sign Sellotaped to it that said, in red capitals, 'CLEARANCE FROM £1.' I felt a sudden impulse and acted on it. I removed the sign from the trolley and stuck it on top of the sign advertising Johnson's book. By chance, they were the same size and format, A4, landscape. I turned around and walked out, but not before taking a quick photograph and posting it on Instagram.

On Tuesday 1 October 2024, I remembered that a new second-hand bookshop had been open in Stoke Newington for a few weeks and I still hadn't been. Did I remember or did Tim Craig remind me? Tim Craig went to my school, is a Nightjar subscriber, lives in Hackney and writes short stories. He's basically me, but a bit younger. On the way to Abney Books, I saw Stewart Lee on his bike and for some reason I didn't say hello. The previous time I'd seen him on his bike, I'd said hello, and he'd said hello back. And when I saw him in the Jolly Butchers, I'd said hello, and he'd said hello back and we'd had a little chat. So, now, by not saying hello on this occasion, I'd undermined the imaginary friendship that I have with Stewart Lee, surely the Funniest Man in Britain. I was also deep into my annual prostate crisis. Every winter, I seem to reach a point where I notice I'm paying more visits to the bathroom and I decide that this means I should be booking a PSA test.

As I get older, more and more of my (male) friends are getting prostate trouble – all right, prostate cancer – and I tend to think, how come they get it and I don't? Don't get me wrong. I don't want to get it. I haven't got a morbid variant of FOMO. I just think, he's got it, so I'm bound to have it. It's the same when I read in the news that someone has died of some cancer I didn't even know you could get. I think, I'm bound to get that. I've probably already got it.

I also saw Emily Thornberry on her bike, in Islington in April 2024, but didn't say hello. I would have done, perhaps, but she was in the distance before I realised it was her. And, the same month, Clive Myrie, in Oxfam Books & Music Islington. He wasn't on his bike, but was donating books, and I did say hello, using the fact of our shared love of Manchester City to initiate a conversation. He had extraordinary charisma and was easy to talk to. On a later visit I bought his copy of Sartre's *Les mains sales* (Folio).

So, Abney Books cheered me up a little. Four books for a tenner. One of my four, Joseph Conrad's *Tales of Unrest* (Penguin Modern Classics), had a Christmas inscription. 'All our unrest is in these covers. Happy Christmas my love.' The signature could be Ken or Kim. I can't be sure.

I liked the young man running the place. He said business had been OK, but was less good when it was raining.

A week or so later, back in Dalston, a Saturday. In Oxfam I selected Tim Burton's *The Melancholy Death of Oyster Boy & Other Stories* (Faber) for its Christmas inscription. It's a lovely inscription – 'Xmas 02. Dearest Chester, Wishing you masses of love & kisses this Christmas. 2003 is going to be the year of all years!! Love you, Spot xxxx' – but if there's one thing that makes me feel unChristmassy, it's publishers indulging celebrities by publishing books like this. It's 113 pages, RRP £12.99 and it took me nine minutes to read in the bath.

In the same shop a couple of months earlier I'd found Jonathan Coe's *What a Carve Up!* (Penguin), which had been given as a present the same Christmas as the Tim Burton. 'To Daniel,' goes the inscription, 'I loved this book! Merry Christmas 2002. With our love as always. The Broadbottom 3 xxx.'

I really want to know who the Broadbottom 3 are.

Manchester City won the FA Cup in 1969, which gave Stanley Paul publishers a good picture to put on the front of *The Manchester City Football Book* edited by Peter Gardner. 'To Jackie, "Merry Christmas 1969" Lots of love, Gillian xxxxxx,' it says on the flyleaf. Is Jackie still a City fan? Has she been enjoying the club's phenomenal success during the last ten years? Does she think Rayan Cherki is the new David Silva? I haven't given any of my treasured football books away. Someone gave this one to Sue Ryder in Didsbury, where I bought it on Halloween, 2024.

I hope Jackie is OK.

In the new year – Sunday 26 January 2025 – my friend Conrad was down in the dumps, so I offered to drive him to Buxton.

And leave him there.

We parked in my usual place, about a mile from Scrivener's, and walked through the icy rain to reach the bookshop. Something made me look inside Nicolas Freeling's *The King of the Rainy Country* (Penguin) and on the inside front cover I found this brief message: 'To Dad, Merry Christmas, with love from

Lesley.' I remembered a contrasting inscription in a hardback edition of Saul Bellow's *Collected Stories* (Viking) that I had bought from Jambala Buddhist charity bookshop the previous April. 'Dearest daddy,' it had begun, 'I hope you enjoy reading this book and get many hours of pleasure doing so. Merry Christmas and Happy New Year, all my love, your delightful daughter, Alex xxxxx.' It was dated December 2001. There was also a boarding pass, at page 81, in the name of Gluck.

But I wasn't done in Scrivener's. I liked the look of a slim hardback in red cloth, Paul Tabori's *Private Gallery* (Sylvan Press), a first edition with very fine wood engravings by Val Biro. In an author's note, Tabori states that the stories in this his first collection were based on real characters and actual events. There's a handwritten dedication on the flyleaf: 'To Miss Ilona Solymossy in friendship and admiration. Xmas 1944. Paul Tabori.'

Paul Tabori (1908–74) was a Hungarian-born author, journalist, screenwriter and psychoanalyst who moved to Britain in 1937 and became a British citizen ten years later.

Ilona Solymossy, a teacher, came to Britain from Hungary in 1938 with her sister Elizabeth. She died on 24 January 1991, at the age of 82, and is buried at St Peter's Church, Edensor.

Conrad bought a Nevil Shute paperback. I've never read Nevil Shute. Am I missing out?

I was walking from Walthamstow to Muswell Hill and had reached Crouch End, when the heavens opened. I sought shelter in the Harington Charity Shop on Hornsey High Street, where I found a copy of Ron Butlin's *The Tilting Room* (Canongate). Ron Butlin's first short story collection, published in 1983, was recommended to me in the 1990s by playwright Richard Cameron in the bar of the Bush Theatre, Shepherd's Bush, where I had just watched a production of his latest play, either *Pond Life* or *Not Fade Away* or perhaps *This Mortal Ash*. I think I saw all three.

It took a while, but eventually I found a copy of *The Tilting Room*, read it and loved it, and became friends with the author – all thanks to a chance remark over a drink.

The copy I found in the Harington shop, on Friday 12 September 2025, contained an inscription: 'Dear Ollie – Will either be weird and good, or weird and rubbish – let's see. Love you – Dad x. Xmas 2022.'

A good choice by Ollie's dad. Definitely 'weird and good', in my opinion. I hope Ollie agreed. Yet there it was in a charity shop not quite three Christmases later.

I had already made a good find that day. In Oxfam Walthamstow I had bought Hilary Mantel's *Wolf Hall* (4th Estate) for an inclusion, at page 225, some family photographs and a letter from the NHS to J. (I later tracked down J at a City law firm and returned her letter and photographs, which she was very pleased to get back.) From Crouch End, once the thunderstorm had passed over, I walked up to Muswell Hill, where writer and book collector WB Gooderham had recommended a new second-hand bookshop, Muswell Hill Books & Parlour. Open less than a week, it was a class act. Cosy, low-wattage bulbs, great selection of books, good prices – owner Chris previously ran Black Gull Books at Camden Lock. I bought Franz Kafka's *The Trial* (Penguin Modern Classics); on the bottom right-hand corner of the flyleaf was written, 'Ma & Pa, Xmas 1979.' Did Ma write that? Or Pa? Or the son or daughter who was the recipient? We'll never know.

After Christmas, the book still not delivered, I got a call from Gareth Evans. You might remember me and Gareth meeting in a café called Bread & Butter in the chapter 'Library fines'. On the phone, excitedly, Gareth began telling me about something that had just happened to him involving the book exchange shelves at Haggerston station. In his role as programmer and host of the *London Review of Books*' 'London Reviewed' series at the Garden Cinema, he had emailed the writer Ronan Bennett to invite him to introduce a screening of Jules Dassin's 1950 noir classic *Night and the City*, adapted from the novel by Gerald Kersh. Bennett accepted Gareth's invitation. The following morning, Gareth stopped by the book exchange at Haggerston station and found three very interesting, quite valuable books. To keep this story short, I'll mention only the pick of the bunch: a UK first edition of *Fowlers End* by Gerald Kersh.

At the time of writing, a search on AbeBooks reveals only one copy like this for sale, at £150.

As Gareth gathered up the three books, another reader – 'a young man in his mid twenties with a thin beard' – pushed in front of him to look at the shelves. Instinct told Gareth that had he arrived at the book exchange a minute later, the books he now held in his arms, one of which would make an excellent token of appreciation for Ronan Bennett's acceptance of his invitation, would have gone.

'Among the many fascinating elements of your trilogy,' Gareth wrote to me later in an email, 'is the acknowledgement of chance in the discovery of certain titles and editions, a quality built into the very DNA of second-hand bookshops.'

That's very kind, I deflected, but I can't possibly put that in my book. For a start, it's practically finished, and secondly, it would feel too, I don't know, self-congratulatory, especially if I slipped it in towards the end of the last chapter.

'We never know, of course, what or who is missed by the

timing of our journeys through the city,' Gareth went on, almost as if I hadn't said anything. 'Synchronicity only reveals itself when it is noticed, when it takes place. In this way, perhaps there is nothing mysterious about it; simply put, it is *what happened*.

'That is not what I think,' Gareth continued. 'Along with Carl Gustav Jung and Paul Auster, to name only two, I feel compelled to believe that more, possibly *much* more, is at play, and at stake, when such occurrences are encountered.'

I knew Gareth would be familiar with the Ballard quote – 'Deep assignments run through all our lives; there are no coincidences' – so didn't even mention it.

'Whatever the source, intention or outcome of such energising juxtapositions,' Gareth added, 'there is no doubt that they enliven urban living immeasurably, making every walk a potential arena of adventure and discovery.'

I'm walking west along the Fallowfield Loop. It's a Tuesday towards the middle of January. I'm reading a print-out of one of the chapters of this book, reading out loud. It's the only way. The only way to catch everything. Which is not to say I think I've caught everything, but by reading out loud I can catch the things that I can catch.

I'm feeling quite good about it, energised by walking and by the process of reading and improving the text as I go, but I can't deny there's a little background anxiety to do with the fact that the book should have been delivered at the end of December.

The floater in my left eye left over from the posterior vitreous detachment (PVD) that happened in December is getting smaller, or I'm just noticing it less. Moorfields Eye Hospital is amazing, by the way. If ever anything goes wrong with your eyes and you're anywhere near London, I strongly recommend heading straight for Moorfields. I was nowhere near London, but I was on my way there. I was 200 miles away on the platform at Stockport station when I suddenly became aware of black ink or thick black smoke curling into my left eye, or so it seemed. It was a bright day, sky the colour of a football shirt. This unannounced blackness was alarming and strangely thrilling at the same time. I thought, I hope not too inappropriately, of Jamaica Kincaid's short story, 'Blackness'. 'How soft is the blackness as it falls. It falls in silence and yet it is deafening, for no other sound except the blackness falling can be heard. The blackness falls like soot from a lamp with an untrimmed wick. The blackness is visible and yet it is invisible, for I see that I cannot see it. The blackness fills up a small room, a large field, an island, my own being.'

The London train was pulling in alongside. I didn't know what to do. Go home or get on? I got on. Maybe if I managed to sleep on the train, it would magically go away after twenty minutes, like the visual auras that I get two or three times a year, my field of vision ringed by flashing lights like the filament of an old light bulb twisted into glowing barbed wire. I closed my eyes, but didn't fall asleep. I gave it twenty minutes and opened my eyes. It was still there. Maybe a little smaller, but still there. If I moved my eye, it moved with the eye, like my eye had become an aquarium, home to a single Black Moor goldfish, which can live for up to twenty years. Thank you, brain, for that particular random fact.

Was I losing my sight? Would I live the last years of my life in darkness, like Borges? Would I still be able to write? Would I finally learn to touch type? Would I dictate my stories, like Borges? Would I never again see my mum's face? My wife's face? My children's faces? The faces of all my loved ones?

When I got to London, my wife suggested we go to Moorfields

where an almost preternaturally serene gentleman called Cornelius suggested I come back the following morning when I would be seen more quickly. Everyone I saw at Moorfields, hailing from almost a complete set of continents and Merseyside ('Do you think you'll win the League?' asked the Liverpool fan who had given up on his club's defending the title), that following morning and in two subsequent visits, was kind, helpful and utterly professional.

It turns out PVD is not uncommon – as you get older.

On the Fallowfield Loop, I look up and see a woman coming towards me, walking quite fast – and reading.

'Excuse me,' I say, and already I'm thinking I've seen this reader-walker before. 'Do you mind if I ask what you're reading? Haven't we, er . . .'

It's Kate Hughes, the woman who was reading Jeremy Cooper's *Brian* last time I saw her, the first time I saw her. This time she's reading Ann Cleeves' *Murder in Paradise*, which I haven't read. I show her what I'm reading and explain that it's a chapter from the book in which I write about meeting her. We chat for a few more minutes and off she goes. It occurs to me once she's gone that our paths crossed in more or less exactly the same spot as on the previous occasion. Maybe fifty yards' difference.

As I set off again, I realise I feel exhilarated, stimulated, full of confidence. I hesitate to mention the word 'colonoscopy' again, which you might remember from the chapter on 'Doubles'. How about if I just mouth it, like the word 'cancer' was often mouthed when I was little? It happened last week and it was mostly normal, and what wasn't normal was not serious, so that definitely helps, but there's no denying the fact that a second chance encounter with a virtual stranger with whom I had a couple of tiny things in common – we both read while we walk and we both like Jeremy Cooper's *Brian* – has had a positive effect on my mood. It was pretty good anyway, but now I am bounding along, already thinking about how I will write this up.

Maybe it will work well at the end of the book. I mean, I'm virtually there now anyway. Let's see.

Acknowledgements

I would like to thank LNER for providing me with a complimentary travel pass between London and Newcastle. Large parts of this book were written in The Art of Tea and Lapwing Deli in Didsbury, Manchester, and Belle Epoque, in Islington, London; staff in these establishments have been very accommodating and regulars good company. Thanks to Catherine Lovich for allowing me to write a regular column for Oxfam's monthly in-house publication *Bookmark*, where some short passages in this book appeared first, in a different form. I would also like to thank the following: Matthew Adamson, Charles Boyle, Michael Caines, JO Carr, Mark Chambers, Joshua Chapman, Richard Clegg, Jonathan Coe, David Collard, Sarah-Clare Conlon, Ailsa Cox, Geoff Cox, Tim Craig, Ian Cunningham, Katie Davies, Peter Davies, Philip de Jersey, Simon Donoghue, Nick Duerden, Martin Edwards, Martin Ellerby, Maz Esnouf, Gareth Evans, Iris Feindt, Dell Fielding, Tibor Fischer, Samuel Fisher, David Gaffney, Andy Gardiner, Anne Gerrish, Jonathan Gibbs, WB Gooderham, Sarah Guy, Kerry Hadley-Pryce, Naomi Hamill, Chris Hamilton-Emery, Jen Hamilton-Emery, Ian Hay, Rosie Hewitson, Hilaire, Kate Hughes, Roger Huss,

FINDERS, KEEPERS: *The Secret Life of Second-hand Books*

Joanne and Simon, Jonathan at LJMU Library, Linda Kabi, Lisa from Broad Road, Nigel Kendall, Kianja, Michael Lacey, Heather McAlister, Alexandra Mckenzie, Brian McMahon, Cliff McNish, Livi Michael, More Maniacs & everyone at Moniack Mhor, Sonya Moor, Adam Morris, Dan Norcott, Emma Oakey, John Oakey, Simon Okotie, Zalan Pall at Phoenix Cinema, Ian Patterson, Paul from Malvern, Chris Pearson, Janet Penny, Brian Radcliffe, Cécile Radcliffe, Julia Ratcliffe, Nick Rogers, David Rose, Bella Royle, Charlie Royle, Jean Royle, Joanna Royle, Julie Royle, Nicholas Royle, Kate Ryan, John Saddler, Ian Sansom, Nicholas Shakespeare, Tim Shearer, Robert Sheppard, Adrian Slatcher, Stephen Smith, Kevin Sommerville, Yuka Sonobe, Joe Stretch, Louise Theodosiou, Jess Thomas, Trevor Mark Thomas, Mark Valentine, Steven Waling, Conrad Williams, Matthew Wright, Zoë from Malvern. Special thanks to my wife, Ros Sales, and apologies to those people I am bound to have forgotten.

Picadors, published between 1972 and 2002, added to main collection since lists in *White Spines* and *Shadow Lines*:

Chinua Achebe, *The African Trilogy*
David Foster, *Moonlite*
F Gonzalez Crussi, *On the Nature of Things Erotic*
Lian Hearn, *Across the Nightingale Floor*
Alice Hoffman, *Turtle Moon*
Mark Leyner, *A Dream Date With Di and Other Pieces*

Picador Classics, published 1980s/90s, added to collection since lists in *White Spines* and *Shadow Lines*:

James Agee, *Let Us Now Praise Famous Men*
Yasunari Kawabata, *Palm-of-the-Hand Stories*
Claude Lévi-Strauss, *Tristes Tropiques*

ALSO BY NICHOLAS ROYLE

NOVELS
Counterparts
Saxophone Dreams
The Matter of the Heart
The Director's Cut
Antwerp
Regicide
First Novel

NOVELLAS
The Appetite
The Enigma of Departure

SHORT STORIES
Mortality
In Camera (with David Gledhill)
Ornithology
The Dummy & Other Uncanny Stories
London Gothic
Manchester Uncanny
Paris Fantastique

ANTHOLOGIES (as editor)
Darklands
Darklands 2
A Book of Two Halves
The Tiger Garden: A Book of Writers' Dreams
The Time Out Book of New York Short Stories
The Ex Files: New Stories About Old Flames
The Agony & the Ecstasy: New Writing for the World Cup
Neonlit: Time Out Book of New Writing
The Time Out Book of Paris Short Stories
Neonlit: Time Out Book of New Writing Volume 2
The Time Out Book of London Short Stories Volume 2
Dreams Never End
'68: New Stories From Children of the Revolution
The Best British Short Stories 2011
Murmurations: An Anthology of Uncanny Stories About Birds
The Best British Short Stories 2012–2025

NON-FICTION
White Spines: Confessions of a Book Collector
Shadow Lines: Searching for the Book Beyond the Shelf

ALSO BY NICHOLAS ROYLE

NOVELS
Counterparts
Saxophone Dreams
The Matter of the Heart
The Director's Cut
Antwerp
Regicide
First Novel

NOVELLAS
The Appetite
The Enigma of Departure

SHORT STORIES
Mortality
In Camera (with David Gledhill)
Ornithology
The Dummy & Other Uncanny Stories
London Gothic
Manchester Uncanny
Paris Fantastique

ANTHOLOGIES (as editor)
Darklands
Darklands 2
A Book of Two Halves
The Tiger Garden: A Book of Writers' Dreams
The Time Out Book of New York Short Stories
The Ex Files: New Stories About Old Flames
The Agony & the Ecstasy: New Writing for the World Cup
Neonlit: Time Out Book of New Writing
The Time Out Book of Paris Short Stories
Neonlit: Time Out Book of New Writing Volume 2
The Time Out Book of London Short Stories Volume 2
Dreams Never End
'68: New Stories From Children of the Revolution
The Best British Short Stories 2011
Murmurations: An Anthology of Uncanny Stories About Birds
The Best British Short Stories 2012–2025

NON-FICTION
White Spines: Confessions of a Book Collector
Shadow Lines: Searching for the Book Beyond the Shelf

This book has been typeset by
SALT PUBLISHING LIMITED
using Granjon, a font designed by George W. Jones
for the British branch of the Linotype company in the United
Kingdom. It has been manufactured using Holmen Book
Cream 65gsm paper, and printed and bound by Clays Limited
in Bungay, Suffolk, Great Britain.

CROMER

GREAT BRITAIN

MMXXVI

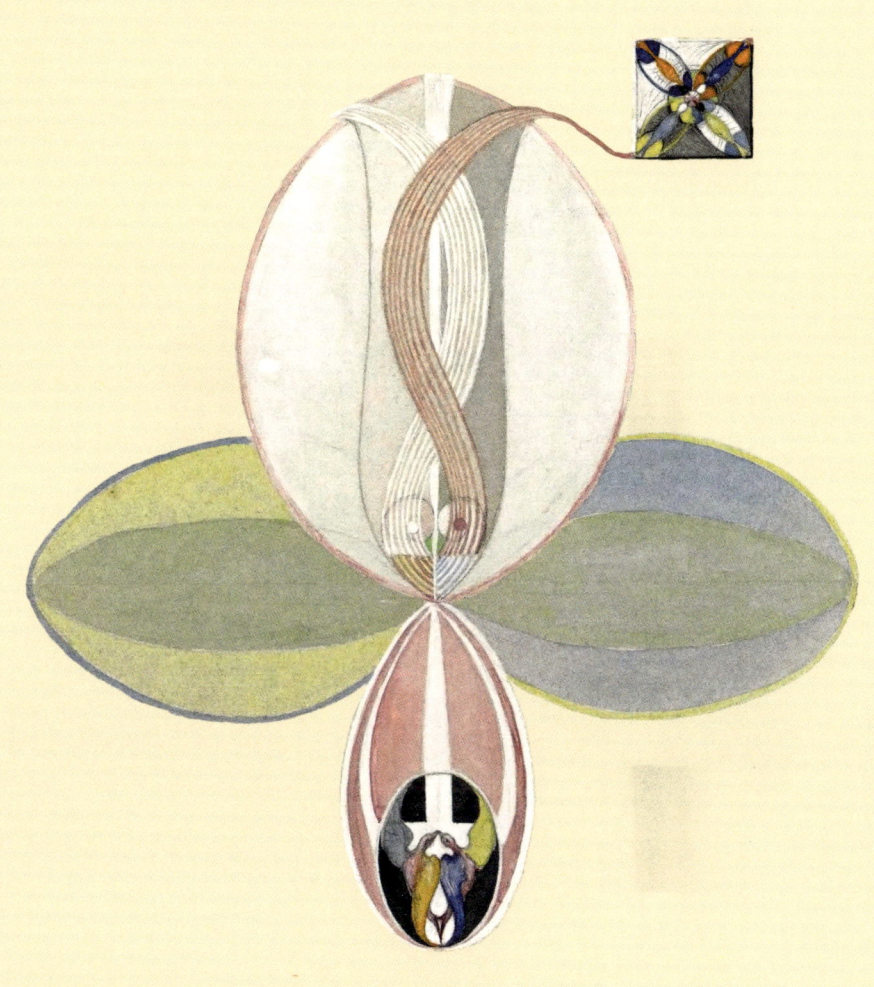

HOPE B. WERNESS

The SECRET LANGUAGE OF PLANTS

ART, NATURE & SYMBOLISM

With 400 illustrations

This volume is dedicated to my mother:

JOANNE HILL BENEDICT
(1920–2014)

An artist and prize-winning quiltmaker,
she loved nature and incorporated many plants
and flowers into her work. She also provided
an environment in which my sister and
I could flourish.

It is also dedicated to the new twig on the family
tree, Charles Severn ('Sev') Werness-Rude.
May he grow and prosper.

And to my husband, George, who died as this
book was being prepared. His enthusiasm,
support and love are greatly missed.

CONTENTS

INTRODUCTION 6

PLANT INDEX 8

TREES 18

FLOWERS 88

FRUIT, VEGETABLES & SEASONINGS 152

GRAINS, GRASSES & VINES 202

ACKNOWLEDGMENTS 226

GLOSSARY 227

NOTES 227

BIBLIOGRAPHY 228

SOURCES OF ILLUSTRATIONS 231

INDEX 236

INTRODUCTION

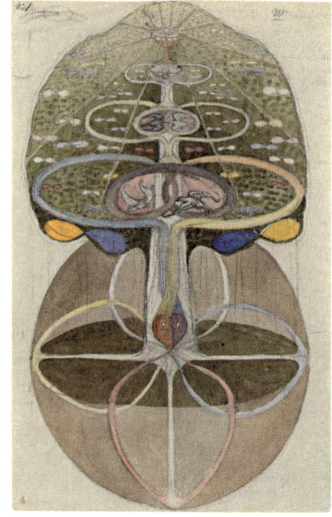

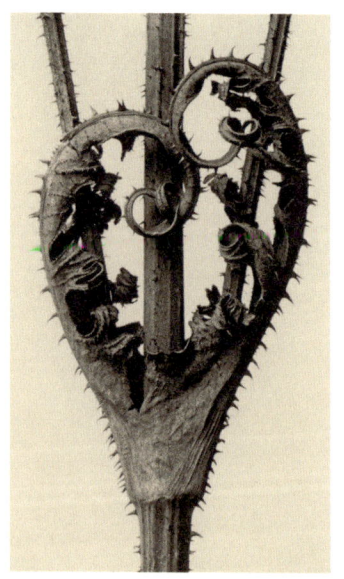

Confucius wrote: 'If you think in terms of a year, plant a seed; if in terms of ten years, plant trees; if in terms of 100 years, teach the people.' But artists and botanists think in millennia or even longer.

According to a list compiled by Botanic Gardens Conservation International using data from its 500 member organizations, there are approximately 400,000 flower species and 60,065 tree species. Of course, not all of them carry symbolic meaning; if they did, this book could never be completed or even begun. Symbolic plants vary from culture to culture, time to time and place to place. Many provide sustenance and shelter and, beyond significance and usefulness, their awesome beauty and abundant life force are sources of endless wonder.[1] Their perceived meanings provide insights that would otherwise go unnoticed, and add to our sum of knowledge.

This book attempts to review and discuss the cultural and art-historical treatment of plants.[2] A new perspective is developing among scholars and artists, stemming from the sweeping ecological changes the world is undergoing. In *Why Look at Plants?* (2018), Giovanni Aloi suggests that John Berger's *Why Look at Animals?* (2009) can be used as a model for current plant studies. Aloi suggests that we must take a different approach, one that does not involve distancing ourselves from and objectifying plants:

> *The hope is that like human-animal studies, the field of plant studies will enrich our perspectives on plants, thus leading to different modalities in what right now constitutes a mostly unacknowledged critical node in the survival of life on the planet...[Instead of counterproductive approaches] contemporary art has the ability to complement, unhinge, problematize, and challenge philosophical concepts – the synergy between the two can constitute a powerful tool just as long as it is put to work to achieve actual change.*

The field of plant studies has grown and changed since the turn of the millennium, resulting in a new, wide-ranging literature that is often international in scope.[3] Not just scientific and environmental in nature, it examines aesthetic, literary, philosophical and spiritual issues. A central theme regards the sentience of plants, replacing the common, long-held idea that they are immobile and unfeeling. Recent fiction, such as Richard Powers's *The Overstory: A Novel* (2018) and Brian Selznick's *Big Tree* (2023), also addresses this subject, drawing attention to the complexity of plant interaction. Contemporary art exemplifies the new approaches, such as the work of John Grade (see 'Cedar', p. 38), Precious Okoyomon (see 'Kudzu', p. 216) and Mark Dion (see 'Hemlock', p. 44). Artists also concern themselves with extinction – not just that of plants, but also that of animals and entire environments.[4] As Dion puts it:

> *Certainly for the things I care about – oceans, forests, wild places and wild things, there is little good news. This is a serious role for the arts – bearing witness and mourning. After all, mourning is a legitimate mode of thinking.*

When I began this book, I thought I'd be doing the 'acorn = strength, fertility' and so on. And I have done that. I have found, however, that plants are being re-evaluated. Artists, art historians, philosophers, scientists and others are looking anew at plants – at their beauty, sentience and life force. Most maintain that we must change our ideas about and relationships with plants. To do so, they believe, could be a crucial step towards making changes that might eventually impact the environmental disasters now occurring.

Readers wishing to find information about specific plants should consult the Plant Index in the following pages.

⊗ Hilma af Klint, *Tree of Knowledge, no. 1*, 1913, watercolour on paper. Potomac, MA: Glenstone Museum.

✳ Karl Blossfeldt, *Dipsacus laciniatus (cutleaf teasel)*, 1928, gelatin silver print. Los Angeles, CA: J. Paul Getty Museum.

❖ William Henry Fox Talbot, *Two Plant Specimens*, 1839, photogenic drawing. Chicago, IL: Art Institute of Chicago.

✻ Tosa Mitsuoki, *Autumn Maples with Poem Slips* (detail), 1670–80, ink, colours, gold leaf and gold powder on silk. Chicago, IL: Art Institute of Chicago.

PLANT INDEX

References are to page numbers for each plant entry. Common names are listed at the bottom of each page.

TREES

28 . . . . ACACIA	32 . . . . BAOBAB	36 . . . . CHESTNUT
30 . . . . SYCAMORE	34 . . . . BIRCH	38 . . . . CEDAR

40 . . . . ORANGE 44 . . . . HEMLOCK 50 . . . . CYPRESS 54 . . . . FIG
42 . . . . LEMON 48 . . . . HAZEL 52 . . . . BEECH

58 . . . . ASH   62 . . . . JUNIPER   66 . . . . OLIVE   70 . . . . PINE
60 . . . . HOLLY   64 . . . . LAUREL   68 . . . . PALM

74 .... ALMOND   82 .... WILLOW   86 .... ELM
78 .... OAK   84 .... YEW

FLOWERS

93 . . . . ANEMONE	98 . . . . DAISY	106 . . . . CROCUS	112 . . . . FOXGLOVE
94 . . . . COLUMBINE	102 . . . . THISTLE	108 . . . . CYCLAMEN	114 . . . . SUNFLOWER
96 . . . . ARUM	104 . . . . CHRYSANTHEMUM	110 . . . . CARNATION	118 . . . . HYACINTH

120. . . . . IRIS	130. . . . . NARCISSUS	138. . . . . POPPY	146. . . . . TULIP
124. . . . . LILY	132. . . . . . . WATER LILY	142. . . . . PASSIONFLOWER	148. . . . . VIOLET
128. . . . . . . HONEYSUCKLE	136. . . . . ORCHID	144. . . . . ROSE	150. . . . . PANSY

FRUIT, VEGETABLES & SEASONINGS

156. . . . . ONION	159. . . . . CELERY	162. . . . . GOURD
158. . . . . PINEAPPLE	160. . . . . CABBAGE	164. . . . . PUMPKIN

166..........ARTICHOKE	172..........STRAWBERRY	180..........NUTMEG
168..........CARROT	174..........APPLE	182..........CHERRY
170..........FENNEL	178..........BANANA	184..........PEACH

187....... POMEGRANATE   192............ RADISH   196......... AUBERGINE   200........... MULLEIN
190.............. PEAR   194............ TOMATO   198............ POTATO

GRAINS, GRASSES & VINES

206 .... CUCUMBER	212 .... IVY	216 .... KUDZU	222 .... GRAPEVINE
208 .... GRASS	214 .... REED	218 .... WHEAT	224 .... CORN

TREES

There are more than 60,000 species of tree – fewer than flower species, but perhaps of greater importance. Trees are larger than humans, outlive us by aeons and have been on earth far longer than us; indeed, many might seem to us to be immortal. They provide shelter – shade and building materials – and flowering trees provide sustenance and nurture in the form of medicine, fruit and nuts. We often refer to our family line as a tree, and use similar words to describe trees and our own bodies: crown, trunk and limbs.

The importance of trees in the environment cannot be overstated. They stabilize the soil and prevent erosion. They breathe, absorbing carbon dioxide and replenishing oxygen. They are abidingly strange and beautiful. We may have been expelled from Eden, but Paradise lives on in national parks, botanical gardens, nature reserves and seed banks, and in the critical work of artists and environmentalists.[5]

Some depictions of trees convey more general meanings. Allison Meier delineated several of these 'types' in the catalogue of an exhibition at the Courtauld Gallery in London in 2014, 'A Dialogue with Nature: Romantic Landscapes from Britain and Germany':

> *The Blasted Tree: a wounded but still living tree –*
>   *the cycle of nature, disruption of pastoral peace.*
> *The Lone Tree: a sometimes damaged but surviving lone*
>   *tree – subtext man lives and dies, but trees continue*
>   *in a longer life; in a Christian context, Resurrection.*
> *Dead Trees: memento mori.*
> *Reaching to the Sky: spiritual symbols connecting earth*
>   *and sky, often with rainbows.*
> *Trees Entwined: in connection with family portraits,*
>   *entwined lives of people.*
> *Gnarled Giants: often anthropomorphic depictions*
>   *of rooted strength.*

In the following pages, all aspects of each tree are considered: the tree itself, its blossom and its fruit or nuts. For separate discussions of fruit, please see the plant index.

H. J. Ruprecht, Trunk and roots of a pine tree cut to show growth rings; microscopic views of wood cells in longitudinal and transverse section and of a root tip, chromolithograph, 1877. London: Wellcome Collection.

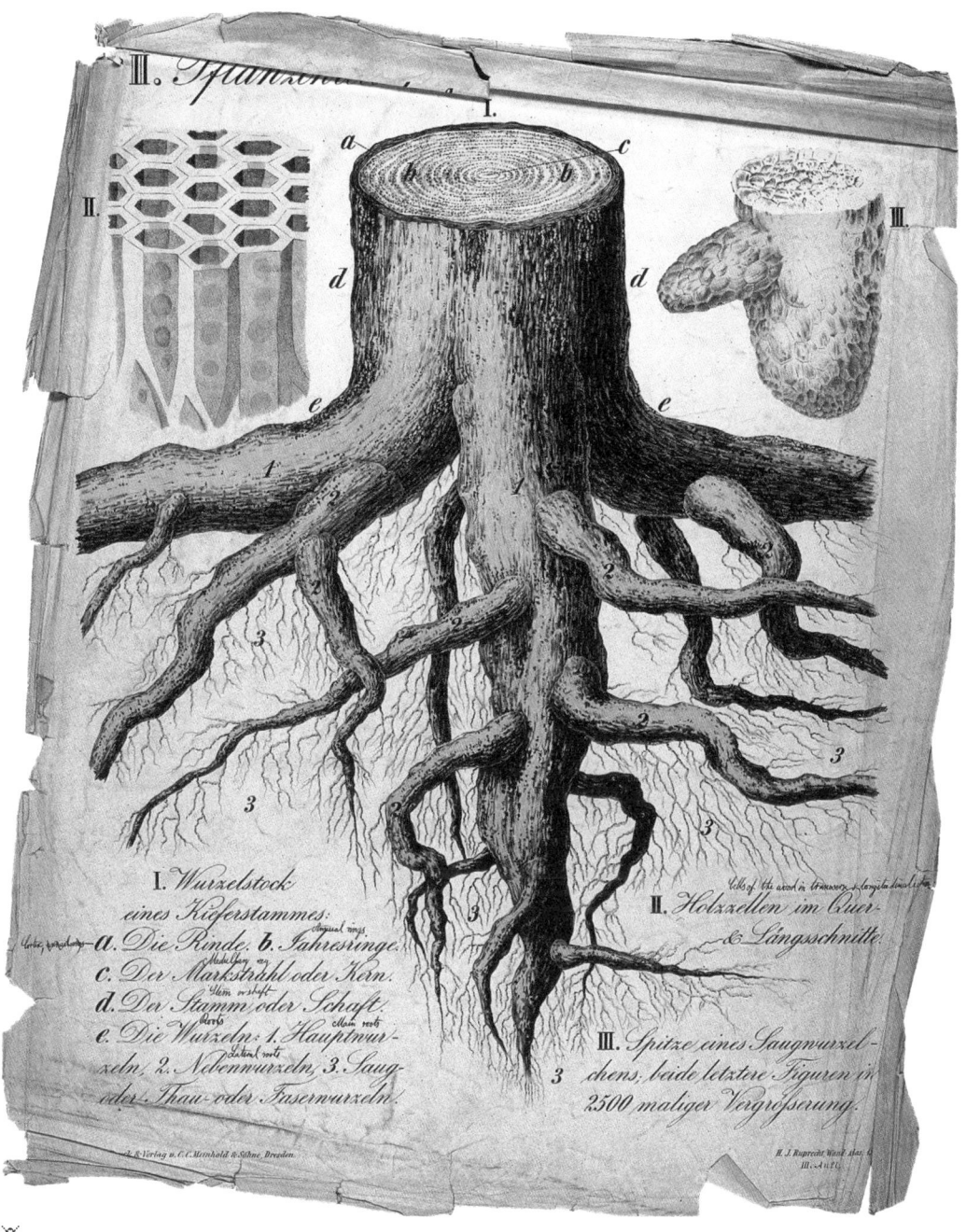

INTRODUCTION

MYTHICAL TREES: TREE OF LIFE

The concept of the Tree of Life is ancient and widespread; perhaps unsurprisingly, since trees are among the most obvious things in the landscape. The Tree of Life is one of the two trees described in the Biblical book of Genesis, the other being the Tree of Knowledge:

> *And out of the ground the Lord God made every tree grow that is pleasant to the sight and good for food. The tree of life was also in the midst of the garden, and the tree of the knowledge of good and evil* (2:9, 16–17)

Since Genesis does not mention a particular species, many candidates have been suggested: acacia, apple, cedar, cherry, dragon tree, elm, fig, palm, persea, pomegranate, quince and sycamore. The tree is seen in Christian images of Paradise, for instance in Albrecht Dürer's *Adam and Eve* (1504). In Eastern Orthodox art, Christ often sits in or hangs crucified from the tree.

The most ancient images of the Tree of Life appear in Egyptian tomb paintings and low-relief carvings from Mesopotamia. In the twelfth-century Jewish mystical tradition the Kabbalah, the Tree is depicted as a diagram called the Sefirot (or Sephirot), a word meaning 'emanations'. In Kabbalist theory, ten creative forces, or emanations, exist between Ein Sof (the infinite, unknowable divine) and the created world.

Gustav Klimt's *Tree of Life* mosaic, one of three commissioned for the dining room of a palace in Brussels, depicts the concept with swirling branches, climbing plants and fragile threads, indicating the energy and complexity of life. Flowers, symbols and glittering surfaces magically convey vitality and immortality.

A 2021 image by the San Francisco artist David Maxim is a poignant example of the Tree of Life. Some years ago Maxim created images of himself hugging trees in the Sierras. In 2021 he was diagnosed with a terminal disease. He writes of a visit to Golden Gate Park:

✤ Gustav Klimt, *Tree of Life*, Stoclet Frieze (detail), 1909, working drawing of a mosaic frieze. Vienna: Museum of Applied Arts.

✤ Sefirotic tree, *The Great Parchment*, copied by James Hepburn, 1606. Oxford: The Bodleian Library.

✤ David Maxim, *Old Man with Young Tree*, 2021, watercolour on paper. Courtesy of the artist.

With my diagnosis fresh in my mind I decided this was a good day for a park visit...I was drawn to the hopeful, promising vision of young trees.

After I set up my camera to capture the right position, I had to get on my knees to find space free of limbs to put my arms around the slender trunk. My body will never hug the mature tree. I whispered to the tree as I would to a small child. With my pose in a prayerful attitude, I imagined an exchange of energy, in my body's touch of the tree, and the tree to me.

I will die very soon compared to this tree with its whole life before it. Yet it seems kindred, family, insofar that our lives may intersect while we are both on the planet at the same time. Man to tree and tree to man. It accepted my connection to it and to the earth deep below. In my embrace of the tree, I engage all of life around me. And its life will all go on and on. I embrace it – a welcome, a farewell, a meditation, a prayer. For now we live together on the planet. The tree is rooted; I am grounded, and at ease with the world around me.

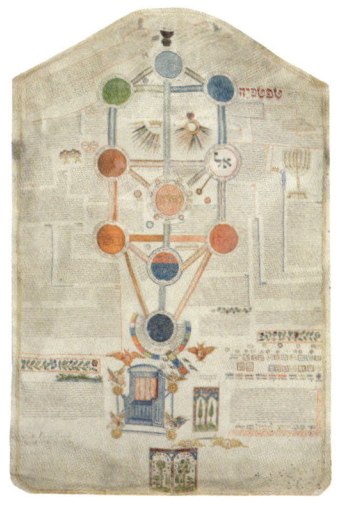

This apparently simple image evokes not only the Tree of Life but other complex themes: life and death, the idiosyncrasies of time and the enormity and endurance of life. The tenderness of the artist's embrace conveys hope, humility, an abiding gratitude and acceptance, and love. The fragile young tree stands at the centre, uniting and connecting all.

WORLD TREE

Although not entirely universal, the concept of a primordial tree that grew at the centre of the universe and connected the heavens, earth and the underworld is widespread. Symbolism is attributed to its branches, trunk, leaves and roots. Stars crown it in the heavens, animals and birds inhabit its branches, and serpents lie at its roots. It is aligned to the cardinal points and springs forth from sacred fountains that sustain it.

Yggdrasil is the World Tree in Scandinavia. Similar trees or pillars occur in ancient Egypt, Persia, India (both Hindu and Buddhist) and Greece (under Alexander the Great), as well as in Islamic and Teutonic traditions. Siberia and Russia also have mythical trees, as does Oceania (Papua New Guinea, Maori Aotearoa New Zealand, Hawai'i, Samoa). Mesoamerica, Maya and some Native North Americans (the Hopi, Navajo and Plains people) also have dramatic World Trees. Various species are candidates for the World Tree: apple, ash, bo/bodhi (pipal), oak, pine and yew.

FOREST

A forest is a mysterious place; in legends and fairy tales, it is the haunt of shadowy and dangerous creatures. It is a place of testing, a realm of death holding the secrets of nature, which must be penetrated to find meaning.

The forest contrasts with various human environments – city, town and village – and that contrast implies the difference between irrationality and rationality, unconscious and conscious, and feminine and masculine. A dramatic instance of this is the wilderness versus the planned and organized garden. The untamed nature of the forest differs dramatically from the controlled safety of the places in which humans live. In his *Dictionary of Symbols* (first published in 1958), Juan Eduardo Cirlot writes:

> *The forest is the place where vegetable life thrives and luxuriates, free from any control or cultivation.*

※ Oluf Olufsen Bagge, *Yggdrasil, The Mundane Tree*, 1847, engraving.

※ William Blake, *The Wood of the Self-Murderers: The Harpies and the Suicides*, 1824–27, graphite, ink and watercolour on paper. London: Tate.

❋ Max Ernst, *The Forest*, 1927–28, oil on canvas. New York: Guggenheim Museum.

INTRODUCTION

*

> *And since its foliage obscures the light of the sun, it is therefore regarded as opposed to the sun's power and as a symbol of the earth...Since the female principle is identified with the unconscious in Man, it follows that the forest is also a symbol of the unconscious.*

Emphasizing the forest as a source of knowledge, in *The Forest in Folklore and Mythology* (1928) Alexander Porteous writes: 'It has been said that the forest knows all and is able to teach all, and there is a French proverb to the effect that the forest, which always listens, has the secret of every mystery'. Udo Becker notes the forest's ambiguous character, suggesting

that, as a favoured dwelling place of hermits and ascetics, the forest represents sanctuary and provides a safe abode for concentration and contemplation.

Beginning in 1824, the English visionary artist William Blake created 102 watercolour images to illustrate an edition of Dante Alighieri's *Divine Comedy*. One of the most memorable is 'The Wood of the Self-Murderers: The Harpies and the Suicides'. Dante and Virgil enter a forest before exploring the levels of the Inferno. In the seventh circle of hell, murderers and suicides (suicide was then considered an immoral act) have been turned into nasty-looking trees and are fed on by harpies.

✳ Anselm Kiefer, *Entrance to Paradise*, 2010, mixed media. Los Angeles, CA: The Broad.

ACACIA

FAMILY Fabaceae

The acacia, native to Africa and Australia, grows throughout the temperate regions of the world. All species bear seed pods and spiny thorns. It has a number of medicinal uses and, combined with other plants, is often an ingredient in incense.

Acacia often serves as a divine attribute linked with male solar gods. Because of its hard wood, it can symbolize victory over death. It was sacred to the ancient Egyptians because of its colour, and some scholars suggest that it functioned as their Tree of Life. The creator goddess Neith resided in the tree; worshipped as early as Pre-Dynastic times, she was mother of Ra and goddess of war, weaving and hunting. The acacia's thorns were thought to repel evil.

In Judeo-Christian thought, the almost incorruptible acacia, with its sharp thorns and white or blood-red blossoms (although some species have yellow flowers), served as a solar symbol of rebirth and immortality. The Ark of the Covenant was made of gold-plated acacia (Exodus 37:1–4). It may have been the burning bush described in Exodus 3:2 and 25:10, 23; the bush instructed Moses to build the Tabernacle of acacia wood. Christ's Crown of Thorns was said to be woven from acacia. The crown has been linked with the marriage of heaven and earth – interpreted as the wedding ring of the Word (Christ) and the earth, virgin and as yet unfertile.

Acacia can be found in coats of arms, and its leaf figures in Masonic symbolism (for more information, see Hans Biedermann).

※ 'Netting Birds, Tomb of Khnumhotep' (detail), Middle Kingdom, c. 1897–1878 BCE. Facsimile by Nina de Garis Davies of painting in Tomb 3, Beni Hasan, Egypt. New York: Metropolitan Museum of Art.

※ James Watts, after E. D. Smith, *Acacia oxycedrus* (sharp-pointed acacia), 1827.

ACER PSEUDOPLATANUS / FICUS SYCOMORUS — SYCAMORE

FAMILY Sapindaceae / Moraceae

The sycamore, sometimes sycamore fig or fig-mulberry – because its leaves resemble those of the mulberry – grows in West Asia and in southern parts of Africa.

In Europe and sometimes the United States, the name refers to a type of maple (*Acer pseudoplatanus*). In the United States, a type of plane tree (*Platanus occidentalis*) is also commonly referred to as sycamore. A relative of the sycamore fig, the Moreton Bay fig (*Ficus macrophylla*), native to Australia, often reaches very large sizes.

The sycamore fig, along with the persea, served as the ancient Egyptians' Tree of Life. Since it was the only tree of any size to which they had access, they also used it to build mummy cases. The tomb of the artisan Sennedjem contains many fine paintings; in one, the regenerated Sennedjem (as indicated by his green flesh) participates in the rebirth of the sun. The calf represents the rising sun, and the god Ra-Horakhty-Atum embodies the risen sun's future triumph. The greenish-blue colour of the trees relates to the turquoise mines of the Arabian and Sinai deserts.

The sycamore was sacred to the goddesses Isis, Hathor and Nut, all of whom are depicted in tomb paintings rising out of trees and reaching out to offer sustenance to the deceased. Since some coffins were made of sycamore wood, the mummy might be thought of as being placed in the womb of a goddess. The souls of the dead,

※ Wolfgang Meyerpick, after Giorgio Liberale, *Ficus sycomorus* (Sycamore fig), 1568.

※ Brian Selznick, 'Merwin (left) and Louise (right)', from *Big Tree*, 2023.

which take the shape of birds (*ba*), rest in the trees just as the living enjoyed the shade and security of the trees. The sycamore fig is now endangered in Egypt.

In Luke (19:1–10), Zacchaeus – a wealthy and detested Jericho tax collector – wished to see Jesus as he passed through the town on the way to Jerusalem. Being short in stature, Zacchaeus was unable to see over the crowd, so he ran ahead and climbed a sycamore tree. As he passed the tree, Jesus looked up and said: 'Zacchaeus, make haste and come down, for today I must stay at your house.' Although the story has been interpreted in various ways, it can be understood as an example of Christ's mission to bring salvation to all.

Big Tree, written and illustrated by Brian Selznick, is an epic saga of cosmic history. His afterword cites the ecologist Suzanne Simard's discovery of the interconnectedness of plant life, called the 'wood-wide web'. Selznick summarizes: 'the forest in real life is not a place where individual trees grow. Rather it's an interdependent community with members that help one another survive'. Selznick notes that sycamore fossils from the Cretaceous Period (65–146 million years ago) exist, but he chose to describe and picture modern sycamores. His main characters are Merwin and Louise, who begin the book as two tiny sycamore seeds.

ADANSONIA — BAOBAB

FAMILY Malvaceae

The baobab tree, which is native to Madagascar, mainland Africa and Australia, can grow up to 30 m (100 ft) tall, with a circumference of 50 m (165 ft).

Baobabs are sometimes nicknamed 'upside down trees' for their canopy, which resembles a root system. They can live for over 1,000 years, and as a result, have become symbols of resilience and endurance. In the 2010s and 2020s, South African baobabs began to die off rapidly, possibly because of dehydration caused by global heating.

Antoine de Saint-Exupéry published *The Little Prince* in 1943, the year before he died. In the story, a pilot crash-lands in the Sahara Desert and meets the little prince, who comes from an asteroid known as B-612, where there grows a rose bush beloved by the prince, and baobab trees, which threaten to take over his planet. The pilot sees the danger of the baobabs and draws three huge, magnificent, entwined trees to warn the prince. They are said to represent fears, problems or habits that, if unchecked, grow ever larger; like the trees, they must be rooted out in a timely way to avoid disaster.

Antoine de Saint-Exupéry, *The Baobabs*, from *The Little Prince*, 1943.

Mme E. Panckoucke and P. J. F. Turpin, *Baobab*, 1833.

Lith Vayron, Baobab (*Adansonia digitata*), 1843–46.

ADANSONIA BAOBAB

BETULA — BIRCH

FAMILY Betulaceae

A deciduous hardwood tree, the birch belongs to the same family as alders, hazels and hornbeams. It serves as an ornamental tree and also has uses in folk medicine.

Birch trees are, perhaps most notably, a source of paper. The bark can be peeled and written on directly, or it can be pulped. The oldest birch-bark manuscripts date back to first-century CE India. In Germany, the inventor Johannes Gutenberg carved letters out of birch bark and wrapped them in paper while still damp; upon unwrapping them, he observed an impression on the paper. From this discovery, the art of printing evolved in Europe.

The birch tree was sacred in Russia and Siberia, as well as among the ancient Celts. Associating it with the sun and moon, the Celts believed it to be a conduit between the heavens and earth – spiritual energy descends and human aspirations ascend. Pliny described its applications in the ancient world, including for switches used by magistrates as punishment; its more positive attributes linked the tree to wedding torches and guardianship.

Gustav Klimt spent summers in Litzlberg, Austria, where he was surrounded by trees and depicted them with a powerful combination of detail and abstraction. He has been called a *Waldschrat*, a solitary wood-dweller. Seen close up in ranks in *Birch Forest*, the trees mostly block out the sky, but with no sense of claustrophobia. Instead, flickering patterns, colour and light fill the pictorial space from side to side and top to bottom in a way that is reminiscent of Byzantine mosaics.

Pancrace Bessa, White Birch (*Betula populifolia*), 1819.

Gustav Klimt, *Birch Forest*, 1903, oil on canvas. Private collection.

BETULA BIRCH

CASTANEA — CHESTNUT

FAMILY Fagaceae

The chestnut tree is a member of the beech family, as is the oak (pp. 78–81). It is native to temperate zones of the northern hemisphere.

The horse chestnut is unrelated (genus: *Aesculus*), and is so named because it produces similar-looking but toxic and inedible nuts. The true chestnut produces nuts covered with spiny husks. The trees have been cultivated since 2000 BCE and were at one time an important food source; later they fell out of favour because they came to be regarded as food for the poor. Chestnut blight has decimated about a billion American chestnuts since the beginning of the twentieth century.

One of the most fabled chestnuts is the Tree of One Hundred Horses on Mt Etna, Sicily. It is believed to be between 2,000 and 4,000 years old, despite being only 8 km (5 miles) from the volcano's crater. The name stems from a legend that a large group of horsemen, caught in a storm, was able to shelter under the canopy of the tree. In 1780, the trunk measured 58 m (190 ft) in circumference, which Guinness World Records has recorded as the 'greatest tree girth ever', although the tree has since split into multiple trunks.

Probably the most famous literary use of this genus is Henry Wadsworth Longfellow's poem 'The Village Blacksmith', which begins 'Under the spreading chestnut-tree...' In Christian art, the chestnut husk has evoked Christ's suffering. The nut itself symbolizes the Immaculate Conception; like the nut within the spiny husk, the Virgin was without thorns, surrounded – but unaffected – by Original Sin. Mary's chastity and purity were also associated with the nut, protected by the husk. The remarkable ability of the tree to regenerate after it is cut led to its association with Christ's Crucifixion and Resurrection.

Charles E. Burchfield's *Summer Solstice* was inspired in part by Julia Ellen Roger's *The Tree Book*, first published in 1905, in which he read about the Tree of One Hundred Horses. He drew and painted chestnuts as early as 1916 and even then was surely aware of their disease and death. Here, the heat of the solstice sun falls on the glowing, mysterious tree, giving it an iconic, visionary quality – alive and safe in memory.

⊗ Giorgio Gallesio, Spanish chestnut (*Castanea sativa*), 1817–39.

※ Charles E. Burchfield, *Summer Solstice* (*In Memory of the American Chestnut Tree*), 1961–66, watercolour on paper. Buffalo, NY: Burchfield Penney Art Center at SUNY Buffalo State.

OTHER CHESTNUT IMAGES
- Samuel Palmer, *A Hilly Scene*, c. 1826–28, watercolour on paper. London: Tate (see p. 220).

※

CEDRUS — CEDAR

FAMILY Pinaceae

Cedar trees comprise four species of evergreen conifer, most of them native to the Mediterranean region, where they functioned as the Tree of Life for some ancient cultures.

The tree is particularly associated with the mountains of Lebanon, where it once grew plentifully. The wood is insect-repellent and resistant to decay, and therefore very useful for building houses, fence posts and furniture, and for use in a variety of folk remedies. Its name comes from a Hebrew word meaning 'to be firm', and the tree's natural properties also made it a symbol of incorruptibility and immortality.

The ancient Egyptians used cedar wood to build ships and coffins, and for sculptures. The wooden parts of Tutankhamun's sarcophagus were carved from cedar, and this and other cedar objects were in remarkable condition when they were excavated in the early twentieth century. Cedar resin was used in mummification and to preserve papyrus documents.

In ancient Judaea, cedar wood was also used for shipbuilding, and Solomon is said to have constructed his Temple at Jerusalem of cedar. Cedar is mentioned often in the Old Testament, as when Noah is reported to have built his ark from a variety of cedars.

Greco-Roman sculptures of immortal gods and ancestors were often made from cedarwood. In Christian art, Christ has been depicted emerging from a cedar tree. The cedar is one of the four trees said to have been used to make Christ's Cross, the other three being cypress, olive and palm.

The contemporary American sculptor John Grade works in wood on a monumental scale. *Treeline* was made primarily of yellow cedar

⊗ J. J. or J. E. Haid, after Georg Dionysius Ehret, *Cedrus*, c. 1750.

✳ John Grade, *Treeline*, 2017, Alaskan yellow cedar and Metasequoia wood. Portland, OR: Karl Miller Center atrium, Portland State University.

salvaged from the building site of a new art gallery at Portland State University. Grade, who worked with PSU students on the sculpture, said: 'We had this beautiful little unusual tree standing where the new building was going to be sited, which inspired thoughts about salvaging it as material and more broadly about trees in general, longevity and legacy.' Displayed at the grand opening of the gallery, the sculpture hangs 3 m (10 ft) above the ground and is 9.5 m high, 3.5 m wide and 3 m deep (31 × 12 × 10 ft). By recycling cedar and other woods, Grade dramatizes the plight of trees and can be said to be recreating and rejuvenating trees that would otherwise die.

CITRUS × AURANTIUM — ORANGE

FAMILY Rutaceae

Oranges are the fruit of various citrus species, a hybrid between pomelo and mandarin. They originated in Asia, and are first mentioned in Chinese literature in 314 BCE.

The sweet orange accounts for about 70 per cent of citrus production worldwide and includes Valencia, navel and blood oranges. Oranges are of great economic importance, supplying fruit, juice, oils, jams/jellies and orange peel, all rich sources of vitamin C and other nutrients.

It is possible that the golden apples of the Hesperides were oranges (see 'Apple', p. 174).

Images of the Virgin and her retinue sometimes contain orange trees, their white blossom symbolizing purity. In Cosmè Tura's *Madonna and Child in a Garden* (*c*. 1455), two orange trees can be seen behind Mary, signifying her virginity. The oranges are green, possibly because the Christ Child is still an infant. Other flowers adorn the foreground, probably also symbols of the Virgin. Botticelli's *Primavera* (p. 90) contains some of the most beautiful orange trees in art, linked with the Virgin Mary as well as with marriage, since it was probably commissioned to celebrate a Medici wedding.

In *The Orchard*, an Art Nouveau tapestry by the designer John Henry Dearle of Morris & Co., female figures and plants symbolize the seasons: summer, at the far left, has fully laden orange trees and assorted flowers. A poem composed by William Morris appears on a banner that unfurls across the tapestry. Here, the orange trees seem to have been chosen to demonstrate the bounty of nature.

The custom of using orange blossom in weddings dates from the Crusades, when

✻ William Morris and John Henry Dearle, 'Summer' (detail) from *The Orchard*, also called *The Seasons*, 1890, tapestry. London: Victoria and Albert Museum.

✻ *Citrus x Aurantium*, 1831.

✻ John Everett Millais, *The Bridesmaid*, 1851, oil on panel. Cambridge, UK: Fitzwilliam Museum.

OTHER ORANGE IMAGES
- Cosmè Tura, *Madonna and Child in a Garden*, c. 1455, tempera on panel. Washington, DC: National Gallery of Art.

Europeans saw Arab brides wearing orange blossom as a double symbol of virginity and fecundity, since both flowers and fruit can appear on the tree at the same time. Eventually, the practice spread throughout Europe and to North America. Both brides and bridal attendants wore these fragrant flowers. But the fruit of the orange was also linked with marriage and fertility. In John Everett Millais's *The Bridesmaid*, a plate at the bottom of the painting holds an orange and a piece of wedding cake. Having been served the cake, according to folk tradition, the bridesmaid will pass a morsel through a ring and place it under her pillow in the hope of dreaming of her future spouse.

CITRUS × LIMON

LEMON

FAMILY Rutaceae

The lemon is a small evergreen tree native to Asia and northeastern India. Its fruit is used in cooking and baking, and the juice is an effective cleaning agent.

According to some sources, Alexander the Great brought lemons to Greece; they arrived in Europe no later than the second century CE, and the first substantial cultivation occurred in Genoa in the fifteenth century. The fruit was believed to have healing properties, to act as a disinfectant and to work as an antidote to poison.

The Greeks believed that lemon trees celebrated the marriage of Zeus and Hera. The Romans certainly knew the plant, since it appeared in Pompeiian frescoes, but it probably wasn't widespread at that point. By the Italian Renaissance, lemons appear in paintings of the Garden of Eden, symbolizing redemption and immortality. A trellis supporting a lemon shrub forms the background of Antonio da Correggio's *Virgin and Child with the Young St John the Baptist*. Expanding on his treatment of the shift towards realism as a celebration of God's creation, Giovanni Aloi notes that the lemon fruit's brilliant yellow colour linked it to the sun. Lemons were also associated with the Virgin Mary.

In the eighteenth and nineteenth-century Netherlands, lemons were linked with fidelity

✣ Charles Dessalines D'Orbigny, *Citrus Limonium*, 1892.

✣ Antonio da Correggio, *Virgin and Child with the Young St John the Baptist* (detail), c. 1515, oil on panel. Chicago, IL: Art Institute of Chicago.

✣ Maria Margaretha van Os, *Still Life with Lemon and Cut Glass*, 1823–26, oil on panel. Amsterdam: Rijksmuseum.

and may also have symbolized the passage of time. They show up in still-life paintings, often with a long curl of peel that allowed the artist to display their skill for the admiration of their patrons. The art historian Mariët Westermann suggests that the lemon indicated that one had arrived in society.

OTHER LEMON IMAGES
- Domenico Ghirlandaio, *The Last Supper*, 1480, fresco. Florence: refectory of the Convent of the Ognissanti.
- Willem Claesz. Heda, *Still Life with a Gilt Cup*, 1635, oil on panel. Amsterdam: Rijksmuseum.

CONIUM / TSUGA — HEMLOCK

FAMILY Apiaceae | Pinaceae

Hemlock refers to both a flowering plant of the carrot family and a tree of the pine family. Native to Europe and North Africa, the plant – which is famously poisonous – can reach heights of up to 3.5 m (12 ft).

Wild carrot, a plant from the same family, is less tall and has hairy stems without hemlock's purple blotches; giant hogweed and cow parsley, which has paler, weaker stems and tiny green leaves, are other plants in the genus.

Hemlock's deadliness has led to it symbolizing treason and death. In ancient Greece, it was used to poison condemned prisoners, the most famous being the philosopher Socrates.

The name also refers to several species in a genus of conifers found in North America and East Asia, so-called because the crushed foliage – which is harmless – smells like poison hemlock. The North American hemlock is seriously threatened by a sap-sucking insect and, in many places, has died out.

In a famous legend of the Northwest Coast Native American people, a great chief was the only one with light, which he kept hidden in a treasure box, causing great suffering for humanity. The trickster Raven disguised himself as a hemlock needle; when the chief's daughter swallowed the needle, she became pregnant, and Raven was born as a human child. The child cried until he was given the box.

- Hemlock (left) and fine-leaved water hemlock (right), 1772–93.
- Jacques-Louis David, *The Death of Socrates* (detail), 1787, oil on canvas. New York: Metropolitan Museum of Art.

Raven, reverting to bird form, opened the box, bringing into the open the light of the sun (shown as a mask in George Hunt Jr's print, overleaf), the moon and the stars, thus illuminating the world.

In 2006, the contemporary conceptual and installation artist Mark Dion completed *Neukom Vivarium*, a large work focused on ecosystems and extinction. With extensive help from donors, he installed an 18.3 m (60 ft) fallen Western hemlock in a purpose-built greenhouse. The tree acts as a nurse log for bacteria, fungi, insects, lichen and plants. Visitors can enter this 'art system' and study it with magnifying glasses and tiles that identify its features. Dion states:

I think that one of the important things about this work is that it's really not an intensely positive, back-to-nature kind of experience. In some ways, this project is an abomination. We're taking a tree that is an ecosystem – a dead tree, but a living system – and we are re-contextualizing it and taking it to another site. We're putting it in a sort of Sleeping Beauty coffin, a greenhouse we're building around it. And we're pumping it up with a life support system – an incredibly complex system of air, humidity, water, and soil enhancement –

- George Hunt Jr., *Raven Releasing the Sun*, 1985, silkscreen on paper. Seattle, WA: Seattle Art Museum.
- Mark Dion, *Seattle Vivarium*, 2002, coloured pencil on paper.
- Mark Dion, *Neukom Vivarium*, 2006, mixed-media installation. Seattle, WA: Olympic Sculpture Park.

to keep it going. All those things are substituting what nature does, emphasizing how, once that's gone, it's incredibly difficult, expensive, and technological to approximate that system – to take this tree and to build the next generation of forests on it. So, this piece is in some way perverse. It shows that, despite all of our technology and money, when we destroy a natural system, it's virtually impossible to get it back. In a sense, we're building a failure.

OTHER HEMLOCK IMAGES
- William Holman Hunt, *The Light of the World*, 1853–54, oil on canvas. Oxford, UK: side chapel, Keble College. Two other versions exist: a smaller one in Manchester and a copy painted in 1900–4 in St Paul's Cathedral, London.
- Joan Mitchell, *Hemlock*, 1956, oil on canvas. New York: Whitney Museum of American Art.
- David Buckley Borden and Aaron M. Ellison, *Hemlock Hospice*, 2017–18, art–science installation and exhibition. Petersham, MA: Harvard Forest.

CORYLUS — HAZEL

FAMILY Betulaceae

The hazel, a member of the birch family, is a genus of deciduous trees and large shrubs native to the temperate northern hemisphere. The fruit is called the hazelnut, or sometimes (erroneously) the filbert.[6]

In Greek mythology, the sons of Zeus, Apollo (god of music and harmony) and Hermes (the messenger god), received gifts intended to better the human condition. Apollo's was the lyre and Hermes's a hazel wand that promoted the exchange of ideas. The wand, the so-called *caduceus*, with wings and two entwined serpents, today symbolizes communication, commerce, writing and eloquence.

A Y-shaped branch of hazel was believed to have supernatural properties, especially divination. The rod of Asclepius, god of healing, has only one snake and no wings, and the use of Hermes's *caduceus* to represent the medical profession is inaccurate.

In ancient Germanic and Nordic cultures, the hazel was sacred to Thor, god of thunder, war and strength, and Idun, goddess of life and fertility. Loki freed Idun from captivity by changing himself into a falcon and carrying her off in the shape of a hazelnut.

The hazel was sacred to the ancient Celts, who associated it with wisdom and inspiration. The tree's protective properties explain why its leaves and nuts are found in ancient burials and why it appears so often in Celtic myths.

The hazel tree appears in the Unicorn Tapestries, a series of Netherlandish tapestries made around the turn of the sixteenth century and now in the Metropolitan Museum of Art. Its presence here may offer protection from evil and even death. The unicorn, symbolizing Christ, dies, but is resurrected in the final image, appearing whole and very much alive.

According to apocryphal Christian tradition, after the expulsion from Eden, God gave Adam a hazel rod that enabled him to create any animal he wished by striking the sea. Adam first created sheep. Eve followed this by creating the wolf, which immediately devoured the sheep. In turn, Adam created the dog, thus saving his sheep and balancing out the wild and the tame. In another Christian legend, the Virgin left the sleeping Christ Child to pick strawberries for him. A viper emerged from the grass and pursued her until she sought refuge in a hazelnut bush. She declared that henceforth the hazelnut would have the power to drive off evil. This may be why Mantegna included hazelnuts in the centre panel of the San Zeno altarpiece. Hazelnuts in their husks appear on a swag of fruit above the Madonna, backed by a relief of *putti* holding a cornucopia.

⊗ Andrea Mantegna, centre panel of San Zeno altarpiece (detail), 1457–60, tempera on panel. Basilica of San Zeno, Verona.

✷ Mary Vaux Walcott, Beaked Hazelnut (*Corylus rostrata*), 1932.

OTHER HAZEL/HAZELNUT IMAGES
- *The Unicorn Is Killed and Brought to the Castle*, Unicorn Tapestries, 1495–1505, wool and silk threads. New York: The Cloisters.

CORYLUS HAZEL

CUPRESSUS — CYPRESS

FAMILY Cupressaceae

Native to the Himalayas, the cypress was introduced into the Mediterranean by the Phoenicians, who colonized the island of Cyprus, from which the tree derived its name. It has been cultivated for ornamental use and for its strong, durable timber.

The Roman poet Ovid tells of a legendary island youth named Cyparissus (a favourite of Apollo), who was accidentally killed by a large stag. Apollo was so grief-stricken that he begged the gods to let his sorrow last forever, and so they turned the youth into a cypress tree, which became a symbol of the immortal soul. In Greco-Roman myth, the tree was related to the gods of the Underworld, Hades, the Fates and the Furies. Cypress wood, believed to preserve bodies, provided the timber for some ancient Egyptian mummy cases, and the ancient Greeks built coffins of it; the tree was also planted in cemeteries.

As do all evergreens, the cypress signifies incorruptibility and immortality. Other deities associated with it include Cronos, Asclepius, Aphrodite, Athena, Artemis, Cybele, Hera and Persephone. Because Orpheus descended into the Underworld and was able to return from it, Orphic initiates believed that, upon entering

Evelyn De Morgan, *The Angel of Death I* (detail), 1880, oil on canvas. Barnsley, UK: De Morgan Collection.

Cypress tree (*Cupressus mas*), 1751.

Henri-Edmond Cross, *Coastal View with Cypress Trees*, 1896, oil on canvas. Geneva: Musée du Petit Palais.

Hades, they would encounter a cypress leaning over a fountain. They were warned not to drink from the Fountain of Lethe (oblivion) but could retain the memory of their past by imbibing from the Fountain of Mnemosyne (memory). The tree's association with death arose because the cypress, once cut, does not grow back.

In Christian art, the cypress sometimes appears in images of martyred saints. Because of its vertical thrust to the heavens, it is also linked with the Virgin Mary, Christ and the Church. Cypress trees appear in Annunciation scenes, and it was thought to have been one of the four trees used to create Christ's Cross, along with the cedar, olive and palm.

Van Gogh painted many images of the cypress, a tree that he considered characteristic of Provence. The flame-like cypress in *The Starry Night* connects the celestial heaven filled with swirling stars and an earthly village with a few lighted windows. The painting may embody an old belief that the souls of the dead travel to the stars, and the cypress provides the bridge.

OTHER CYPRESS IMAGES
- Arnold Böcklin, *Island of the Dead*, 1886, oil on wood. Leipzig: Museum der bildenden Künste.
- John Singer Sargent, *Cypress Trees at San Vigilio*, 1912, oil on canvas. Andover, MA: Addison Gallery, Phillips Academy.

FAGUS — BEECH

FAMILY Fagaceae

Beech trees, native to the temperate regions of the world, have between ten and thirteen species. Beechwood can be used in construction, but has traditionally been preferred as firewood.

The ancient Greek oracle at Dodona, while primarily sacred to the oak, sometimes used beech leaves in prophecy. The Roman writer and naturalist Pliny wrote of beech groves sacred to Diana and Juno. The beech was apparently favoured for carving lovers' names, as in Shakespeare's *As You Like It*, and has also been connected with study and knowledge because its smooth, pale bark can be written on.

Paul Nash painted trees frequently, including beeches, as well as other plants. For him, they were a mysterious part of the living world, as he wrote in 1912:

True, I have tried to paint trees as tho they were human beings. . .because I sincerely love & worship trees & know that they are people & wonderfully beautiful people. . .Do you realise the full significance of 'tree' or what it would try to mean to you: A shelter, a shade, a consoling old thing, a strong kind friend to come to.

Wittenham Clumps in Berkshire are said to be the oldest human-planted beech trees in England, at more than 280 years old. The chalky Sinodun Hills on which they stand were late

⌧ Pierre-Joseph Redouté, *Fagus silvatica*, 1801–19.

⌧ Paul Nash, *The Wood on the Hill (Wittenham Clumps)*, 1912, pen-and-ink drawing. Oxford: Ashmolean Museum.

Bronze Age hill forts, inhabited by people who herded animals and farmed wheat and barley, and the site, abandoned around 300 BCE, was later used by the Romans. Nash powerfully captured the connection between trees and landforms. His image of Wittenham Clumps conveys the continuity of life – a path, probably the remains of a Roman road, follows the contour of the hill – in both human lives and nature. Nash was only twenty-three when he made this drawing, but he produced several images of the trees, hills and path.

FICUS   FIG

FAMILY Moraceae

The common fig is a flowering plant in the mulberry family and has been known since ancient times. Native to the Mediterranean region and Asia, it is now also grown widely in North America and Europe. It is one of the earliest plants to have been cultivated by humans.

In the Greco-Roman world, the earth goddess Gaia ordered a fig tree to protect her son, the Titan Sykeus, from Zeus' thunderbolts. It is for this reason that the fig is said to be impervious to lightning strikes. The tree was also associated with the founding of Rome, since Romulus and Remus, abandoned on the Tiber River, providentially stopped beneath a fig tree.

Most garden images in the destroyed city of Pompeii are found in reception rooms, but those in the House of the Orchard occupy two smaller rooms that served for relaxation. The central painting of one room depicts a snake winding around the trunk of a fig tree, said to be a symbol of prosperity.

In Genesis, when Adam and Eve understood that they were naked, 'they sewed fig leaves together and made themselves coverings' (Genesis 3:7). Fig trees are sometimes included in depictions of the infant Jesus, where they recall the Tree of Knowledge and Adam and Eve's Fall, remedied by Christ's Crucifixion and Resurrection. This explains why Grünewald included the tree in his *Birth of Jesus*. The setting is a *hortus conclusus* (secluded garden) and the Virgin's red rose appears on the right.

The gesture known as the 'sign of the fig' – the fist with the thumb protruding between the index and middle finger – is believed to ward off the evil eye. Amulets representing the sign are made in a variety of materials, a favourite being red coral. The gesture can also be obscene, meaning sexual intercourse or contempt.

In 2022, the art historian Giovanni Aloi curated an exhibition entitled 'Lucian Freud: Plant Portraits' at the Garden Museum in London. Aloi points out that Freud painted his own potted plants – some of which embodied his family history – and gardens. Freud excluded traditional symbolism, often choosing plants that have no meaning in European traditions. He focused instead on details, creating images that treated the plants as individuals, capturing their essence. The plants move beyond the Christian symbolism of seventeenth-century art and the objectifying, legislated realism of eighteenth-century botanical illustration. As in all his art, Freud eschewed beauty, here creating small-scale, silent images that engage the viewer.

A large fig leaf conceals most of the girl's face except for her wide-open, unblinking left eye.[7] Although most of the artist's plant images lack symbolic meaning, this work may be an exception. The fig leaf's long history, from Adam and Eve's 'coverings' to concealing genitals in Renaissance images, implies sin and shame. Here the leaf covers her right eye and mouth, giving the print an enigmatic character, partially blocking vision and speech. The staring left eye may signify Freud's intense and silent study of the figures and plants.

⊗ Roman fresco from House of the Orchard or of the Floral Cubicles (detail), first century CE. Pompeii, Italy.

※ Giorgio Gallesio, *Fico Pissaluto* (*Ficus carica sativa*), 1817–39.

❖ Lucian Freud, *Girl with a Fig Leaf*, 1947, etching. Private collection.

OTHER FIG TREE IMAGES
- Hieronymus Bosch, *The Garden of Earthly Delights* (left panel), 1490–1500, oil on oak. Madrid: Museo del Prado.

FICUS FIG

FRAXINUS — ASH

FAMILY Oleaceae

The ash is a candidate for the World Tree (p. 24), the tree that grows at the centre of the universe, houses all life and connects all realms. According to Norse myth, the Great Mother/Goddess was born from the elm, and her consort from the ash.

During the troubled late 1970s, the sculptor David Nash planted a circle of twenty-two ash trees near his home in Wales. Of the circle, which is still growing today, he says:

To make a gesture by planting something for the twenty-first century, which was what Ash Dome is about, was a long-term commitment, an act of faith. I did not know what I was letting myself in for.

The dense wood of the European ash was used to make tools. It was also important in folklore and medicine; belief in its healing powers gave rise to the ritual of passing sick children through clefts in the trunk, and its leaves, bark and sap were used to treat various ailments.

A fungal pathogen from East Asia, first identified in Britain in 2012, may result in the death of eighty per cent of English ash trees in a matter of decades. One can only hope that Nash's circle survives. A similar threat currently affects the ash in the United States and Canada, but the cause is a beetle, the emerald ash borer. Introduced from Asia in 2002, it kills all species of North American ash. So far it has wiped out tens of millions of ash trees in twenty-five states, and it is advancing westwards. Although treatments are available for individual trees, the scope of the problem makes prevention close to impossible.

⊗ David Nash, *Ash Dome*, 1977. Eryri/Snowdonia, Wales: closely guarded secret location.

❋ H. Fletcher, after J. van Huysum, Flowering ash (*Fraxinus ornus* L.): flowering stem, c. 1730.

ILEX
HOLLY

FAMILY Aquifoliaceae

These evergreen flowering plants – trees, shrubs and climbers – are found in the tropics and temperate zones worldwide.

Holly was sacred to Saturn, the Roman god of agriculture, and featured in Saturnalia, which was celebrated in mid-December. In medieval European survivals of Saturnalia, three kings – oak, ivy and holly – symbolized wildness and the eternal and enduring forces of nature. When paired with ivy (pp. 212–13), holly has been said to symbolize the male principle in nature and the return of light and life. The being associated with holly, also known as the Green Knight or Wildman, appears in the thirteenth-century long poem *Sir Gawain and the Green Knight*. A huge, mysterious green being appears at an Arthurian New Year's Eve feast riding a mammoth green horse, holding a holly branch in one hand and an axe in the other. There are many translations of the poem, and various interpretations have been offered. It has been understood as involving the opposition of nature and culture, an interpretation relevant to the environmental challenges that are currently facing the world.

In Germany, holly berries symbolized the life-giving blood of the Teutonic Underworld goddess Holle, and its evergreen leaves signified immortality. As a Mother Goddess, Holle was a patron of newborns and named them, an equivalent to giving them their souls.

Holly leaves symbolized Christ's Crown of Thorns, and its berries stood for his blood. It has also been linked with St Jerome and John the Baptist, both of whom were connected with Christ's Passion. The ubiquitous appearance of holly in Christmas decorations, like that of mistletoe, combines its Christian and pre-Christian symbolism.

- Rebecca Hey, Holly, 1837.

- Carlton Alfred Smith, *Christmas Eve* (detail), 1901, oil on canvas. Private collection.

- *The Unicorn Surrenders to a Maiden* (detail), Unicorn Tapestries, 1495–1505, wool and silk threads. New York: The Cloisters.

ILEX HOLLY

JUNIPERUS — JUNIPER

FAMILY Cupressaceae

These coniferous trees in the cypress family are widely distributed throughout the northern hemisphere and grow at some of the highest altitudes of any tree.

Some junipers are given the common name cedar and widely used as timber. Juniper berries are used as a spice, as an essential oil, in herbal remedies and for flavouring alcoholic drinks like gin and jenever. Its oldest recorded use – 1500 BCE – was in ancient Egypt, where its berries were used to treat tapeworm. The Romans used juniper berries for purification and stomach ailments.

The juniper has long been associated with chastity, because its berries are protected by thorny leaves, much as the chestnut is protected by its husk. Pliny wrote of the tree's incorruptibility, giving as an example a Spanish temple in perfect condition, sacred to Artemis, that had been built of juniper beams some 200 years before the Trojan War. This symbolism continued in Christian art, where it sometimes appears in Nativity scenes, while the tree's thorny leaves recall Christ's Passion and the Crown of Thorns. In portraiture its presence sometimes relates to the sitter's name, as in

Leonardo's *Portrait of Ginevra de' Benci* (1474–75), which features a juniper on the reverse.

The Brothers Grimm are believed to have adapted the fairytale entitled 'The Juniper Tree' from the German Romantic artist Philipp Otto Runge. It is indeed a grim tale involving an evil stepmother, murder and unwitting cannibalism. The tree itself serves as a burial place. Illustrated volumes include images of the tree; the English artist Walter Crane contributed one showing a bird arising from the tree, implying the survival of the soul (1882).

The Canadian artist and writer Emily Carr painted trees over and over again. Junipers as well as other trees signify the spiritual connection and boundless energy she found in nature – as is clear from a passage in her journal:

Go into the woods alone and look at the earth crowded with growth, new and old bursting from their strong roots hidden in the silent, live ground, each seed according to its own kind expanding, bursting, pushing its way upward toward the light and air, each one knowing what to do, each one demanding its own rights on the earth.

⊗ Pierre-Joseph Redouté, *Juniperus communis* (Common juniper), *Juniperus oxycedrus* (Prickly juniper), 1801–19.

✻ Emily Carr, *A Rushing Sea of Undergrowth*, 1935, oil on canvas. Vancouver, British Columbia: Vancouver Art Gallery, Emily Carr Trust.

LAURUS   LAUREL

FAMILY Lauraceae

The laurel – also known as bay laurel, sweet bay or true laurel – is an evergreen shrub or small tree. Native to the Mediterranean, it now grows worldwide.

It is commonly an ornamental plant, and its leaves are used for seasoning, as well as having medicinal purposes. The bay leaf is sometimes categorized as a herb.

In ancient Greece, the plant was called *daphne*, after the nymph of the same name. Apollo pursued her, and she pleaded with Gaia, Mother Earth, who transported her to Crete and left a laurel tree in her place. Ovid says that she was immediately transformed into a tree. Apollo took the laurel as a personal symbol, and so it came to symbolize inspiration and immortal fame. Laurel leaves and crowns adorn artists, athletes, rulers, soldiers and philosophers, and the modern title Laureate means 'laurel-crowned one'. Laurel is associated with several other Greco-Roman deities: Artemis, Dionysus, Hera and Zeus; the priestesses of the Delphic oracle chewed its leaves to promote prophecies.

One of the most memorable depictions of Ovid's story can be found in Piero del Pollaiuolo's *Apollo and Daphne* of about 1470–80 at the National Gallery, London. Daphne is shown undergoing transformation, her arms sprouting into leafy branches. Apollo appears as an aristocratic youth, and the scene is set in the Florentine countryside. The painting is small and would probably have been kept in a velvet bag when not on display. The museum's

- Girolamo dai Libri, *Madonna and Child with Saints*, *c.* 1520, tempera and oil on canvas. New York: Metropolitan Museum of Art.

- William Clark, Bay laurel (*Laurus nobilis*), 1834.

- Lorenzo Lotto, *Venus and Cupid* (detail), 1520, oil on canvas. New York: Metropolitan Museum of Art.

caption mentions the literary connection to Petrarch's fourteenth-century verses about the unattainable Laura, a platonic passion that became the ideal form of courtly love and the pursuit of beauty. The laurel tree and its leaves were sometimes also included in portraits of individuals who shared the plant's name: Laura or Lorenzo, for example.

The subject of Daphne and Apollo would be incomplete without mention of Gian Lorenzo Bernini's breathtaking sculpture (1622–25), now in the Galleria Borghese, Rome. Here, too, Daphne is caught mid-transformation, and marble mimics bark, slowly embracing her leg and her hair, while her fingertips sprout leaves.

The tree's symbolism of immortality also featured in Christian art. The Virgin Mary's intimate connection with the plant inspired Girolamo dai Libri to place her and the infant Jesus under the tree in his painting *Madonna and Child with Saints*. In Renaissance works such as Lorenzo Lotto's *Venus and Cupid*, Venus holds a laurel crown; in others, winged, allegorical figures of Victory convey laurel crowns.

See also 'Mullein', pp. 200–1, for a discussion of the laurel in Bellini's *St Francis in the Desert*.

OLEA — OLIVE

FAMILY Oleaceae

Evergreen olive trees are cultivated in all countries in the Mediterranean basin, as well as in the Americas, Africa, China and Australia.

The fruit, also called the olive, is of major agricultural importance, olive oil being a core ingredient of Mediterranean cuisine. The tree may have originated some 20–40 million years ago.

The olive tree, together with its fruit and oil, is replete with symbolism: peace, fruitfulness, purification, strength, victory and reward. A small replica of an olive branch in gold was left on the moon by the astronauts of NASA's *Apollo 11* in 1969 to represent the wish for peace on earth.

According to Greek legend, Athena and Poseidon competed for the honour of giving a name to a newly created city. Poseidon threw his trident and a salty spring issued forth – or, according to some versions, a horse. Athena struck the ground with her spear and an olive tree sprang up. The gods declared Athena the winner, since her tree symbolized peace as well as being more useful, and the city was named Athens. Descendants of the original tree are said to flourish on the Acropolis today. Victors in Athena's Panathenaic games were crowned with wreaths of olive leaves. The sacred grove at Olympia was made up of olive trees, and

※ Benoît Chirat, Olive (*Olea europea*): fruiting branch, *c.* 1850.

❋ Attic red-figure *skyphos* with Athena's owl and olive, *c.* mid-fifth century BCE. New York: Metropolitan Museum of Art.

❖ Vincent van Gogh, *Olive Trees*, 1889, oil on canvas. Minneapolis, MN: Minneapolis Institute of Art.

branches were presented to the winners of the games.

In the Torah the olive branch symbolizes safety, since when the dove returned with it, Noah knew the waters of the Great Flood had abated. Olive oil is poured on troubled waters; Jacob poured oil on the stone of Bethel after his dream of the ladder extending to heaven, and in Hebrew *messiah* means 'the anointed one'. Olive oil was used to treat wounds and, mixed with balsam and aromatic herbs, made the chrism (consecrated oil) used for Christian baptism, confirmation, holy orders and the anointing of the sick.

OTHER OLIVE IMAGES
- Dove and olive branch, fourth century CE, fresco. Catacomb of San Lorenzo, Rome.
- El Greco, *Christ in the Olive Garden*, c. 1600, oil on canvas. Lille, France: Palais des Beaux-Arts.

PHOENIX / PALM

FAMILY Arecaceae

There are many different species of palm, though this entry refers primarily to the genus *Phoenix*, the date palm.

Important as a food source in the ancient Mediterranean, the palm has long been a candidate for the Tree of Life, since it grows in arid lands and desert oases. Almost universally, palm branches symbolize triumph, victory and immortality.

The Egyptian date palm was a sacred tree, its branches symbolizing the god Heh, the personification of eternity. The god held a palm branch with several notches, each symbolizing a year, so that the branch signified never-ending life. This meaning also applies to Virgil's *Aeneid* and to the Eleusinian Mysteries of ancient Greece. In Greco-Roman culture the palm served as a symbol of military success – a meaning shared by many later societies – and Romans returning victorious from campaigns were met with palm bearers, as was Christ when he entered Jerusalem.

Images of martyred saints bear palms as a symbol of their triumph over death. A fourth-century Roman martyr born into a wealthy family, St Lucy was persecuted, tortured and killed for attempting to distribute her riches to the poor. Lucy's story was expanded in the thirteenth-century *Golden Legend*, a collection of lives of the saints. Her captors had gouged out her eyes, but while her body was being prepared for burial, they were miraculously restored. Lucy is thus the patron saint of the blind and of those suffering from eye ailments. In Francesco del Cossa's painting, Lucy holds the martyr's palm in one hand and, in the other, her eyes, which look rather like strange little flowers on a single stem.

The Virgin Mary's association with the palm comes from the Song of Solomon (7:8): 'This stature of yours is like a palm tree, and your breasts like its clusters.' The Archangel Gabriel sometimes holds palm fronds in Annunciation scenes, and they appear again in the Virgin's death scenes. She apparently asked that they be carried in her funeral procession.

Images depicting the Holy Family's journey to Egypt usually include a palm bending so that Joseph could pick the fruit. The story of

the flight is told briefly in Matthew 2:13–18, without mention of the palm tree. A more complete version appears in the apocryphal eighth–ninth-century Pseudo-Matthew, chapter 20. Images of the flight were popular with Renaissance and Baroque artists, such as Caravaggio, Gerard David, Albrecht Dürer, Lucas van Leyden, Hans Memling, Joachim Patinir and Martin Schongauer. Not all the elements of Pseudo-Matthew's text are included; other types of tree are sometimes substituted, since many European artists had never seen a palm. Indeed, most of the landscapes look decidedly un-Egyptian.

Fr. Eugen Köhler, *Areca catechu* (Areca palm), 1890.

Francesco del Cossa, *Saint Lucy*, c. 1473–74, tempera on panel. Washington, DC: National Gallery of Art.

OTHER PALM IMAGES
- Funeral ritual in a garden, facsimile by Charles K. Wilkinson of an image from the Tomb of Minnakht, Egypt, c. 1479–1425 BCE. New York: Metropolitan Museum of Art.
- Martin Schongauer, *The Flight into Egypt*, c. 1470–75, engraving. Washington, DC: National Gallery of Art.
- Andrea del Verrocchio and Leonardo da Vinci, *The Baptism of Christ*, c. 1470–75, tempera and oil on panel. Florence: Le Gallerie degli Uffizi.

PINUS — PINE

FAMILY Pinaceae

Pines are evergreen, coniferous trees native to the northern hemisphere and may live for 1,000 years or more ('Methuselah', a bristlecone pine, is said to be about 4,600 years old).

They are thought to have evolved about 153 million years ago. Outside the wild, pines are grown largely for timber, harvested when the trees reach twenty-five years of age. Pines were used medicinally in China, and pine nuts are an important by-product. The word 'pine' can be traced to an Indo-European root word meaning 'resin'. Before the nineteenth century, pines were often referred to as fir trees.

In common with all evergreen trees, the pine and pine cones symbolize immortality. Many myths tell of the transformation of the dead into pine trees, and the rustling of their needles has been said to be the voices of gods. In Greece and Rome, the pine was sacred to Cybele, a fertility goddess. The Roman cult of Cybele conducted a multi-day spring ritual in which a pine was cut down and carried to the Palatine Temple, where it was bandaged like a corpse and wreathed with violets to represent the body of Cybele's lover Attis. On the final day, the rebirth of Attis was celebrated with great rejoicing.

Pine cones appear in art all over the world, usually with meanings of fertility and immortality. The ancient Egyptians depicted a pine cone encircled by twin cobras atop the staff of the god Osiris. Some scholars have claimed that pine cones also adorned the top of the ivy-entwined staff – the *thyrsus* – carried by Dionysus and his maenads, but more recently that shape has been linked with the artichoke (p. 166). The world's largest pine cone was created or commissioned by the Roman

Caspar David Friedrich, *Winter Landscape*, probably 1811, oil on canvas. London: National Gallery.

Publius Cincius Salvius, whose name appears on its base. The bronze cone was 3.4 m (11 ft) tall, and probably graced a fountain, water being another symbol of fertility. Unearthed near the Pantheon, the sculpture was moved in 1608 to the Vatican's Cortile della Pigna, where it now rests at the top of a double staircase designed by Michelangelo.

The pine tree was also important among the ancient Celts and possibly provided one of the letters in the ogham alphabet. There is a Germanic story about a church steeple bent by the wind and subsequently straightened by a shepherd, who attached it to a pine and uttered invocations. In 1492, the Virgin Mary is said to have appeared in a pine tree and spoken to the bishop of Gran Canaria. The basilica that was built as a result of this revelation contains an extraordinary statue of the Virgin (patron saint of the island) that is thought to have healing properties.

One of the miracles of St Francis of Assisi involved a pine. Taking refuge on the island of San Francesco del Deserto in the Venetian lagoon during a storm, Marilyn Aronberg Lavin, Jinyu Liu and Adam Gitner write that the saint is said to have taken a limb of pine to serve as a walking stick: 'Before leaving the island, Francis planted his staff in the ground where it miraculously germinated, becoming a pine tree that grew to an extraordinary height.' The island subsequently housed a Franciscan monastery, and the tree 'flourished in the monastery cloister until it had to be taken down. The remains now rest in a side chapel.' Lavin, Liu and Gitner suggest that the story serves as a metaphor for Francis's spreading of the holy word.

The symbolism of the pine continued to be evident in Romantic art, as in the work of the German artist Caspar David Friedrich.

In *Winter Landscape*, a group of conifers occupies the foreground, their shape repeated in the misty silhouette of a church in the background. Having cast his crutches aside, a man rests against a boulder and prays before a crucifix standing in the trees. Taken together, the dawn light, church, cross and trees symbolize hope and rebirth. The trees are identified as firs on the National Gallery website; however, because of their clustered needles, they are likely to be pines.

The pine cone has been associated with the third eye and the pineal gland, defined by Merriam-Webster's Dictionary as follows: 'a small, typically cone-shaped structure in the brain that arises from the third ventricle, is enclosed by the pia mater, and functions primarily as an endocrine gland secreting the sleep-influencing hormone melatonin'. Thought to be a vestigial eye, the pineal gland became associated with enlightenment, as did its pine-cone-like shape. Both the pine cone and the third eye figure in Masonic symbolism.

The pine cone also forms a perfect logarithmic (or equiangular) spiral. This pattern is found frequently in nature, such as in the growth of plants – in cacti, the seeds of the sunflower (pp. 114–17), and elsewhere – the chambered nautilus and spiral galaxies. The spiral's beauty, energy and endlessness probably explain the frequency with which pine cones appear in symbolic art.

※ Jersey pine (*Pinus inops*), 1837.

PRUNUS AMYGDALUS — ALMOND

FAMILY Rosaceae

Native to Iran and surrounding regions in West Asia and North Africa, almond trees are now cultivated elsewhere. The tree is one of the earliest domesticated, beginning around 3000 BCE.

A traditional symbol of sweetness and delicacy, almond trees are among the first to bloom in the spring and are therefore vulnerable to frost. The precise knowledge of the plant's life cycle acquired by its early farmers led to its symbolism: the tree's early bloom makes it a symbol of rebirth, survival and immortality.

In Jewish folklore, the almond fruit is regarded as female and the tree as male. The word *luz* means almond, and is also the name of a mysterious city, one of the 'Seats of the Immortals', which can be accessed at the foot of an almond tree. Thus, the tree is associated with immortality. In Exodus (25:31–40), God reveals the design of the golden menorah to Moses – it was to have cups shaped like almond flowers with buds and blossoms. The menorah from the Second Temple was carried off by the Romans in 70 CE, and it is depicted among the spoils of war on the Arch of Titus in Rome. Moses's elder brother Aaron's rod of almond wood, a symbol of authority, flowered, signifying divine favour, and in Jewish art, the almond is a symbol of Aaron. In the Christian New Testament, Joseph's rod also flowered, with the same symbolism; by extension, it signified the Virgin's purity.

The almond nut signifies awakening, revival, spring, hope, divine approval, virginity and fruitfulness. As Jean Chevalier puts it,

⊗ Giorgio Gallesio, Almond, 1817-39.

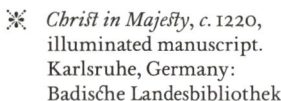

✳ *Christ in Majesty*, *c*. 1220, illuminated manuscript. Karlsruhe, Germany: Badische Landesbibliothek.

PRUNUS AMYGDALUS ALMOND

❖ Vincent van Gogh, *Almond Blossom*, 1890, oil on canvas. Amsterdam: Van Gogh Museum.

'in common parlance', to eat an almond means to have sexual intercourse. He also suggests that passing from its secular to sacred symbolism serves only to strengthen its connotation of the primordial womb, the beginning of time and creation.

Myth has it that the Greek and Phrygian god of vegetation, Attis, was conceived from an almond. The Greek traveller Pausanias recounts a complex story of abandonment, madness, self-castration, death and rebirth – all from an almond. Almond oil was also linked with Zeus, regarded as his seed.

Mandorla, the Italian word for almond, describes the almond-shaped halo of light surrounding the body of Christ and other holy beings. The mandorla first appeared in the fifth-century mosaics of the Church of Santa Maria Maggiore in Rome. From the sixth until the early fifteenth century, it became common in depictions of the Transfiguration and many other Christian subjects. It is often found in Eastern Orthodox art and in medieval architectural sculpture, where the frame may be adorned with decorative mouldings filled with inscriptions or symbols, such as Alpha and Omega (A and Ω), stars and/or flowers (such as the five-petalled almond blossom), but the device was abandoned by Renaissance artists as being unrealistic.

The mandorla can also take the form of a lens (the intersection of two circles) called the *vesica piscis* (Latin for 'bladder of a fish'). The *ichthys* (fish), the secret symbol of early Christians, consisted of similarly intersecting arcs, extending on one side to create the fish's tail. The Greek letters were additionally linked with Christ's name (I=Iesous/Jesus, C=Christos, Q=Theou/God's, U=Uios/Son, S=Soter/Saviour).

The almond within its skin symbolizes Christ – the divine nature hidden within the human form. More generally, the almond in its skin signifies substance hidden by external accident: spirituality masked by dogma and ritual, reality concealed by appearance, the yet-to-be-revealed truth.

Probably the most famous almond blossom in the history of art is the charming painting Van Gogh created for his newborn nephew and namesake, born in early 1890, drawing on the early-blooming tree's symbolism of spring and abundant yet vulnerable new life. The artist wrote to his own mother:

How glad I was when the news came...I should have greatly preferred him [Vincent's brother Theo] to call the boy after Father, of whom I have been thinking so much these days, instead of after me; but seeing it has now been done, I started right away to make a picture for him, to hang in their bedroom, big branches of white almond blossom against a blue sky.

Theo elected to hang the painting over the piano after Vincent sent it to Paris in April. The artist's viewpoint is unusual; the blossoms are shown close up, as if seen from below. One need not look far to see it as a new flowering of the Van Gogh family tree. The Van Gogh Museum website entry states: 'Unsurprisingly, it was this work that remained closest to the hearts of the Van Gogh family.'

QUERCUS — OAK

FAMILY Fagaceae

Native to the northern hemisphere, oaks can be either deciduous or evergreen. North America has the most oak species, spread throughout the United States and Mexico. Oaks' fruit are called acorns, and both leaves and acorns are poisonous to livestock when consumed in large amounts.

※ Pierre-Joseph Redouté, *Quercus robur* (Pedunculate Oak, Truffle Oak, Common Oak, English Oak, Irish Dair), 1801–19.

※ Samuel Palmer, *Oak Tree and Beech, Lullingstone Park*, 1828, pen-and-ink drawing. New York: Morgan Library and Museum.

※ Patricia Day, *Whispering Oak*, 2023, pastel on paper. Courtesy of the artist.

Ancient cultures venerated the oak because it was widely believed to be the first tree, from which humans sprang. Its sacred status among the Hebrews stemmed from the meeting of Abraham and the angel beneath an oak. In Greco-Roman culture, the oak functioned as the World Tree. The presence of oaks at the oracle at Dodona linked the tree and its fruit, the acorn, to the king of the gods, Zeus or Jupiter, as well as to thunder, lightning and rain. It also stood for the Roman goddess Diana and the 'Kings of the Wood', her lovers.

Ancient Egyptian tomb paintings and mummy cases show crowns made of oak leaves and acorns, and some ancient rulers also wore oak crowns. Roman soldiers who saved civilians received a prestigious crown formed of oak leaves and acorns. The acorn was also important in Greco-Roman culture, since the oak was sacred to Zeus, representing strength and immortality. Many museum collections contain gold acorn jewelry, and some of the pendants may have originally adorned wreaths similar to the one illustrated overleaf, which may also reflect Egyptian models. Soldiers carried acorns into battle for protection, and women wore them to preserve their youthfulness.

In a Catholic context, the acorn symbolizes the power of the spirit and the virtue of truth, which probably explains the acorns on the cords of Catholic cardinals' hats, said to signify

the spiritual growth that comes from a kernel of truth.

Sacred to Thor among the Teutons of northern Europe, the oak also served as the Tree of Life there. The oak's identification as the Tree of Life continued after the rise of Christianity, and, because its wood was held to be incorruptible, it came to symbolize immortality. Its attributes of strength, longevity and steadfastness made it an analogue of the Christian faith in the face of adversity.

Samuel Palmer's *Oak Tree and Beech, Lullingstone Park* was commissioned by his friend and mentor, the painter John Linnell. The artist's approach appears to be distinctly anthropomorphic. In a letter, he described the tree as having a 'muscular belly and shoulders; the twisted sinews'. After meeting William

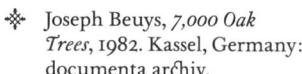

- Joseph Beuys, *7,000 Oak Trees*, 1982. Kassel, Germany: documenta archiv.

- Gold funerary wreath, imperial Rome, first or second century CE. New York: Metropolitan Museum of Art.

OTHER OAK IMAGES
- Caspar David Friedrich, *Abtei im Eichwald* (*Abbey among Oak Trees*), 1809/10, oil on canvas. Berlin: Alte Nationalgalerie.
- Limbourg Brothers, 'November', from the *Belles Heures* of Jean de France, Duc de Berry, 1405–8/9, tempera, gold and ink on vellum. New York: The Cloisters.
- Frida Kahlo, *Portrait of Luther Burbank*, 1931, oil on panel. Mexico City: Museo Dolores Olmedo.

Blake, Palmer combined naturalism with a visionary approach, resulting in memorable Romantic images. In this drawing, the close-up details powerfully suggest strength, endurance and longevity.

Joseph Beuys's *7,000 Oak Trees* project began with a mound of black basalt rocks piled in front of a museum in Kassel. From above, the rocks formed an arrow pointing at a single oak tree. Beuys said a rock could be moved from the pile, but only if a tree were planted next to it. In 1982, the artist, with the help of volunteers, started planting 7,000 trees; the work was completed on the anniversary of Beuys's death in 1987 by his son. Initially controversial, the project is now a valued part of Kassel's cityscape. In a conversation with the gallerist Richard Demarco, Beuys said of the project:

I think the tree is an element of regeneration which in itself is a concept of time. The oak is especially so because it is a slowly growing tree with a kind of really solid heartwood. It has always been a form of sculpture, a symbol of this planet...The tree planting enterprise provides a very simple but radical possibility...when we start with the seven thousand oaks.

The contemporary artist Patricia Day lives on the edge of a ravine populated by California live oaks. Her recent work focuses on trees, especially the oaks' entwined structure, strength and resilience despite urban pollution and the threat of fire.

SALIX   WILLOW

FAMILY Salicaceae

Willows, also called sallows (for those with broad leaves) and osiers (narrow leaves), are a group of deciduous trees and shrubs primarily found in moist soils in the northern hemisphere.

Willow bark has been known since 500 BCE as an analgesic because of its high concentration of salicylic acid, the ingredient in aspirin.

Willow symbolism, while not uniform, encompasses water, grief, healing and eternal life. The willow is also sometimes linked to the moon.

The ancient Egyptians saw the willow as sacred and protective, and linked it with miraculous births. Osiris was found in a willow clump, and Moses, abandoned at birth, was discovered floating safely on the Nile in a willow basket. In ancient Greece and Rome, both Homer and Pliny attached negative symbolism to the willow, holding it to be infertile, since it sheds fruit before it ripens. The goddess Hera was said to have been born on the island of Samos under a willow tree, which was long preserved in her temple there.

The willow is one of four trees associated with the Jewish Feast of Tabernacles (Leviticus 23:40). Participants circle the Torah table seven times, then strike the ground with willow branches; the branches symbolize repentance, and the action signifies the beating out of sin.

In Christian art, the tree was both positive (symbolizing faith and the faithful) and negative (sin and grief). The negative reading comes from Psalms, and the positive from Isaiah 44:4, in which God promises Jacob to bless his descendants: '[who] will spring up among the grass like willows by the watercourses'.

The weeping willow is associated with death in Western art. Favoured in the nineteenth century as an embroidery image, the weeping

⊗ Gravestone with weeping willow, nineteenth century. Rainham, Kent.

✻ Babylon Willow (*Salix Babylon*), n.d.

⊗

willow sometimes adorned *memento mori* samplers complete with the name and date of the deceased. It also appears frequently as a motif of grief and loss on Victorian gravestones.

The popular blue 'Willow Pattern' was obtained from Chinese sources by Minton, an English ceramics firm, in 1780. The design includes a story of forbidden love, elopement, pursuit by a parent and, finally, the transformation of the lovers into turtle doves.

Willow branches were used as divining rods to locate water, presumably because willows like to have their roots wet and grow prolifically near rivers and streams.

OTHER WILLOW IMAGES
- Albrecht Dürer, *St Jerome Seated Near a Pollard Willow Tree*, 1512, drypoint print. London: British Museum.
- Mary Bechler, mourning sampler, *c.* 1830. Private collection.
- Vincent van Gogh, *Garden with Weeping Willow*, 1888, oil on canvas. Private collection.
- Piet Mondrian, *Haystack with Willow Trees*, 1897/98, oil on canvas. Private collection.
- Claude Monet, *Weeping Willow* series, several variations by 1919 in various museums.
- Brothers Hildebrandt, 'Old Man Willow', illustration for a calendar after J. R. R. Tolkien's *The Lord of the Rings*, 1978.

TAXUS BACCATA — YEW

FAMILY Taxaceae

An evergreen conifer, the common yew is native to most of Europe as well as parts of Africa and Asia. Also called the English or European yew, it is grown primarily as an ornamental.

Fred Hageneder, an ethnobotanist and the author of *Yew: A History* (2007), believes that the yew is the original World Tree, the only tree that has existed throughout the entire territory of cultures with a World Tree tradition.

Sacred to the Greek goddess Hecate (witchcraft, death, necromancy), the tree was said to purify the dead as they entered Hades. In the British Isles, the yew was traditionally associated with war because the wood was so hard that shields, longbows and spears were commonly made from it. It was revered by pagans as the oldest tree of all, and is now often found in cemeteries; indeed, such trees are often older than the church next to which they grow.[8] New sprigs appear when old branches touch the ground, or from dead or dying stumps, and so perhaps unsurprisingly the yew has served as a symbol of immortality, rebirth and connection to ancestors. The tree was sacred to the Druids, for whom it carried a range of meanings – from death to resurrection.

In the UK, the Ancient Yew Group is dedicated to identifying and protecting veteran (400 to 900 years old) and ancient (over 900 years old) yews.

✺ Yew (Ground Hemlock), 1862–69.

✷ Old yew trees, north door of St Edward's Church, Stow-on-the-Wold, Gloucestershire, twelfth to fifteenth century. The door itself dates from the seventeenth or eighteenth century.

The seeds of the sticky red fruit and the needles are highly toxic; the flesh of the fruit is the only non-toxic part of the tree. The Pacific yew (*T. brevifolia*), on the other hand, is the source of paclitaxel, an anti-cancer drug. Stripping the bark kills the tree, but it has since been discovered that the drug can also be produced from the leaves of the English yew.

ULMUS — ELM

FAMILY Ulmaceae

Elm trees first appeared about twenty million years ago, in Central Asia. They flourished and, before the appearance of Dutch elm disease in the twentieth century, spread over most of the northern hemisphere.

Caused by a microfungus dispersed by bark beetles, the disease killed most mature elms in Europe and North America, although the development of disease-resistant cultivars has now begun to restore the elm to forests and urban landscaping. The oldest elms in the world were planted in the 1860s by Frederick Law Olmsted in Central Park, New York. Most of the 1,200 elms – which make up half of the trees in the park – were saved from disease by aggressive management.

Elm wood is quite hard, and in ancient times it was used to make ploughs and chariots. The elm is sometimes associated with the Great Mother, and it has been suggested that Adam and Eve were born from the Goddess's Tree of Life, rather than created as is reported in Genesis. The Goddess was herself born from the elm, and her male consort was born from the ash. Elm symbolism is complex. On the one hand, it symbolizes birth, life and immortality, but the tree is also linked with death and the Underworld, and its wood was commonly used to make coffins. After Orpheus failed to rescue Eurydice from Hades, it is said that a grove of elm trees sprang up upon hearing his lyre played in mourning.

Constable's *Study of the Trunk of an Elm Tree* is almost photographic in its realism. It embodies the artist's humble attitude towards nature, and captures a sense of the impetus of life. Lucian Freud admired Constable deeply and attempted to copy the elm painting when he was a student, but gave up because it was so difficult. In 2002 Freud arranged an exhibition of Constable's work at the Grand Palais in Paris, and created an etching entitled *After Constable's Elm* for the catalogue.

⊗ Thomas S. Sinclair, Thomas's Elm (*Ulmus racemosa*), 1842–49.

※ John Constable, *Study of the Trunk of an Elm Tree*, c. 1821, oil on paper. London: Victoria and Albert Museum.

ULMUS ELM

FLOWERS

Sandro Botticelli, *Primavera*, c. 1480, tempera on wood. Florence: Le Gallerie degli Uffizi.

Jeff Koons, *Puppy*, 1992, stainless steel, soil and flowering plants. Bilbao: Guggenheim Museum.

Joseph Stella, *Flowers, Italy*, 1931, oil on canvas. Phoenix, AZ: Phoenix Art Museum.

It seems that flowers have always been loved and regarded as meaningful – although in ways that vary by era, fashion and geography.[9] Before the second half of the seventeenth century, flowers were categorized by smell, taste, colour and medicinal use; botanical classification occurred fairly late.

Both the flower and the blossom are universal symbols of young life and of beauty, and their transitory nature is sometimes used to evoke *joie de vivre* or the fragile quality of childhood. Colour has a great deal to do with symbolism: red stands for love, passion and blood; white for innocence and blamelessness, or sometimes death. Udo Becker adds that yellow signifies the sun; blue, dreams and mystery.

Flowers are connected to all aspects of love, from the fresh innocence of young love and spring to lust, passion and the realm of the erotic. They have been especially linked to the vulva and used as a symbol of purity or virginity.

Scattered flowers often mean joy, especially in the context of wedding flower-bearers.

Individual flowers carry specific meanings, many of which begin in the ancient world. The popular and widespread *Language of Flowers*, originating in Persia, was introduced to Europe in the early eighteenth century. Flowers have also functioned as personal, national or state symbols and appear in calendars of the months and seasons.

Some artists depict individual blooms to convey specific meanings. Combinations of flowers appear in still-life images and in landscapes. One of the most sumptuous of all is Botticelli's masterpiece *Primavera*. Tiny, identifiable flowers (the *millefleur* style is said to be anachronistic, recalling medieval tapestries) are sprinkled like stars throughout the landscape, and more spill from the mouth of Chloris. Several theories have been proposed to explain this enigmatic, complex painting. Most agree that it celebrates spring. Additional suggestions include the occasion of a Medici wedding or a celebration of the senses, smell in particular, as well as love and beauty – both human and natural. More than 500 species are depicted, among them approximately 190 flowers, of which 130 have been identified.

In the hippy culture of the 1960s, as consumerism began to be questioned and social consciousness grew, flowers became symbols of peace and love. Widespread sentiment against authority, shown by anti-war and student demonstrations, also led to overt reactions against the exploitation of nature. More recently, Jeff Koons's *Puppy* incorporates flowers into a 13-metre-high (43 ft) living sculpture of a West Highland terrier, reprised from an image of his own little white dog in 1993. It refers to both eighteenth-century elite topiary gardens and the excesses of modern pop culture (sentimentality and Hallmark-card-cute puppies set against the reality of puppy farms). Despite the negative implications of the sculpture, the public response has been overwhelmingly positive, inspiring optimism, love, joy and, as Koons himself intended, 'confidence and security'. The flowers are renewed in May (begonias, impatiens and petunias) and October (pansies), and fed and watered by a network of pipes inside the artwork.

LANGUAGE OF FLOWERS

A Persian tradition, the *Language of Flowers* was introduced to Europe by the Swedish king Charles II on his return to Sweden from exile in Turkey in 1714. The tradition became widespread, nearly universal, in the eighteenth and nineteenth centuries.

Two others are credited with bringing the *Language* to Europe: the writer and medical pioneer Mary Wortley Montagu (England, 1717) and the traveller Aubry de La Mottraye (Sweden, 1727). Throughout the nineteenth century, the symbolism of the *Language of Flowers* could be found in the composition of wreaths, baskets, bouquets, Valentines and other greetings cards, *billets-doux* and visiting cards, as well as tussie-mussies and posies. Modern florists continue to find it of interest, as is evident in the many commercial websites that list flowers and their meanings as a sales pitch.

Books devoted to floriography were published all over Europe and in the United States. The historian and Orientalist Joseph Hammer-Purgstall's *Dictionnaire du langage des fleurs* (1809) may be the earliest, but among the most popular (and still in print) is Kate Greenaway's *Language of Flowers* (1884). In Vanessa Diffenbaugh's novel *The Language of Flowers* (2011), the main character gradually comes to realize that flowers have multiple meanings, sometimes contradictory. She devises her own 'Language' by studying plant characteristics and selecting suitable meanings.

Dorothea Tanning depicted a dozen newly created flowers in her collection *Another Language of Flowers* (1998). She did not wish to rival nature, but rather to pay homage. The flowers, accompanied by poetry, have fictional names that convey meaning. For instance, *Windwort* initially seems to be a rather indistinct flower, but a closer look reveals its hybrid nature, with female breasts on the right and a profile face on the left. A nude female body arches over the delicate petals. The circular hole in the centre recalls other forms – apples, melons, cabbage – associated with sexuality and fecundity. Tanning's last work, these paintings convey the mysteries of nature and the marvel that is the artist's imagination.

- Dorothea Tanning, *Zephirium apochripholiae (Windwort)*, 1997–98, oil on canvas. From *Another Language of Flowers: Paintings* by Dorothea Tanning, James Ingram Merrill et al., Braziller, 1998.

- John William Waterhouse, *The Awakening of Adonis* (detail), 1899, oil on canvas. Private collection.

- J. M. Seligmann, *Anemone plant*, c. 1768.

ANEMONE

FAMILY Ranunculaceae

The anemone, native to temperate zones, is nearly always bluish violet, white, pink or red; one species is yellow.

The word *anemone* means 'daughter of the wind' in Greek, and the flower is said to herald spring breezes. It can stand alone, letting the wind ruffle its petals, but a strong gust may pluck it – thus the flower embodies both the profusion of life and its transience.

In Book 10 of the *Metamorphoses*, Ovid tells how Venus loved a mortal hunter named Adonis so much that she neglected heaven. Adonis ignored her warnings of the danger of hunting and was gored by a wild boar. The goddess heard his dying groans and declared that his blood would become a flower. A bloom sprang up, but 'the joy it gives to man is short-lived, for the winds which give the flower its name, Anemone, shake it right down'. The flower thus became a symbol of death and sorrow. In John William Waterhouse's painting Venus awakens Adonis with a kiss; her garden is in full flower, anemones included, signifying the renewal of nature.

The anemone may be the flower referred to in the Bible as the 'lily of the fields', since there are no white lilies in Palestine, but anemones are widely distributed. Anemones are also said to have sprouted from Christ's blood and thus to have grown at the foot of the Cross. The flower may also signify the blood of saints.

Anemones appear in many still-lifes, especially Dutch *vanitas* paintings, and in decorative ceramics.

OTHER ANEMONE IMAGES
- Nicolas-Bernard Lépicié, *Adonis Transformed by Venus into an Anemone*, 1782, oil on canvas. Versailles, France: Petit Trianon.
- Pierre-Joseph Redouté, 'Anemone Simple', from *Choix des Plus Belles Fleurs*, 1827.
- Raoul Dufy, *Anemones*, 1937, lithograph after a watercolour.

AQUILEGIA — COLUMBINE

FAMILY Ranunculaceae

Perennial columbine plants are found in meadows and woodlands.

The Latin name of the genus comes from the word for eagle (*aquila*), because the petals are said to resemble an eagle's claw. By contrast, the common name comes from the Latin word for dove (*columba*), because the inverted flowers look like five doves clustered together. The flower is closely related to those of *Actaea* (baneberry) and *Aconitum* (monkshood), and is, like them, poisonous.

The columbine is associated with many goddesses. In Norse mythology it was sacred to Freya, and among the ancient Greeks it was the symbol of Aphrodite.

In Christian art, the flower symbolizes the dove of the Holy Spirit. Six doves signify the gifts of the Holy Spirit – identified by the prophet Isaiah as wisdom and understanding, counsel and might, knowledge and fear of the Lord (11:2) – and the flower often bears six blooms on a stem. The leaves have three lobes and thus can also symbolize the Trinity. The flower appears in paintings depicting the Virgin Mary, specifically symbolizing

- *Aquilegia nikolicii*, 1935; Frederick A. Walpole, Columbine (*Aquilegia formosa*), 1900.

- Hugo van der Goes, *Adoration of the Shepherds* (detail), centre panel of the Portinari altarpiece, 1475–78, oil on wood. Florence: Le Gallerie degli Uffizi.

her sorrows. This led, in turn, to the Renaissance association of this flower with the Passion of Christ and the death of the Virgin.

Hugo van der Goes seems to have loved painting flowers. The columbine appears in a lovely still life sited below the kneeling Virgin in the centre panel of the Portinari altarpiece, foreshadowing the Virgin's grief over the suffering and death of Christ. The painting also includes carnations, red, blue and white irises, scattered violets and stalks of wheat.

OTHER COLUMBINE IMAGES
- Hans Multscher, Wurzach altarpiece, 1437, tempera on panel. Berlin: Gemäldegalerie.
- Hugo van der Goes, Monforte altarpiece, c. 1470, oil on panel. Berlin: Gemäldegalerie.
- Anon., *Spinola Hours*, c. 1510–20, illuminated manuscript. Los Angeles, CA: J. Paul Getty Museum.

ARUM

FAMILY Araceae

Various species of arum are widespread throughout Europe, North Africa and West Asia.

The plant goes by several common names, such as Adam and Eve, Jack-in-the-pulpit, lords-and-ladies and naked girls/boys. Many have sexual implications because the shape of the plant is reminiscent of male and female genitalia, suggesting copulation. Because of its sexual connotations, the plant was often touted as an aphrodisiac. The growth stages involve a cone-shaped flower with an erect central male spathe; in the autumn the lower ring of flowers transforms into vertical clusters of bright red berries. Despite its links with sex, the plant is extremely poisonous. The flower resembles, but is unrelated to, the calla lily.

The arum isn't depicted often in art, although it symbolizes the Virgin Mary in medieval paintings. This may have come about because of the phonetic similarity between arum and Aaron, Mary and her cousin Elizabeth being descended from the house of Aaron.

Van Gogh drew arum lilies in the garden of the asylum at Saint-Rémy, and included them in a painting of a moth that he mistakenly identified as a death's-head hawkmoth (it is actually a giant peacock moth). Not wishing to kill the moth for his studies, he made quick drawings that he later referred to when creating the painting. The painting also includes the later berry stage of the arum in the upper centre. The regenerative symbolism of the arum may counteract the deathly associations of the death's-head hawkmoth, which gets its name from the skull-like pattern on its thorax.

John Curtis, *Arum italicum*, 1823.

Vincent van Gogh, *Giant Peacock Moth*, 1889, oil on canvas. Amsterdam: Van Gogh Museum.

BELLIS — DAISY

FAMILY Asteraceae

The daisy is one of the less showy members of the family Asteraceae, in which are also classified the chrysanthemum (pp. 104–5) and the sunflower (pp. 114–17). The common name comes from the Saxon *daes eage*, 'day's eye', describing its bright yellow centre. Uses include food and herbal medicine.

The name of the genus stems from Roman legend. Vertumnus, the god of vegetation and the seasons, fell in love with a nymph or dryad named Belides. He pursued her, and to avoid his unwanted attention she transformed herself into a daisy.

Towards the end of the fifteenth century – possibly for the first time in paintings by Botticelli – daisies appear in Annunciation scenes, symbolizing the Christ Child's innocence and purity; they were thought to be more fitting than the austere lily, which represents the same attributes in his mother. Botticelli painted daisies not only in images of the Virgin and Child but also in *The Birth of Venus*, in which they are embroidered on the robe held out by the Hora (a minor Greek goddess) of Spring. The Neoplatonic concepts of the time may have suggested a link between Aphrodite/Venus and the Virgin Mary, in terms of human and divine love.

Daisies are among the blooms scattered throughout the landscape of Botticelli's *Primavera* (see p. 90). The flower also appears in Giovanni Bellini's *St Francis in the Desert* (see 'Mullein', pp. 200–1), where it may indicate the saint's guileless simplicity and virtue. In his *Annunciation* of 1482, Domenico Ghirlandaio adorned the Virgin's writing desk with a vase of roses, daisies and jasmine, symbolizing love, innocence and divine hope.

✻ Sandro Botticelli, *The Birth of Venus*, c. 1485, tempera on canvas. Florence: Le Gallerie degli Uffizi.

❖ Jane Elizabeth Giraud, Daisies, 1846.

❋ Richard Dadd, *The Fairy Feller's Master-Stroke*, 1855–64, oil on canvas. London: Tate.

BELLIS DAISY

CARDUUS, CIRSIUM AND OTHER GENERA — THISTLE

FAMILY Asteraceae

Thistle is the common name for a group of prickly flowering plants. Medicinally, thistles may provide remedies for headaches, mouth ulcers, vertigo and jaundice.

The thistle has been the national emblem of Scotland since the thirteenth century; it appears in Scots heraldry and in coinage, badges and tattoos. Many thistle images can be found in botanical illustrations, and the flower was popular in Art Nouveau and Arts and Crafts jewelry, textiles and ceramics.

Some thistles are troublesome and/or poisonous weeds (such as the yellow starthistle, *Centaurea solstitialis*), but others are important sources of nectar for butterflies and honeybees.

In ancient times thistles were believed to guard against evil and demonic powers, and possibly to have aphrodisiac potential. Medieval medicinal uses of the plant included the treatment of internal disorders.

The thistle, along with the thorn (Genesis 3:17–18), functioned as a Christian symbol of sorrow and sin; thistles often appear at the foot of the Cross in paintings by northern European artists and have symbolized Christ's suffering. Martyred saints are sometimes depicted grasping thistles.

At the age of twenty-two, having just completed his apprenticeship, Albrecht Dürer painted a self-portrait holding a thistle to symbolize conjugal fidelity. He married (not altogether happily, it would turn out) the year it was painted, and judging from the symbol, intended to be faithful to his wife. He may also have been aware of medieval herbalists' belief that the thistle could combat depression. Indeed, the portrait may reflect the artist's melancholic temperament, religious intentions and philosophic doubts. He added an inscription next to the date; translated, it reads: 'My affairs follow the course allotted to them on high. Marriage has in part determined his destiny – the Bridegroom puts his future life in the hands of God'.

OTHER THISTLE IMAGES
- Hans Hoffmann, *A Hare in the Forest*, c. 1585, oil on panel. Los Angeles, CA: J. Paul Getty Museum.
- J. J. Grandville, *Les Fleurs animées*, 1847.

❋ Albrecht Dürer, *Portrait of the Artist Holding a Thistle* (detail), 1493, oil on parchment over canvas. Paris: Musée du Louvre.

❋ Alice Carmen Gouvy, *Thistle 215*, 1902.

CHRYSANTHEMUM

FAMILY Asteraceae

Chrysanthemums are native to East Asia and northern Europe, and are popular as a cut flower. They have traditionally symbolized cheerfulness in adversity and a love of truth, but also slighted love.

Beginning in 1897, Piet Mondrian drew and painted hundreds of images of flowers, which vary from naturalistic to semi-abstract. Often just single blossoms, the flowers stand centred and isolated against neutral grounds. This enabled the artist to devote his full attention to rendering subtle geometry and minute detail. 'Mums' bloom late in the year, providing brilliant colour when other flowers are absent. Mondrian must have appreciated this, and apparently wished to show the cycle of life, since some of his chrysanthemums exude energy and life force, while others begin to droop and decay.

This early *Chrysanthemum* is said to reflect Mondrian's interest in the work of Van Gogh and in theosophy. From 1875, members of the British Theosophical Society had sought to grasp the hidden essence of reality through transcendent spiritual states. According to the activist and president of the society Annie Besant, flowers emit auras that link with higher spheres of existence; the chrysanthemum is said to evoke the moon, while the sunflower (pp. 114–17) recalls the sun. The energetic symmetry of this bloom seems to disclose what the artist identified as 'the deeper beauty' hidden within. He apparently saw the chrysanthemum as an ideal embodiment of this beauty, and may have depicted as many as 150 of these flowers.

- Piet Mondrian, *Chrysanthemum*, c. 1908–9, crayon on paperboard. New York: Guggenheim Museum.

- Pieter de Pannemaeker after Jean Linden, Autumn chrysanthemum hybrids, 1888.

CROCUS

FAMILY Iridaceae

A genus of flowering plants in the iris family, the crocus is native to woodland and meadows nearly worldwide. The spice saffron comes from the stigmas of *Crocus sativus*, which is common in the Mediterranean, notably on the islands of Crete and Santorini.

The ancient Minoans of Bronze Age Crete depicted the natural world around them with enthusiasm and accuracy. The crocus was the source of saffron, an important commodity, used in medicine, dye and perfume, and traded throughout the Mediterranean. According to the archaeologist Rachel Dewan, it also played a role in Minoan worship of the Mother Goddess and served as a symbol of Minoan female identity. It may have been at this time that saffron came to be considered an aphrodisiac.

According to Greek legend, the flower is named after a youth who unrequitedly loved a shepherdess named Smilax. When he pined away and died, the gods changed him into the crocus flower. Because of this association with love, the flower became linked with weddings. The Romans grew it and sprinkled its blooms to perfume banquet halls, gardens and courtyards.

The crocus continues to be a significant source of saffron, and is still mostly grown in Greece. Brilliant yellow clothing dyed with saffron symbolized light and majesty, and often adorns gods and kings.

The colour of Buddhist robes varies according to culture. The Buddha himself wore robes made from discarded cloth that was dyed by being boiled with vegetable matter and spices such as turmeric or saffron, which gives cloth a yellow-orange colour. The colour of the robes indicated that the monks were fulfilling their vows of poverty.

OTHER CROCUS IMAGES
- *The Saffron Walden Charter*, 1514. Saffron Walden, Essex: Saffron Walden Museum.
- Raymond C. Booth, *Crocus*, 1962, oil on canvas. Warrington, Cheshire: Warrington Museum & Art Gallery. A bird's skull rests beneath the crocus flowers.

✤ Crocus (*Crocus stellaris*): entire flowering plant and its anatomical segments, *c.* 1812.

✶ 'Saffron Gatherers', detail of fresco, *c.* 1500 BCE. Xeste 3, Akrotiri, Santorini.

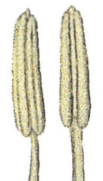

CYCLAMEN

FAMILY Primulaceae

A genus of twenty-three species of flowering plant native to Europe and the Mediterranean, cyclamen are grown today for decorative use both indoors and outside.

Theophrastus claimed that the cyclamen was an aphrodisiac that promoted conception. Sacred to Hecate, who presided over all magical spells, it was believed to purify the ground on which it grew. In Christian art, it became sacred to the Virgin Mary. The little red spots sometimes found on the inside of the flower symbolized her sorrow over Christ's death.

Moshe Gershuni's work is autobiographical, recalling his childhood in Israel. His series *Hai Cyclamen* (*18 Cyclamens*) relates to war, regeneration and atonement. The number eighteen, *Chai* in the Kabbalah, means world or life, and donations to synagogues are made in multiples of this figure. Persian cyclamen (*Cyclamen persicum*) grows wild across the Levant and North Africa. After the 1948 Arab–Israeli War, the cyclamen became a national symbol of Israel. Hebrew inscriptions around the edges of the painting (opposite) refer to Psalms, expressing forgiveness and reconciliation.

In Japanese culture, the cyclamen is a sacred flower to lovers and is often given as a gift on Valentine's Day.

⊗ James Sowerby, Cyclamen (*Cyclamen coum*), 1787.

✳ Moshe Gershuni, *Hai Cyclamen*, 1984, mixed media on paper. Private collection.

OTHER CYCLAMEN IMAGES
- Ernst Ludwig Kirchner, *Cyclamen*, 1918–19, oil on canvas. New York: Metropolitan Museum of Art.
- Ellsworth Kelly, several cyclamen lithographs, 1966. New York: Museum of Modern Art.

DIANTHUS CARYOPHYLLUS — CARNATION

FAMILY Caryophyllaceae

Imported from Tunisia in the thirteenth century, the carnation has been cultivated for about 2,000 years.

Its Greek name, *dianthus*, mentioned by Theophrastus and taken up by the naturalist Carolus Linnaeus in the eighteenth century as its botanical name, comes from the words for divine (*dios*) and flower (*anthos*). According to legend, the goddess Artemis, having been rejected by a shepherd boy, took revenge by tearing out his eyes. When the eyes fell to the ground, they sprouted, becoming carnations. The flower was used in Greco-Roman ceremonial crowns.

In Christian imagery, carnations sometimes appear in the Virgin's or Christ's hand, or in the Garden of Eden. Medieval legend attributes the flower's origin to the tears shed by the Virgin Mary at the Crucifixion.

In northern Europe, the flower was commonly worn by brides and became associated with marriage. Indicating a promise of marriage or a pledge of love, carnations sometimes appear in Flemish portraits. They also appear in still lifes, most notably in Dutch Baroque *vanitas* works, where they and the other objects recall the brevity of life and pleasure, and serve as a reminder of the dangers of overindulgence.

✣ Francisco Goya, *The Marquesa de Pontejos* (detail), c. 1786, oil on canvas. Washington, DC: National Gallery of Art.

✣ Augusta Withers, Tree carnation, 1857.

✣ John Singer Sargent, *Carnation, Lily, Lily, Rose*, 1885–86, oil on canvas. London: Tate.

Carnations, lilies and roses appear in John Singer Sargent's *Carnation, Lily, Lily, Rose*. The title comes from 'Ye Shepherds Tell Me', a song by the British composer Joseph Mazzinghi popular in the 1880s. The refrain asks, 'Have you seen my Flora pass this way?' '[B]eauty's queen' – and goddess of flowers – in the song, Flora wears a wreath of lilies, carnations and roses, symbolic of love, purity and spring rebirth. Although it is unclear whether Sargent meant this painting to be symbolic, it certainly celebrates the beauty of nature and flowers, as well as the innocence of childhood.

The carnation has been the emblem of Mother's Day in the United States since 1907, and red and pink carnations are the symbol of Parents Day in Korea.

OTHER CARNATION IMAGES
- Leonardo da Vinci, *The Madonna of the Carnation*, 1478–80, oil on panel. Munich: Alte Pinakothek.
- Nicolaes van Verendael, *Flowers in a Glass Vase on a Stone Ledge*, between 1657 and 1691, oil on canvas. Aachen: Suermondt Ludwig Museum.

DIGITALIS — FOXGLOVE

FAMILY Plantaginaceae

Native to and widespread throughout temperate Europe, this plant is popular in gardens worldwide. It is the source of digoxin, a heart medicine.

The colour of the blossoms varies; typically purple in their wild form, when cultivated the plants may bear pink, yellow or white blooms. The flowering stem can measure between 0.9 and 1.8 m (3–6 ft) tall, and the plant is poisonous to varying degrees.

Probably the most famous foxglove in art appears in Van Gogh's *Portrait of Dr Gachet*. There are two versions: the earliest is now in an unknown private collection, and the second, originally owned by Gachet himself, is in the Musée d'Orsay in Paris. The doctor, a homeopath and amateur artist, cared for Van Gogh after his release from the asylum at Saint-Rémy. Van Gogh, who felt a kinship with Gachet, wrote that he had attempted to create a modern portrait to capture 'the deeply sad [often translated as heartbroken] expression of our times'. The foxglove in both versions of the painting reflects the doctor's role as both healer and fellow sufferer.

The contemporary Irish artist Dorothy Cross spent twenty years studying the foxglove, creating sculptures of individual specimens in bronze and thereby, according to Giovanni Aloi, elevating the plant to mythological status. The artist's interest in the plant stemmed from her childhood, when she was warned of its dangers. One wonders whether Cross was aware of suggestions that Van Gogh suffered from digitalis intoxication, since other aspects of her work deal with altered states of mind induced by psychotropic substances, poison and sex.

OTHER FOXGLOVE IMAGES
- Paul Ranson, *Digitalis*, 1899, tempera on canvas. Tokyo: National Museum of Western Art.

✹ Vincent van Gogh, *Portrait of Dr Gachet*, 1890, oil on canvas. Paris: Musée d'Orsay.

✺ James Sowerby, *Foxglove*, 1785.

✻ Dorothy Cross, *Foxglove*, 2007, bronze.

DIGITALIS FOXGLOVE

HELIANTHUS — SUNFLOWER

FAMILY Asteraceae

All species except one are native to North and Central America, domesticated in Mexico around 2100 BCE. The common or giant sunflower was brought back to Europe by Spanish explorers. Sunflowers provide edible seeds and oil and are used as fertilizer. The sunflower's face is said to follow the sun across the sky, and its petals spread out like the sun's rays – hence the genus name, from the Greek *hēlios*, 'sun'.

Baroque artists – such as Anthony van Dyck, who painted a self-portrait holding a sunflower – played on its meaning of unconditional devotion, related to the way its flowers turn to face the sun. In Van Dyck's case, it signified his allegiance to Charles I of England, for whom he served as court painter.

The flower was beloved by the Pre-Raphaelites, and a little later in the nineteenth century sunflowers were also popular as decorative motifs in the Arts and Crafts Movement. The sunflower became Oscar Wilde's iconic symbol after a caricature of him appeared in *Punch* in 1881; Wilde adopted the sunflower, praising its 'gaudy leonine beauty'. Thereafter, the flower became associated with the Aesthetic Movement.

Dorothea Tanning's *Eine Kleine Nachtmusik* dates from the artist's time in Arizona, where she lived with Max Ernst. A huge sunflower head rests at the top of a stairway on a red carpet. Two girls occupy the hallway, one of them apparently especially threatened by the flower, to the extent that her hair is literally standing on end. Tanning, who connected the flower with the intense Arizona sun, wrote of the painting:

It's about confrontation. Everyone believes he/she is his/her drama. While they don't always have giant sunflowers (most aggressive of flowers) to contend with, there are always stairways, hallways,

⊗ William Clark, Sunflower, 1826.

✳ Dorothea Tanning, *Eine Kleine Nachtmusik*, 1943, oil on canvas. London: Tate.

✻

even very private theatres where the suffocations and the finalities are being played out.

Vincent van Gogh painted sunflowers before he left Paris and created many more to adorn Paul Gauguin's room in Arles, where the artists shared a house – known as the Yellow House – for several weeks in late 1888. He hoped Gauguin would be a mentor and looked forward to discussing art and literature with the older painter, so the flowers doubtless embody his admiration. Unfortunately, the feeling wasn't reciprocated, and Gauguin's visit famously ended in a violent quarrel.[10]

Van Gogh's celebrated sunflowers continue to inspire contemporary art, for instance Faith Ringgold's story quilt *The Sunflower Quilting Bee at Arles* (part of her *French Collection*), of which several versions exist. The quilts depict influential African American women and feature Van Gogh himself holding a sunflower still life. The works celebrate community, creativity and the challenges these women overcame. One of the quilts includes the Yellow House. The quilts highlight the contribution of Black women as well as honouring Van Gogh.

Anselm Kiefer, among the twenty-first century's most complex and important artists, works in diverse media. Plants play a significant role in his art. For instance, huge sunflowers appear in *The Orders of the Night*,[11] hovering over the supine body of a man, a self-portrait.[12] The sunflowers symbolize adoration; but these appear to be dying, their seeds falling to earth to grow again. His works are unstable; surfaces crack, bloom and grow. Building on Van Gogh's visions, Kiefer evokes the vast, eternal cycles of nature, divine mystery and human strength and frailty.

❖ Anselm Kiefer, *Die Orden der Nacht* (*The Orders of the Night*), 1996, acrylic, emulsion and shellac on canvas. Seattle, WA: Seattle Art Museum.

❖ Faith Ringgold, *The Sunflower Quilting Bee at Arles*, 1991, acrylic on canvas with pieced fabric border. Private collection.

OTHER SUNFLOWER IMAGES
- Anthony van Dyck, *Self-Portrait with a Sunflower*, 1633, oil on canvas. Private collection.
- Charles de La Fosse, *Clytie Transformed into a Sunflower*, 1688, oil on canvas. Versailles: Grand Trianon, Palace of Versailles.
- Edward Linley Sambourne, caricature of Oscar Wilde as a sunflower, *Punch*, 1881.

HYACINTHUS — HYACINTH

FAMILY Asparagaceae

This small genus of perennial flowering plants is native to the eastern Mediterranean and known by the common name hyacinth. The bulbs are poisonous.

⊗ Pierre-Joseph Redouté, *Hyacinthus orientalis*, 1827.

✳ Ellsworth Kelly, *Hyacinth*, 1949, ink on paper. Private collection.

The hyacinth's name comes from the Greek poet Homer, or possibly from Ovid. There are several variants of the story: in some, the youth Hyacinth was killed by Apollo and in others by the wind god Zephyrus. A number of sources suggest that the relationship between Apollo and Hyacinth was sexual. In all versions, Apollo changes Hyacinth's blood into the hyacinth flower. It has also been suggested that Hyacinth was a pre-Hellenic vegetation deity whose importance was eclipsed by the Olympian gods.

The hyacinth appears in the garden of Flora in Renaissance art, growing at the lower edge of Botticelli's *Primavera* (p. 90), and it also graces still lifes. In Christian art, it is a symbol of prudence, depicted only rarely. It sometimes appears in Nativity scenes.

While living in Paris in 1949, Ellsworth Kelly bought a potted hyacinth to cheer up his room. Kelly drew throughout his life, often returning to accurate line drawings of plants, perhaps as a foil to the increasing abstraction of his paintings. While his plant drawings may not have had any deeper meaning, they clearly convey his appreciation for the simple beauty of the world around him.

Hyacinths often appear in botanical illustrations and are favourites with contemporary floral artists. William Morris combined the hyacinth with other flowers in a stunning wallpaper design; it also appears in pattern #480, manufactured in 1917 after his death.

IRIS

FAMILY Iridaceae

The Iris's name comes from the Greek goddess of the rainbow, possibly referring to its many colours. Irises grow in nearly all temperate zones of the northern hemisphere, and are widely cultivated as an ornamental. Their uses include aromatherapy, the flavouring and colouring of alcoholic drinks, and perfume. They have also been used in plantings for water purification, but can become invasive.

The ancient Egyptians placed the iris on the brow of the Sphinx, symbolizing power. The Greek goddess Iris also acted as the female messenger of the gods, paired with Hermes. Iris led the souls of dead women to the Elysian Fields, and irises were planted on women's graves.

In Christianity, the iris is one of the flowers linked with the Virgin. It sometimes takes the place of the lily in Annunciation scenes, probably because of another of its common names: sword lily. The sharp leaves may also signify the Virgin's sorrow over the death of Christ, as stated in the Gospel of Luke: 'a sword will pierce through your own soul also' (2:35). According to a medieval French legend, the petals of all irises were golden until Christ's death, when they turned purple as a sign of mourning.

The flower served as a symbol of French royalty as early as the first century CE. The first twelve Louis signed their names with an iris or perhaps a lily (pp. 124–27), giving rise to the *fleur-de-lys* emblem that is still associated with France today. The three large petals signified

Vincent van Gogh, *Irises*, 1889, oil on canvas. Los Angeles, CA: J. Paul Getty Museum.

Kazumasa Ogawa, *Iris Kæmpferi*, 1896, coloured collotype. Los Angeles, CA: J. Paul Getty Museum.

OTHER IRIS IMAGES
- Hugo van der Goes, *Adoration of the Shepherds*, centre panel of Portinari altarpiece, 1475–78, oil on wood. Florence: Le Gallerie degli Uffizi.
- James Atkinson Grimshaw, *Iris, Spirit of the Rainbow*, 1876, oil on canvas. Leeds: Leeds Museums and Galleries.
- Fernand Khnopff, *Portrait of Yvonne Suys*, 1890, oil on panel. Private collection.
- Louis Comfort Tiffany, *Magnolias and Irises*, c. 1908, stained-glass window. New York: Metropolitan Museum of Art.

faith, wisdom and valour, and the purple colour stood for royalty and nobility.

Among the most famous of all iris images is Van Gogh's *Irises*. The artist voluntarily admitted himself to the asylum at Saint-Paul de Mausole in May 1889. As soon as he was able to go out into the hospital garden, he began this painting. Most of the flowers are purple, but there is a single white iris, as well as marigolds. The individuality of the flowers is evidence of Van Gogh's very close observation, while the single white flower among the deep purples is sometimes said to represent his loneliness.

* Pierre-Joseph Redouté, *Iris squalens* (brown-flowered iris), *Iris germanica* (German flag iris), 1805–16.

* Georgia O'Keeffe, *Black Iris*, 1926, oil on canvas. New York: Metropolitan Museum of Art.

LILIUM — LILY

FAMILY Liliaceae

Lilies belong to a genus of flowering plants that grow from bulbs, most of them native to the temperate northern hemisphere.

Generally symbolizing femininity, the lily is the sacred flower of motherhood and fruitfulness in Mediterranean and Egyptian mythology. In ancient Greece and Rome, it was sacred to Hera/Juno. The lily is said to have sprung from Hera's milk, some drops of which fell to earth when the Milky Way was created.

According to Semitic legend, the flower sprang from Eve's tears after leaving the Garden of Eden and finding that she was pregnant. In Christianity the lily represents purity, innocence and chastity, and is the favoured symbol of the Virgin Mary. The flower appears in Annunciation scenes from the medieval period, and since the Renaissance, three lilies have been favoured, signifying the Trinity – Father, Holy Spirit and yet-to-be-born Christ. Examples can be found in Leonardo and Botticelli, and later in Rossetti.

Simone Martini's *Annunciation with St Margaret and St Ansanus* was painted for the altar of St Ansanus in the transept of Siena Cathedral. The archangel Gabriel, bearing the olive branch of peace, appears to a startled Virgin Mary. A vase of lilies occupies the centre

Simone Martini, *Annunciation with St Margaret and St Ansanus* (detail), 1333, tempera on wood with gold background. Florence: Le Gallerie degli Uffizi.

Charlotte Sowerby, *Lilium speciosum*, 1857.

❖ Dante Gabriel Rossetti, *The Blessed Damozel*, 1871–78, oil on canvas. Cambridge, MA: Fogg Museum/Harvard Art Museums.

❋ David Hockney, *Mr and Mrs Clark and Percy*, 1970–71, acrylic on canvas. London: Tate.

OTHER LILY IMAGES
- Francisco de Zurbarán, *Christ and the Virgin in the House at Nazareth*, c. 1640, oil on canvas. Cleveland, OH: Cleveland Museum of Art.
- Paul Gauguin, *Contes barbares*, 1902, oil on canvas. Essen: Museum Folkwang.
- Stanley Spencer, *The Resurrection, Cookham*, 1924–27, oil on canvas. London: Tate.

of the composition, symbolizing the Virgin's chastity, innocence and purity.

Lilies also appear in images of the Assumption of the Virgin and, focusing on the flower's attributes of purity and innocence, in depictions of the Christ Child. The lily is associated with saints including Catherine of Siena, Clare, Philomena, Joseph, Anthony of Padua and Francis of Assisi. A lily and a sword in images of the Last Judgment symbolize the separation of the innocent and the sinful.

The lily became a favoured heraldic symbol, primarily of the city of Florence and the kings of France. There is some disagreement as to whether the lily or the iris is the basis for the *fleur-de-lys* (see 'Iris', pp. 120–23).

The Blessed Damozel was inspired by a poem Rossetti wrote when he was eighteen, taking the theme of separated lovers who will be rejoined in heaven from Dante's *La Vita Nuova* (1294). The Damozel holds three lilies, which are said to symbolize purity (or possibly the Trinity). Her lover appears in the 'earthly sphere' below, an arrangement reminiscent of Italian Renaissance altarpieces.

LONICERA
HONEYSUCKLE

FAMILY Caprifoliaceae

Honeysuckle symbolizes pure happiness. Because of its tenacious, clinging habit, it also signifies affection, love and everlasting bonds, while its fragrance links it to sweet pervasiveness.

Honeysuckle has also been believed to repel evil and protect the home. Medicinally, the flowers are natural antibiotics, and can be used to treat staphylococcus infections and upper respiratory problems.

In Greek mythology, the lovers Daphnis and Chloe could remain together only while the honeysuckle bloomed. Daphnis asks Eros, the god of love, to make the plant flower for longer, and it is said to be for this reason that some honeysuckle species bloom for an extended time.

The Druids gave the honeysuckle a place in the ogham alphabet, the twenty-third letter of which is usually ascribed to this flower. Later, Scottish farmers hung honeysuckle wreaths over barn doors or around the necks of cattle as a form of protection.

In 1609, Peter Paul Rubens painted an image of himself and his first wife, Isabella Brant, just before their marriage. The couple is seated on a honeysuckle branch, the foliage of which surrounds and embraces them. The artist thus established a symbolic setting for wedded bliss. Tragically, Isabella died at the age of thirty-four from bubonic plague.

OTHER HONEYSUCKLE IMAGES
- Dante Gabriel Rossetti, *La Ghirlandata*, 1871–74, oil on canvas. London: Guildhall Art Gallery.
- Dante Gabriel Rossetti, *Venus Verticordia*, 1868, oil on canvas. Bournemouth: Russell-Cotes Art Gallery & Museum.

⊗ John T. Curran, Tiffany & Co., *Loving Cup*, 1891, silver gilt. New York: Metropolitan Museum of Art.

※ H. Fletcher after J. van Huysum, Honeysuckle (*Lonicera* species): three varieties, 1730.

❖ Peter Paul Rubens, *Honeysuckle Bower* (detail), *c.* 1609–10, oil on canvas. Munich: Alte Pinakothek.

NARCISSUS

FAMILY Amaryllidaceae

A genus of spring-flowering perennial plants, narcissi were well known in ancient cultures both medicinally and botanically, and became increasingly popular in Europe after the sixteenth century. The plant may be poisonous if accidentally ingested.

An ancient Greco-Roman myth tells of a semi-divine youth, Narcissus, who was so pampered by his mother and the other nymphs that he became extremely conceited. The nymph Echo fell in love with him, but he was too self-obsessed to notice, and she wasted away until only her voice remained. Incensed by his behaviour, Nemesis, the goddess of vengeance, caused him to fall in love with his own reflection in a pool of water. Narcissus, unable to reach his beloved, died and became a flower. Thus we are to understand that narcissism – excessive egotism – will eventually be punished. The flower was also connected with sleep, apparently because its bulb dies back but blooms again each spring. It was often planted on graves, linking death with sleep.

In Christian art, the narcissus appears in representations of Eden and in Annunciations as a symbol of the triumph of divine love over death, egotism and sin. Negative meanings include an allegory of self-love and stupidity.

Salvador Dalí depicted the myth of Narcissus in his memorable *Metamorphosis of Narcissus*. Narcissus appears on the left-hand side of the painting, while on the right, a stone hand clutches a cracked stone egg from which the flower emerges. In a small book about the painting in 1937, Dalí wrote: 'If one looks for some time, from a slight distance and with a certain "distant fixedness", at the hypnotically immobile figure of Narcissus, it gradually disappears until at last it is completely invisible'. Dalí met Sigmund Freud the year after painting *Metamorphosis of Narcissus*. He took the painting to their meeting in order to discuss his theory of narcissism, which he had developed based on Freud's concept of paranoia.

✵ Salvador Dalí, *Metamorphosis of Narcissus*, 1937, oil on canvas. London: Tate.

✵ Pierre-Joseph Redouté, *Narcissus gouani* (Double daffodil), 1827.

OTHER NARCISSUS IMAGES
- Lucian Freud, *Narcissus*, 1948, ink on paper. London: Tate.

NYMPHAEA WATER LILY

FAMILY Nymphaeaceae

The water-lily family consists of aquatic herbs with large round leaves, and includes the plant known in ancient Egypt as the lotus. Rooted in the quiet riverbed, the flower rests on the surface of the water. It thus symbolizes life force and the eternal cycle of life.

With flowers that open in the morning and close at night, the lotus symbolized the sun, creation and rebirth. It was sacred to Horus, the Egyptian hawk-headed god associated with the sun and the moon. He was the son of Osiris and Isis, and after his father's murder Isis hid him in the marshes of the Nile, where the lotus proliferates. When he grew up, Horus was strong enough to fight Seti, his father's killer, and assume the throne of Egypt; he is thus also linked with power and the pharaohs, who believed they were his descendants. Images of Egyptian water lilies – blue (*Nymphaea caerulea*) and white (*N. lotus*) – as symbols of power often appear in depictions of rulers and in tomb paintings, and inspire many column designs.

The Egyptian deity Nefertem emerged as a lotus from the primordial waters, signifying both sunlight and the delightful aroma of the lotus. A beautiful New Kingdom wooden head found in Tutankhamun's tomb is known as the 'Head of Nefertum' and is said to depict Tutankhamun as a child, emerging at the moment of lotus-birth. Wilson notes that the image links earthly political power with the divine regenerative powers of the gods.

The ancient Egyptian priesthood apparently used the lotus as a narcotic, and the elite classes soaked the petals in wine – with results both aphrodisiac and soporific.

The lotus is a sacred flower in Buddhism and Hinduism, representing enlightenment and resurrection. The lotus flower features prominently in much Asian art. In Hinduism the lotus is often featured alongside the divinities Lakshmi and Vishnu. In Buddhist art, the Buddha is usually shown on a lotus throne.

Among the most admired water-lily paintings are those created by the French Impressionist artist Claude Monet. When

Head of Nefertem, 18th Dynasty, 1332–1323 BCE. Cairo: Egyptian Museum.

Louis van Houtte, *Nymphaea stellata*, 1845.

he purchased the house he had previously rented in Giverny, northern France, he began lavishing his attention on the garden, particularly the water-lily pond. To establish this, he diverted a local stream – causing problems with his neighbours, who also objected when he introduced water lilies imported from foreign sources. He spent the last three decades of his life painting approximately 250 images of them, ranging from small to mural-sized works.[13]

Giovanni Aloi looks at Monet's water lilies without 'disciplinary-specific filters'. He notes that Monet's love affair with water lilies began with the exhibition of hybrids raised by the botanist Joseph Bory Latour-Marliac at the 1889 World's Fair in Paris:

Open form and lack of detail free the represented body from many economic, social, and cultural implications – if there is a symbolic register to be found in these extremely open paintings, it is that the water lilies are interconnected with everything else around them: the sky, the water, the grass, the trees hanging over them, and the human perceiving them. There's an eco-continuity and interconnectedness at play in these paintings that is unprecedented in the history of representation.

✤ Nakht and family fishing and fowling (detail), *c.* 1400–1370 BCE, tempera facsimile by Norman de Garis Davies and Lancelot Crane of image from the Tomb of Nakht, east wall, south side of offering chapel, 1908–10. New York: Metropolitan Museum of Art.

✱ Claude Monet, *Nymphéas*, 1897–98, oil on canvas. Los Angeles, CA: Los Angeles County Museum of Art.

*

Indeed, these paintings incorporate and go beyond the aims of Impressionism by capturing not only the fall of light and colour, but also the interconnectedness, eternal restlessness and movement of nature. Additionally, as embodiments of tranquillity and peace, they stand outside a modern world racked with troubles. Aloi also points out that Monet's water lilies resulted from selective breeding and hybridization, a fact that gives his paintings of them a 'more modern edge'.

OTHER EGYPTIAN LOTUS AND WATER-LILY IMAGES
- The hawk-headed god Horus holding a bouquet of lotus blossoms, *c.* 237 BCE. Edfu, Egypt: Temple of Horus.
- 'William' the hippo, 12th Dynasty, 1961–1878 BCE, faience. New York: Metropolitan Museum of Art.
- Banksy, *Forgive Us Our Trespassing*, 2011, acrylic, spray-paint and marker pens on wooden panels. Commissioned by the Museum of Contemporary Art, Los Angeles.

ORCHIDACEAE — ORCHID

FAMILY Orchidaceae

Orchids comprise one of the two most numerous flowering plant families in the world, the other being the daisy family (Asteraceae). They evolved some 78–84 million years ago; a bee trapped in amber bearing orchid pollen has been dated to 15–20 million years ago. Orchids appear in almost every environment, even glaciers.

In the ancient world, the name orchid comes from the Greek word for testicle because of the shape of the flower's bulbs. The Romans claimed that orchids sprang forth from the semen of copulating satyrs, or from the scattered body parts of the ritually sacrificed Orchis, son of a satyr. The orchids that appear on the Ara Pacis Augustae altar in Rome are the oldest orchid images in Western art.

Not surprisingly, given the flower's sexual associations, it was connected with potency and was a common ingredient in love potions. In the *Language of Flowers* it conveyed seduction.

In the second half of the nineteenth century 'Orchid Mania' took over, and orchids were valued above all other flowers. The demand led to ecological disaster, wiping out many orchids in the wild. Strangely, by the twentieth century it had become valued as a floral gift for dates and school proms, possibly because of their expense.

Orchids in low relief, 9 BCE. Rome: Ara Pacis Augustae.

John Nugent Fitch, *Cattleya velutina*, 1882–97.

OTHER ORCHID IMAGES
- Martin Johnson Heade, *Orchid with Two Hummingbirds*, 1871, oil on panel. Winston-Salem, NC: Reynolda House Museum of American Art.

PAPAVER — POPPY

FAMILY Papaveraceae

Poppies are herbaceous annuals, biennials or short-lived perennials. They come in many colours and bloom in the spring and early summer in temperate zones.

Opium is produced from the seeds of the opium poppy (*Papaver somniferum*), but despite the drug's popularity, little is known of its ancient history. It originated in the Neolithic period, and the locations suggested vary across West Asia and Europe. Egyptian doctors used poppy seeds to relieve pain, and poppy images occur in both Greek and Assyrian art of the fifth millennium BCE. It is possible that the poppy symbolized sleep and death in ancient Egypt, since poppies were included in the floral collars from Tutankhamun's embalming cache.

The ancient Greek god of sleep, Hypnos, is usually depicted wearing a crown of poppies. Ovid describes the realm of sleep as a hidden cavern, with at one end a lush field of poppies and at the other herbs of drowsiness that night gathers to sprinkle over the lands. The poppy was also linked with Morpheus, the god of dreams, and over time it became associated with death and eternal sleep. Poppies also figure in Virgil's *Georgics*, which tells how the Shades were placated by a gift of poppies. This later facilitated the fictional Dante's entry into Hades in search of Beatrice in the *Divine Comedy*.

Because of the flower's bright red colour, Christian doctrine took it as a symbol of Christ's Passion and blood, and it appears in some Crucifixion scenes. Wild poppies grow in wheatfields, thus conveying a Eucharistic connection.

The poppy in Rossetti's *Beata Beatrix* symbolizes death and grief, both Dante Alighieri's for his beloved Beatrice and Rossetti's

Roman sarcophagus with the myth of Selene and Endymion, early third century, marble. New York: Metropolitan Museum of Art.

Papaver somniferum, 1887.

PAPAVER POPPY

for the death of his wife, Elizabeth Siddal, the model for the image. Siddal died of an accidental overdose of laudanum, an opium tincture. A dove brings Beatrice a white poppy. The dove symbolizes the Holy Spirit, and the poppy signifies death; Rossetti additionally envisioned the bird as a messenger of love, and depicts Beatrice as if in a dream-like ecstasy, transformed, he writes in a letter in 1873, by 'sudden spiritual transfiguration'. The sundial shows the moment of her death, nine o'clock on 9 June 1290.

A Canadian doctor, John McCrae, noticing poppies growing amid the graves of First World War dead in the graveyard of Ypres, wrote a poem entitled 'In Flanders Fields' (1915). The poem led, in part, to the establishment of Remembrance Sunday, on which the fallen of various conflicts are honoured by wearing red poppies.

In 2014, the contemporary artist Paul Cummins, with the set designer Tom Piper and volunteers, created 888,246 ceramic poppies, one for each British and colonial soldier who died during the First World War. It took several thousand volunteers to install the poppies in the moat of the Tower of London. The first poppy was planted on 28 July 2014 and the last on 11 November 2014, and the flowers were subsequently sold to recoup expenses and for charity.

- Dante Gabriel Rossetti, *Beata Beatrix* (detail), *c.* 1864–70, oil on canvas. London: Tate.

- Paolo Veneziano, *Madonna of the Poppy* (detail), *c.* 1325, oil on panel. Venice: San Pantalon.

- Paul Cummins and Tom Piper, *Blood Swept Lands and Seas of Red*, 2014, ceramic poppies. Installation at the Tower of London.

OTHER POPPY IMAGES
- Michelangelo, *Night*, 1526–31, marble. Florence: Medici chapel (New Sacristy), San Lorenzo.
- Emil Nolde, *Poppies*, *c.* 1934, oil on canvas. Copenhagen: Statens Museum for Kunst.

PASSIFLORA — PASSIONFLOWER

FAMILY Passifloraceae

A fast-growing perennial climbing plant, the passionflower has large, intricate flowers and grows wild as well as in cultivated environments.

The passionflower is native to South and Central America and the southern United States. It was used traditionally as an anti-inflammatory and a calming herb, as well as being cultivated for food and drink.

Jesuit settlers in South America understood the flower as symbolic of the Passion of Christ, hence their name for it. Its radial filaments represent the Crown of Thorns; the three-pronged stigma indicates the three nails; the petals refer to the ten faithful Apostles; the five anthers represent Christ's five sacred wounds; and the central vertical element is the pillar to which he was tied before being beaten.

Charles Allston Collins depicted many flowers in his painting *Convent Thoughts*. A nun stands in a *hortus conclusus* holding what appears to be an illuminated book of hours; she studies a passionflower (representing Christ's Passion and Crucifixion), and there are forget-me-nots (remembrance), lilies (the Madonna's purity) and honeysuckle (constancy). Water lilies (purity of heart) float in the pond at her feet. Collins was not a member of the Pre-Raphaelite Brotherhood, although the painting clearly reflects the style of that group of painters, and the frame, ornamented with lilies, was created by John Everett Millais, who was a member. Debra Mancoff suggests that the painting shows

✣ John Everett Millais, *Isabella* (detail), 1849, oil on canvas. Liverpool: Walker Art Gallery.

✣ *Passiflora holosericea*, 1815.

✣ Charles Allston Collins, *Convent Thoughts*, 1851, oil on canvas. Oxford: Ashmolean Museum.

the novice learning lessons of piety from nature and symbolic flowers, and 'confirm[ing] her commitment to her calling'.

Passionflowers are found carved into gravestones as well as in church decor. In the US, several cemeteries feature gravestones by Louis Comfort Tiffany, many of them adorned with flowers; in Green-Wood Cemetery, Brooklyn, passionflowers emerge from the granite of the so-called Child's cross (1913). Tiffany, who died in 1933, is buried nearby.

OTHER PASSIONFLOWER IMAGES
- Tiffany Studios, Child's cross, *c.* 1913. Brooklyn, New York: Green-Wood Cemetery (National Historic Landmark).

ROSA — ROSE

FAMILY Rosaceae

The rose is a perennial flowering plant; the term is also used to refer to the flower itself. Most species are native to Asia, with smaller numbers being native to Europe, North America and northwestern Africa.

Roses are among the most valued and favoured plants in human history and, along with the lotus, the most symbolically significant. Symbolism varies by colour and by the number of petals. The blue rose, for instance, symbolizes impossibility.

Based on fossil evidence, the rose is around 35 million years old and has been cultivated for some 5,000 years in China. Consisting of a large number of species, it is one of the most widespread, cultivated and hybridized plants in history. It is not surprising, then, that the rose is one of the most frequently represented flowers in art, nor that it is associated with some of the most important figures in world culture. In most world cultures, roses were linked with goddesses – Aphrodite, Cybele, Psyche, the Three Graces, Flora and Eve – the Virgin Mary, who was believed to have been conceived while her mother, Anne, was smelling a rose, and female saints. Roses symbolize love, beauty, youth, war and politics.

In ancient Greece, the rose was sacred to Athena and Aphrodite. An origin story tells of Chloris, the goddess of flowers, who, when walking in the woods, found the dead body of a beautiful nymph. Wishing to give the nymph new life by transforming her into a flower, she called upon the other gods to help, and each contributed something to the creation of the rose. According to another myth, the rose was white until Aphrodite's lover Adonis was mortally wounded. The goddess, running to

him, pricked herself on a thorn, and her blood coloured the rose red.

The term *sub rosa* originated from the practice of attaching a rose to the ceiling of council chambers to swear all present to secrecy. In Rome, the rose was associated with death, and Rosalia, a celebration of roses, was linked with the cult of the dead.

In Christian art, the white rose signifies the Virgin's purity. She is called 'the rose without thorns', since she was untouched by Original Sin (it is said that roses grew thorns only after the Fall). The red rose symbolizes Christ's blood and his Passion, and the Christ Child sometimes holds a rose as he is depicted sitting in his mother's lap. The enthroned Virgin and Child often appear in a rose arbour or a *hortus conclusus* filled with roses. The German artist

Stefan Lochner loved plants and includes many in the work pictured here; not just red and white roses, but also lilies, strawberries and possibly a tiny apple.

Roses are a favourite flower in heraldic emblems and coats of arms, signifying nobility, sacrifice, triumph, war (the Romans believed the war god Mars was born from a rose), generosity and discretion. Another connection of the rose with war stems from the English Wars of the Roses (1455–85), fought between the houses of Lancaster (the red rose) and York (the white rose). The conflict ended with the establishment of the Tudor monarchy, the emblem of which includes both a white and a red rose, symbolizing peace.

The use of strings of beads as a mnemonic for prayer originated in antiquity and is found in several Asian religions. The Catholic version, the rosary, served as a meditation on the mysteries of the Virgin Mary. Rosaries have long been made of compressed rose petals. The word itself comes from the Latin *rosarium*, meaning a garden or garland of roses and, by association, a garden or bouquet of prayers.

OTHER ROSE IMAGES
- Pieter Vanderlyn, attrib., *Young Lady with a Rose*, 1732, oil on canvas. New York: Metropolitan Museum of Art.
- Dante Gabriel Rossetti, *The Beloved* ('*The Bride*'), 1865–66, oil on canvas. London: Tate.
- Herman de Vries, *Rosa Damascena*, 1984, dried flowers. Installation at 56th Venice Biennale.

✺ Stefan Lochner, *Madonna of the Rose Bower* (detail), c. 1440–42, oil on panel. Cologne: Wallraf-Richartz Museum.

✶ Pierre-Joseph Redouté, *Rosa centifolia*, 1817–24.

TULIPA   TULIP

FAMILY   Liliaceae

Tulips grew wild in West Asia and the Mediterranean, and were being cultivated in Istanbul by the mid-eleventh century. They are perennials that grow from bulbs and flourish in temperate climates.

In Persia, the flower – believed to have sprung from the tears of a disappointed lover – stood for perfect love. The petals are edible, but there is some question as to the toxicity of the bulbs.

The herbalist Conrad Gesner first described and illustrated the tulip for Europeans in 1561. It was brought to Vienna by an Austrian politician in the second half of the sixteenth century and soon spread throughout Europe. It reached the height of popularity in Holland, bringing about 'tulipomania', which resulted in great fortunes for some and financial ruin for others, until the entire market collapsed in 1657.

Dutch still lifes often included tulips alongside many other plants. Since many of these paintings depicted flowers that bloomed at different times, they have been called 'fantasy bouquets'. The Denver Art Museum website points out that such paintings were a 'cheap' alternative to buying real flowers; they lasted longer and could still be enjoyed in the winter. The flower also appears in *vanitas* paintings, where tulips in various stages of life, from fresh to wilted, signify the fragility and brevity of existence.

The presence of so many plant and flower species in Van Oosterwyck's sumptuous painting, opposite, relate to the fragility and brevity of life. The striped tulip on the left – a beautiful symbol of worldly greed and ephemeral wealth – seems to confront the sunflower (pp. 114–17), the ultimate symbol of the sun and the divine.

⊗   Charles Dessalines D'Orbigny, *Tulipa gesneriana*, 1849.

✳   Maria van Oosterwyck, *Bouquet of Flowers in a Vase*, c. 1670s, oil on canvas. Denver, CO: Denver Art Museum.

VIOLA   VIOLET

FAMILY Violaceae

The names 'violet' and 'viola' usually refer to small-flowered annuals or perennials, including wild species. Most are found in the temperate northern hemisphere.

Violets serve as garden plants, for decorative culinary use and for medicinal purposes (as antioxidants, and for insomnia and skin conditions). *Viola odorata* is also used as a source of scent in the perfume industry.

The violet symbolizes modesty and humility. It also stands for the balance between heaven and earth, sense and spirit, passion and reason, and love and wisdom. Clarity of mind and deliberate action are qualities associated with this flower.

In mythology, the violet is said to have grown from the blood of the Phrygian god of vegetation, Attis, who incited the jealousy of Cybele; she, driven mad by him, struck him so that he self-mutilated and died. Cybele, regaining her sanity, begged Zeus to keep Attis's corpse from decaying, resulting in the bloom. Another story involving jealousy is told of Zeus, who loved Io and, to avoid Hera's wrath, turned the mortal into a white heifer. When the heifer shed tears on the grass, Zeus transformed her tears into violets, more suited to her delicate

OTHER VIOLET IMAGES
- Pauline Powell Burns, *Violets*, *c.* 1890, oil on cardboard. Washington, DC: Smithsonian National Museum of African American History and Culture.

taste. Because of violets' association with incorruptibility, the Romans decorated graves with the flower on *dies violaris*, violet day.

The flower's core symbolism led to its association with the Virgin Mary, as well as Christ in his humble human form. The flower appears in paintings of the Madonna and Child, in Adoration scenes and, although rarely, at the foot of the Cross. In medieval art Christ sometimes wears a purple robe, the colour of the violet, symbolizing both his humble humanity and the acceptance of divinity.

❈ Stefan Lochner, *Virgin with the Violet* (detail), *c.* 1450, oil and tempera on wood. Cologne: Kolumba Museum.

❈ Ford Madox Brown, *The Convalescent (A Portrait of the Artist's Wife)*, 1872, pastel on paper. New York: Metropolitan Museum of Art.

❈ Jacques Le Moyne de Morgues, Violets, *c.* 1575.

VIOLA × WITTROCKIANA — PANSY

FAMILY Violaceae

The pansy is derived from the hybridization of *Viola tricolor* and other wild violets, and the words pansy, violet and viola are sometimes used interchangeably.

Pansies have two petals pointing up and three to the sides and downwards, although *V. melanium* has four upward-pointing petals. The flower's name comes from the French *pensée*, the feminine form of the verb *penser*, to think or ponder something. The French word was derived from the Latin *pensare* or *pendare*: to consider, to take everything into consideration; by extension, to remember. Early herbals, referring to the 'heartsease pansy', touted the plant's curative powers, especially for painful disorders of the heart. Wild varieties of the plant are still often called heartsease.

The flower, which can also symbolize humility and love, has been a favourite of writers and poets, including Shakespeare, Ben Jonson, Edmund Spenser, Wordsworth, Nathaniel Hawthorne and D. H. Lawrence. In *A Midsummer Night's Dream*, the fairy king Oberon tells how the once white pansy turned 'purple with love's wound' when shot by Cupid's arrow. Older names for the flower linked it with wanton affection.

Pansies were a popular subject in nineteenth-century art. In Van Gogh's painting, opposite, a basket of pansies rests on a small stool shaped like a tambourine. Such stools and tables graced the Café du Tambourin in Paris, which Van Gogh frequented and where he exhibited his own art and a selection from his collection of Japanese prints. He had a brief relationship with the proprietor, Agostina Segatori, so the flowers may signify his affection and indicate that she was in his thoughts.

OTHER PANSY IMAGES
- Henri Fantin-Latour, *Still Life with Pansies*, 1874, oil on canvas. New York: Metropolitan Museum of Art.
- Georgia O'Keeffe, *Black Pansy and Forget-Me-Nots*, 1926, oil on canvas. Brooklyn, NY: Brooklyn Museum.
- Joe Brainard, *Three Pansies*, 1967, watercolour on paper. New York: Metropolitan Museum of Art.

- J. Vandamme, *Viola tricolor* (1. *Gloire de Bellevue*; 2. *Reine des Panachées*), 1854.

- Vincent van Gogh, *Basket of Pansies*, 1887, oil on canvas. Amsterdam: Van Gogh Museum.

- British Queen Elizabeth I's embroidered bookbinding, created at the age of eleven for her stepmother Katherine Parr, 1544. Oxford: Bodleian Library.

FRUIT, VEGETABLES & SEASONINGS

Like flowers, fruit and vegetables often appear in art because of their beauty and sensuous appeal. This aspect of their symbolism is most evident in still lifes.

The earliest depictions of fruit are found in ancient Egypt, where paintings of food appear on tomb walls. The Egyptians believed the images became tangible in the afterlife and thus provided sustenance for the dead.

Mosaic *emblemata* representing fruit and other food adorned the walls of wealthy Romans, signifying the hospitality that would be extended to guests. The images also presented a visual celebration of the seasons.

Later depictions of fresh fruit convey fertility, vitality, youth and abundance. In a state of decay, they signify transience and mortality. This can be seen in Cézanne's *Still Life with Skull*, in which a prominent piece of decaying fruit has dark cavities that mimic the skull's eye and nasal holes.

Vegetables are classified in various ways. The most useful system divides them by the part of the plant that is consumed: bulbs (such as onion), flowers (broccoli), leaves (lettuce), stalks (celery), tubers (potato) and roots (carrot).

When it comes to seasonings, the words 'spice' and 'herb' are often used interchangeably, but they are actually two different things, made from different parts of plants and processed in different ways. Spices are generally more highly flavoured because they come from parts of the plant that contain essential oils. Even so, the distinction between herb and spice is not always clear, and some plants provide both herbs and spices. Coriander (*Coriandrum sativum*) produces a seed that is ground to serve as a spice. The leaves that provide the herb are also known as coriander (cilantro in the United States). Dillweed, mustard and myrrh's seeds also all provide spices, while their leaves are used as herbs.

❈ Vincent van Gogh, *Grapes, Lemons, Pears, and Apples* (detail), 1887, oil on canvas. Chicago, IL: Art Institute of Chicago.

❈ Adriaen van Utrecht and Theodoor Rombouts, *An amorous couple with lettuce, artichokes, peas and other vegetables, with a squirrel* (detail), *c.* 1630, oil on canvas. Private collection.

❈ Paul Cézanne, *Nature morte au crâne* (*Still Life with Skull*), 1890–93, oil on canvas. Philadelphia, PA: Barnes Foundation.

INTRODUCTION

ALLIUM CEPA — ONION

FAMILY Amaryllidaceae

The onion, like garlic, spring onions, shallots, chives and leeks, is a member of the amaryllis family, and is categorized as a vegetable. It has been cultivated for 7,000 years.

Onions were known to the ancient Egyptians, and Homer mentioned them in his writings. The Romans substituted onions and fish for human heads in sacrificial ceremonies to Jupiter. Onions figure in folk medicine and have been viewed as an aphrodisiac. In Europe, they have also carried the reputation of being food for poor people, due in part to the fact that they are cheap to buy or grow.

Giuseppe Arcimboldo arranged fruit and vegetables to form human heads. Aside from their immediate whimsicality, the artist's works show his keen appreciation and knowledge of plants; *Spring* (1573) contains some eighty identifiable plants. *The Vegetable Gardener* features an onion cheek. The bountiful vegetables have sexual connotations, like the fleshy mushrooms that make up the lips; the onion has been compared to a woman's breast, the tangle of roots positioned where a nipple would be. Inverted, the image becomes a bowl with vegetables in it. Arcimboldo's work has been interpreted as criticizing the wealthy elite's behaviour and their frivolous approach to nature. Aloi suggests that the images served as an 'attention-seeking device' that expressed anthropocentric concerns.

Broadly speaking, onions, because they cause eye irritation, are regarded as useful but superficially unpleasant – suggestive of life's woes. With its many concentric rings, the onion sometimes also serves as a metaphor for mystery and life.

- Pierre-Joseph Redouté, *Allium fragrans* (fragrant onion), 1805–16.

- Giuseppe Arcimboldo, *L'Ortolano* (*The Vegetable Gardener*), 1587–90, oil on panel. Cremona, Italy: Museo Civico Ala Ponzone.

ANANAS — PINEAPPLE

FAMILY Bromeliaceae

A tropical plant with edible fruit, the pineapple originated in South America, where it was an important source of food and medicine to the Tupinambá people in the Amazon region. It is thought to have symbolized hospitality and fertility.

First cultivated in Europe in the seventeenth century, it became a symbol of wealth and luxury. Though they are not native to the islands, Hawai'i is now the most active producer of pineapples.

As a symbol of hospitality, sculpted and painted pineapples ornament architecture and interiors. In colonial Virginia, sailors placed a pineapple on the gatepost to announce their safe return home. The 'Dunmore Pineapple' summerhouse in Scotland, built for the 4th Earl of Dunmore, last Governor of Virginia, announced his return home somewhat more dramatically. Acquired by the Scottish National Trust in the 1970s, it is now a holiday guest house.

- Sir William Chambers, 'The Dunmore Pineapple', after 1777. Dunmore, Scotland.

- Georg Ehret, *Ananas aculeatus* (pineapple), c. 1742.

- Terracotta *pinax* (votive tablet) showing Persephone and Hades enthroned, 500–450 BCE. Reggio Calabria, Italy: Museo Nazionale.

- Cesare Ubertini, Wild celery (*Apium graveolens* L.), 1772–93.

158

FRUIT, VEGETABLES & SEASONINGS

APIUM GRAVEOLENS VAR. *DULCE*   CELERY

FAMILY Apiaceae

Celery was first cultivated in the ancient Mediterranean. It is a diuretic and has been known as an aphrodisiac, an effect that some researchers attribute to androsterone, a steroid that acts as a pheromone.

Celery leaves were found in garlands in the tomb of Tutankhamun, and the Cairo Agricultural Museum owns a wreath with celery leaves from the grave of a Theban nobleman. The Greeks and Romans also garlanded their dead with celery, and victorious athletes were crowned with the plant, possibly reflecting its links with bravery and victory.

Celery had conflicting meanings in classical Greece. It plays an aphrodisiac role in Homer's *Odyssey*, growing on the isle of the nymph Calypso and possibly inflaming her lust for Odysseus. It was linked to the lusty god Silenus, but was also believed to have sprouted from the blood of an Underworld deity, and thus associated with death. In this votive tablet from the Sanctuary of Persephone at Locri in southern Italy, Hades, god of the Underworld, holds a plant that has been identified as celery.

In the eighteenth century, Mme de Pompadour served King Louis XV celery soup for its aphrodisiac properties; it was also reputedly consumed by the adventurer Giacomo Casanova. Celery became an irresistible luxury in nineteenth-century Europe and North America, and in 1912 it was served in first class on the Titanic.

BRASSICA OLERACEA VAR. *CAPITATA* — CABBAGE

FAMILY Brassicaceae

The cabbage is generally regarded as a humble vegetable and a symbol of the everyday and ordinary. Formerly a member of the mustard family, it now has its own family. Brassicaceae contains many plants that have been domesticated and altered, including broccoli, Brussels sprouts, cauliflower and kale, as well as ornamentals like candytuft and honesty.

Stanley Spencer's *The Dustman* shows a family retrieving items from the rubbish. An overripe cabbage occupies the centre of the canvas. Spencer celebrates ordinariness, writing: 'All the signs and tokens of home life, such as cabbage leaves and teapot, which I have so much loved that I have had them resurrected from the dustbin because they are reminders of home life and peace'.

The Romans apparently used cabbage to alleviate hangovers. They placed its leaves on wounds and mixed it with honey to salve the eyes. In the sixteenth and seventeenth centuries the cabbage symbolized female sexuality and hidden beauty.

Leonora Carrington created a portrait of a red cabbage, of which she wrote: 'it...screams when dragged out of the earth and plunged into boiling water or grease – forgive us, cabbage...the cabbage is still the alchemical rose'. For Carrington, the 'ordinary' cabbage was extraordinary, sentient and mystical. Her cabbage is a Chinese cabbage (*Brassica rapa*), with a tightly packed head inside the graceful leaves.

✵ Anselmus Boëtius de Boodt, Cabbage (*Brassica oleracea*), 1596–1610.

✵ Stanley Spencer, *The Dustman* or *The Lovers* (detail), 1934, oil on canvas. Newcastle upon Tyne: Laing Art Gallery.

✤ Leonora Carrington, *Cabbage*, 1987, acrylic on canvas. Private collection.

OTHER CABBAGE IMAGES
- Pieter Aertsen, *Market Scene*, 1569, oil on wood. Stockholm: Hallwylska Museet.
- Nathaniel Bacon, *Cookmaid with Still Life of Vegetables and Fruit*, 1620–26, oil on canvas. London: Tate.

CUCURBITA / CRESCENTIA / LAGENARIA AND OTHER GENERA — GOURD

FAMILY Cucurbitaceae

Gourds include the fruit of flowering plants such as pumpkins, cucumbers, squash, courgettes and various melons.

In the context of art, the hollow shells of bottle gourds (also known as calabash, *Lagenaria siceraria*, and found on archaeological sites dating from as early as 13,000 BCE) served not only as musical instruments but also as decorated containers.

In some translations of 1 Kings 6 and 7, sacred gourds adorned the interior of the Temple of Solomon and the basin that held water for ritual use. They represent fertility, new life and the sunrise. The solar symbolism stems from the gourd's mature shape, which swells like God's emblem, the sun, as it rises in the morning.

Albrecht Dürer's *St Jerome in His Study* depicts the contemplative ideal of the Christian scholar. One odd feature is the huge gourd hanging from the ceiling. St Jerome mistranslated the Latin word *cucurbita* in the story of the prophet Jonah as a type of ivy, and debate ensued in letters he exchanged with St Augustine in 403–4 CE. By placing the gourd in the saint's study, Dürer refers to this erudite discussion.

The gourd symbolizes both transience and salvation, since God provided Jonah with a gourd as a shelter from the elements, and then sent a worm to destroy it. In Dürer's image, the hanging gourd relates to the skull on the windowsill, serving as a *memento mori*, a reminder of the brevity of life and, one could assume, philological discussions.

The many seeds of the gourd link it to fertility, but because it grows and withers quickly, it also symbolizes the brevity and fragility of life. In modern times, all over the world, gourds are carved, painted and inlaid for decorative purposes.

Albrecht Dürer, *St Jerome in His Study* (detail), 1514, engraving.

Elizabeth Twining, *Cucurbitaceae*, The Gourd Tribe, 1849–55.

CUCURBITA / CRESCENTIA / LAGENARIA AND OTHER GENERA GOURD

CUCURBITA — PUMPKIN

FAMILY Cucurbitaceae

The pumpkin often symbolizes prosperity, growth and abundance. It is native to the Americas and had reached Europe by the sixteenth century, first appearing in the Villa Farnesina, Rome, in festoons painted between 1515 and 1518.

Raphael supervised work in the Villa Farnesina's Loggia of Psyche; the fruit and vegetables there allude to love and sexuality. Giovanni Martini da Udine painted the bountiful festoons with more than 170 species, identified by Caneva and Janick as including a huge variety of cucurbits. Agostino Chigi, a banker and the original owner of the villa, was also pivotal in cultivating plants from the Americas in Europe.

The pumpkin is now linked most closely with Halloween, as jack-o'-lanterns that illuminate porches and shine from windows, traditionally a form of protection. The journalist Blane Bachelor writes in *National Geographic* that

- Giovanni Martini da Udine, fruits, flowers and vegetables (detail), including *Cucurbita maxima* (pumpkin), 1515–81, fresco. Rome: Villa Farnesina, Loggia of Cupid and Psyche.
- Cesare Ubertini, *Cucurbita aspera Pyriformis* (Pumpkin), 1772–93.
- Yayoi Kusama, *Pumpkin*, 1994. Naoshima: Benesse Art Site.

representations of the human head relate to the Celtic festival of Samhain, originally celebrated on 1 November. To ward off wandering spirits, the Celts carved scary faces into root vegetables such as beetroot, turnips and potatoes. The jack-o'-lantern is said to have been introduced to the United States by Irish immigrants, who quickly replaced the root vegetables of their homeland with pumpkins. A carved pumpkin appeared on the cover of *Harper's Weekly* in 1867, but perhaps the most memorable comes from Washington Irving's short story 'The Legend of Sleepy Hollow' (1820). And, of course, Cinderella's coach was a pumpkin. The demand for pumpkins today explains why in the US in 2022, more than a billion pounds were harvested. Professional pumpkin carvers work all year round. Some duplicate masterpieces of art, while others, such as Ray Villafane, depict squashed and manipulated heads.

Yayoi Kusama claims that, the first time she ever saw one as a child, the pumpkins on her family's seed farm spoke to her. The rotund forms she first created while in her teens brought her poetic peace, and symbolized her childhood, life and fertility. She says, 'I love pumpkins because of their humorous form, warm feeling and human-like quality and form. My desire to create works of pumpkins... continues. I have enthusiasm as if I were still a child'. Her pumpkins still speak to her, and have made her one of Japan's most important contemporary artists.

OTHER PUMPKIN IMAGES
- Disney Enterprises, *Cinderella*, 1950.
- Arthur Rackham, 'The Headless Horseman', from Washington Irving's 'The Legend of Sleepy Hollow', 1928.

CYNARA CARDUNCULUS VAR. *SCOLYMUS*   ARTICHOKE

FAMILY Asteraceae

The globe artichoke (also known as the French artichoke or green artichoke) is a variety of thistle that is cultivated as food.

The edible part of the vegetable consists of the leaves and central 'choke' before the flowers bloom. Artichokes can also be made into a herbal tea and the Italian liqueur Cynar, and artichoke leaf powder is being investigated for medicinal use to reduce cholesterol.

The ancient Greeks and Romans consumed artichokes, even though Pliny referred to them as monstrosities of nature. The thyrsus, a staff held by Dionysus and his maenads, was formerly said to be topped with a pine cone – but lately it has been re-identified as an artichoke.

After visiting Strawberry Hill, the former home of Horace Walpole, in west London in 2017, Caroline Murray wrote:

The artichoke (Cynara cardunculus var. scolymus) has to be one of the vegetables least likely to have been discovered to be edible – what desperate early inhabitant of the Mediterranean area first took the trouble to wrestle one into submission and find that this particular giant thistle was concealing something rather delicious under all the sharp points and choking bits?

Murray also writes about the plant's contradictory meanings: sadness, hope for a prosperous future, disappointment, and – since it has a heart – love and devotion. This latter symbolism may be at work in the so-called *Bedford Double Portrait*, of which four versions exist. Mary Tudor and Charles Brandon, Duke of Suffolk, appear hand in hand. Mary's brother Henry VIII wished to cement political alliances by marrying her to the much older Louis XII of France, first by proxy and later in reality, but Louis died abruptly eighty-two days after the wedding, possibly thanks to his enthusiastic reception of the beautiful Mary. After a great deal of intrigue, Mary and Brandon returned to England and were married. The artichoke in Mary's hand has been compared to a royal orb and may relate to her brief stint as queen of France, but it is more likely to signify the love she felt for Brandon.

※ Dancing maenad holding a thyrsus (detail), Roman copy after fifth-century BCE Greek original, attributed to Callimachus. Madrid: Museo del Prado.

※ British School, *Mary Tudor and Charles Brandon, 1st Duke of Suffolk* (detail), after 1515, oil on canvas. Cambridge, UK: Anglesey Abbey.

❖ Basilius Besler, *Fructus artischochi* (artichoke), 1613.

DAUCUS CAROTA — CARROT

FAMILY Apiaceae

Carrots are associated with health, abundance and fertility, in part because, like other elongated, cylindrical fruit and vegetables, they are vaguely phallic.

The wild carrot probably originated in Persia, and evidence of its presence in Europe dates from as early as 3000 BCE. Heirloom carrots come in many colours; the characteristic orange developed from selective breeding in the seventeenth century. The bright orange colour comes from the concentration of beta-carotenes (sadly, despite all tales to the contrary, it doesn't improve vision). Carrots are also a good source of vitamins K and B6.

Along with myriad fruit and other vegetables, carrots appear in many images from the sixteenth century onwards, among them Dutch market and kitchen paintings. One of the more entertaining European images is by an unknown French artist and depicts a fantastic women's headpiece. This whimsical arrangement possibly stemmed from the earlier practice of lacing headdresses with carrot foliage as a substitute for feathers. Outrageously tall headdresses, apparently a craze begun by Queen Marie Antoinette of France in the late eighteenth century, incorporated faux materials of all sorts; caricatures of the period show servants following women with tools to keep their headdresses from tipping backwards. In addition to the carrots large and small in the illustrated headdress, lettuce and possibly *haricots verts* (green beans) appear.

The Surrealist René Magritte often played with plants in his art, creating hybrid images, mysterious forests and realistic bottles. The

⊗ Unknown artist (French), 'Fantastic Hairdress with Fruit and Vegetable Motif', eighteenth century, watercolour on canvas over board. New York: Metropolitan Museum of Art.

✳ Maubert, Edible roots, 1864–69.

❖ René Magritte, *L'Explication* (*The Explanation*), 1952, oil on canvas. Private collection.

❖

first bottle, painted in 1940, probably reflects wartime material shortages, and he is said to have done it to amuse his friends. Magritte returned to the bottle form in sculpture and painting into the 1960s, and more than thirty survive. One of the most puzzling paintings is *The Explanation*. A bottle is depicted on the left next to another bottle that seems to be transforming into a carrot, its form a pointed cylinder. A rather anaemic-looking carrot lies in the foreground. The scholarly literature on Magritte lacks an explanation. The empty bottle may convey inebriation, and in combination with the the carrot's association with male genitalia and the bullet- or bomb-shaped cylinder, could be read as a suggestion, even explanation, of where things have gone wrong.

FOENICULUM — FENNEL

FAMILY Apiaceae

A flowering plant in the carrot family, fennel is indigenous to the Mediterranean basin and now widely naturalized elsewhere. It is classified as a herb, used to flavour absinthe, and various parts of the plant are also used in cooking.

It produces aromatic seeds that are sometimes confused with those of anise, which are similar in taste and appearance, although smaller.

According to Pliny, fennel cleared vision and provided spiritual rejuvenation. The herb was sacred to fire-making gods such as Prometheus, who was said to have brought fire down from the heavens as a gift to human beings. Greek islanders traditionally carried fire from place to place in the stalks of giant fennel, since the pith is fire-resistant. And in present-day Italy, ceremonial battles are fought with fennel stalks in a traditional attempt to avert agricultural disasters. The plant, when eaten by snakes, was believed to cause shedding, so it has also symbolized periodic renewal and rejuvenation.

In *The Blind Leading the Blind*, painted the year before the artist's death, Pieter Bruegel the Elder depicted a Flemish proverb, probably based on Matthew 15:14, in which Christ, referring to the Pharisees, says, 'They are blind leaders of the blind. And if the blind leads the blind, both will fall into a ditch.' The powerful painting not only illustrates several forms of blindness, but also contains symbolic plants. Guy de Chauliac, a contemporary doctor, wrote that blindness was caused by 'corrupt fumes, mounting from the stomach to the brain'.

Sufferers could chew on cloves, cinnamon, fennel, anise, coriander and nuts of maquette, resulting in gentle, curative breath. The surface of the painting was abraded at some point, but plants that can be identified include fennel (immediately behind the figure in blue, second from the right) and an iris (above the fallen man on the far right).

⊗ Pieter Bruegel the Elder, *The Blind Leading the Blind*, 1568, distemper on canvas. Naples, Italy: Museo e Real Bosco di Capodimonte.

✳ Cesare Ubertini, *Crithmum maritimum* (Sea fennel), 1772–93.

FOENICULUM FENNEL

FRAGARIA — STRAWBERRY

FAMILY Rosaceae

Strawberries are cultivated worldwide for their fruit, which is appreciated for its sweetness, aroma and bright red colour.

Technically, the fruit is not a berry, because its flesh does not come from the ovary of the flower. The first garden strawberries were transplanted from the wild in the Middle Ages.

The strawberry is a symbol of harmony and spiritual nourishment. Although no mention of the fruit occurs in the Bible, it has often been considered part of the earthly paradise. The strawberry also appears in scenes of the Nativity and the Adoration, as well as in depictions of the Holy Family. The three-lobed leaves relate to the Trinity, the little white flower suggests innocence and humility, and, above all, the red fruit evokes blood and the Passion of Christ. For this reason, it also appears in some Crucifixion and Deposition scenes.

In the medieval period, strawberries were carved on altarpieces and atop columns. They often appeared in illuminated manuscripts, partly for their decorative appeal but also as symbols of innocence and fruitfulness, the latter because of their many seeds. Probably for this reason, the strawberry is also associated with the Virgin Mary. Strawberry plants with fruit often adorn the Virgin's gardens, especially the *hortus conclusus*. This inclusion of strawberries in garden settings continued during the Renaissance.

Luscious-looking strawberries appear in the centre panel of *The Garden of Earthly Delights* by Hieronymus Bosch. The panel, representing humanity after Adam and Eve's expulsion from Eden, depicts a multitude of naked figures cavorting about. Set in a lush, intricate landscape, they indulge in delicious-looking

edibles, amorous activities and other earthly pleasures. Bosch lived in a strict religious community, and some critics have suggested that the painting warns against most of the seven deadly sins, especially lust. Strawberries supposedly had aphrodisiac properties, but they may also signify the dangers of another deadly sin, gluttony. One detail shows a man embracing and biting a large berry; elsewhere, a ring of naked figures huddle beneath a giant strawberry that they seem almost to be worshipping. Generally, the centre panel sets out all sorts of sins, tempting but ephemeral. The huge strawberry pins the figures down, in much the same way sin ensnares and weighs down the soul. The consequences of sin are made evident in the gloomy, menacing right-hand panel.

Fray José de Sigüenza, an early seventeenth-century monk and librarian at El Escorial, Spain, suggested that the strawberries in this painting symbolized the ephemeral, transient nature of earthly pleasures.

❈ Hieronymus Bosch, *The Garden of Earthly Delights* (detail of centre panel), 1490–1500, oil on oak. Madrid: Museo del Prado.

❋ Upper Rhenish Master, *Madonna in den Erdbeeren* (*Madonna of the Strawberries*) (detail), *c.* 1425, mixed media on spruce wood. Solothurn, Switzerland: Kunstmuseum Solothurn.

❖ G. Severeyns, Strawberries, 1851.

OTHER STRAWBERRY IMAGES
- Anon. (possibly Polish), *The Madonna with Wild Strawberry, c.* 1465–77, oil on panel. Kraków, Poland: Stanisław Wyspiański Museum.

MALUS   APPLE

FAMILY Rosaceae

Having originated in Central Asia, apples are now cultivated worldwide. A large number of species exist that vary in tree size and fruit yield.

In secular art, the apple can symbolize the cosmos or totality thanks to its perfectly spherical shape. In portraits, emperors and kings often hold an 'imperial apple' (orb) along with a sceptre. Apples were also linked with many goddesses and came to be regarded as magical fruit that granted immortality. The apple tree served as the World Tree in many cultures.

The fruit that tempted Eve in Eden is not named in Genesis, and many possibilities have been suggested. Having eaten the fruit, Adam and Eve obtained forbidden knowledge (Genesis 3:5), contrary to the Creator's will, and were banished from Eden. One reason for identifying the apple as the forbidden fruit is that the Latin word *malum* (from which the genus name comes) means both apple and evil.

The ancient Greeks believed that Dionysus, the god of wine and intoxication, created the apple, which he gave to Aphrodite, the goddess of love. Apples were also associated with beauty and sexuality. When Eris, the goddess of discord, called for 'the judgment of Paris', she threw down a golden apple and demanded that he choose the most beautiful goddess. Paris chose Aphrodite, who rewarded him with Helen of Troy. Helen's abduction led to the Trojan War.

The most famous apples in antiquity were the golden ones in Hera's garden at the ends of the earth, guarded by nymphs called the Hesperides and a 100-headed dragon. The apples, which granted immortality, were Gaia's wedding gift to Hera when she married Zeus. Obtaining the apples formed the eleventh labour of Hercules. The hero needed Atlas's help and agreed to hold the heavens aloft while the giant fetched the apples. When Atlas returned, he thought he would leave Hercules holding the heavens, but was, inevitably, tricked into taking the weight back.

In Christian art, Christ often reaches out for or holds an apple, signifying his role as a

※ Orchard Painter (attrib.), *Women Gathering Apples*, obverse of a red-figure column krater, *c.* 460 BCE. New York: Metropolitan Museum of Art.

※ Giorgio Gallesio, *Malus appenninensis* (Pupina apple), 1817–39.

redeemer from sin and death. His birth returns the world to the state of innocence before the Temptation and Fall. In the Venetian painter Carlo Crivelli's *Madonna and Child*, a swag of apples and a cucumber-like gourd hang above the Virgin's head, signifying salvation.

One of the most famous twentieth-century apples appears in Magritte's *Son of Man* (1963). It started out as a self-portrait in response to a commission by Harry Torczyner, the artist's friend, advisor and patron. The face-obscuring apple and the title could refer to Original Sin and expulsion from Eden. The apple, the enigmatic setting and the bowler-hatted, well-dressed but rigid figure all recur in Magritte's work, evoking mystery and ambiguity. For Magritte, the painting involved the tension between the visible and the hidden. The whites of the eyes – just visible on either side of the apple – the flattened coat and the left arm, which seems to bend back at the elbow, add to the enigma of sight, the conflict between seen and unseen.

OTHER IMAGES OF APPLES
- Mary Cassatt, *Baby Reaching for an Apple*, 1893, oil on canvas. Private collection.
- Carlo Crivelli, *Madonna and Child*, c. 1480, tempera and gold on panel. New York: Metropolitan Museum of Art.
- René Magritte, *La Chambre d'écoute (The Listening Room)*, 1952, oil on canvas. Houston: Menil Collection.
- Gabriël Metsu, *La Peleuse de pommes (The Apple Peeler)*, 1662, oil on wood. Paris: Musée du Louvre.

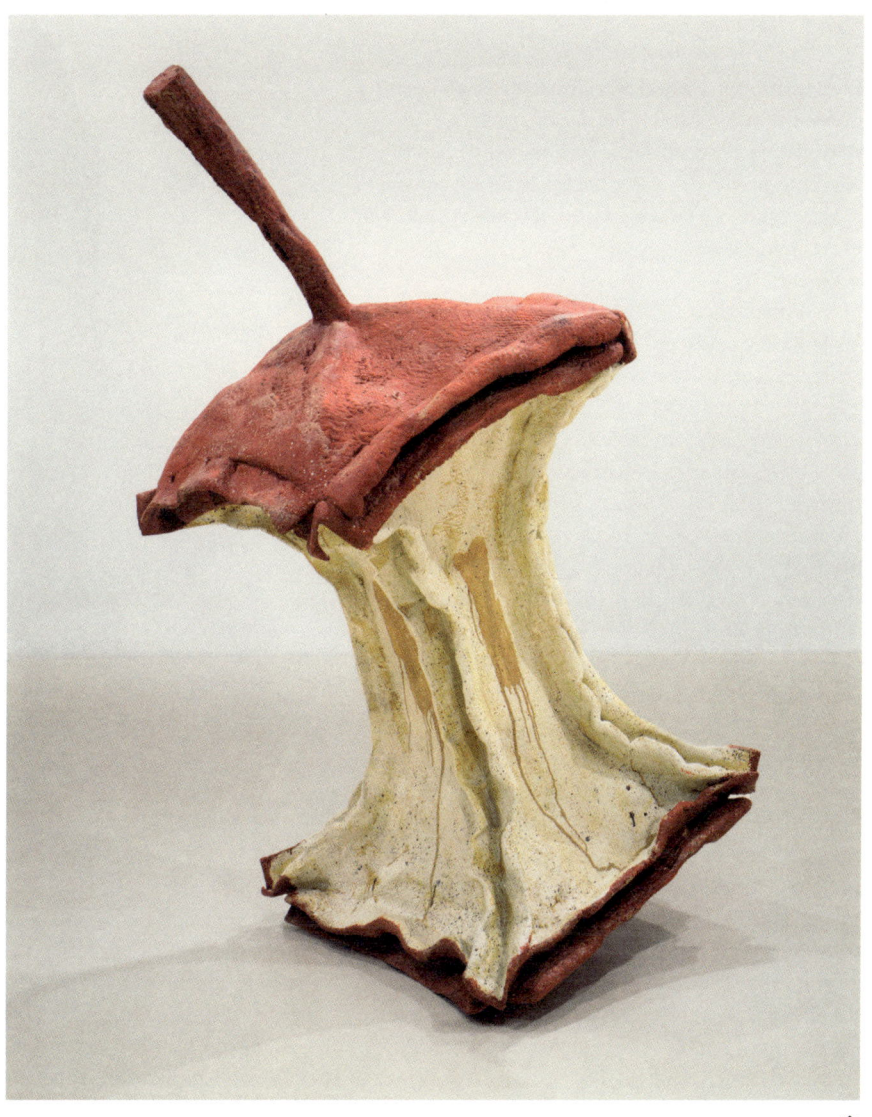

❖ René Magritte, *The Son of Man*, 1964, oil on canvas. Private collection.

✸ Claes Oldenburg and Coosje van Bruggen, *Geometric Apple Core*, 1991, latex paint, polyurethane and steel. San Francisco, CA: Museum of Modern Art.

MUSA — BANANA

FAMILY Musaceae

The banana is an elongated fruit (technically a berry) of several large flowering herbaceous plants. The words 'banana' and 'plantain' are sometimes used interchangeably. Generally, botanists do not consider the plant to be a tree since its 'trunk' consists entirely of entwined leaves.

First domesticated in Polynesia, bananas now grow in 135 countries around the world. The fruit develops all year round in large clusters of approximately twenty, in between three and twenty tiers. Touted as a good source of potassium, bananas in fact deliver less of that nutrient than raw spinach, skinless cooked potatoes and soybeans, but according to Alex Abella's *The Total Banana* (1979) they do still have substantial benefits, including providing important vitamins, assisting with weight reduction and maintaining healthy digestion.

As they became more widespread in Europe and North America, bananas came to represent ideas of the 'exotic'. In 1924, Josephine Baker danced semi-naked at the Folies Bergère in Paris with only a string of artificial bananas around her waist, drawing on and challenging such imagery. Bananas have since featured in other costumes: in the 1930s, Carmen Miranda's costume included a fruit-bowl hat full of bananas and other tropical fruit; excessive numbers of oversized (not to mention suggestive) bananas appeared in Busby Berkeley's film *The Gang's All Here* (1943), which starred Miranda. Her popularity may have induced United Fruit to invent the brand name Chiquita Banana.

When bananas appear in art, it is often as a symbol of the erotic. De Chirico's *The Uncertainty of the Poet* depicts a rather twisted

antique sculpture that is said to represent Aphrodite, side by side with a cluster of twenty-three bananas that appear to have been ripped from a tree. One of the artist's most important paintings, it contains elements typical of de Chirico, among them a train belching smoke, long shadows and a sharply tilted arcade. The conjunction of bananas and the classical torso evokes both exoticism and a sort of mysterious, constrained eroticism.

In the twenty-first century, various banana-related works have raised questions about consumption and gender. Maurizio

Cattelan's *Comedian* consisted of a banana duct-taped to the wall at Art Basel, Miami, in 2019. The 'edition' of three bananas sold for between $120,000 and $150,000 each, with purchasers buying the concept and a certificate of authenticity. The Dadaist conceptual work attracted such crowds that the banana had to be removed. *Consumer Art*, a video work from the 1970s by the Polish artist Natalia LL showing herself eating bananas suggestively, was removed from view in Warsaw's National Museum in 2019. Almost 1,000 people gathered outside and ate bananas in protest, prompting the museum to put the video back on display.

- Berthe Hoola van Nooten, *Musa paradisiaca L.* (plantain banana), c. 1885.

- Giorgio de Chirico, *The Uncertainty of the Poet*, 1913, oil on canvas. London: Tate.

MYRISTICA FRAGRANS — NUTMEG

FAMILY Myristicaceae

A seed or ground spice, nutmeg originated in Indonesia. Its health benefits are unclear, and in large amounts it can be hallucinogenic and even toxic.

The Indonesian Banda Islands remained its only source until the nineteenth century. In the seventeenth century, the Dutch East India Company killed, starved, exiled and enslaved the Bandanese in order to control the nutmeg market.

Today, nutmeg is an important crop in Grenada, having been introduced by English merchants in 1843. The spice mace, which features prominently in Caribbean food, comes from nutmeg's bright red seed cover.

The Norwegian sculptor Lene Kilde received a scholarship from Arts Council Norway that enabled her to travel to Grenada in 2014. Grenada's Underwater Sculpture Park, one of twenty-five gardens created by Jason deCaires Taylor, contains ecologically friendly sculptures that encourage marine growth and keep tourists away from nearby fragile coral reefs. Kilde's sculpture *The Nutmeg Princess*, inspired by a book of the same name by a Grenadian author, Richardo Keens-Douglas, stands 3.4 m (11 ft) tall. In the book, the Nutmeg Princess, who knows when the nutmeg is ripe, can be seen only by the brave and pure of heart. She encourages the children to believe in themselves and follow their dreams. Kilde's figure, eyes closed and apparently arising from a giant nutmeg, reaches upwards, her hands full of nutmeg. Once installed, Kilde notes, the sculpture has changed 'day by day, providing hiding places for marine life, and surfaces for corals and sponges to attach and grow'. The figure's rapt expression and pose convey generosity, contemplation and joy.

Lene Kilde, *The Nutmeg Princess*, 2014, concrete. Grenada: Underwater Sculpture Park at Molinere Bay.

Myristica fragrans Houtt., 1890.

MYRISTICA FRAGRANS NUTMEG

PRUNUS CERASUS — CHERRY

FAMILY Rosaceae

The cherry originated in the Mediterranean and is now grown worldwide. In Denmark and Lithuania, probably before the introduction of Christianity, demons were thought to live in cherry trees.

As a Christian symbol, the deep red cherry represents Christ's blood, which is why the fruit sometimes appears on the table in depictions of the Last Supper or his appearance at Emmaus. Cherries often appear in Renaissance images of the Madonna and Child, as sumptuous fruit and a harbinger of Christ's death and Resurrection. Sometimes Northern Renaissance painters substitute a cherry tree for the palm (pp. 68–69) in scenes of the 'Rest on the Flight to Egypt', possibly never having seen a palm.

Giovanna Garzoni is regarded as the finest Italian Baroque miniature painter. She served several aristocratic patrons, even becoming an official miniaturist in the Medici court. Few of her miniatures survive, however, and she is now better known for her painstaking still-life watercolours. Flowers, fruit and living creatures such as birds, bees, beetles and snails were rendered with great accuracy. Unusually for an Italian painter, her work often resembles Dutch Baroque *vanitas* images in style.

The art historian Mary Garrard notes the vitality and sensuality of Garzoni's still lifes and suggests that, during the plague, looking at them might have been thought to promote health. Garrard also sees in them associations with the human body (such as melons being equated with plump breasts). The images may therefore have conveyed the magic of sexual and cyclical regeneration in nature.

✡ Giovanna Garzoni, *Cherries in a Dish, a Pod and a Bumblebee*, c. 1642–51, gouache on parchment. Florence: Galleria Palatina.

✺ Pierre-Joseph Redouté, *Cerasus semperflorens* (Allsaints cherry), 1801–19.

OTHER CHERRY IMAGES
- Giovanni Pietro Rizzoli, called Giampietrino, *Madonna of the Cherries* or *Madonna and Child by a Window*, 1508–10, oil on panel. Private collection. (Mid-sixteenth-century copies exist, apparently by Joos van Cleve and/or his workshop.)
- Marco d'Oggiono (attrib.), *Girl with Cherries*, c. 1491–95, oil on panel. New York: Metropolitan Museum of Art.
- Titian, *Madonna of the Cherries*, c. 1515, oil on panel. Vienna: Kunsthistorisches Museum.

PRUNUS CERASUS CHERRY

PRUNUS PERSICA — PEACH

FAMILY Rosaceae

The deciduous peach tree originated between two and six million years ago in China, from where it migrated to Persia, then Europe.

The *Prunus* genus includes several other fruit trees; the nectarine, although distinguished commercially, is identical to the peach, but without the fuzzy skin. The tree and the fruit are particularly important in Asian cultures.

Tradition has it that the peach was brought to Greece by Alexander the Great following his conquests in Persia. Its presence in the Roman Empire is evident from a beautiful fresco in the ruined city of Herculaneum, where the peaches promote a sense of hospitality.

Peach trees bloom early and thus symbolize spring. The three parts of the fruit – flesh, stone and seed within the stone – link it to the Holy Trinity. The Christ Child sometimes holds a peach instead of an apple in depictions of the Madonna and Child, and in such images it has the same meaning as the fruit of salvation.

Renaissance artists revived an ancient tradition that the leaf and stem of the peach together symbolized the heart and tongue. It therefore signifies truth, in the sense of speaking the truth from the heart. The fruit also symbolized fertility. The four pieces of fruit on the left-hand side of Van Eyck's *The Arnolfini Portrait*, a painting widely discussed for its symbolism, have been identified as peaches and/or oranges. If they are oranges, they may signify wealth; if they are peaches, they may instead suggest the hope for a fruitful marriage.

Peaches adorned *vanitas* still-lifes throughout the Baroque period in the Netherlands, and

✣ Giorgio Gallesio, *Persica Magdalena* (Peach), 1817–39.

✣ Jan van Eyck, *The Arnolfini Portrait*, 1434, oil on oak. London: National Gallery.

PRUNUS PERSICA PEACH

Pierre-Auguste Renoir, *Still Life with Peaches*, 1881, oil on canvas. New York: Metropolitan Museum of Art.

Greek vase in the form of a pomegranate, eighth century BCE, terracotta. New York: Metropolitan Museum of Art.

Pierre-Joseph Redouté, *Grenadier punica* (Pomegranate), 1827–33.

have continued to appear in European art long afterwards. Their fuzzy surface and variegated colours posed no challenge for Renoir, whose *Still Life with Peaches* depicts a pyramid of delicious-looking peaches, seen from different vantage points, in a faience jardinière. On the white cloth, complete with folds and violet shadows, rest two pears, an apple and a smaller green fruit. This arrangement is backed by a tapestry or wallpaper that adds to the energy and liveliness of the painting, contributing to the overall sense of *joie de vivre* and sensuous appeal.

Roald Dahl's children's story *James and the Giant Peach* (1961) has been reprinted with new illustrations several times. The story tells of an unhappy orphan boy who finds a tunnel into a giant peach, where he meets various giant-sized bugs that take him on magical adventures. The peach represents a nurturing, safe place where James can grow.

OTHER PEACH IMAGES

- Still life with peaches and a water jar, from Herculaneum, *c.* 62–69 CE. Naples, Italy: Museo Archeologico Nazionale.
- Carlo Crivelli, *Madonna col Bambino* (*Madonna and Child*), *c.* 1482, tempera on panel. Bergamo, Italy: Accademia Carrara.

PUNICA GRANATUM — POMEGRANATE

FAMILY Lythraceae

The pomegranate originated in Afghanistan, Iran and northern India, and travelled westwards; it was introduced into the Americas in the sixteenth century.

Today, it is widely cultivated for juice and used in cooking, baking, garnishes and alcoholic drinks. The fruit is a rich source of dietary fibre and is high in several vitamins, although its precise health benefits are the subject of debate.

The pomegranate has a long history in art, beginning in the ancient Mediterranean. It is one of the candidates for the Tree of Knowledge in Eden, and is mentioned among the fruits of Paradise in the Qur'an. Pomegranates occur in several passages in the Old Testament; the fruit is one of the plants listed among the valued products of Israel.

The Greeks associated the pomegranate with female fertility; it was sacred to Aphrodite and Hera, as well as playing a role in the abduction of Persephone. The daughter of Demeter and Zeus, Persephone was picking flowers when Hades carried her off to the Underworld. Demeter, the goddess of agriculture, became so grief-stricken that famine ensued. Zeus interceded, ordering Hades to return the girl to her mother. But Persephone had eaten a pomegranate seed (in some tellings, several) while in the Underworld, so she could spend only certain months with Demeter each year; the months she spent in the Underworld correspond to the barren fields after harvest. Pomegranates are common in Greek art as early as the Geometric period, and the object illustrated below is one of many terracotta pomegranates. Probably because of its association with Persephone's release from the Underworld, the fruit often appears on ancient gravestones. Figures of young women holding pomegranates may have been devotees of Hera.

The dining-room frescoes from the Villa of Livia at Prima Porta (30–20 BCE; now in the

- *The Unicorn Rests in a Garden*, Unicorn Tapestries, *c.* 1495–1505, wool and silk threads. New York: The Cloisters.

- Sandro Botticelli, *Virgin and Child with Angels* ('Madonna of the Pomegranate', also known as 'Madonna of the Magnificat') (detail), *c.* 1487, tempera on wood. Florence: Le Gallerie degli Uffizi..

- Dante Gabriel Rossetti, *Proserpine* (detail), 1874, oil on canvas. London: Tate.

Palazzo Massimo in Rome) feature many species of bird and plant, including pomegranate trees bursting with fruit. Here they would seem to indicate sheer energy and the bounty of life. This symbolism of bounty, fertility and rebirth continued into the medieval period and seems to have reached its height in the Italian Renaissance.

In *The Unicorn Rests in a Garden* (sometimes called *The Unicorn in Captivity*) from the Cloisters' Unicorn Tapestries, the unicorn – often said to symbolize Christ – reclines in a fenced circle beneath a pomegranate tree, its fruit having apparently dripped onto its white coat. The pomegranate symbolizes fertility, but the red spots on the unicorn resemble blood – signifying the immortality made possible by Christ's sacrifice. It has been suggested that the tapestries were created to celebrate a wedding; thus, the image may also indicate the desire for a fruitful marriage.

Italian painters included pomegranates in many images of the Virgin and Child, probably because the fruit's red juice, like wine, foreshadowed the Last Supper and Christ's death and Resurrection. In Botticelli's *Virgin and Child with Angels* the skin has burst, and some of the fruit's many seeds are visible. Just as seeds produce new plants, so Christ's sacrifice signifies rebirth. Pomegranates also appear in the works of Fra Angelico, Gentile da Fabriano, Filippino Lippi, Lorenzo di Credi and Raphael, among others.

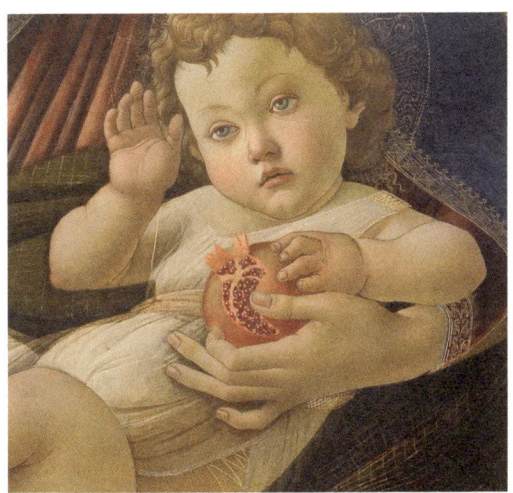

OTHER POMEGRANATE IMAGES
- Botanic Garden of Thutmosis III, Festival Hall, Temple of Amon-Re, Karnak, Egypt, *c.* 1450 BCE.

PYRUS   PEAR

FAMILY Rosaceae

The pear tree is a member of the rose family. Among the most important fruit trees, pears are cultivated worldwide in temperate zones.

The fruit is eaten fresh or canned, although some species are mainly decorative. The common pear (*Pyrus communis*), probably of European origin, has been cultivated since ancient times. The Williams cultivar is the most popular type in America, where it is known as the Bartlett pear.

    Pausanias wrote that in Tiryns and Mycenae, the two greatest cities of the Bronze Age Mycenaean civilization, statues of Hera were carved from pear wood. The fruit was sacred to Aphrodite as well as Hera. Pliny called it the 'Aphrodite' pear because the rounded lower form recalled the shape of the female body.

The pear tree is one of many candidates for the Tree of Knowledge in the Garden of Eden. Pears often also appear in images of the Madonna and Child, alluding to redemption and the sweetness of virtue. Crivelli frequently included fruit in his images of this subject; the example opposite features two ripe pears in the upper left-hand corner, and an apple on the right. The cherry on the balustrade is said to symbolize Christ's blood.

OTHER PEAR IMAGES
- Giovanni Bellini, *Madonna col Bambino* (*Madonna and Child*), 1485–*c.* 1487, oil on panel. Bergamo: Accademia Carrara.
- Albrecht Dürer, *Madonna and Child with a Pear*, 1511. Engraving.
- Luis Egidio Meléndez, *Still Life with Melon and Pears*, *c.* 1772, oil on canvas. Boston, MA: Museum of Fine Arts.

    ✣   Giorgio Gallesio, *Pera Campana, Pyrus Pompeiana* (Pears), 1817–39.

    ✣   Carlo Crivelli, *Madonna and Child*, *c.* 1490, tempera on panel. Washington, DC: National Gallery of Art, Kress Collection.

PYRUS PEAR

RAPHANUS — RADISH

FAMILY Brassicaceae

The radish is a vegetable in the mustard family. Thought to have originated in China, radishes have been cultivated for thousands of years.

Medicinally, the radish has antibacterial and antifungal properties, and also helps to clear phlegm from a cold. The Romans linked it with Mars, god of war, and therefore with quarrel and strife – probably in part because it is commonly bright red, though some varieties are different colours. It is also said to be an attribute of wind and weather gods. Counterbalancing this stormy symbolism, the radish was consecrated, traditionally on the day of the Catholic festival of the Chair of St Peter.

The contemporary American artist Jennifer Knaus has created a series of strikingly original portraits reminiscent of both Surrealism and the work of Arcimboldo. Her delicate, detailed paintings depict mostly female figures wearing luscious arrangements of various fruit and vegetables. She bridges portraiture and still life in ways that are mysterious and evocative. In *Radish Head*, as well as the red radishes, there are white flowers in the background, which may be daffodils. Whether the images reflect aspects of the sitter's personality or serve some other symbolic purpose is unclear, but they certainly make remarkable use of plants.

✵ Cesare Ubertini, *Raphanus minor* (radish), 1772–93.

❋ Jennifer Knaus, *Radish Head*, 2014, oil on panel.

SOLANUM LYCOPERSICUM — TOMATO

FAMILY Solanaceae

Technically, the tomato is the berry of a species that originated in South and Central America. It was domesticated by about 500 BCE.

The tomato was first encountered by Europeans when the Spanish conquered the Aztec empire and took the fruit back to Spain, from where it spread during the sixteenth century. Although tomatoes are classified as fruit, they are generally used in the kitchen as vegetables.

In ancient times, the tomato was believed to be an aphrodisiac, and there was some thought that it might be poisonous. It appears in Baroque still lifes, including paintings by Luis Egidio Meléndez. Bartolomé Esteban Murillo's *The Angels' Kitchen*, commissioned by the Franciscans of Seville for the cloister of their monastery, depicts a monastery kitchen and a Franciscan friar in ecstatic prayer. Two angels separate the friar from the kitchen, where celestial cooks prepare food, with one dish featuring tomatoes and squash.

Andy Warhol's *Campbell's Soup Cans* is synonymous with Pop Art and its appropriation of popular and commercial images. The version in the Museum of Modern Art, New York, consists of thirty-two canvases measuring 51 × 41 cm (20 × 16 in.), with an instruction to install them 7.6 cm (3 in.) apart. The canvases resemble mass-produced advertisements, but they are, in fact, hand-painted, with a hand-stamped *fleur-de-lys* pattern on the base of the can. Warhol said he had the soup for lunch for twenty years, like the repeated can images, 'over and over again'.

OTHER TOMATO IMAGES
- Bartolomé Esteban Murillo, *Un miracle du frère Francisco* (*The Miracle of Brother Francisco*; better known as *The Angels' Kitchen*), 1646, oil on canvas. Paris: Musée du Louvre.
- Luis Egidio Meléndez, *Still Life with Cucumbers, Tomatoes and Vessels*, 1774, oil on canvas. Madrid: Museo del Prado.

※ Pierre Joseph de Pannemaeker, a bunch of tomatoes (*Lycopersicon esculentum*), c. 1854.

※ Andy Warhol, *Campbell's Soup Cans*, 1962, acrylic and enamel paint on canvas. New York: Museum of Modern Art.

SOLANUM LYCOPERSICUM TOMATO

SOLANUM MELONGENA — AUBERGINE

FAMILY Solanaceae

Possibly originating in India, the aubergine, brinjal or eggplant was known in Europe by the thirteenth century. Its fruits can be white, yellow, violet and rich purple, and all other parts of the plant are poisonous.

Aubergine has been associated with a number of health benefits, including stimulation of the appetite, improved digestion and lower cholesterol. It has long had sexual connotations, as a phallic symbol, and since 2010 the aubergine emoji has been a popular choice for suggestive messages.

Unknown in the Greco-Roman world, the aubergine was introduced to Spain in the eighth century by its Arab rulers. It is mentioned frequently in medieval and Renaissance documents, but in the Middle Ages attitudes towards the fruit were ambiguous, and some claimed it promoted anger and melancholy, even insanity. Its aphrodisiac associations are evident in a miniature from the eleventh-century health handbook *Tacuinum sanitatis* (*The Maintenance of Health*), depicting a screen of plants with globular purple fruit. An amorous dancing couple feels its effects, while a single female remonstrates with them.

Renaissance herbalists also attributed aphrodisiac properties to the aubergine. It appears in the sixteenth-century festoons in the Villa Farnesina in Rome; the painter Giuseppe Arcimboldo depicted them; and in 1601 they were forged into the bronze doors of Pisa Cathedral. It is found in seventeenth-century painting, but perhaps the best images of the aubergine come from the eighteenth-century heyday of botanical illustration.

✥ *Melongiana* (aubergine) in a copy of *Tacuinum sanitatis* (detail), 1385–90. Vienna: Austrian National Library.

✻ Paul Cézanne, *Still Life with a Ginger Jar and Eggplants* (detail), 1893–94, oil on canvas. New York: Metropolitan Museum of Art.

❈ Basilius Besler, Aubergine, 1613.

SOLANUM MELONGENA AUBERGINE

SOLANUM TUBEROSUM — POTATO

FAMILY Solanaceae

The potato is a tuber in the nightshade family. The wild potato originated in what is now Peru, and was domesticated independently by many different Indigenous groups.

Spanish explorers introduced the potato to Europe in the second half of the sixteenth century, and early in the twenty-first century it became the world's fourth-largest food crop, after corn (maize), wheat and rice. There are now 5,000 different types of potato! As well as being food, potatoes are used to brew alcoholic drinks (most famously vodka). In popular culture, Mr Potato Head, invented in 1949 and marketed by Hasbro in 1952, is a popular toy and the first to be advertised on television. Originally, a real potato was used as the base for eyes, ears and mouth; newer versions are made of plastic.

Like the onion (see pp. 156–57), for centuries the potato was seen as a food of the lower classes. Some nineteenth-century artists, among them Anton Mauve and Jean-François Millet, depicted peasants eating and harvesting potatoes. Probably the most notable such painting is Vincent van Gogh's *The Potato Eaters*, which

depicts five labourers at a table eating their evening meal. The artist showed the harsh effects of their reality in their coarse, distorted features and bony hands, but nevertheless the meal has a sacramental quality, evoking a sense of endurance and pious gratitude for what little they have. Van Gogh wrote to his brother in 1885:

You see, I really have wanted to make it so that people get the idea that these folk, who are eating their potatoes by the light of their little lamp, have tilled the earth themselves with these hands they are putting in the dish, and so it speaks of manual labour and – that they have thus honestly earned their food… [O]ne would be wrong, to my mind, to give a peasant painting a certain conventional smoothness. If a peasant painting smells of bacon, smoke, potato steam – fine – that's not unhealthy – if a stable smells of manure – very well, that's what a stable's for – if the field has an odour of ripe wheat or potatoes or – of guano and manure – that's really healthy – particularly for city folk. They get something useful out of paintings like this. But a peasant painting mustn't become perfumed.

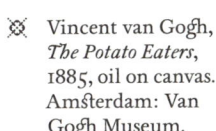

Vincent van Gogh, *The Potato Eaters*, 1885, oil on canvas. Amsterdam: Van Gogh Museum.

J. Vreugdenhil, *Solanum tuberosum* (potato), n.d.

SOLANUM TUBEROSUM   POTATO

VERBASCUM — MULLEIN

FAMILY Scrophulariaceae

Common mullein (*V. thapsus*) is a herb with a substantial anecdotal history of medicinal use, having been mentioned as early as 64 CE. With worldwide distribution, it is sometimes regarded as a weed.

Mullein stalks can measure between 1.5 and 2 m (5–7 ft) tall and are densely packed with tiny five-petalled flowers. Medicinal products derived from the leaves can alleviate ear pain, coughs and other upper respiratory conditions and inflammation.

In ancient times, the plant was said to be able to drive off demons. From this may come the belief that it provided protection and inner strength. The Romans used dried mullein stalks, dipped in tallow, as torches, and for this reason they called the plant *candelaria*.

Notable appearances in art include Giovanni Bellini's *St Francis in the Desert*, in which the plant grows out of a small, raised garden directly behind St Francis. It appears to be a cultivated plant, and may protect the saint as he undergoes a transformational, supernatural experience, or encourage him to fulfil his destiny. Francis is said to have suffered from a number of maladies, so the mullein may also have served to alleviate his pain.

Writing about Bellini's masterpiece, the art historian James Elkins notes the important roles played by plants. He suggests that Bellini, uncomfortable with depicting supernatural beings, embedded the miracle in the landscape: 'Because nothing is quite what it should be, everything is partly sacred'. The saint has stepped away from his desk and stands barefoot, arms wide, absorbing radiant supernatural light. The Tuscan landscape, frozen in the moment as the saint receives the transformative stigmata, contains myriad symbolic plants that range from barren to healthy; several are undergoing rejuvenation. These include a laurel tree (symbolizing honour and victory over death, the burning bush[14]) and a grapevine (for the Eucharist and the saint's devotion to Christ). There are also bindweed, daisies (for innocence), two fig trees (redemption), a juniper (chastity), olive, a reed cross and gate, and a Crown of Thorns; James Elkins adds briars, ivy and maidenhair fern. Medicinal plants include orris and mullein. Bellini combines Italian Renaissance macrocosmic spirituality with Northern Renaissance microcosmic naturalism.

※ *Verbascum thapsus* (mullein), n.d.

※ Giovanni Bellini, *St Francis in the Desert* (detail), c. 1475–80, oil on panel. New York: Frick Collection.

OTHER IMAGES OF MULLEIN
- Martin Schongauer, *The Flight into Egypt*, c. 1470–75, engraving. Washington, DC: National Gallery of Art.
- Caravaggio, *St John the Baptist in the Wilderness*, 1604, oil on canvas. Kansas City, MO: Nelson-Atkins Museum of Art.
- Gian Lorenzo Bernini, *Fountain of Four Rivers*, opened 1677. Rome: Piazza Navona. (Depicts thirty-four species associated with the rivers' environments.[15])
- W. G. Smith, *Common Mullein*, c. 1863, lithograph. London: Wellcome Collection.

GRAINS, GRASSES & VINES

The grass family includes all the major cereals (including wheat, rice, barley and oats), and most of the grains (corn, rye and millet, among others) as well. Grasses are the most important flowering plants, providing nutrition for both animals and humans, and preventing soil erosion by way of their mat-forming root systems. They are among the largest families of flowering plants, numbering some 10,000 species, and – from evidence of fossilized grass pollen – have been around for at least sixty-six million years. The tallest grass is bamboo, which can grow up to 30 m (100 ft) high.

Vines are plants that require support and climb by tendrils, or twine or creep along the ground. The word 'vine' often refers to the grapevine (pp. 222–23). The prehistoric Mother Goddess was known as 'The Goddess of the Vines', a source of natural creation. Vines in ancient Syria and Judaea were trained on fig trees (pp. 54–57), both plants being symbols of peace and abundance. A golden vine is said to have adorned the eastern wall of the temple in Jerusalem; in 70 CE it was carried off by the Romans and displayed as part of the spoils of war. The Jewish people regarded the vine and the olive (pp. 66–67) as the two Messianic plants, and the vine may actually have been identified with the Tree of Life in Eden. The Jewish Messiah, compared to the vine, became the true symbol of the Chosen People.

The vine functioned as one of the earliest symbols of Christ: 'I am the vine, you [the apostles] are the branches' (John 15:5). Vine paintings ornamented the walls of both pagan and early Christian catacombs. Under Emperor Constantine, the vine became the sole symbol of Christianity. Its symbolism extended to every human soul; God planted the vine, Christ the Messiah visited the vineyard, and his blood redeemed all souls. Cultivated relatively late in Greece, the vine was linked with Dionysus, god of the mysteries of wine, fruitfulness and vegetation, but also madness.

Vines, because of their varying habits, enjoy complex meanings. Their ability to grow and cling signifies strength and energy (using trees, walls or other supports, ivy can reach impressive heights, for instance). Many vines flower and bear fruit, relating them to plenty and resurgence. Vines can also mean friendship, support and intimate companionship (see 'Honeysuckle', pp. 128–29). It is this meaning that perhaps explains the popularity of modern vine tattoo designs.

There are scores of types of vine, and Darwin categorized them by their climbing habits. Some, such as liana and kudzu, are extremely invasive. Many have medical uses. Others – among them bougainvillea, clematis, morning glory, nasturtium, philodendron and wisteria – make excellent garden plants, providing glorious decoration as well as privacy.

※ Arthur Hughes, *The Long Engagement*, 1859, oil on canvas. Birmingham, UK: Birmingham Museum & Art Gallery.

※ Hieronymus Bosch, *The Haywain Triptych*, c. 1516, oil on panel. Madrid: Museo del Prado.

CUCUMIS SATIVUS — CUCUMBER

FAMILY Cucurbitaceae

A widely cultivated creeping plant with large leaves and tendrils that enable it to grow on trellises. It has been cultivated for 3,000 years, having originated in India and been introduced elsewhere by the Greeks and Romans.

✵ F. Domingo, *Cucumis sativus* (cucumber), 1877–83.

✻ Carlo Crivelli, *Madonna and Child*, c. 1480, tempera and gold on wood. New York: Metropolitan Museum of Art.

According to Pliny, Emperor Tiberius ate cucumbers every day in the summer and winter, probably grown in some form of greenhouse. The Romans used cucumbers to treat scorpion bites and bad eyesight, and to repel mice. Women wishing for children sometimes wore cucumbers, which were then discarded by the midwives once the wished-for child was born. In the eighth and early ninth centuries, the Carolingian king Charlemagne's gardens featured cucumbers, and Christopher Columbus introduced the vegetable to the Americas in the late fifteenth century.

In Christian art, the cucumber often appears in images of the Virgin Mary. A passage in Isaiah prefigures the Immaculate Conception: 'As a hut in a garden of cucumbers, as a besieged city' (1:8), the Virgin, surrounded by sin, remained pure. Carlo Crivelli included a cucumber in his *Madonna and Child*, opposite. The cucumber and several apples dangle from the upper corners, overlapping a folded cloth that hangs behind the Virgin. The Christ Child holds a goldfinch and looks down at a large fly on the balustrade. In this painting, the apples and the fly are symbols of sin and evil, counteracted by the bird and the cucumber, which signify redemption and the soul.

GRAINS, GRASSES & VINES

CUCUMIS SATIVUS CUCUMBER

CYNODON / *FESTUCA* / *LOLIUM* / *POA* AND OTHER GENERA   GRASS

FAMILY Poaceae

Grass is one of the single most important plants in the world, both in the form of natural grasses (grassland) and cultivated grasses, such as corn and wheat.

Grasses appear in all environments, even in Antarctica. This entry refers to what is commonly thought of as grass: grassland or perennials such as Bermuda grass (Cynodon dactylon), bluegrass (Poa species) and fescue (Festuca species), to name just a few.

Grass can represent the idea of a homeland – as in the popular song 'The Green, Green Grass of Home', versions of which were recorded by Elvis Presley, Johnny Cash and Tom Jones – or, when pulled, surrender or conquest of land or territory. In places where it grows prolifically, it has also often been a symbol of usefulness, as a humble common plant. Grass can also signify evanescence, being quick to grow but also to wither and die. 'Under the grass' is a term commonly associated with burial and death.

Grass is tenacious. It is one of the first plants to appear after such natural disasters as floods, wildfires and snowstorms, and many types will grow up through the slightest crack, enlarging fissures in rock or concrete and filling gaps between paving stones.

Albrecht Dürer took great pains to depict the natural world based on careful observation. His watercolour *Great Piece of Turf* (1503) is generally seen as a study undertaken to help him render plants more realistically. Indeed, the slightly larger-than-life-sized plants are so detailed that they can be identified accurately, and include several kinds of meadowgrass, plantain, speedwell, daisy leaves, hound's tongue and yarrow. The clarity and focus, as well as the scene's detachment from a larger setting, suggest timelessness and a sort of pantheistic perfection.

In Walt Whitman's 'Song of Myself', part of his great *Leaves of Grass* (1855), the poet, asked by a child 'What is the grass?', suggests that grass, like life, is fundamentally unknowable and inexplicable. He guesses at what it might mean, evoking macrocosmically everything in existence. The microcosm is evoked in the following line from Verse 31: 'I believe a leaf of grass is no less than the journey-work of the stars.'

A powerful contemporary example of the regenerative and enduring qualities of grass can be seen in Ansel Adams's photograph of grass sprouting in the crevice of a burned tree in Yosemite Valley. The artists Heather Ackroyd and Dan Harvey, meanwhile, collaborate on works in which they manipulate light to create human–grass hybrids, shown opposite, symbolically looking towards a future of human–plant harmony.

⊗   Ackroyd & Harvey, *Mother and Child* (*Heather and Adèle*), 1998, staygreen grass, clay and jute. Commissioned for Santa Barbara Museum of Art, CA.

❋ Albrecht Dürer, *Great Piece of Turf*, 1503, watercolour and body colour on vellum. Vienna: Albertina.

❖ A. F. Lydon, *Bromus asper, Hordeum sylvaticum* and *Avena flavescens*, 1858.

HEDERA HELIX — IVY

FAMILY Araliaceae

Ivy is an evergreen, ground-creeping woody plant native to most of Europe and parts of Africa and Asia. It is now also widespread in North America and Australia. Ivy climbs trees, rocky outcrops and buildings, with a reach of up to 10 m (35 ft).

In ancient Greece, ivy was called *cissos*. According to myth, it was named after the nymph Cissus or Kissos, who danced so energetically at a feast of the gods that she fell dead at Dionysus' feet. Moved, he turned her into the vigorous plant.

When Dionysus, god of vegetation, was born of a union between Zeus and Semele, his cradle was hidden from Hera, queen of the gods', wrath by being covered in ivy. The plant was dedicated to him; his devotees, including the maenads, are often shown wearing or otherwise ornamented with ivy, and even today ivy decorates taverns and wine shops.

The dancing figure illustrated here, from a famous kylix, carries an ivy-covered staff and a leopard, and wears a serpent diadem and a leopard skin. Ivy also adorned images of satyrs and sileni, who, like the followers of Dionysus, enjoyed life's pleasures. The Romans used ivy boiled in wine to alleviate hangovers.

Because of its clinging habit, ivy is associated with loyalty and undying affection. Owing to its trilobed shape, it can also symbolize the Trinity. Green ivy in medieval Christian art often signifies the immortality of the soul after death, and because of its tenacity, it can also represent the passage of time. In Dutch Baroque *vanitas* paintings such as Rachel Ruysch's, illustrated below, where the vine twines around a skull, ivy symbolizes immortality. The plant was a popular motif among Art Nouveau artists and is commonly incorporated into tattoos today.

- Rachel Ruysch (attrib.), *Vanité* (*Vanity*), c. 1690, oil on canvas. La Fère, France: Museé Jeanne d'Aboville.

- J.P. Del, *Glechoma hederacea* (ground ivy), 1835.

- Maenad with thyrsus ornamented with ivy leaves, Attic white-ground *kylix*, 490–480 BCE, from Vulci. Munich: Staatliche Antikensammlungen.

OTHER IMAGES OF IVY
- Limestone beardless male head with ivy wreath, Cypriot, late sixth–early fifth century BCE. New York: Metropolitan Museum of Art.
- Henri Matisse, *Ivy in Flower*, 1953, mixed media on paper over canvas. Dallas, TX: Dallas Museum of Art.

HEDERA HELIX   IVY

PHRAGMITES AND OTHER GENERA — REED

FAMILY Various

Reed is a common name used for several tall, grass-like plants that grow in wetlands. The various families include Poaceae (the grass family), Cyperaceae (sedges), Typhaceae (cattails) and Restionaceae (restiads). Reeds are both flexible and fragile, and have uses as varied as thatching and musical instruments.

The symbolic Egyptian *djed* pillar was made of reeds, and the architectural form of reed-bundle columns may have derived from reed-built homes. The ancient Egyptians called the afterlife the Field of Reeds (A'aru or Iaru) and envisaged it as an agrarian paradise, part of one's eternal journey. Boats were fashioned from reeds in order to travel there. The afterlife duplicated temporal life, but without pain or fear of death. Accompanied by loved ones, the deceased carried out the same activities as they had while alive. The painting of A'aru, below, illustrates one of the spells from the so-called Book of the Dead. In their tomb, the Ancient Egyptian artisan Sennedjem and his wife honour various gods and work at agricultural activities.

Papyrus (*Cyperus papyrus*) and lotus plants are also referred to as reeds, and all played major roles in ancient Egyptian art and architecture. Reed sceptres were borne by some deities; in Egypt, Set – the god of violence, chaos and storms – bore one.

A Greek myth tells of a nymph named Syrinx, who was pursued by Pan and escaped at the river's edge by transforming into reeds. Pan cut the reeds and made his first set of pipes from them.

In the Old Testament, speaking of the coming Messiah, Isaiah wrote: 'A bruised reed He will not break... He will bring forth justice for truth. He will not fail nor be discouraged, till He has established justice in the earth' (42: 3–4). In Christian art, the reed became associated with Christ, and reeds are often woven into the shape of a cross at Easter.

⊗ A'aru (The Field of Reeds), Tomb of Sennedjem, Deir-el-Medina, Egypt, c. 1200 BCE. Facsimile by Charles K. Wilkinson, 1922. New York: Metropolitan Museum of Art.

✻ Johann Ibmayer, *Arundo donax* (giant reed), 1809.

PUERARIA — KUDZU

FAMILY Fabaceae

Kudzu is a group of climbing and trailing vines native to parts of Asia and some Pacific islands, where it has been cultivated for centuries and is celebrated for its ability to flourish in even the most depleted soil.

'Kudzu' comes from the plant's Japanese name, *kuzu*, and it has also been known as Japanese arrowroot. Its fibres have been used to make clothing and paper, and it is also used in food and traditional medicine throughout East Asia.

Kudzu was first planted in North America as an ornamental vine, but became widely cultivated and promoted as a soil enhancer and a form of erosion control. It is an invasive species in Europe and North America, and became particularly notorious in the southern United States as the 'vine that ate the South'.

The work of Precious Okoyomon involves transforming spaces into living environments that convey historical or social ideas. *Earthseed*, installed in the Museum für Moderne Kunst, Frankfurt, involved covering the gallery floor with a thick layer of topsoil, in which the artist planted young kudzu vines in the spring.[16] By autumn, the artist's six yarn and lambswool figures had been enveloped by the vines. Crickets, spiders, butterflies and even snails moved in. Okoyomon's installation drew attention to the resilience of nature – as they put it, 'our entanglement with nature'. Using plant material of this kind serves as a reminder of unintended consequences. As Coco Romack suggests, the artist warns against destroying nature, while celebrating its energy and chaos.

Mary Emily Eaton, *Pueraria thunbergiana* (kudzu), 1930.

Precious Okoyomon, *Earthseed*, 2020, mixed media. Frankfurt, Germany: Museum für Moderne Kunst.

TRITICUM — WHEAT

FAMILY Poaceae

Wheat is a grass widely cultivated for its seed, a cereal grain with worldwide distribution and use, and the leading source of vegetable protein globally. Archaeological evidence shows that it was first cultivated in the Levant as early as 9600 BCE.

The Egyptian gods Osiris and Nepra (the god of grain, considered an aspect of Osiris) were both linked with wheat. According to Plutarch, Osiris's main festival began at Abydos with a commemoration of the god's death and planting of wheat on the same day. The Egyptologist Emily Teeter writes that 'Osiris beds' were constructed in the shape of the god, filled with soil and sown with seed; the germinating wheat symbolized Osiris's resurrection from the dead.

In ancient Greece, in the secret rites of the Eleusinian Mysteries, a grain of wheat was displayed to remind the participants of the eternal cycle of life. Wheat is planted, cultivated and finally harvested to provide not only the sustenance of bread but also seed for the next cycle. The origin of wheat was mysterious and therefore regarded as a gift of the gods.

Around the time of Christ, Jewish people made unleavened bread for Passover from both wheat and barley. At the Last Supper, during the Passover meal, Christ broke bread with his disciples and likened it to his body and wine to his blood; they were to consume both in memory of him. Despite considerable variation in both doctrine and practice among later Christians, the Eucharist reflects the ancient symbolism of life's constant renewal and the promise of rebirth brought about by Christ's sacrifice.

A sheaf of wheat appears with other symbolic plants in Hugo van der Goes's Portinari Altarpiece (c. 1475, see p. 95). The wheat indicates not only Bethlehem (the word means 'house of bread' in Hebrew), but also the cyclical immortality granted by Christ's death and

⊗ 'Sennedjem and His Wife Harvest Wheat in the Fields of Osiris', Tomb of Sennedjem, Deir el-Medina, *c.* 1300 BCE. Tempera facsimile (detail) by Charles K. Wilkinson, 1922. New York: Metropolitan Museum of Art.

✳ Charlotte M. Yonge, *Triticum aestivum* (wheat and bearded wheat) and *Avena sativa* (oats), 1858.

OTHER IMAGES OF WHEAT
- Ceres (Demeter) rising from the ground with sheaves of wheat, Roman, Augustan period (27 BCE –14 CE), bas-relief.
- Hieronymus Bosch, centre panel of *The Haywain Triptych*, *c.* 1512–15, oil on panel. Madrid: Museo del Prado.
- Pieter Bruegel the Elder, *The Harvesters*, 1565, oil on wood. New York: Metropolitan Museum of Art.

Resurrection. On gravestones, a sheaf of wheat suggests that the individual lived a long life.

Wheat symbolizes plenty and fertility, and has long been an artistic subject. Among the finest depictions is Samuel Palmer's *A Hilly Scene* (*c.* 1826–28), which represents what the Tate website calls 'an ideal image of pastoral contentment'. The enormous flowering horse chestnut (spring) and the ripe autumn wheat may reflect Edmund Spenser's *Faërie Queene* (1596): 'There is continuall spring, and harvest there.'

❋ Samuel Palmer, *A Hilly Scene*, c. 1826–8, watercolour on paper. London: Tate.

❋ Thomas Hart Benton, *Wheat*, 1967, oil on wood. Washington, DC: Smithsonian American Art Museum.

VITIS VINIFERA — GRAPEVINE

FAMILY Vitaceae

Grapes have been cultivated possibly since between 6000 and 4000 BCE, and evidence of wine-making dates back almost as far. Grapevines originated in North Africa and the Levant, and often appear as decorative elements in art and architecture.

Generally, grapes are symbols of wine: intoxication, hospitality (even orgies) and youthfulness. In the ancient world, grapes were an attribute of Dionysus/Bacchus – the god of wine-making, fertility, insanity and religious ecstasy, among other things – and his followers, who sometimes wore grapevine crowns.

In Christian art, grapes symbolize the wine of the Eucharist, transformed into the blood of Christ. By extension, grapes refer to the Last Supper, the Passion and Redemption. The grapevine symbolizes Christ, as in John 15:1: 'I am the true vine.' Late Roman and early Christian art made use of the vine as a proselytizing device, to smooth the transition to Christian symbolic meaning. A wonderful example can be found in a Roman mausoleum. A portrait of Costanza, the daughter of Emperor Constantine (the first Christian ruler), appears in the middle of one of the ambulatory mosaics. Her image is surrounded by twining grapevines, with *putti* harvesting, transporting and stamping the grapes. Some of the same imagery appears on her porphyry sarcophagus, which is decorated with garlands and grapevines, acanthus scrolls and cupids treading grapes.

St Augustine, among other early theologians, compared Christ to a cluster of grapes from the Promised Land, crushed in a press. This interpretation gave rise to the motif of Christ in a wine press, popular in art from about 1100 until the eighteenth century – one of the few medieval Catholic images that is also found in Protestant art.

In Giovanni Bellini's *St Francis in the Desert* (see also 'Mullein', pp. 200–1), grapevines – recalling the Eucharist and Christ's blood – overhang the entrance to the saint's al fresco shelter. This remarkable image suggests oneness with the divine, subtly conveyed through the humble details of the material world.

OTHER IMAGES OF GRAPES AND THE GRAPEVINE
- Roman sarcophagus with garlands, heroes and scenes of sacrifice, 140–50 CE. Rome: Museo Nazionale Romano, Palazzo Massimo.
- Frans Snyders, *Fruit Stall*, 1618–21, oil on canvas. St Petersburg: State Hermitage Museum.
- Henri Matisse, *Vine*, 1958, lithograph.

※ W. Clark after William Hooker, *Vitis vinifera cv.* (Black Corinth grape): fruiting branch, *c.* 1835.

✻ Cupids harvesting grapes, detail of ambulatory mosaic, fourth century. Mausoleum of Santa Costanza, Rome.

❖ Sandro Botticelli, *Virgin and Child with an Angel* (detail), 1470–74, tempera on panel. Boston, MA: Isabella Stewart Gardner Museum.

VITIS VINIFERA GRAPEVINE

ZEA MAYS — CORN

FAMILY Poaceae

What we today call corn, and sometimes maize, originated in Mexico and spread throughout the Americas. This tall annual cereal grass was originally domesticated over 9,000 years ago by Indigenous groups in southern Mexico and is now grown worldwide for its ears of starchy seeds, its production outpacing that of all other grains.

As a widespread foodstuff, eaten by humans and animals, corn is often seen as a symbol of prosperity and plenty. It is also used to produce alcoholic drinks; in the US, 40 per cent of all corn production is used for ethanol. In 2009, genetically modified corn made up 85 per cent of the American crop.

In his still lifes, the Dutch Baroque painter Cornelis de Heem depicted many flowers, fruit and vegetables that served as reminders of the beauty, fragility and brevity of life – so-called *vanitas* images. Species that grow in different seasons are shown together in these still lifes, again emphasizing the passage of time, while their rarity is an indication of the wealth and sophistication of his patrons. Corn was a relative newcomer to Europe, having been brought there from the Americas by Christopher Columbus around the turn of the sixteenth century. The earliest depictions come from Renaissance Italy, in the 1510s.

⊗ Otto Wilhelm Thomé, *Zea Mays* (Corn), 1903.

✻ Grant Wood, *Corn Cob Chandelier for Iowa Corn Room*, 1925–26, copper, iron and paint. Cedar Rapids, IA: Cedar Rapids Museum of Art.

❋ Cornelis de Heem (attrib.), *Fruit and Flowers* (detail), 1662, oil on canvas. London: Victoria and Albert Museum.

American Regionalist painters, inspired by the landscape of the Midwest, often painted corn. In 1926 Grant Wood created *Corn Room*, a mural commissioned by the hotelier Eugene C. Eppley and consisting of several nearly abstract panels. It was papered over and lost until recently, but is now displayed in the Sioux City Art Center. Wood also created remarkable corn-cob chandeliers for the dining room of the Montrose Hotel in Cedar Rapids, Iowa. Perhaps the whimsy of the chandeliers inspired patrons to order corn on the cob!

Maria Fernanda Cardoso, a Colombian-born artist now practising in Australia, began working with corn as early as 1989. The importance of corn in the Americas consumed her, and while undertaking a Masters degree at Yale she grew corn in as many types and colours as possible, threading together hundreds of dried corncobs to create sculptural coils. These art forms evoke the significance of corn in everyday life in Colombia, and the variety of ways in which they can be used.

This book would not have been possible without the stellar education I received many years ago, particularly the mentorship of Henri Dorra and Alfred Moir. Additionally, during my years of teaching, my students' interest in symbolism served to encourage me, as did the ongoing support and enthusiasm of my family.

The contributions of the Thames & Hudson 'dream team' – Kate Edwards, Ben Hayes, India Jackson, Lise Seguin, Rosie Fairhead, Aman Phull, Sadie Brookes and Ginny Liggitt – made this the splendid book that it is. The enthusiastic help of the many artists whose work is illustrated is also much appreciated.

GLOSSARY

Agrostology The scientific study of grasses. Also called graminology.

Annual A plant that completes its life cycle in one year, then dies.

Biennial A plant that completes its life cycle in two years, flowering in the second year, then dies.

Botanical nomenclature The naming system of plants, dating as far back as the Greeks. Beginning with Carolus Linnaeus's mid-eighteenth-century binomial organization, the system became more formal, ranking plants from the largest to the smallest groups: kingdom, phylum (or division), class, order, family, genus, species, subspecies. Many plants are also known by common names, which vary according to time and place.

Deciduous A plant that sheds its leaves annually.

Emblem An abstract or representational image that signifies a concept, place or person (such as roses in coats of arms).

Endemic Natural distribution confined to one area. Compare **Native**.

Family See **Botanical nomenclature**

Genus See **Botanical nomenclature**

Graminology See **Agrostology**

Herbaceous Describes a plant that has no woody stem, typically **biennial** or **annual**; also of or relating to herbs and grasses.

Hybrid The offspring of two plants or animals of different varieties.

Keystone species A species that is vital to the health of the surrounding habitat.

Millefiori/millefleur Literally 1,000 flowers. An all-over pattern of small and diverse flowers, popular in weaving and somewhat rare in painting (but see Botticelli's *Primavera*). Medieval manuscripts supply some examples, and the practice was regarded as passé by the Renaissance.

Native Naturally occurring in one area, but not confined to it. Compare **Endemic**.

Neoplatonic A philosophy that emerged in the third century CE, was linked to Renaissance humanism and continues to the present. It holds that the material world is experienced indirectly through human senses, while the apex, ideal level is known only through mysticism. Time and beauty are implied through ideal forms.

Perennial Describes a plant that grows, irrespective of season, for more than two years.

Species See **Botanical nomenclature**

Taxonomy The grouping or classifying of plants.

Understorey Plant life below the forest canopy.

NOTES

1 This volume focuses on the visual arts. Informative studies of plants in literature include Judith Farr and Louise Carter's *The Gardens of Emily Dickinson*, Cambridge, MA, 2004; and Randy Laist and Jim Horwitz, *Plants and Literature: Essays in Critical Plant Studies*, New York, 2013.

2 Tompkins and Bird's *The Secret Life of Plants* recounts the history of the scientific recognition of plant sentience – a patchy and largely ignored area until the twentieth century.

3 See, for example, Jim Ellis's *Intertwined Histories: Plants in their Social Contexts*, Calgary, 2019; and Gibson.

4 Harrison and Kirkham (12) estimate that some 8,000 tree species are under threat of extinction.

5 See Harrison and Kirkham for an extensive overview of trees, in particular the chapter 'Healers and Killers', 115ff. They also provide a vocabulary for describing important tree characteristics: 'godfather tree' (a tree planted by one generation that doesn't bear fruit until several generations later; 116), 'survivor trees' (those that flourish despite poor environments or other obstacles; 183) and 'keystone species' (trees that are vital to the health of the surrounding habitat; 205).

6 The filbert nut is in fact more elongated than the hazelnut and comes from a different species (Harrison and Kirkham 48).

7 Sources do not identify the girl, although the eye and brow resemble those of Lady Caroline Blackwood (an admired and prolific writer, and Freud's second wife from 1953 to 1959). A close-up by Freud of her right eye, painted in 1950, resurfaced in 2015, having been in a private collection for many years.

8 Harrison and Kirkham suggest that yews were planted near pagan temples because of their symbolic significance, and that the builders of Christian churches used the same grounds and meaning. The writers also list several very old British yews (58ff.).

9 Stephen Buchmann's *The Reason for Flowers* begins with an excellent preface. The book contains everything one might wish to know about flowers, enhanced by the author's stunning photographs.

10 Incidentally, it is possible that Van Gogh knew of the Wilde caricature, since he pored over British periodicals such as *The Graphic* and the *Illustrated London News* and kept up to date with the art scene. He owned prints from *Punch* as well. These are now in the Van Gogh Museum, including twenty-eight unidentified prints by Sambourne (Jansen et al., Letter 235).

11 One might read *Offices* instead of *Orders*, since the works may reflect the Catholic Church's canonical daily offices that are marked by prayer, which would have been well known to Kiefer.

12 The Metropolitan Museum's text accompanying a woodcut of the same subject suggests that the prone figure may be Robert Fludd, a sixteenth-century English occultist who believed that every plant in the world had its own equivalent star in the firmament.

13 See Gibson's discussion of the water lily and eco-feminism (128–30), and Monet (130f.).

14 Lavin notes that although the burning bush is usually depicted as a bush, Bellini instead depicted a noble laurel, which supposedly had the ability to withstand fire (244). Lavin also explains the desert reference in the painting's title: it refers to an island in the Venice lagoon called Isola di San Francesco del Deserto, where the saint took refuge during a storm (234).

15 Giulia Caneva et al., 'Plant Iconography and Its Message: Realism and Symbolic Message in the Bernini Fountain of the Four Rivers in Rome', *Rendiconti Lincei. Scienze Fisiche e Naturali*, 31 (2020), 1011–26, doi.org/10.1007/s12210020-00946-2. The mullein is associated with the Danube River.

16 Okoyomon obtained the kudzu from Amsterdam. Called 'the vine that ate the South', kudzu was imported to the United States to alleviate soil erosion. Despite good intentions, the project backfired and the plant took over the environment. It is now banned there.

BIBLIOGRAPHY

BOOKS AND PERIODICALS

Abella, Alex, *The Total Banana*, New York, 1979
Aloi, Giovanni, ed., *Botanical Speculations*, Newcastle upon Tyne, 2018
——, *Why Look at Plants?*, Critical Plant Studies, vol. 5, Leiden, 2019
——, *Lucian Freud: Plant Portraits*, London, 2022
Becker, Udo, ed., *The Continuum Encyclopedia of Symbols*, trans. Lance W. Garmer, London and New York, 1996
Biedermann, Hans, *Dictionary of Symbolism*, trans. James Hulbert, New York, 1992
Bisanz, Rudolf M., *German Romanticism and Philipp Otto Runge: A Study in Nineteenth-Century Art Theory and Iconography*, Ithaca, NY, 1970
Buchmann, Stephen, *The Reason for Flowers: Their History, Culture, Biology, and How They Change Our Lives*, New York, 2015
Caneva, G., et al., 'Plant Iconography and Its Message: Realism and Symbolic Message in the Bernini Fountain of the Four Rivers in Rome', *Rendiconti Lincei Scienze Fisiche e Naturali*, xxxi (2020), pp. 1011–26
Chevalier, Alexandre, Elena Marinova and Leonor Peña-Chocarro, eds, *Plants and People: Choices and Diversity through Time*, Oxford and Philadelphia, 2014
Chevalier, Jean, and Alain Gheerbrant, *The Penguin Dictionary of Symbols*, trans. John Buchanan-Brown, London, 1996 (2nd edn)
Cirlot, J. E., *A Dictionary of Symbols*, Mineola, NY, 2002 (2nd edn)
Dahl, Roald, *James and the Giant Peach*, New York, 1961 (1st edn)
D'Ancona, Mirella Levi, *The Garden of the Renaissance: Botanical Symbolism in Italian Painting*, Florence, 1977
Diffenbaugh, Vanessa, *The Language of Flowers*, London, 2011
Draguet, Michel, *Fernand Khnopff: Portrait of Jeanne Kéfer*, Los Angeles, 2004
Etheredge, Laura, *Egypt*, New York, 2011
Garrard, Mary D., 'The Not-So-Still Lifes of Giovanna Garzoni', in *'The Immensity of the Universe' in the Art of Giovanna Garzoni*, ed. Sheila Barker, Florence, 2020
Gibson, Prudence, *The Plant Contract: Art's Return to Vegetal Life*, Leiden, 2018
Goossen, E. C., *Ellsworth Kelly*, New York, 1973
Greenaway, Kate, *Language of Flowers* [1884], many recent editions
Haig, Elizabeth, *The Floral Symbolism of the Great Masters* [1913], reprinted London, 2018
Hall, James, *Illustrated Dictionary of Symbols in Eastern and Western Art*, New York, 1994
Hansson, Ann-Marie, and Andreas G. Heiss, eds, 'Plants Used in Ritual Offerings and in Festive Contexts', in Chevalier, Marinova and Peña-Chocarro, *Plants and People*, pp. 311–83
Harrison, Christina, and Tony Kirkham, *Remarkable Trees*, London, 2019, reprinted 2020
Hulton, P. H., *Flowers in Art from East and West*, London, 1979
Impelluso, Lucia, *Nature and Its Symbols*, Los Angeles, 2004
Janick, Jules, and Harry S. Paris, 'The Cucurbit Images (1515–1518) of the Villa Farnesina, Rome', *Annals of Botany*, xcvii/2 (February 2006), pp. 165–76, doi: 10.1093/aob/mcj025
Koerner, J. L., *The Moment of Self-Portraiture in German Renaissance Art*, Chicago, 1997
Lehner, Ernest, and Johanna Lehner, *Folklore and Symbolism of Flowers, Plants and Trees* [1960], Eastford, CT, 2012
Mancoff, Debra N., *The Pre-Raphaelite Language of Flowers*, Munich, 2002
Milner, John, *Mondrian*, London, 1995
Olderr, Steven, *Symbolism: A Comprehensive Dictionary*, Jefferson, NC, and London, 2012 (2nd edn)
Porteous, Alexander, *The Forest in Folklore and Mythology* [1928], Mineola, NY, 2002
Saint-Exupéry, Antoine de, *The Little Prince*, New York, 1943
Selznick, Brian, *Big Tree*, New York, 2023
Snider, Tui, *Understanding Cemetery Symbolism: A Field Guide for Historic Graveyards*, n.p., 2017
Sylvester, David, *Magritte: The Silence of the World*, New York, 1992
Taft, Catherine, et al., *Yayoi Kusama*, London, 2017
Tanning, Dorothea, *Another Language of Flowers*, New York, 1998
Tompkins, Peter, and Christopher Bird, *The Secret Life of Plants* [1973], New York, 2002
Torczyner, Harry, *Magritte: Ideas and Images*, New York, 1977
Tresidder, Jack, *Dictionary of Symbols*, San Francisco, 1997
Walker, Barbara, *The Woman's Dictionary of Symbols & Sacred Objects*, San Francisco, 1988
Wilkinson, Charles K., and Marsha Hill, *Egyptian Wall Paintings: The Metropolitan Museum of Art's Collection of Facsimiles*, New York, 1983
Williams, C. A. S., *Outlines of Chinese Symbolism and Art Motifs* [1932], Shanghai, 1976
Wilson, Matthew, *Symbols in Art*, London and New York, 2020
——, *The Hidden Language of Symbols*, London and New York, 2022
Woldbye, Vibeke, ed., *Flowers into Art*, The Hague, 1991
Zohary, Daniel, and Maria Hopf, *Domestication of Plants in the Old World* [1988], Oxford, 2000

ONLINE RESOURCES

'7,000 Oaks', Wikipedia, http://wikipedia.org/wiki/7000_Oaks (accessed July 2024)
Alcover-Cateura, Pablo José and Antoni Riera Melis, 'The Presence of Cherries in the Gothic Altarpieces in the Museu Nacional d'Art de Catalunya: A Brief History of Medieval Fruit', 23 April 2020, https://blog.museunacional.cat/en/the-presence-of-cherries-in-the-gothic-altarpieces-in-the-museu-nacional-dart-de-catalunya-a-brief-history-of-medieval-fruit
Anderson, Heather Arndt, 'Celery was the Avocado Toast of the Victorian Era', *Taste*, 23 August 2017, www.tastecooking.com/celery-was-the-avocado-toast-of-the-victorian-era
Art Gallery of Victoria, 'Picturing the Giants: The Changing Landscapes of Emily Carr', *AGGV Magazine*, 1 March 2020, http://emagazine.aggv.ca/picturing-the-giants-the-changing-landscapes-of-emily-carr
Barkham, Patrick, 'Britain's Ancient Yews: Mystical, Magnificent – and Unprotected', *The Guardian*, 28 September 2019, www.theguardian.com/environment/2019/sep/28/britain-ancient-yews-mystical-magnificent-and-unprotected
Bass-Krueger, Maude, 'A Brief History of Food in European Art', Google Arts & Culture, http://artsandculture.google.com/story/tQURN-8DeIXhIg (accessed July 2024)
Blessing, Jennifer, 'Piet Mondrian: Chrysanthemum', Guggenheim, www.guggenheim.org/artwork/2999 (accessed July 2024)
'Bouquet of Flowers in a Vase', Denver Art Museum, www.denverartmuseum.org/edu/object/bouquet-flowers-vase (accessed July 2024)
Bowen, Monica, 'Strawberries as an "Earthly Delight"', 9 July 2011, 'Alberti's Window' blog, www.albertis-window.com/2011/07/strawberries-as-an-earthly-delight

British Museum, 'Egyptian Life and Death', www.britishmuseum.org/collection/galleries/egyptian-life-and-death (accessed July 2024)

Brotherton, Barbara, 'Object of the Week: Raven Releasing the Sun', Seattle Art Museum, 2 July 2021, https://samblog.seattleartmuseum.org/2021/07/raven-releasing-the-sun-george-hunt-jr

Cary, Zulma, 'Top 10 Most Famous Trees in The World', Earth&World, 21 May 2018, www.earthnworld.com/top-10-most-famous-trees-in-the-world

Chandler, Graham, 'Walnuts and First Forest Farms', AramcoWorld, March/April 2017, www.aramcoworld.com/articles/march-2017/walnuts-and-the-first-forest-farms

Christie's, 'Paul Nash: The Three', 18 June 2008, www.christies.com/lotfinder/lot/paul-nash-1889-1946-the-three-5097384-details.aspx

Daunay, Marie-Christine, and Jules Janick, 'History and Iconography of Eggplant', *Chronica Horticulturae*, xlvii/3 (January 2007), pp. 16–22, www.hort.purdue.edu/newcrop/chronicaeggplant.pdf

Elkins, James, 'Weeping over Bluish Leaves', 2009, www.jameselkins.com/wp-content/uploads/2009/12/Tears-5.pdf

Ewbank, Anne, 'Ancient Greek Funerals Were Decked Out in Celery', 23 October 2018, *Atlas Obscura*, www.atlasobscura.com/articles/history-of-funeral-wreaths

'Gardiner's Sign List of Egyptian Hieroglyphs', *Egyptian Hieroglyphs*, www.egyptianhieroglyphs.net/gardiners-sign-list (accessed July 2024)

Gerry in Art, 'Paul Nash at Tate Britain: Searching for Another Angle of Vision', 'How the Light Gets In' blog, 2016, www.gerryco23.wordpress.com

Gholson, Christien, 'Noise and Silence: The World of Leonora Carrington, Part II: The Alchemical Kitchen', 12 April 2012, www.christiengholson.blogspot.com/2012/04/world-of-leonora-carrington-part-ii.html

Gill, N. S., 'Adonis and Aphrodite: The Story by Ovid from *Metamorphoses* X', ThoughtCo, 7 April 2019, www.thoughtco.com/adonis-and-aphrodite-111765

Goodeve, Thyrza Nichols, 'Mark Dion: Mourning Is a Legitimate Mode of Thinking', *Brooklyn Rail*, May 2016, www.brooklynrail.org/2016/05/art/mourning-is-a-legitimate-mode-of-thinking

Gottesman, Sarah, 'A Brief History of Flowers in Western Art', Artsy.net, 1 July 2017, www.artsy.net/article/artsy-editorial-van-gogh-okeeffe-art-historys-famous-flowers

Gurney, Tom, 'Great Piece of Turf: Albrecht Dürer', History of Art, 19 June 2020, www.thehistoryofart.org/albrecht-durer/great-piece-of-turf

Hageneder, Fred, 'Yew and Misconceptions in Religious History' (interview), *Fred Hageneder's Gateway to the Meaning of Trees in Culture and Consciousness*, 2007, www.themeaningoftrees.com/yew-and-misconceptions-in-religious-history

Harris, Alexandra, 'Top of the Crops: Cabbages in Art', *The Guardian*, 1 December 2010, www.theguardian.com/artanddesign/2010/dec/01/alexandra-harris-cabbages-art-first-book-award

'The History of Roses', University of Illinois Extension, www.extension.illinois.edu/roses/history (accessed July 2024)

'Honeysuckle', Ebrary.net, www.ebrary.net/27948/environment/honeysuckle (accessed July 2024)

'House of the Orchard or of the Floral Cubicles', Pompeii, http://pompeiisites.org/en/archaeological-site/house-of-the-orchard-or-of-the-floral-cubicles (accessed July 2024)

'Interview: *Neukom Vivarium*, Mark Dion', Art:21, n.d., www.art21.org/read/mark-dion-neukom-vivarium

Jackson, Kitty, 'Symbolism: Honeysuckle in Rubens' *Honeysuckle Bower*', *Artdependence Magazine*, 28 February 2019, www.artdependence.com/articles/symbolism-honeysuckle-in-rubens-honeysuckle-bower

Janick, Jules, 'The Pear in History, Literature, Popular Culture, and Art', *Acta Horticulturae*, December 2002, www.hort.purdue.edu/newcrop/pearinhistory.pdf

——, 'Fruits and Nuts of the Villa Farnesina', *Arnoldia*, 2012, www.hort.purdue.edu/newcrop/pdfs/70-2_03_villa_farnesina.pdf

——, and Giulia Caneva, 'The First Images of Maize in Europe', *Maydica*, I/I (January 2005), pp. 71–80, www.hort.purdue.edu/newcrop/maize/images_of_maize.pdf

——, and Anna Whipkey, 'The Fruits and Nuts of the Unicorn Tapestries', *Chronica Horticulturae*, liv/1 (2014), www.hort.purdue.edu/newcrop/pdfs/unicorn-tapestry-plants.pdf

Jansen, Leo, Hans Luijten and Nienke Bakker, eds, *Vincent van Gogh, The Letters*, 2009, www.vangoghletters.org

Jobson, Christopher, 'Ash Dome: A Secret Tree Artwork in Wales Planted by David Nash in 1977', Colossal, 9 May 2016, www.thisiscolossal.com/2016/05/ash-dome-david-dash

John Grade Studio, '*Treeline*', www.johngrade.com/projects/treeline (accessed July 2024)

Kargère, Lucretia Goddard, 'Two Sculptures in Deep Conversation at The Met Cloisters', Metropolitan Museum of Art, 22 May 2018, www.metmuseum.org/blogs/collection-insights/2018/virgin-and-child-sculptures-met-cloisters-heavenly-bodies

Kim, Hae-in, 'The Spiritual Depths of the Feminine Soul in Rossetti's "The Blessed Damozel"', Victorian Web, 2004, www.victorianweb.org/authors/dgr/hikim5.html

Kinver, Mark, 'World Is Home to "60,000 Tree Species"', BBC News, 5 April 2017, www.bbc.co.uk/news/science-environment-39492977

Knaus, Jennifer, www.jenniferknaus.com

Landmark Trust, 'The Pineapple', www.landmarktrust.org.uk/search-and-book/properties/pineapple-10726

Laqueur, Thomas W., 'Beneath the Yew Tree's Shade', *Paris Review*, 31 October 2015, www.theparisreview.org/blog/2015/10/31/beneath-the-yew-trees-shade

Larkin, Deirda, '*The Medieval Garden Enclosed*: The Holly and the Ivy', Metropolitan Museum of Art, 18 December 2008. www.metmuseum.org/articles/medieval-garden-enclosed-holly-and-ivy

Lavin, Marilyn Aronberg, Jinyu Liu and Adam Gitner, 'The Joy of St Francis: Bellini's Panel at the Frick Collection', *Artibus et Historiae*, xxviii/56 (2007), pp. 231–56, www.jstor.org/stable/20067174

Lemonedes, Heather, 'Bits of Rainbows', 21 December 2015, *Cleveland Art*, www.clevelandart.org/articles/bits-rainbows

Linsley, Alice C., 'The Gourd in Biblical Symbolism', 'Biblical Anthropology' blog, 12 December 2015, www.biblicalanthropology.blogspot.com/2015/12/the-gourd-in-biblical-symbolism.html

Lobell, Jarrett A., 'The Emperor's Orchids', *Archaeology*, January/February 2013, www.archaeology.org/issues/january-february-2013/digs-discoveries/roman-ara-pacis-altar-flowers

McCouat, Philip, 'Perception and Blindness in the 16th Century: Bruegel's *The Blind Leading the Blind*', *Journal of Art in Society*, October 2018, www.artinsociety.com/perception-and-blindness-in-the-16th-century.html

McNally, Ross, 'Ash to Ashes: The Vikings' Tree of Life Is under Threat', *Sussex Bylines*, 11 November 2022, www.sussexbylines.co.uk/news/environment/ash-to-ashes-the-vikings-tree-of-life-is-under-threat

'Mark Dion', Lenfest Center for the Arts, Columbia University School of the Arts, October 2021, http://arts.columbia.edu/events/mark-dion

Marks, Tasha, 'Lemons and Lobsters and Cabbages, Oh My! Symbolic Food in Painting', Art UK, 22 April 2020, www.artuk.org/discover/stories/lemons-and-lobsters-and-cabbages-oh-my-symbolic-food-in-painting

Meagher, Jennifer, 'Food and Drink in European Painting, 1400–1800', Metropolitan Museum of Art, May 2009, www.metmuseum.org/toah/hd/food/hd_food.htm

Meier, Allison, 'The Romantic Symbolism of Trees', Hyperallergic, 10 June 2014, www.hyperallergic.com/131541/the-romantic-symbolism-of-trees

Meistere, Una, 'Woodstock, Raves and the Image Recycler', 20 August 2020, Arterritory, www.arterritory.com/en/visual_arts/interviews/25074-woodstock_raves_and_the_image_recycler

Murray, Caroline M., entries in 'Professor Hedgehog's Journal' blog, The Artichoke', 16 February 2019, www.professorhedgehogsjournal.uk/2019/02/16/the-artichoke; 'Plant of the Month [Pineapple]: June 2017', 21 June 2017, www.professorhedgehogsjournal.uk/2017/06/21/plant-of-the-month-june-2017

O'Brien, Barbara, 'The Buddha's Robe: An Overview of Robes Worn by Buddhist Monks and Nuns', Learn Religions, 5 April 2023, www.learnreligions.com/the-buddhas-robe-450083

Olszewski, Edward, 'Dionysus's Enigmatic Thyrsus', *Proceedings of the American Philosophical Organization*, clxiii/2 (June 2019), pp. 153–73, www.amphilsoc.org/sites/default/files/2020-03/attachments/Olszewski.pdf

Paris, Harry S., et al., 'First Known Image of *Cucurbita* in Europe, 1503–1508', *Annals of Botany*, xcviii/1 (July 2006), pp. 41–47, www.ncbi.nlm.nih.gov/pmc/articles/PMC2803533

'Paul Nash: *Solstice of the Sunflower*', National Gallery of Canada, www.gallery.ca/collection/artwork/solstice-of-the-sunflower

Phaidon, 'Why Does Yayoi Kusama Love Pumpkins?', 21 March 2018, www.phaidon.com/agenda/art/articles/2018/march/21/why-does-yayoi-kusama-love-pumpkins

Protas, Allison, et al., 'Dictionary of Symbolism', Fantasy and Science Fiction website, University of Michigan, 1997/2001, www.umich.edu/~umfandsf/symbolismproject/symbolism.html

Real, Carol, 'Lene Kilde: The Nutmeg Princess', Art Summit, 9 April 2018, www.art-summit.com/lenekilde

Riggs, Terry, 'Salvador Dalí, *Metamorphosis of Narcissus*', The Tate, 1998, www.tate.org.uk/art/artworks/dali-metamorphosis-of-narcissus-t02343

Romack, Coco, 'The Artist Who Transforms Galleries into Forests and Fields', *New York Times Style Magazine*, 3 May 2021, www.nytimes.com/2021/05/03/t-magazine/precious-okoyomon-artist-shed.html

Ruiz, Carme, *Salvador Dalí and Science: Beyond a Mere Curiosity*, 2010, Fundació Gala – Salvador Dalí, www.salvador-dali.org/en/research/archives-en-ligne/download-documents/16/salvador-dali-and-science-beyond-a-mere-curiosity

Saffron Walden Museum, 'Saffron', 14 November 2017, www.saffronwaldenmuseum.swmuseumsoc.org.uk/saffron

Dr Samanthi, 'Difference between Pine and Fir', DifferenceBetween.com, 23 August 2011, www.differencebetween.com/difference-between-pine-and-vs-fir

'Samuel Palmer', www.themorgan.org/drawings/item/247415

Sanders, David, 'Introduction to the Tree of Life', The Kabbalah Experience, www.kabbalahexperience.com/introduction-to-the-tree-of-life (accessed July 2024)

Sargent, John Singer, *Carnation, Lily, Lily, Rose*, The Tate, www.tate.org.uk/art/artworks/sargent-carnation-lily-lily-rose-n01615

Schaechter, Moselio (Elio), and Roberto Kolter, 'Small Things Considered' blog, American Society for Microbiology, n.d., http://schaechter.asmblog.org/schaechter/about-small-things-considered.html

'Sennedjem and Iineferti in the Fields of Iaru', Metropolitan Museum, www.metmuseum.org/art/collection/search/548354 (accessed July 2024)

'Sennedjem – TT1', Osirisnet: The Tombs of Ancient Egypt, www.osirisnet.net/tombes/artisans/sennedjem1/e_sennedjem1_01.htm (accessed July 2024)

Sexton, Chrissy, 'Fibonacci Spirals: An Unexpected Twist in Plant Evolution', 16 June 2023, www.earth.com/news/fibonacci-spirals-an-unexpected-twist-in-plant-evolution/

Spanish National Research Council (CSIC), 'A First-ever Find in Egypt: 4,000-year-old Funerary Garden at Tomb Entrance', Science Daily, 4 May 2017, www.sciencedaily.com/releases/2017/05/170504093225.htm

Stańska, Zuzanna, 'Nature in Art: Gustav Klimt's Enchanting Depictions of Trees', 21 June 2024, *Daily Art Magazine*, www.dailyartmagazine.com/gustav-klimt-trees-paintings

Storl, Wolf D., 'A Curious History of Vegetables: Aphrodisiacal and Healing Properties...', Publicism, 2016, http://publicism.info/gardening/curious/7.html

Sullivan, Kerry, 'Wittenham Clumps: Ancient Earthworks Haunted by Gods Long Forgotten', Ancient Origins, 3 October 2016, www.ancient-origins.net/ancient-places-europe/wittenham-clumps-ancient-earthworks-haunted-gods-long-forgotten-006755

'Tower of London Remembers: WWI Centenary Commemorations at the Tower of London', Historic Royal Palaces, www.hrp.org.uk/tower-of-london/history-and-stories/tower-of-london-remembers (accessed July 2024)

'*Treeline*: John Grade', Jordan Schnitzer Museum of Art at PXU, www.pdx.edu/museum-of-art/treeline (accessed March 2024)

'Virgin del Pino', Wikipedia, http://en.wikipedia.org/wiki/Virgen_del_Pino (accessed July 2024)

'What Does a Willow Tree Symbolize?', Reference, 4 August 2015, www.reference.com/article/willow-tree-symbolize

SOURCES OF ILLUSTRATIONS

INTERIOR

Dimensions are given in centimetres followed by inches; height precedes width precedes depth, unless otherwise stated.

a = above; b = below
l = left; r = right

Images in the Plant Index are all details taken from images reproduced elsewhere in the book.

Endpapers Front Maria van Oosterwyck, *Bouquet of Flowers in a Vase* (detail), *c.* 1670s. Oil on canvas, 73.7 × 55.9 (29 × 22). Funds by exchange from T. Edward and Tullah Hanley in honor of longtime director, Otto Bach and his wife Cile Bach. Denver Art Museum (1997.219); Dante Gabriel Rossetti, *Beata Beatrix* (detail), *c.* 1864–70. Oil on canvas, 86.4 × 66 (34 ⅛ × 26). Tate, London (N01279). Photo Tate Images; Hilma af Klint, *Tree of Knowledge*, No. 5 (detail), 1913–15. Watercolour, gouache, graphite and ink on paper, 46 × 30 (18 × 11 ⅞). Glenstone Museum, Potomac, Maryland; *The Unicorn Rests in a Garden (from the Unicorn Tapestries)* (detail), 1495–1505. Wool warp with wool, silk, silver, and gilt wefts, overall: 368 × 251.5 (144 ⅞ × 99). Gift of John D. Rockefeller Jr., 1937. The Metropolitan Museum of Art, New York (37.80.6) **Back** René Magritte, *L'Explication (The Explanation)* (detail), 1952. Oil on canvas, 46 × 35 (18 ⅛ × 13 ¾). Private Collection. © ADAGP, Paris and DACS, London 2025; Charles Allston Collins, *Convent Thoughts* (detail), 1851. Oil on canvas, 84 × 59 (33 ⅛ × 23 ¼). Bequeathed by Mrs Thomas Combe, 1893. Ashmolean Museum, Oxford (WA1894.10)

1 *The Unicorn Rests in a Garden (from The Unicorn Tapestries)* (detail), 1495–1505. Wool warp with wool, silk, silver, and gilt wefts, overall: 368 × 251.5 (144 ⅞ × 99). Gift of John D. Rockefeller Jr., 1937. The Metropolitan Museum of Art, New York (37.80.6) **2** Francesco del Cossa, *Saint Lucy* (detail), *c.* 1473–74. Tempera on panel, 77.2 × 56 (30 ⅜ × 22 ¹/₁₆). Samuel H. Kress Collection. National Gallery of Art, Washington, D.C. (1939.1.228) **4** Joanne Hill Benedict, *California Palms*, 1999. Watercolour on paper, 35.6 × 25.4 (14 × 10). Private Collection. © Joanne Hill Benedict **6a** Hilma af Klint, *Tree of Knowledge*, No. 1, 1913–15. Watercolour, gouache, graphite, and ink on paper, 46 × 30 (18 × 11 ⅞). Glenstone Museum, Potomac, Maryland **6b** Karl Blossfeldt, *Dipsacus laciniatus*, 1928. Gelatin silver print, 25.9 × 19.8 (10 ³/₁₆ × 7 ¹³/₁₆). J. Paul Getty Museum, Los Angeles (84.XM.142.3) **7a** William Henry Fox Talbot, *Two Plant Specimens*, 1839. Photogenic drawing, 22.1 × 18 (8 ¾ × 7 ⅛). Edward E. Ayer Endowment in memory of Charles L. Hutchinson. Art Institute of Chicago (1972.325) **7b** Tosa Mitsuoki, *Autumn Maples with Poem Slips* (detail), 1670–80. Ink, colours, gold leaf and gold powder on silk, 144 × 286 (56 ¾ × 112 ⅝). Kate S. Buckingham Endowment. Art Institute of Chicago (1977.157) **18** Girolamo dai Libri, *Madonna and Child with Saints* (detail), *c.* 1520. Tempera and oil on canvas, 398.8 × 207 (157 × 81 ½). Fletcher Fund, 1920. The Metropolitan Museum of Art, New York (20.92) **21** H.J. Ruprecht, Trunk and roots of a pine tree cut to show growth rings; microscopic views of wood cells in longitudinal and transverse section and of a root tip. Chromolithograph, 1877. Wellcome Collection, London (27043i) **22** Gustav Klimt, *Tree of Life*, working drawing of the execution of a mosaic frieze for the dining hall of Stoclet House, Brussels. Tracing paper, coloured pencil, gold, pastel, platinum, silver, bronze, gouache, 200 × 102 (78 ¾ × 40 ¼). MAK, Vienna (MAL 226-4) **23a** Sefirot, *The Great Parchment*, copied by James Hepburn, 1606. Parchment, 108 × 75 (42 ⅞ × 29 ⅝). The Bodleian Library, Oxford (MS Hunt. Add. E) **23b** David Maxim, *Old Man with Young Tree*, 2021. Watercolour on paper, 35.6 × 27.9 (14 × 11). © David Maxim **24** Oluf Olufsen Bagge, *Yggdrasil, The Mundane Tree*, from the *Prose Edda*, 1847 **25a** William Blake, *The Wood of the Self-Murderers: The Harpies and the Suicides*, 1824–27 (from Illustrations to Dante's *Divine Comedy*). Graphite, ink and watercolour on paper, 37.2 × 52.7 (14 ⅝ × 20 ¾). Tate, London (N03356). Photo Tate Images **25b** Max Ernst, *The Forest*, 1927–28. Oil on canvas, 96.3 × 129.5 (37 ⅞ × 51). The Solomon R. Guggenheim Foundation Peggy Guggenheim Collection, Venice, 1976 (76.2553.72). © ADAGP, Paris and DACS, London 2025 **26–27** Anselm Kiefer, *Entrance to Paradise*, 2010. Oil, emulsion, acrylic, shellac, thorn bushes, photographs, and lead on canvas in glazed steel frames, 282 × 768 × 35 (111 × 302 ⅜ × 13 ¾). The Broad Art Foundation, Los Angeles. Photo Charles Duprat. © Anselm Kiefer **28** 'Netting Birds, Tomb of Khnumhotep', *c.* 1897–1878 BCE. Facsimile by Nina de Garis Davies. Tempera on paper, 101 × 260 (39 ¾ × 102 ⅜). Rogers Fund, 1933. The Metropolitan Museum of Art, New York (33.8.18) **29** James Watts, after E. D. Smith, *Acacia oxycedrus*, 1827. 203 × 125 (80 × 49 ¼) from Robert Sweet's *Flora Australasica*, James Ridgway, 1827 **30** Wolfgang Meyerpick, after Giorgio Liberale, *Ficus sycomorus*, 1568, from *I discorsi di M. Pietro Andrea Matthioli*, Presso Nicolò Pezzana, 1712. Photo SuperStock/Album/Florilegius/Album Archivo **31** Brian Selznick, *Merwin and Louise*, from *Big Tree*, Scholastic Press, 2023. © 2023 by Brian Selznick. Reprinted by permission of Scholastic Inc. **32a** Antoine de Saint-Exupéry, *The Baobabs*, from Saint-Exupéry's *The Little Prince*, Reynal & Hitchcock, 1943 **32b, 33l** Mme E. Panckoucke and P.J.F. Turpin, *Baobab*, from F.P. Chaumeton, Chamberet et Poiret's *Flore Médicale*, C.L.F. Panckoucke, 1833 **33r** Lith Vayron, Baobab, from Étienne Denisse's *Flore d'Amérique*, Gihaut, 1843–46 **34** Pancrace Bessa, White Birch, from François André Michaux's *The North American Sylva*, C. D'Hautel, 1819 **35** Gustav Klimt, *Birch Forest*, 1903. Oil on canvas, 110.1 × 109.8 (43 ⅜ × 43 ¼). Private Collection **36** Giorgio Gallesio, Spanish chestnut, from Gallesio's *Pomona Italiana*, Niccolò Capurro, 1817–39. The New York Public Library (b13674913) **37** Charles E. Burchfield, *Summer Solstice (In Memory of the American Chestnut Tree)*, 1961–66. Watercolour on paper, 137.2 × 152.4 (54 × 60). Burchfield Penney Art Center at SUNY Buffalo State, Buffalo, New York **38** J.J. or J.E. Haid, after Georg Dionysius Ehret, *Cedrus*, *c.* 1750. Coloured engraving, 45.5 × 29.6 (18 × 11 ⅞). Wellcome Collection, London (18377i) **39** John Grade, *Treeline*, 2017. Alaskan yellow cedar and Metasequoia wood, 9.5 × 3.7 × 3 m (31 × 12 × 10 ft.). Karl Miller Center atrium, Portland State University. Courtesy John Grade **40l** William Morris and John Henry Dearle, *The Orchard* (detail), 1890. Tapestry woven in wool, silk and mohair on a cotton warp, 221 × 472 (87 ⅛ × 185 ⅞). Victoria and Albert Museum, London (154-1898) **40r** *Citrus Aurantium*, from David Nathaniel Friedrich Dietrich's *Flora Medica*, August Schmid, 1831 **41** John Everett Millais, *The Bridesmaid*, 1851. Oil on panel, 27.9 × 20.3 (11 × 8). The Fitzwilliam Museum, Cambridge (499*) **42l** *Citrus Limonium*, from Charles Dessalines D' Orbigny's *Dictionnaire Universel d'histoire Naturelle*, MM. Renard, Martinet et cie, 1892 **42r** Antonio da Correggio, *Virgin and Child with the Young St. John the Baptist* (detail), *c.* 1515. Oil on panel, 64.2 × 50.2 (25 ¼ × 19 ¾). Clyde M. Carr Fund. Art Institute of Chicago (1965.688) **43** Maria Margaretha van Os, *Still Life with Lemon and Cut Glass*, 1823–26. Oil on panel, 27 × 23 (10 ⅝ × 9 ⅛). Rijksmuseum, Amsterdam (SK-A-1107) **44** Hemlock (l) and fine-leaved water hemlock (r), from Giorgio Bonelli et al., *Hortus Romanus*, Bouchard et Gravier, 1772–93.

Rare Book Division, The New York Public Library (b14444147) **45** Jacques-Louis David, *The Death of Socrates* (detail), 1787. Oil on canvas, 129.5 × 196.2 (51 × 77 ¼). Catharine Lorillard Wolfe Collection, Wolfe Fund, 1931. The Metropolitan Museum of Art, New York (31.45) **46** George Hunt Jr., *Raven Releasing the Sun*, 1985. Silkscreen on paper, 50.8 × 38.1 (20 × 15). Gift of R. Bruce and Mary-Louise Colwell. Seattle Art Museum (2018.29.191). © George Hunt Jr. **47a** Mark Dion, *Seattle Vivarium*, 2002. Coloured pencil on paper, 23 × 30.5 (9 × 12). Courtesy the artist and Tanya Bonakdar Gallery, New York, Los Angeles **47b** Mark Dion, *Neukom Vivarium*, 2006. Mixed media installation, Greenhouse structure length: 24.38 m (80 ft.). Gift of Sally and William Neukom, American Express Company, Seattle Garden Club, Mark Torrance Foundation and Committee of 33, in honour of the 75th Anniversary of the Seattle Art Museum, 2007. Commissioned from the artist by Seattle Art Museum (funds from donors), 2003. Photo Paul Macapia. Courtesy the artist and Tanya Bonakdar Gallery, New York, Los Angeles **48** Andrea Mantegna, centre panel of San Zeno altarpiece (detail), 1457–60. Tempera on wood, 220 × 115 (86.6 × 45.2). Basilica of San Zeno, Verona **49** Mary Vaux Walcott, Beaked Hazelnut, 1932. Watercolour on paper, 25.5 × 17.9 (10 × 7). Gift of the artist. Smithsonian American Art Museum, Washington, D.C. (1970.355.63) **50l** Evelyn De Morgan, *The Angel of Death I* (detail), 1880. Oil on canvas, 93 × 112.8 (36 ⅝ × 44 ½). De Morgan Collection, Barnsley (P_EDM_0021) **50r** Cypress Tree, from Joseph Miller's *A Curious Herbal*, John Nourse, 1751. George Arents Collection, The New York Public Library (b10121930) **51** Henri-Edmond Cross, *Coastal View with Cypress Trees*, 1896. Oil on canvas, 65 × 92 (25 ⅝ × 36 ¼). Musée du Petit Palais, Geneva **52** Pierre Joseph Redouté, *Fagus silvatica*, from M. Duhamel du Monceau's *Traité des Arbres et Arbustes*, Didot ainé, 1801–19. Rare Book Division, The New York Public Library (b14485031) **53** Paul Nash, *The Wood on the Hill (Wittenham Clumps)*, 1912. Pen and ink drawing, 34 × 33.4 (13 ½ × 13 ¼). Ashmolean Museum, Oxford (WA2001.60). Photo Ashmolean Museum/Bridgeman Images **55** Roman fresco from House of the Orchard or of the Floral Cubicles (detail), Pompeii, 1st century. Photo Berk Ozdemir/Alamy **56** Giorgio Gallesio, *Fico Pissaluto*, from Gallesio's *Pomona Italiana*, Niccolò Capurro, 1817–39. The New York Public Library (b13674913) **57** Lucian Freud, *Girl with a Fig Leaf*, 1947. Etching on paper, 29 × 23.5 (11 ½ × 9 ⅜). Private Collection. © The Lucian Freud Archive. All Rights Reserved 2025/Bridgeman Images **58** David Nash, *Ash Dome*, 1977. Closely guarded location, Eryri/Snowdonia, Wales. Photo, 2009 © Jonty Wilde; Courtesy David Nash **59** Jacob van Huysum, Flowering ash, 1730. Engraving with watercolour, 37 × 25.5 (14 ⅝ × 10 ⅛). Wellcome Collection, London (20537i) **60** Rebecca Hey, *Holly*, from Hey's *The Spirit of the Woods*, Longman, Brown, Green, and Longmans, 1837 **61l** Carlton Alfred Smith, *Christmas Eve* (detail), 1901. Watercolour, 75 × 123 (29.5 × 48.4). Private Collection **61r** *The Unicorn Rests in a Garden (from The Unicorn Tapestries)* (detail), 1495–1505. Wool warp with wool, silk, silver, and gilt wefts, overall: 368 × 251.5 (144 ⅞ × 99). Gift of John D. Rockefeller Jr., 1937. The Metropolitan Museum of Art, New York (37.80.6) **62, 63l** Pierre Joseph Redouté, *Juniperus communis, Juniperus oxycedrus*, from M. Duhamel du Monceau's *Traité des Arbres et Arbustes*, Didot ainé, 1801–19. Rare Book Division, The New York Public Library (b14485031) **63r** Emily Carr, *A Rushing Sea of Undergrowth*, 1935. Oil on canvas, 112.8 × 69 (44 ½ × 27 ¼). Emily Carr Trust. Vancouver Art Gallery (VAG 42.3.17) **64** Girolamo dai Libri, *Madonna and Child with Saints*, c. 1520. Tempera and oil on canvas, 398.8 × 207 (157 × 81 ½). Fletcher Fund, 1920. The Metropolitan Museum of Art, New York (20.92) **65l** William Clark, Bay laurel, from John Stephenson and James Morss Churchill's *Medical Botany*, J. Churchill, 1834 **65r** Lorenzo Lotto, *Venus and Cupid* (detail), 1520. Oil on canvas,

92.4 × 111.4 (36 ⅜ × 43 ⅞). Purchase, Mrs. Charles Wrightsman Gift, in honor of Marietta Tree, 1986. The Metropolitan Museum of Art, New York (1986.138) **66l** Benoît Chirat, Olive branch, lithograph with watercolour, c. 1850. Wellcome Collection, London (27084i) **66r** Terracotta skyphos, Greek, mid-5th century BCE. Red-figure, 5.8 × 12.1 × 7.2 (2 ¼ × 4 ¾ × 2 ¹³⁄₁₆). Rogers Fund, 1941. The Metropolitan Museum of Art, New York (41.162.100) **67** Vincent van Gogh, *Olive Trees*, 1889. Oil on canvas, 73.66 × 92.71 (29 × 36 ½). The William Hood Dunwoody Fund. Minneapolis Institute of Art (51.7) **68** Areca catechu, from Köhler's *Medizinal-Pflanzen*, Fr. Eugen Köhler, 1890 **69** Francesco del Cossa, *Saint Lucy*, c. 1473–74. Tempera on panel, 77.2 × 56 (30 ⅜ × 22 ¹⁄₁₆). Samuel H. Kress Collection. National Gallery of Art, Washington, D.C. (1939.1.228) **70–71** Caspar David Friedrich, *Winter Landscape*, probably 1811. Oil on canvas, 32.5 × 45 (12 ⅞ × 17 ¾). The National Gallery, London (NG6517) **72** Pinus inops, 1837, from Aylmer Bourke Lambert's *A Description of the Genus Pinus*, George White, 1837. Rare Book Division, The New York Public Library (b13640523) **74** Giorgio Gallesio, *Mandorla del Diavolo*, from Gallesio's *Pomona Italiana*, Niccolò Capurro, 1817–39. Rare Book Division, The New York Public Library (b13674913) **75** *Christ in Majesty*, from The Speyer Evangelist, c. 1220. 33.2 × 25.3 (13 ⅛ × 10). Badische Landesbibliothek (Cod. Bruchsal 1, fol.1v) **76** Vincent van Gogh, *Almond Blossom*, 1890. Oil on canvas, 73.3 × 92.4 (28 ⅞ × 36 ½). Van Gogh Museum, Amsterdam (Vincent van Gogh Foundation) **78** Pierre Joseph Redouté, *Quercus robur*, from M. Duhamel du Monceau's *Traité des Arbres et Arbustes*, Didot ainé, 1801–19. Rare Book Division, The New York Public Library (b14485031) **79a** Samuel Palmer, *Oak Tree and Beech, Lullingstone Park*, c. 1828. Pen, ink, graphite, watercolour and opaque watercolour on paper, 29.6 × 47 (11 ⅝ × 18 ½). The Morgan Library and Museum, New York (2006.53) **79b** Patricia Day, *Whispering Oak*, 2023. Pastel on paper, 14 × 21.6 (5.5 in. × 8.5). Courtesy the artist **80** Joseph Beuys, *7000 Oak Trees*, 1982. documenta archiv, Kassel. Photo © documenta archiv/Dieter Schwerdtle. Artwork © DACS 2025 **81** Gold funerary wreath, Rome, 1st–2nd century. Gold, 31.8 (12 ½). Gift of Mrs. Wallace Phillips, 1957. The Metropolitan Museum of Art, New York (57.59) **82** Gravestone with weeping willow, 19th century. St Mary's churchyard, Rainham, Kent. Photo courtesy Carole Tyrrell **83** Babylon Willow, n.d. Photo DeAgostini Picture Library/Getty Images **84** Yew (Ground Hemlock), 1862–69. Lithograph, 9.8 × 5.6 (3 ⅞ × 2 ³⁄₁₆). The Jefferson R. Burdick Collection, Gift of Jefferson R. Burdick. The Metropolitan Museum of Art, New York (Burdick 627, W13.12) **85** Old Yew Trees, North Door of St. Edward's Church, Stow-on-the-Wold, Gloucestershire, 12th–15th century. The door itself dates from the 17th or 18th century. Photo SuperStock/David Hall/Loop Images **86** Thomas S. Sinclair, Thomas's Elm, from Thomas Nuttall's *The North American Sylva*, J. Dobson, 1842–49 **87** John Constable, *Study of the Trunk of an Elm Tree*, c. 1821. Oil on paper, 30.6 × 24.8 (12 × 9 ¾). Victoria & Albert Museum, London (786-1888) **88** Salvador Dalí, *Metamorphosis of Narcissus* (detail), 1937. Oil on canvas, 51.1 × 78.1 (20 ⅛ × 30 ¾). Tate, London (T02343). Photo Tate Images. © Salvador Dalí, Fundació Gala-Salvador Dalí, DACS 2025 **90** Sandro Botticelli, *Primavera*, c. 1480. Tempera on wood, 207 × 319 (81 ½ × 125 ⅝). Uffizi Galleries, Florence (1890 n. 8360) **91a** Jeff Koons, *Puppy*, 1992. Stainless steel, soil and flowering plants. Guggenheim Museum Bilbao (GBM1997.29). Photo KarSol/Alamy. Artwork © Jeff Koons **91b** Joseph Stella, *Flowers, Italy*, 1931. Oil on canvas, 189.8 × 189.8 (74 ¾ × 74 ¾). Gift of Mr. and Mrs. Jonathan Marshall. Phoenix Art Museum **92** Dorothea Tanning, *Zephirium apochriphoniae (Windwort)*, 1997–98. Oil on canvas, 97 × 130 (38 ¼ × 51 ⅛). © ADAGP, Paris and DACS, London, 2025 **93l** John William Waterhouse, *The Awakening of Adonis* (detail), 1899. Oil on canvas, 95.9 × 188 (37 ⅞ × 74 ⅛). Private Collection. Photo The Maas Gallery, London/Bridgeman Images **93r** Johann

Michael Seligmann, *Anemone plant*, *c.* 1768. Engraving with watercolour and gouache. Wellcome Collection, London (20471i) **94l** *Aquilegia nikolicii*, from *Curtis's Botanical Magazine* N.9405, 1935 **94r** Frederick A. Walpole, Columbine, Fisch, Sitka, Alaska, June 26, 1900, from Harriman, et al. *Alaska*. Doubleday, Page, 1901. **95** Hugo van der Goes, *Adoration of the Shepherds* (detail), centre panel of the Portinari altarpiece, 1477–78. Oil on wood, 274 × 652 (107 ⅞ × 256 ¾). Uffizi Galleries, Florence (1890 nn. 3191, 3192, 3193) **96** John Curtis, *Arum italicum*, from John Sims' *Curtis's Botanical Magazine* vol.50, 1823 **97** Vincent van Gogh, *Giant Peacock Moth*, 1889. Oil on canvas, 33.5 × 24.5 (13 ¼ × 9 ¾). Van Gogh Museum, Amsterdam (Vincent van Gogh Foundation) **98–99** Sandro Botticelli, *The Birth of Venus*, *c.* 1485. Tempera on canvas, 172.5 × 278.5 (68 × 109 ¾). Uffizi Galleries, Florence (1890 n. 878) **100** Jane Elizabeth Giraud, Daisies, 1846. The New York Public Library (b13501092) **101** Richard Dadd, *The Fairy-Feller's Master-Stroke*, 1855–64. Oil on canvas, 54 × 39.4 (21 ⅜ × 15 ⅝). Tate, London (T00598). Photo Tate Images **102** Albrecht Dürer, *Portrait of the Artist Holding a Thistle* (detail), 1493. Oil on parchment over canvas, 56.5 × 44.5 (22.2 × 17.2). Musée du Louvre, Paris (RF 2382) **103** Alice Carmen Gouvy, *Thistle 215*, 1902. Watercolour on paper, 64 × 45 (25 ¼ × 17 ¾). Rakow Research Library, Corning, NY (88923 1000074694) **104** Piet Mondrian, *Chrysanthemum*, *c.* 1908–9. Crayon on paperboard, 25.4 × 28.6 (10 × 11 ¼). Solomon R. Guggenheim Museum, New York (61.1589) **105** Pieter de Pannemaeker, after Jean Linden, Autumn chrysanthemum hybrids, from Jean Linden's *L'Illustration Horticole*, 1888. Photo Florilegius/Universal Images Group/Getty Images **106, 107b** Crocus, coloured etching, *c.* 1812. Wellcome Collection, London (26412i) **107a** 'Saffron Gatherers', detail of fresco, *c.* 1500 BCE, Xeste 3, Akrotiri, Santorini **108** James Sowerby, Round-Leaved Cyclamen, from William Curtis' *Botanical Magazine*, vol.1, 1787 **109** Moshe Gershuni, *Hai Cyclamen*, 1984. Mixed media on paper, 200 × 140 (78 ¾ × 55 ⅛). Private Collection. © The Moshe Gershuni Art Trust **110l** Francisco Goya, *The Marquesa de Pontejos* (detail), *c.* 1786. Oil on canvas, 210.3 × 127 (82 13/16 × 50). Andrew W. Mellon Collection. National Gallery of Art, Washington (1937.1.85) **110r** Augusta Withers, *Tree carnation*, from Edward George and Andrew Henderson's *The Illustrated Bouquet*, E.G. Henderson & Son, 1857 **111** John Singer Sargent, *Carnation, Lily, Lily, Rose*, 1885–86. Oil on canvas, 174 × 153.7 (68 ⅝ × 60 ⅝). Tate, London (N01615). Photo Tate Images **112** Vincent van Gogh, *Portrait of Dr Paul Gachet*, 1890. Oil on canvas, 68.2 × 57 (26 ⅞ × 22 ½). Musée d'Orsay, Paris (RF1949-16) **113l** James Sowerby, *Foxglove*, from William Withering's *An Account of the Foxglove*, M. Swinney, 1785. Wellcome Collection, London (ESTC T55002) **113r** Dorothy Cross, *Foxglove*, 2007. Bronze, 70 × 20 × 16 (27 ⅝ × 7 ⅞ × 6 ⅜). Courtesy the artist **114** William Clark, *Sunflower*, from Richard Morris' *Flora Conspicua*, Longman, Rees, Orme, Brown, and Green, 1826 **115** Dorothea Tanning, *Eine Kleine Nachtmusik*, 1943. Oil on canvas, 40.7 × 61 (16 ⅛ × 24 ⅛). Tate, London (T07346). Photo Tate Images. © ADAGP, Paris and DACS, London 2025 **116** Anselm Kiefer, *Die Orden der Nacht* (*The Orders of the Night*), 1996. Acrylic, emulsion, and shellac on canvas, 356 × 463 (140 ⅛ × 182 ¼). Gift of Richard and Elizabeth Hedreen. Seattle Art Museum (99.85). Photo Prudence Cuming Associates Ltd. © Anselm Kiefer **117** Faith Ringgold, *The Sunflower Quilting Bee at Arles*, 1991. Acrylic on canvas with pieced fabric border, 188 × 203.2 (74 × 80). Private Collection. © 2025 Faith Ringgold/ARS, NY and DACS, London **118** Pierre Joseph Redouté, *Hyacinthus orientalis*, from Redouté's *Choix des Plus Belle Fleurs et des Plus Beaux Fruits*, Panckoucke, 1827. The Minnich Collection, The Ethel Morrison Van Derlip Fund, 1966. Minneapolis Institute of Art (P.18,330) **119** Ellsworth Kelly, *Hyacinth*, 1949. Ink on paper, 41.9 × 30.5 (16 ½ × 12). Private Collection. Image courtesy Ellsworth Kelly Studio. © Ellsworth Kelly Foundation **120** Vincent van Gogh, *Irises*, 1889. Oil on canvas, 74.3 × 94.3 (29 ¼ × 37 ⅛). J. Paul Getty Museum, Los Angeles (90.PA.20) **121** Kazumasa Ogawa, *Iris Kæmpferi*, 1896. Colored collotype, 27.9 × 20.8 (11 × 8 3/16). J. Paul Getty Museum, Los Angeles (84.XB.759.6.7) **122** Pierre Joseph Redouté, *Iris squalens* and *Iris germanica*, from Redouté's *Les Liliacées*, Imprimerie de Didot Jeune, 1805–16. Rare Book Division, The New York Public Library (b10808712) **123** Georgia O'Keeffe, *Black Iris*, 1926. Oil on canvas, 91.4 × 75.9 (36 × 29 ⅞). Alfred Stieglitz Collection, 1969. The Metropolitan Museum of Art, New York (69.278.1). © Georgia O'Keeffe Museum/DACS 2025 **124** Simone Martini, *Annunciation with St Margaret and St Ansanus* (detail), 1333. Tempera on wood, 184 × 168 (72 ½ × 66 ¼). Uffizi Galleries, Florence (1890 nos. 451, 452, 453) **125** Charlotte Sowerby, *Lillium speciosum*, from William Robyn's *The Illustrated Bouquet*, E.G. Henderson & Son, 1857. Rare Book Division, The New York Public Library (b14454923) **126** Dante Gabriel Rossetti, *The Blessed Damozel*, 1871–78. Oil on canvas, 136.8 × 96.5 (53 ⅞ × 38). Bequest of Grenville L. Winthrop. Harvard Art Museums/Fogg Museum, Cambridge, MA (1943.202) **127** David Hockney, *Mr and Mrs Clark and Percy*, 1970–71. Acrylic on canvas, 213.4 × 304.8 (84 × 120). Tate, London (T01269). Photo Tate Images. © David Hockney **128l** John T. Curran, Tiffany & Co., *Loving Cup*, 1891. Silver gilt, 23.2 × 15.9 (9 ⅛ × 6 ¼). Anonymous Gift, 2010. The Metropolitan Museum of Art, New York (2010.286.1) **128r** H. Fletcher, after J. van Huysum, Honeysuckle, 1730. Engraving with watercolour, 37 × 25.5 (14 ⅝ × 10 ⅛). The Wellcome Collection (20536i) **129** Peter Paul Rubens, *Honeysuckle Bower* (detail), *c.* 1609–10. Oil on canvas, 178 × 136.5 (70 ⅛ × 53 ¾). Bavarian State Painting Collections - Alte Pinakothek Munich (334) **130** Salvador Dalí, *Metamorphosis of Narcissus*, 1937. Oil on canvas, 51.1 × 78.1 (20 ⅛ × 30 ¾). Tate, London (T02343). Photo Tate Images. © Salvador Dali, Fundació Gala-Salvador Dalí, DACS 2025 **131** Pierre-Joseph Redouté, *Narcissus gouani*, 1827. Hand-coloured stipple engraving, 27.94 × 21.59 (11 × 8 ½). The Minnich Collection The Ethel Morrison Van Derlip Fund, 1966. Minneapolis Institute of Art (P.18,349) **132** Head of Nefertem, 18th Dynasty, 1332–1323 BCE. Wood and paint, 30 (12) high. Egyptian Museum, Cairo (JE 60723) **133** Louis van Houtte, *Nymphaea stellata*, from van Houtte's *Flore des Serres et des Jardins de l'Europe*, Louis van Houtte Éditeur, 1845–80 **134** Nakht and family fishing and fowling, *c.* 1400–1370 BCE, facsimile (detail) by Norman de Garis Davies and Lancelot Crane of image from the Tomb of Nakht, east wall, south side of offering chapel, 1908–10. Tempera on paper, 194.3 × 203.8 (76 ½ × 80 ¼). Rogers Fund, 1915. The Metropolitan Museum of Art, New York (15.5.19e) **135** Claude Monet, *Nympheas*, 1897–98. Oil on canvas, 66 × 104.1 (26 × 41). Mrs. Fred Hathaway Bixby Bequest. Los Angeles County Museum of Art (M.62.8.13) **136** Orchids in Low Relief, Ara Pacis Augustae, Rome, 9 BCE. Photo Jean-Pierre Dalbéra **137** John Nugent Fitch, *Cattleya velutina*, 1882–97, from Robert Warner and Benjamin Samuel Williams' *The Orchid Album*, B. S. Williams **138** Roman Sarcophagus with the myth of Selene and Endymion, early 3rd century. Marble, 72.39 (28 ½). Rogers Fund, 1947. The Metropolitan Museum of Art, New York (47.100.4a,b) **139** *Papaver somniferum*, 1887, from Köhler's *Medizinal-Pflanzen*, Fr. Eugen Köhler, 1883–1914 **140l** Dante Gabriel Rossetti, *Beata Beatrix* (detail), *c.* 1864–70. Oil on canvas, 86.4 × 66 (34 ⅛ × 26). Tate, London (N01279). Photo Tate Images **140r** Paolo Veneziano, *Madonna of the Poppy* (detail), *c.* 1325. Oil on panel, 98 × 184 (38 ⅝ × 72 ½). San Pantalon, Venice. Photo Mondadori Portfolio/Getty Images **141** Paul Cummins and Tom Piper, *Blood Swept Lands and Seas of Red*, 2014. Ceramic poppies. Installation at the Tower of London. Photo Zefrog/Alamy **142l** John Everett Millais, *Isabella* (detail), 1849. Oil on canvas, 103 × 142.8 (40 ⅝ × 56 ¼). Purchased by the Walker Art Gallery in 1884. Walker Art Gallery, Liverpool (WAG 1637) **142r** *Passiflora holosericea*, 1815, from Sydenham

Edwards and James Ridgway's *The Botanical Register*, Printed for James Ridgway, 1815–28 **143** Charles Allston Collins, *Convent Thoughts*, 1851. Oil on canvas, 84 × 59 (33 ⅛ × 23 ¼). Bequeathed by Mrs Thomas Combe, 1893. Ashmolean Museum, Oxford (WA1894.10) **144** Stefan Lochner, *Madonna of the Rose Bower* (detail), *c.* 1440–42. Oil on panel, 50.5 × 40 (20 × 15 ¾). Bequest of F. J. von Herwegh, 1848. Wallraf-Richartz-Museum, Cologne (WRM 0067). Photo DeAgostini/Getty Images **145** Pierre Joseph Redouté, *Rosa Centifoliar*, from Redouté's *Les Roses*, Firmin Didot, 1817–24. The Miriam and Ira D. Wallach Division of Art, Prints and Photographs: Print Collection, The New York Public Library (b13999305) **146** Charles Dessalines D' Orbigny, *Tulipa gesneriana*, from D'Orbigny's *Dictionnaire Universel d'Histoire Naturelle*, MM. Renard, Martinet et Cie., 1849 **147** Maria van Oosterwyck, *Bouquet of Flowers in a Vase*, *c.* 1670s. Oil on canvas, 73.7 × 55.9 (29 × 22). Funds by exchange from T. Edward and Tullah Hanley in honor of longtime director, Otto Bach and his wife Cile Bach. Denver Art Museum (1997.219) **148l** Stefan Lochner, *Virgin with the Violet* (detail), *c.* 1450. Oil and tempera on wood, 121.5 × 102 (47 ⅞ × 40 ¼). Kolumba Museum, Cologne **148r** Ford Madox Brown, *The Convalescent (A Portrait of the Artist's Wife)*, 1872. Pastel on paper, 46.7 × 44.1 (18 ⅜ × 17 ⅜). Rogers Fund, 1910. The Metropolitan Museum of Art, New York (10.46) **149** Jacques Le Moyne de Morgues, *Violets and red admiral butterfly*, *c.* 1575. Watercolour, 27.3 × 18.7 (10 ¾ × 7 ⅜). Victoria and Albert Museum, London (AM.3267A-1856) **150** J. Vandamme, *Viola tricolor* (I. *Gloire de Bellevue*; 2. *Reine des Panachées*), from Charles Antoine Lemaire's *L'Illustration Horticole*, Imprimerie et lithographie de F. et E. Gyselnyck, 1854 **151a** Vincent van Gogh, *Basket of Pansies*, 1887. Oil on canvas, 46 × 55 (18 ⅛ × 21 ¾). Van Gogh Museum, Amsterdam (Vincent van Gogh Foundation) **151b** British Queen Elizabeth I's embroidered bookbinding, 1544. Bodleian Libraries, University of Oxford. Photo The Picture Art Collection/Alamy **152** Hieronymus Bosch, *The Garden of Earthly Delights* (detail of centre panel), 1490–1500. Oil on oak, 185.8 × 172.5 (73 ¼ × 68). Museo del Prado, Madrid (P002823) **154a** Vincent Van Gogh, *Grapes, Lemons, Pears, and Apples* (detail), 1887. Oil on canvas, 46.5 × 55.2 (18 ¼ × 21 ¾). Gift of Kate L. Brewster. Art Institute of Chicago (1949.215) **154b** Adriaen van Utrecht and Theodoor Rombouts, *An amorous couple with lettuce, artichokes, peas and other vegetables, with a squirrel* (detail), *c.* 1630. Oil on canvas, 148.9 × 129.9 (58 ⅝ × 51 ⅛). Private Collection **155** Paul Cezanne, *Still Life with Skull*, 1890–93. Oil on canvas, 54.3 × 65.4 (21 ⅜ × 25 ¾). The Barnes Foundation, Philadelphia (BF329) **156** Pierre Joseph Redouté, *Allium fragrans*, from Redouté's *Les Liliacées*, Impr. de Didot Jeune, 1805–16. Rare Book Division, The New York Public Library (b10808712) **157** Giuseppe Arcimboldo, *L'Ortolano (The Vegetable Gardener)*, 1587–90. Oil on panel, 36 × 24 (14 ¼ × 9 ½). Museo Civico Ala Ponzone, Cremona **158l** Sir William Chambers, 'The Dunmore Pineapple', after 1777. Photo Ivan Vdovin/Alamy **158r** George Ehret, *Ananas aculeatus*, *c.* 1742, from Georg Ehret and Christoph Trew's *Plantae Selectae*, 1750–73 **159l** Terracotta *pinax* (votive tablet) showing Persephone and Hades enthroned, 500–450 BCE. Museo Archeologico Nazionale di Reggio Calabria (inv. 21016 26.2010) **159r** Cesare Ubertini, Wild celery, from Giorgio Bonelli et al., *Hortus Romanus*, Bouchard et Gravier, 1772–93. Rare Book Division, The New York Public Library (b14444147) **160l** Anselmus Boëtius de Boodt, Cabbage, 1596–1610. Watercolour on paper, 26.6 × 17.7 (10 ½ × 7). Loan from private collection. Rijksmuseum, Amsterdam (RP-T-BR-2017-1-9-61) **160r** Stanley Spencer, *The Dustman or The Lovers* (detail), 1934. Oil on canvas, 115 × 123.5 (45 ⅜ × 48 ⅝). Laing Art Gallery, Newcastle upon Tyne (TWCMS:B7412). Tyne & Wear Archives & Museums/© Estate of Stanley Spencer. All rights reserved 2025/Bridgeman Images **161** Leonora Carrington, *Cabbage*, 1987. Acrylic on canvas, 91.5 × 61 cm. Private collection.

© Estate of Leonora Carrington/ARS, NY and DACS, London, 2025 **162** Albrecht Dürer, *St Jerome in his Study* (detail), 1514. Engraving, 24.6 × 18.9 (9 ¹¹⁄₁₆ × 7 ⁷⁄₁₆). Fletcher Fund, 1919. The Metropolitan Museum of Art, New York (19.73.68) **163** Elizabeth Twining, *Cucurbitaceae*, The Gourd Tribe, from Twining's *Illustrations of the Natural Orders of Plants*, Day and Son, 1849–55. 40.6 × 26 (16 × 10 ¼). The Minnich Collection The Ethel Morrison Van Derlip Fund, 1966. Minneapolis Institute of Art (P.18,661) **164l** Giovanni Martini da Udine, fruits, flowers and vegetables, including *Cucurbita maxima*, fresco detail from Loggia of Cupid and Psyche, Villa Farnesina, Rome, 1515–81. Photo Kim Petersen/Alamy **164r** Cesare Ubertini, *Cucurbita aspera Pyriformis*, from Giorgio Bonelli et al., *Hortus Romanus*, Bouchard et Gravier, 1772–93. Rare Book Division, The New York Public Library (b14444147) **165** Yayoi Kusama, *Pumpkin*, 1994, Benesse Art Site Naoshima. Photo Kat Davis/Alamy. © YAYOI KUSAMA **166l** Dancing maenad holding a thyrsus (detail), Roman copy after 5th century BCE Greek original, attributed to Callimachus. White marble, 141 × 79 × 12 (55 ⅝ × 31 ⅛ × 4 ¾). Museo del Prado, Madrid (E000046). Photo SuperStock/Album/Album Archivo **166r** British School, *Mary Tudor and Charles Brandon, 1st Duke of Suffolk* (detail), after 1515. Oil on panel, 41.5 × 44.5 (16 ⅜ × 17 ⅝). National Trust, Anglesey Abbey, Cambridge (NT 515735) **167** Basilius Besler, *Fructus artischochi*, from Besler's *Hortus Eystettensis*, 1613 **168l** Unknown artist (French), 'Fantastic Hairdress with Fruit and Vegetable Motif', 18th century. Watercolour on canvas over board, 43.8 × 55.9 (17 ¼ × 22). Alfred W. Hoyt Collection, Bequest of Rosina H. Hoppin, 1965. The Metropolitan Museum of Art, New York (65.692.8) **168r** Maubert, *Edible roots*, from Aristide Dupuis & Jean-Augustin Barral's *Le Règne Végétal*, T. Morgand, 1864–69. Bibliothèque nationale de France, Paris (S-8442) **169** René Magritte, *L'Explication (The Explanation)*, 1952. Oil on canvas, 46 × 35 (18 ⅛ by 13 ¾). Private Collection. © ADAGP, Paris and DACS, London 2025 **170** Pieter Bruegel the Elder, *The Blind Leading the Blind*, 1568. Distemper on canvas, 86 × 154 (33 ⅞ × 60 ¾). Museo e Real Bosco di Capodimonte, Naples **171** Cesare Ubertini, *Crithmum maritimum*, from Giorgio Bonelli et al., *Hortus Romanus*, Bouchard et Gravier, 1772–93. Rare Book Division, The New York Public Library (b14444147) **172l** Hieronymus Bosch, *The Garden of Earthly Delights* (detail of centre panel), 1490–1500. Oil on oak, 185.8 × 172.5 (73 ¼ × 68). Museo del Prado, Madrid (P002823) **172r** Upper Rhenish Master, *Madonna in den Erdbeeren (Madonna of the Strawberries)*, *c.* 1425. Mixed media on spruce wood, 144.5 × 87.5 (57 × 34 ½). Kunstmuseum, Solothurn (AI 32) **173** G. Severeyns, Strawberries, from Charles Morren's *La Belgique Horticole*, La Direction Générale, 1851 **174** Orchard Painter, *Women Gathering Apples*, red-figure column krater, *c.* 460 BCE. Terracotta, 44.1 × 46 (17 ⅜ × 18 ⅛). Rogers Fund, 1907. The Metropolitan Museum of Art, New York (07.286.74) **175** Giorgio Gallesio, *Malus appenninensis*, from Gallesio's *Pomona Italiana*, Niccolò Capurro, 1817–39 **176** René Magritte, *The Son of Man*, 1964. Oil on canvas, 116 × 89 (45 ⅝ × 35). Private Collection. © ADAGP, Paris and DACS, London 2025 **177** Claes Oldenburg and Coosje van Bruggen, *Geometric Apple Core*, 1991. Latex paint, polyurethane and steel 233.7 × 139.7 × 106.7 (92 × 55 × 42). The Doris and Donald Fisher Collection. San Francisco Museum of Modern Art. Photo Bill Jacobson, courtesy Pace Gallery. © The Estate of Claes Oldenburg **178** Berthe Hoola van Nooten, *Musa paradisiaca*, *c.* 1885. Chromolithograph. The Wellcome Collection (16359i) **179** Giorgio de Chirico, *The Uncertainty of the Poet*, 1913. Oil on canvas, 106 × 94 (41 ¾ × 37 ⅛). Tate, London (T04109). Photo Tate Images. © DACS 2025 **180** Lene Kilde, *The Nutmeg Princess*, 2014. Molinere Bay Underwater Sculpture Park, Grenada. Photo © Howard Clarke. Artwork © Lene Kilde **181** *Myristica fragrans Houtt.*, from Köhler's *Medizinal-Pflanzen*, Fr. Eugen Köhler, 1890 **182** Giovanna Garzoni, *Cherries in* a Dish, a Pod and a Bumblebee, c. 1642–51. Gouache on parchment, 24.5 × 37.5 (9 ¾ × 14 ⅞). Galleria Palatina, Florence **183** Pierre Joseph Redouté, *Cerasus semperflorens*, from M. Duhamel du Monceau's *Traité des Arbres et Arbustes*, Chez Didot ainé, au Louvre..., 1801–19. Rare Book Division, The New York Public Library (b14485031) **184** Giorgio Gallesio, *Persica Magdalena*, from Gallesio's *Pomona Italiana*, Niccolò Capurro, 1817–39. The New York Public Library (b13674913) **185** Jan van Eyck, *The Arnolfini Portrait*, 1434. Oil on oak, 82.2 × 60 (32 ⅜ × 23 ⅝). The National Gallery, London (NG186) **186** Pierre-Auguste Renoir, *Still Life with Peaches*, 1881. Oil on canvas, 53.3 × 64.8 (21 × 25 ½). Bequest of Stephen C. Clark, 1960. The Metropolitan Museum of Art, New York (61.101.12) **187l** Greek vase in the form of a pomegranate, 8th century BCE. Terracotta, 10.2 × 8.3 (4 × 3 ¼). Rogers Fund, 1912. The Metropolitan Museum of Art, New York (12.229.8) **187r** Pierre Joseph Redouté, *Grenadier punica*, from Redouté's *Choix des plus belles fleurs*, Panckoucke, 1827–33 **188** *The Unicorn Rests in a Garden*, Unicorn Tapestries, c. 1495–1505. Wool and silk threads, 368 × 251.5 (144 ⅞ × 99). Gift of John D. Rockefeller Jr., 1937. The Metropolitan Museum of Art, New York (37.80.6) **189a** Sandro Botticelli, *Virgin and Child with Angels* ('*Madonna of the Pomegranate*') (detail), c. 1487. Tempera on wood, diameter 143.5 (56 ½). Uffizi Galleries, Florence (1890/1607) **189b** Dante Gabriel Rossetti, *Proserpine* (detail), 1874. Oil paint on canvas, 125.1 × 61 (49 ⅜ × 24 ⅛). Tate, London (N05064). Photo Tate Images **190** Giorgio Gallesio, *Pera Campana, Pyrus Pompeiana*, from Gallesio's *Pomona Italiana*, Niccolò Capurro, 1817–39. The New York Public Library (b13674913) **191** Carlo Crivelli, *Madonna and Child*, c. 1490. Tempera on panel, 32.8 × 24.7 (12 ¹⁵⁄₁₆ × 9 ¾). Samuel H. Kress Collection. National Gallery of Art, Washington, D.C. (1939.1.264) **192** Cesare Ubertini, *Raphanus minor*, from Giorgio Bonelli et al., Hortus Romanus, Bouchard et Gravier, 1772–93. Rare Book Division, The New York Public Library (b14444147) **193** Jennifer Knaus, *Radish Head*, 2014. Oil on panel, 30.5 × 30.5 (12 × 12). © Jennifer Knaus **194** Pierre Joseph de Pannemaeker, A bunch of tomatoes, chromolithograph, c. 1854. Wellcome Collection, London (28073i) **195** Andy Warhol, *Campbell's Soup Cans*, 1962. Acrylic and enamel paint on canvas, 50.8 × 40.6 (20 × 16) each. The Museum of Modern Art, New York (476.1996.1-32). © 2025 The Andy Warhol Foundation for the Visual Arts, Inc./Licensed by DACS, London **196a** *Melongiana* in Tacuinum Sanitatis (detail), 1385–90. Austrian National Library, Vienna. Photo SuperStock/Album/Prisma/Album Archivo **196b** Paul Cézanne, *Still Life with a Ginger Jar and Eggplants* (detail), 1893–94. Oil on canvas, 72.4 × 91.4 (28 ½ × 36). Bequest of Stephen C. Clark, 1960. The Metropolitan Museum of Art, New York (61.101.4) **197** Basilius Besler, Aubergine, from Besler's *Hortus Eystettensis*, 1613 **198** Vincent van Gogh, *The Potato Eaters*, 1885. Oil on canvas, 82 × 114 (32 ⅜ × 45). Van Gogh Museum, Amsterdam (Vincent van Gogh Foundation) **199** J. Vreugdenhil, *Solanum tuberosum*, n.d. Coloured lithograph. Naturalis Biodiversity Center, Leiden (L.0939623) **200** *Verbascum thapsus*, n.d. Botanical educational poster, 62.2 × 94 (24 ½ × 37 ⅛). Stichting Academisch Erfgoed, Amsterdam **201** Giovanni Bellini, *St. Francis in the Desert* (detail), c. 1475–80. Oil on panel, 124.6 × 142 (49 ¹⁄₁₆ × 55 ⅞). Henry Clay Frick Bequest. The Frick Collection, New York (1915.1.03) **202** Rachel Ruysch (attrib.), *Vanity* (detail), c. 1690. Oil on canvas, 70 × 90 (27 ⅝ × 35 ½). Musée Jeanne d'Aboville, La Fère (MJA323). Photo GrandPalaisRmn/Benoît Touchard **204** Arthur Hughes, *The Long Engagement*, 1859. Oil on canvas, 107 × 53.3 (42 ¼ × 21). Birmingham Museums Trust (1902P13) **205** Hieronymus Bosch, *The Haywain Triptych*, c. 1516. Oil on panel, 147.1 × 224.3 (58 × 88 ⅜). Museo Del Prado, Madrid (P002052) **206** F. Domingo, *Cucumis sativus*, from Fr. Manuel Blanco's *Flora de Filipinas*, 1877–83 **207** Carlo Crivelli, *Madonna and Child*, c. 1480. Tempera and gold on wood, 37.8 × 25.4 (14 ⅞ × 10). The Jules Bache

Collection, 1949. The Metropolitan Museum of Art, New York (49.7.5) **209** Ackroyd & Harvey, *Mother and Child (Aka Heather and Adèle)*, 1998, Staygreen grass, clay, jute, 1.2m × 1.8m. Image imprinted on molecular level through process of photographic photosynthesis. Image courtesy of the artists **210** Albrecht Dürer, *Great Piece of Turf*, 1503. Watercolour and body colour on vellum, 40.3 × 31.1 (15 ⅞ × 12 ¼). The Albertina Museum, Vienna **211** A.F. Lydon, *Bromus asper, Hordeum sylvaticum* and *Avena flavescens* from Edward Joseph Lowe's *A Natural History of British Grasses*, Groombridge, 1858 **212** Rachel Ruysch (attrib.), *Vanity* (detail), c. 1690. Oil on canvas, 70 × 90 (27 ⅝ × 35 ½). Musée Jeanne d'Aboville, La Fère (MJA323). Photo GrandPalaisRmn/Benoît Touchard **213l** J.P. Del, *Glechoma hederacea*, from William Baxter's *British Phaenogamous Botany*, W. Baxter Botanic Garden, 1835 **213r** Maenad with thyrsus, ornamented with ivy leaves, Attic white-ground kylix, Vulci, 490–480 BCE. Staatliche Antikensammlungen, Munich **214** A'aru (The Field of Reeds), Tomb of Sennedjem, Deir-el-Medina, Egypt, c. 1200 BCE. Facsimile by Charles K. Wilkinson, 1922. Tempera on paper, 54 × 84.5 (21 ¼ × 33 ¼). Rogers Fund, 1930. The Metropolitan Museum of Art, New York (30.4.2) **215** Johann Ibmayer, *Arundo donax*, from Nicolai Thomae Host's *Icones et Descriptiones Graminum Austriacorum*, A. Schmidt, 1809 **216** Mary Emily Eaton, *Pueraria thunbergiana*, from *Addisonia*, vol.15, New York Botanical Garden, 1930 **217** Precious Okoyomon, *Earthseed*, 2020, mixed media. Exhibition view at the Museum für Moderne Kunst, Frankfurt, 2020. Photo Axel Schneider. © Precious Okoyomon **218** Sennedjem and his wife in the Fields of A'aru (detail), c. 1300 BCE. Facsimile by Charles K. Wilkinson, 1922. Tempera on paper, 54 × 84.5 (21 ¼ × 33 ¼). Rogers Fund, 1930. The Metropolitan Museum of Art, New York (30.4.2) **219** Charlotte M. Yonge, *Triticum aestivum* and *Avena sativa*, from Yonge's *The Instructive Picturebook, or Lessons from the Vegetable World*, Edmonston & Douglas, 1858. Photo SuperStock/Album/Florilegius/Album Archivo **220** Samuel Palmer, *A Hilly Scene*, c. 1826–28. Watercolour on paper, 20.6 × 13.7 (8 ⅛ × 5 ½). Tate, London (N05805). Photo Tate Images **221** Thomas Hart Benton, *Wheat*, 1967. Oil on wood, 50.8 × 53.3 (20 × 21). Gift of Mr. and Mrs. James A. Mitchell and museum purchase. Smithsonian American Art Museum, Washington D.C. (1991.55). © 2025 T.H. and R.P. Benton Trusts/Licensed by Artists Rights Society (ARS), New York & DACS, London **222** W. Clark, after William Hooker, *Vitis vinifera cv.*, c. 1835. Coloured etching. The Wellcome Collection, London (26391i) **223a** Cupids harvesting grapes, detail of ambulatory mosaic, 4th century. Mausoleum of Santa Costanza, Rome. Photo akg-images/Pirozzi **223b** Sandro Botticelli, *Virgin and Child with an Angel* (detail), 1470–74. Tempera on panel, 85 × 64.5 (33 ⁷⁄₁₆ × 25 ⅜). Isabella Stewart Gardner Museum, Boston (P27w73) **224** Otto Wilhelm Thomé, *Zea Mays*, from Prof. dr. Thomé's *Flora von Deutschland*, Eugen Köhler, 1903 **225l** Grant Wood, *Corn Cob Chandelier for Iowa Corn Room*, 1925–26. Copper, iron and paint, 238.8 × 81.3 × 86.4 (94 × 32 × 34). Gift of John B. Turner II. Cedar Rapids Museum of Art (81.17.3) **225r** Cornelis de Heem (attrib.), *Fruit and Flowers* (detail), 1662. Oil on canvas, 83.1 × 59 (32 ¾ × 23 ¼). Victoria and Albert Museum, London (4641-1858) **226** Indian (Kalighat) School, A woman pulling giant aubergines from a tree, n.d.. Watercolour and pencil on paper, 46.1 × 28.4 (18 ¼ × 11 ¼). The Wellcome Collection, London (26113i)

INDEX

Bold page numbers indicate main illustrated entries for individual plants; *italic* page numbers refer to other illustrations.

A

Aaron (Biblical figure) 74, 96
Abella, Alex, *The Total Banana* 178
Abraham (patriarch) 78
abundance, symbols of 40, 77, 154, 164, 168, 189, 204, 219, 224
acacia (*Acacia*) 8, 22, **28–9**
Ackroyd, Heather 208; *Mother and Child* 208, *209*
acorns 7, 78–9
Adam and Eve (Biblical figures) 22, 48, 54, 86, 96, 124, 144, 172, *172*, 174, 175
Adams, Ansel 208
Adonis (mythological figure) 93, *93*, 144
Aesthetic Movement 114
afterlife 154, 214; *see also* heaven; Underworld
Alexander the Great 24, 42, 184
almond (*Prunus amygdalus*) 11, **74–7**
Aloi, Giovanni 54; *Why Look at Plants?* 6, 42, 112, 134, 156
anemone (*Anemone*) 12, **93**
Angelico, Fra 189
anise (*Pimpinella anisum*) 170, *171*
Anne, St 144
Anthony of Padua, St 127
aphrodisiacs 96, 102, 106, 108, 132, 156, 159, 173, 194, 196
Aphrodite (goddess) 50, 94, 98, 144, 174, 178, 187, 190
Apollo (god) 48, 50, **64–5**, 118
apple (*Malus*) *15*, 22, 24, 40, 92, 145, *154*, **174–7**, 184, *186*, 190, 206
Ara Pacis Augustae altar (Rome) 136, *136*
Arcimboldo, Giuseppe 192, 196; *Spring* 156; *The Vegetable Gardener* 156, *157*
Ark of the Covenant 28
Art Nouveau 40, 102, 212
Artemis (goddess) 50, 62, 64, 110
Arthurian legend 60
artichoke (*Cynara cardunculus* var. *scolymus*) *15*, 70, *154*, **166–7**
Arts and Crafts Movement 102, 114
arum (*Arum*) 12, **96–7**
Asclepius (god) 48, 50

ash (*Fraxinus*) 10, 24, **58–9**, 86
Athena (goddess) 50, 66, *66*, 144
Atlas (mythological figure) 174
Attis (god) 70, 77, 148
aubergine (*Solanum melongena*) 16, **196–7**
Augustine, St 162, 222

B

Bacchus (god) 222
Bachelor, Blane 164–5
Bagge, Oluf Olufsen, *Yggdrasil, The Mundane Tree* 24, *24*
Baker, Josephine 178
banana (*Musa*) *15*, **178–9**
baobab (*Adansonia*) 8, **32–3**
barley (*Hordeum*) 53, 204, *211*, 218
Baroque 69, 110, 114, 182, 184, 194, 212, 224
bay *see* laurel (*Laurus*)
Becker, Udo 26–7, 90
Bedford Double Portrait (16th century) *166*, 167
beech (*Fagus*) 9, 36, **52–3**, *79*
Belides (nymph) 98
Bellini, Giovanni: *Madonna and Child* 190; *St Francis in the Desert* 65, 98, 200, *201*, 222
Benedict, Joanne Hill, *California Palms* 4
Benton, Thomas Hart, *Wheat* 221, *221*
Berkeley, Busby, *The Gang's All Here* 178
Bernini, Gian Lorenzo: *Apollo and Daphne* 65; *Fountain of Four Rivers* 201
Besant, Annie 104
Besler, Basilius: *Artichoke* 167, *167*; *Aubergine* 197, *197*
Bessa, Pancrace, *White Birch* 34, *34*
Beuys, Joseph, *7,000 Oak Trees* 80, *80*, 81
Bible: Exodus 28, 74; Genesis 22, 54, 86, 102, 174; Isaiah 82, 94, 206, 215; Kings 162; Leviticus 82; Luke 31, 120; Matthew 69, 170; Psalms 82, 108; Pseudo-Matthew 69; Song of Solomon 68
birch (*Betula*) 8, **34–5**, 48
Blake, William 81; *The Wood of the Self-Murderers* 24, *25*, 27
blindness and eye ailments 68, 156, 170–1, 206
Blossfeldt, Karl, *Dipsacus laciniatus* 6, *7*
bodhi (*Ficus religiosa*) 24

Boëtius de Boodt, Anselmus, *Cabbage* 160, 161
Book of the Dead 214
Bosch, Hieronymus: *The Garden of Earthly Delights* 56, *152*, 172–3, *172*; *The Haywain Triptych* 205, *205*, 219
Botticelli, Sandro 98, 124; *The Birth of Venus* 98, **98–9**; *Primavera* 40, 90, *90*, 98, 118; *Virgin and Child with an Angel* 223, *223*; *Virgin and Child with Angels* 188, 189, *189*
Brandon, Charles, 1st Duke of Suffolk *166*, 167
Brant, Isabella 128, *129*
brinjal *see* aubergine (*Solanum melongena*)
broccoli (*Brassica oleracea* var. *italica*) 154, 160
Brown, Ford Madox, *The Convalescent (A Portrait of the Artist's Wife)* 148, 149
Bruegel, Pieter the Elder: *The Blind Leading the Blind* 170–1, *170*; *The Harvesters* 219
Buddhism 24, 106, 132
Burchfield, Charles E., *Summer Solstice* 36, *37*
burning bush (Biblical event) 28, 200
Burns, Pauline Powell, *Violets* 148

C

cabbage (*Brassica oleracea* var. *capitata*) 14, 92, **160–1**
calabash (*Lagenaria siceraria*) 162
Callimachus 167
Caneva, Giulia 164
Caravaggio 69; *St John the Baptist in the Wilderness* 201
Cardoso, Maria Fernanda 225
carnation (*Dianthus caryophyllus*) 12, 95, **110–11**
Carr, Emily 63; *A Rushing Sea of Undergrowth* 63, *63*
Carrington, Leonora, *Cabbage* 160, *161*
carrot (*Daucus carota*) *15*, 44, 154, **168–9**, 170
Casanova, Giacomo 159
Catherine of Siena, St 127
Cattelan, Maurizio, *Comedian* 178–9
cedar (*Cedrus*) 8, 22, **38–9**, 51, 62
celery (*Apium graveolens* var. *dulce*) 14, 154, **159**
Celtic 34, 48, 73, 165

cemeteries *see* graves, tombs and cemeteries
Cézanne, Paul: *Still Life with a Ginger Jar and Eggplants* 196, 197; *Still Life with Skull* 154, *155*
Chair of St Peter festival 192
Chambers, Sir William, 'The Dunmore Pineapple' 158, *158*
Charlemagne 206
Charles I, King of England 114
Charles II, King of Sweden 92
chastity 36, 62, 124, 127, 200
Chauliac, Guy de 170–1
cherry (*Prunus cerasus*) *15*, 22, **182–3**, 190
chestnut (*Castanea*) 8, **36–7**, 62
Chevalier, Jean 74, 77
Chigi, Agostino 164
Chinese cabbage (*Brassica rapa*) 160, *161*
Chirat, Benoît, Olive 66, *66*
Chloris (goddess) 91, 144
Christ: Adoration 149, 172; blood 93, 144, 172, 182, 190, 200, 204, 222; Crown of Thorns 28, 60, 62, 142, 200; Crucifixion 22, 36, 38, 51, 54, 93, 102, 110, 120, 138, 142, 149, 172, 215; Deposition 172; entry into Jerusalem 31, 68; as infant 40, 48, 54, *64*, 98, 127, 144, 149, 175, 182, 184, 189, *189*, 190, *191*, 206, *207*; Last Supper 43, 182, 189, 218, 222; mandorla 77; Nativity 54, 62, 118, 172; Passion 60, 62, 95, 138, 142, 144, 172, 222; as redeemer 174–5, 189, 204, 218, 222; Rest on the Flight to Egypt 69, 182, 201; Resurrection 20, 36, 48, 54, 182, 189, 218
Christ in Majesty (illuminated manuscript) 74, *75*
Christmas 60
chrysanthemum (*Chrysanthemum*) 12, 98, **104–5**
Cinderella (film; 1950) 165
Cirlot, Juan Eduardo, *Dictionary of Symbols* 24–6
Cissus (nymph) 212
Clare, St 127
Clark, William: Bay laurel 64, *65*; Black Corinth Grape *222*, 223
coffins and sarcophaguses 30, 38, 50, 86, *138*, 138, 222
Collins, Charles Allston, *Convent Thoughts* 142–3, *143*

236

columbine (*Aquilegia*) 12, 94–5
Columbus, Christopher 206, 224
Confucius 6
Constable, John, *Study of the Trunk of an Elm Tree* 86, *87*
Constantine, Roman Emperor 204, 222
coriander (*Coriandrum sativum*) 154, 171
corn (*Zea mays*) 17, 198, 204, 208, **224**–5
Correggio, Antonio da, *Virgin and Child with the Young St John the Baptist* 42, *42*
Cossa, Francesco del, *Saint Lucy* 2, 68, *69*
Costanza, St 222
Crane, Lancelot, Nakht and family fishing 134, *134*
Crane, Walter 63
Credi, Lorenzo di 189
Crivelli, Carlo, *Madonna and Child* 175, 186, 190, *191*, 206, *207*
crocus (*Crocus*) 12, **106**–7
Cronos (god) 50
Cross, Dorothy 112; *Foxglove* 112, *113*
Cross, Henri-Edmond, *Coastal View with Cypress Trees* 51, *51*
cucumber (*Cucumis sativus*) 17, 162, 175, 194, **206**–7
Cummins, Paul, *Blood Swept Lands and Seas of Red* 140, *141*
Cupid (god) 65, *65*, 150
Curran, John T., *Loving Cup* 128, *129*
Curtis, John, *Arum italicum* 96, *96*
Cybele (goddess) 50, 70, 144, 148
cyclamen (*Cyclamen*) 12, **108**–9
cypress (*Cupressus*) 9, 38, **50**–1, 62

D

Dadaism 179
Dadd, Richard, *The Fairy Feller's Master-Stroke* 100, *101*
daffodil *see* narcissus (*Narcissus*)
Dahl, Roald, *James and the Giant Peach* 186
daisy (*Bellis*) 12, **98**–101, 136, 200, 208
Dalí, Salvador, *Metamorphosis of Narcissus* 88, *130*, 131
Dante Alighieri 138; *Divine Comedy* 27, 138, 140; *La Vita Nuova* 127
Daphne (nymph) 64–5
Daphnis and Chloe (mythological figures) 128
Darwin, Charles 205
date palm *see* palm (*Phoenix*)

David, Gerard 69
David, Jacques-Louis, *The Death of Socrates* 44, *45*
Davies, Norman de Garis, Nakht and family fishing 134, *134*
Day, Patricia 81; *Whispering Oak* 78, *79*
de Chirico, Giorgio, *The Uncertainty of the Poet* 178, *179*
de Heem, Cornelis 224; *Fruit and Flowers* (attrib.) 224, *225*
De Morgan, Evelyn, *The Angel of Death I* 50, 51
Dearle, John Henry, *The Orchard* 40, *40*
death, symbols and associations 20, 28, 44, 51, 68, 82–3, 84, 90, 140, 154, 162, 208; *see also* coffins and sarcophaguses; funeral wreaths; graves, tombs and cemeteries
Del, J.P., *Glechoma hederacea* 213, *213*
Demeter (goddess) 187, 219
Dewan, Rachel 106
Diana (goddess) 52, 78
Diffenbaugh, Vanessa, *The Language of Flowers* 92
Dion, Mark 7; *Neukom Vivarium* 45–7, *47*; *Seattle Vivarium* 46, *47*
Dionysus (god) 64, 70, 166, 174, 204, 212, 222
Dodona oracle 52, 78
Domingo, F., *Cucumis sativus* 206, *206*
D'Orbigny, Charles Dessalines: *Citrus Limonium* 42, *43*; *Tulipa gesneriana* 146, *146*
dragon tree (*Dracaena*) 22
Druids 84, 128
Dunmore, John Murray, 4th Earl of 158
Dürer, Albrecht 69, 208; *Adam and Eve* 22; *Great Piece of Turf* 208, *210*; *Madonna and Child with a Pear* 190; *Portrait of the Artist Holding a Thistle* 102, *102*, 103; *St Jerome in His Study* 161, *162*; *St Jerome Seated Near a Pollard Willow Tree* 83

E

Easter 218
Eaton, Mary Emily, *Pueraria thunbergiana* 216, *216*
Echo (nymph) 130
Eden, Garden of 20, 22, 42, 48, 110, 124, 130, 172, 174, 175, 187, 190, 204
eggplant *see* aubergine (*Solanum melongena*)

Ehret, Georg 38; *Ananas aculeatus* 158, *158*
Eleusinian Mysteries 68, 218
Elizabeth I, Queen 151, *151*
Elkins, James 200
Ellison, Aaron M., *Hemlock Hospice* 47
elm (*Ulmus*) 11, 22, 58, **86**–7
Eppley, Eugence C. 225
Eris (goddess) 174
Ernst, Max 114; *The Forest* 24, *25*
Eros (god) 128
Eucharist 138, 200, 218, 222

F

Fantin-Latour, Henri, *Still Life with Pansies* 150
fennel (*Foeniculum*) 15, **170**–1
fertility symbols 41, 70, 73, 92, 162, 168, 184, 187, 189, 219, 222
fig (*Ficus*) 9, 22, 30, **54**–7, 200, 204
Fitch, John Nugent, *Cattleya velutina* 136, *137*
Fletcher, H.: Flowering Ash 59, *59*; Honeysuckle 128, *129*
fleur-de-lys emblem 120–1, 127, 194
Flora (goddess) 144
floriography 91, 92
forests 24–7
forget-me-not (*Myosotis*) 142, 150
foxglove (*Digitalis*) 12, **112**–13
Francis of Assisi, St 73, 127, 200, *201*
Freud, Lucian 54, 86; *After Constable's Elm* 86; *Girl with a Fig Leaf* 54, *57* Narcissus 131
Freud, Sigmund 131
Freya (goddess) 94
Friedrich, Caspar David: *Abbey among Oak Trees* 80; *Winter Landscape* 70–1, 73
funeral wreaths 78, 80, *81*, 159

G

Gabriel, Archangel 68, 124
Gaia (goddess) 54, 64, 174
Gallesio, Giorgio: Almond 74, *74*; *Fico Pissaluto* 56, *56*; *Malus appenninensis* 174, *175*; *Pera Campana*, *Pyrus Pompeiana* 190, *190*; *Persica Magdalena* 184, *184*; Spanish chestnut 36, *37*
Garrard, Mary 182
Garzoni, Giovanna 182; *Cherries in a Dish* 182, *183*
Gauguin, Paul 115; *Contes barbares* 126
Gentile da Fabriano 189
Gershuni, Moshe 108; *Hai Cyclamen* 108, *109*

Gesner, Conrad 146
Ghirlandaio, Domenico: *Annunciation* 98; *The Last Supper* 43
Giampietrino (Giovanni Pietro Rizzoli), *Madonna of the Cherries* 183
Giraud, Jane Elizabeth, Daisies 100, *100*
Gitner, Adam 73
gourd (*Cucurbita*, *Crescentia*, *Lagenaria* and other genera) 14, **162**–3, 175
Gouvy, Alice Carmen, *Thistle* 215 103, *103*
Goya, Francisco, *The Marquesa de Pontejos* 110, *111*
Grade, John 7, 38; *Treeline* 38–9, *39*
grapevine (*Vitis vinifera*) 17, 154, 200, 204, **222**–3
grass (*Cynodon*, *Festuca*, *Lolium*, *Poa* and other genera) 17, 204, **208–11**, 214, 218
graves, tombs and cemeteries 50, 82, 83, 84, 120, 132, 143, 149, 154, 159, 208, 214, 219
Great Mother (goddess) 58, 86
Greenaway, Kate, *Language of Flowers* 92
grief, symbols of 50, 82–3, 95, 138
Grimm, Brothers, 'The Juniper Tree' 63
Grünewald, Matthias, *Birth of Jesus* 54
Gutenberg, Johannes 34

H

Hades (god) 50–1, 86, 138, 159, *159*, 187
Hageneder, Fred 84
Haid, J.J. or J.E., *Cedrus* 38, *38*
Halloween 164–5
Hammer-Purgstall, Joseph, *Dictionnaire du langage des fleurs* 92
Harvey, Dan 208; *Mother and Child* 208, *209*
Hathor (goddess) 30
Hawthorne, Nathaniel 150
hazel (*Corylus*) 9, 34, **48**–9
headdresses 168, *168*
heaven 28, 67, 148
Hecate (goddess) 84, 108
Heh (god) 68
Helen of Troy 174
hemlock (*Conium* and *Tsuga*) 9, **44**–7
Henry VIII, King 167
Hepburn, James, Sefirotic tree 22, *23*
Hera (goddess) 42, 50, 82, 124, 148, 174, 187, 190, 212

INDEX 237

heraldry 28, 102, 127, 145
Hercules (god) 174
Hermes (god) 48, 120
Hesperides (nymphs) 40, 174
Hey, Rebecca, *Holly* 60, *60*
Hinduism 24, 132
Hockney, David, *Mr and Mrs Clark and Percy* 126, *127*
Holle (goddess) 60
holly (*Ilex*) 10, **60–1**
Holy Spirit 94, 140
Homer 82, 118, 156; *Odyssey* 159
honeysuckle (*Lonicera*) 13, **128–9**, 142, 205
Hooker, William 223
Hoola van Nooten, Berthe, *Musa paradisiaca 178*, 179
Hora (goddess) 98
horse chestnut (*Aesculus*) 36, 219
hortus conclusus 54, 142, 144, 172
hospitality 154, 158, 184, 222
Horus (god) 132, 135
Hughes, Arthur, *The Long Engagement* 204, *205*
Hunt, George Jr, *Raven Releasing the Sun* 45, *46*
hyacinth (*Hyacinthus*) 12, **118–19**
Hyacinth (mythological figure) 118
Hypnos (god) 138

I
Ibmayer, Johann, *Arundo* 215, *215*
Idun (goddess) 48
immortality, symbols of 28, 38, 42, 50, 60, 65, 68, 70, 74, 78, 79, 82, 84, 86, 174, 189, 212, 218
Impressionism 132–5
innocence, symbols of 90, 98, 111, 124, 127, 172, 200
Io (mythological figure) 148–9
Iris (goddess) 120
iris (*Iris*) 13, 95, 106, **120–3**, 127, 171
Irving, Washington, 'The Legend of Sleepy Hollow' 165
Isis (goddess) 30, 132
ivy (*Hedera helix*) 17, 60, 70, 162, 200, 204, **212–13**

J
jack-o'-lanterns 164–5
Jacob (patriarch) 67, 82
Janick, Jules 164
jasmine (*Jasminum*) 98
Jerome, St 60, 83, 162
John the Baptist, St 42, 60, 201
Jonah (Biblical figure) 162
Jonson, Ben 150
Jose de Sigüenza, Fray 173
Joseph, St 68, 74, 127
juniper (*Juniperus*) 10, **62–3**, 200

Juno (goddess) 52, 124
Jupiter (god) 78, 156

K
Kabbalah 22, 82, 108
Keens-Douglas, Richardo 180
Kelly, Ellsworth 118; cyclamen lithographs 108; *Hyacinth* 118, *119*
Kiefer, Anselm 115–16; *Entrance to Paradise* 26–7; *The Orders of the Night* 115, 116, *116*
Kilde, Lene, *The Nutmeg Princess* 180, *180*
Klimt, Gustav 34; *Birch Forest* 34, *35*; *Tree of Life* 22, *22*
Klint, Hilma af, *Tree of Knowledge, no. 1* 6, 7
Knaus, Jennifer 192; *Radish Head* 192, *193*
Köhler, Fr. Eugen, *Areca catechu* 68, *69*
Koons, Jeff, *Puppy* 91, *91*
kudzu (*Pueraria*) 17, 205, **216–17**
Kusama, Yayoi, *Pumpkin* 164, 165, *165*

L
La Mottraye, Aubry de 92
Language of Flowers (floriography) 91, 92, 136
Last Judgment 127
laurel (*Laurus*) 10, **64–5**, 200
Lavin, Marilyn Aronberg 73
Lawrence, D. H. 150
Le Moyne de Morgues, Jacques, *Violets* 149, *149*
lemon (*Citrus* x *limon*) 9, **42–3**, 154
Leonardo da Vinci 124; *The Baptism of Christ* 69; *The Madonna of the Carnation* 111; *Portrait of Ginevra de' Benci* 63
lettuce (*Lactuca sativa*) 154, *154*, 168
Libri, Girolamo dai, *Madonna and Child with Saints 18*, *64*, 65
lily (*Lilium*) 13, 93, 96, 98, 111, 120, **124–7**
Linnaeus, Carolus 110
Linnell, John 79
Lippi, Filippino 189
Liu, Jinyu 73
Lochner, Stefan: *Madonna of the Rose Bower* 144, *145*; *Virgin with the Violet* 148, 149
Loki (god) 48
Longfellow, Henry Wadsworth, 'The Village Blacksmith' 36
Lotto, Lorenzo, *Venus and Cupid* 64, *65*
lotus (*Nymphaea*) *see* water lily
Louis XII, King of France 167

Louis XV, King of France 159
Lucas van Leyden 69
Lucy, St 2, 68 *69*
Lydon, A.F., *Bromus Asper* 211, *211*

M
madness 148, 196, 204, 222
Madonna *see* Mary, Virgin
maenads (mythological figures) 166, *166*, 167, 213, *213*
maize *see* corn
Mancoff, Debra 142–3
mandorla 77
Mantegna, Andrea, San Zeno altarpiece 48, *48*, 49
maple (*Acer*) 30
Marie Antoinette, Queen of France 168
marriage *see* weddings and marriage
Mars (god) 145, 192
Martini, Simone, *Annunciation with St Margaret and St Asanus* 124, *124*, 127
Martini da Udine, Giovanni, Villa Farnesina fresco 164, *164*
martyrdom 51, 68, 102
Mary, Virgin 48, 73, 94–5, 96, 108, 110, 120, 172; Annunciation 51, 68, 98, 120, 124, *124*, 127, 130; Assumption 127; death and funeral 68, 95; Immaculate Conception 36, 144, 206; Madonna and Child images 40, 42, *42*, 64, 65, 149, 175, 182, 183, 184, 186, 188, 189, 189, 190, *191*, 206, *207*; mysteries of the rosary 145; purity and chastity 36, 40, 74, 124, 127, 142, 144
Mary Tudor, Queen of France 166, 167
Masonic symbolism 28, 73
Maubert, Édouard, *Edible Roots* 168, *169*
Mauve, Anton 198
Maxim, David, *Old Man with Young Tree* 22–3, *23*
Mazzinghi, Joseph, 'Ye Shepherds Tell Me' 111
McCrae, John, 'In Flanders Fields' 140
Meier, Allison 20
Meléndez, Luis Egidio 194; *Still Life with Cucumbers, Tomatoes and Vessels* 194; *Still Life with Melon and Pears* 190
melon (*Cucurbita*) 92, 162, 182, 190
Memling, Hans 69

Meyerpick, Wolfgang, *Ficus sycomorus* 30, *30*
Michelangelo 73; *Night* 141
Millais, Sir John Everett 142; *The Bridesmaid* 41, *41*; *Isabella* 142, 143
Millet, Jean-François 198
Miranda, Carmen 178
Mitsuoki, Tosa, *Autumn Maples with Poem Slips* 7
Mondrian, Piet 104; *Chrysanthemum* 104, *104*; *Haystack with Willow Trees* 83
Monet, Claude 132–5; *Nympheas* 134–5, *135*; *Weeping Willow* series 83
Montagu, Lady Mary Wortley 92
moon 34, 66, 82, 104, 132
Morpheus (god) 138
Morris, William 40, 118; *The Orchard* 40, *40*
Moses (Biblical figure) 28, 74, 82
Mother goddesses 58, 60, 86, 106, 124, 204; *see also* Gaia
Mother's Day 111
mourning, symbols of 7, 86, 120
mullein (*Verbascum*) 16, **200–1**
Murray, Caroline 166–7

N
Nakht (Egyptian scribe) 134, *134*
Narcissus (mythological figure) 130, 131
narcissus (*Narcissus*) 13, **130–1**, 192
Nash, David, *Ash Dome* 58, *58*, 59
Nash, Paul, *The Wood on the Hill (Wittenham Camps)* 52–3, *53*
Natalia LL, *Consumer Art* 179
Nefertem (god) 132, *132*, 133
Neith (goddess) 28
Nemesis (goddess) 130
Nepra (god) 218
'Netting Birds, Tomb of Khnumhotep' (Egyptian painting) 28, *28*
Noah (Biblical figure) 38, 67
Norse 48, 58, 94
Nut (goddess) 30
nutmeg (*Myristica fragans*) 15, **180–1**

O
oak (*Quercus*) 11, 24, 36, 52, 60, **78–81**
oats (*Avena*) 204, *211*, 219
Ogawa, Kazumasa, *Iris Kæmpferi* 120, *121*
O'Keeffe, Georgia: *Black Iris* 122, *123*; *Black Pansy and Forget-Me-Nots* 150

Okoyomon, Precious 7, 216; *Earthseed* 216, *217*
Oldenburg, Claes, *Geometric Apple Core* 177, *177*
olive (*Olea*) 10, 38, 51, **66–7**, 124, 200, 204
Olmsted, Frederick Law 86
onion (*Allium cepa*) 14, 154, **156–7**, 198
opium 138, 140
orange (*Citrus* x *aurantium*) 9, **40–1**, 184
Orchard painter (attrib.), *Women Gathering Apples* 174, *174*
orchid (*Orchidaceae*) 13, **136–7**
Original Sin 36, 144, 175
Orpheus (mythological figure) 50–1, 86
Osiris (god) 70, 82, 132, 218
Ovid 50, 64, 118, 138; *Metamorphoses* 93

P
palm (*Phoenix*) 10, 22, 38, 51, **68–9**, 182
Palmer, Samuel: *A Hilly Scene* 37, 219, *220*, *221*; *Oak Tree and Beech, Lullingstone Park* 78, 79–81, *79*
Pan (god) 215
Panckoucke, Mme E., *Baobab* 32, *32*
Pannemaeker, Pierre Joseph, *A bunch of tomatoes* *194*, *195*
Pannemaeker, Pieter de, *Autumn chrysanthemum hybrids* 104, *105*
pansy (*Viola* x *wittrockiana*) 13, 91, **150–1**
papyrus (*Cyperus papyrus*) 214
Paris (mythological figure) 174
passionflower (*Passiflora*) 13, **142–3**
Passover 218
Patinir, Joachim 69
Pausanias 77, 190
peace, symbols of 66, 91, 135, 204
peach (*Prunus persica*) 15, **184–6**
pear (*Pyrus*) 16, 154, *155*, 186, **190–1**
persea (*Persea*) 22, 30
Persephone (goddess) 50, 159, *159*, 187
Petrarch 65
Philomena, St 127
pine (*Pinus*) 10, 20, *21*, 24, 44, 70–3, 166
pineapple (*Ananas*) 14, **158**
Piper, Tom, *Blood Swept Lands and Seas of Red* 140, *141*
plane tree (*Platanus*) 30
plantain (*Musa*) 178, *179*, 208

Pliny 34, 52, 62, 82, 166, 170, 190, 206
Plutarch 218
poisonous plants 44, 78, 85, 94, 96, 102, 112, 118, 130, 196
Pollaiuolo, Piero del, *Apollo and Daphne* 64–5
pomegranate (*Punica granatum*) 16, 22, **187–9**
Pompadour, Jeanne Antoinette, Madame de 159
Pompeii and Herculaneum frescoes 42, 54, *55*, 184, 186
Pop Art 194
poppy (*Papaver*) 13, **138–41**
Porteous, Alexander, *The Forest in Folklore and Mythology* 26
Poseidon (god) 66
potato (*Solanum tuberosum*) 16, 154, 165, 178, **198–9**
Powers, Richard, *The Overstory: A Novel* 7
Pre-Raphaelite Brotherhood 114, 142
Prometheus (god) 170
protection, symbols of 48, 78, 82, 128, 165, 200
Psyche (mythological figure) 144, 164
pumpkin (*Cucurbita*) 14, 162, **164–5**
purity, symbols of 36, 40, 74, 90, 98, 111, 124, 127, 142, 144

Q
Qur'an 187

R
Ra (god) 28, 30
Rackham, Arthur, 'The Headless Horseman' 165
radish (*Raphanus*) 16, **192–3**
rainbows 20, 120, 121
Raphael 164, 189
rebirth, symbols of 28, 73, 74, 77, 84, 111, 132, 189, 218
Redouté, Pierre-Joseph: *Allium fragrans* 156, *156*; 'Anemone Simple' *93*; *Cerasus semperflorens* 183, *183*; *Fagus silvatica* 52, *52*; *Grenadier punica* 186, *187*; *Hyacinthus orientalis* 118, *118*; *Iris squalens* 122, *122*; *Juniperus communis* 62, *63*; *Narcissus gouani* 131, *131*; *Quercus robur* 78, *78*; *Rosa centifolia* 145, *145*
reed (*Phragmites* and other genera) *17*, 200, **214–15**
remembrance 140, 142
Renoir, Pierre-Auguste, *Still Life with Peaches* 186, *186*
rice (*Oryza*) 198, 208
Ringgold, Faith, *The Sunflower Quilting Bee at Arles* 115, *117*

Roger, Julia Ellen, *The Tree Book* 36
Romack, Coco 216
Rombouts, Theodoor, *An amorous couple* 154, *155*
Romulus and Remus (mythological figures) 54
rose (*Rosa*) 13, 32, 54, 98, 111, **144–5**, 190
Rossetti, Dante Gabriel 124; *Beata Beatrix* 138–40, *140*, *141*; *The Beloved* ('*The Bride*') 145; *The Blessed Damozel* 126, *127*; *La Ghirlandata* 129; *Prosperine* 188, *189*; *Venus Verticordia* 129
Rubens, Sir Peter Paul, *Honeysuckle Bower* 128, *129*
Ruprecht, H.J., Trunk and roots of a pine tree 20, *21*
Ruysch, Rachel (attrib.), *Vanity* 202, 212, *212*

S
saffron 106
Saint-Exupéry, Antoine de, *The Little Prince* 32, *32*
Samhain festival 165
Santorini frescoes 106, *107*
sarcophaguses *see* coffins and sarcophaguses
Sargent, John Singer: *Carnation, Lily, Lily, Rose* 111, *111*; *Cypress Trees at San Vigilio* 51
Saturn (god) 60
Schongauer, Martin 69; *The Flight into Egypt* 69, 201
Segatori, Agostina 150
Selene and Endymion (mythological figures) 138, *138*
Seligmann, J.M., *Anemone plant* 92, *93*
Selznick, Brian, *Big Tree* 7, 31, *31*
Semele (mythological figure) 212
Sennedjem (Ancient Egyptian artisan) 30, 214, *218*, 219
Set (god) 214
Severeyns, G., *Strawberries* 172, *173*
sexual symbolism 54, 90, 92, 96, 136, 156, 160, 164, 168, 174, 182, 196
Shakespeare, William 150; *A Midsummer Night's Dream* 150; *As You Like It* 52
Siddal, Elizabeth 140, *140*
Silenus (god) 159
Sinclair, Thomas S., *Thomas's Elm* 86, *86*
Sir Gawain and the Green Knight (poem) 60
sleep 73, 130, 132, 138, 148

Smith, Carlton Alfred, *Christmas Eve* 60, *61*
Socrates 44, *45*
Solomon, King 38, 162
Sowerby, Charlotte, *Lilium speciosum* 124, *125*
Sowerby, James: *Cyclamen* 108, *108*; *Foxglove* 113, *113*
Spencer, Sir Stanley: *The Dustman* 160, *160*; *The Resurrection, Cookham* 126
Spenser, Edmund 150; *Faërie Queene* 219
Spinola Hours (illuminated manuscript) 95
spirals, logarithmic 73
squash (*Cucurbita*) 162, 194
Stella, Joseph, *Flowers, Italy* 90, *91*
strawberry (*Fragaria*) 15, 48, 145, **172–3**
Suffolk, Charles Brandon, 1st Duke of 166, *167*
sun and solar symbolism 28, 30, 34, 42, 45, 90, 104, 114, 132, 146, 162
sunflower (*Helianthus*) 12, 73, 98, 104, **114–17**, 146
Surrealism 168–9, 175, 192
sycamore (*Acer pseudoplatanus* / *Ficus sycomorus*) 8, 22, **30–1**
Syrinx (nymph) 215

T
Tacuinum sanitatis (health handbook) 196, *196*, 197
Talbot, William Henry Fox, *Two Plant Specimens* 7
Tanning, Dorothea: *Another Language of Flowers* 92, *92*; *Eine Kleine Nachtmusik* 114–15, *115*
tattoos 102, 205, 212
Taylor, Jason deCaires 180
Teeter, Emily 218
Theophrastus 108, 110
theosophy 104
thistle (*Carduus, Cirsium* and other genera) 6, *12*, **102–3**, 166–7
Thomé, Otto Wilhelm, *Zea Mays* 224, *224*
Thor (god) 48, 79
Three Graces (goddesses) 144
Tiberius, Roman Emperor 206
Titanic, RMS 159
tomato (*Solanum lycopersicum*) 16, **194–5**
tombs *see* graves, tombs and cemeteries
Torah 67, 82
Torczyner, Harry 175
Tree of Knowledge 6, 7, 22, 54, 187, 190

INDEX 239

Tree of Life 22–3, 28, 30, 68, 79, 86, 204
Trinity, Holy 94, 124, 127, 172, 184, 212
tulip (*Tulipa*) 13, **146–7**
Tura, Cosmè, *Madonna and Child in a Garden* 40, *41*
Turpin, P.J.F., *Baobab* 32, *32*
Tutankhamun (pharaoh) 38, 132, 138, 159
Twining, Elizabeth, *Cucurbitaceae* 162, *163*

U
Ubertini, Cesare: *Apium graveolens L.* 158, *159*; *Crithmum maritimum* 171, *171*; *Cucurbita aspera Pyriformis* 164, *164*; *Raphanus minor* 192, 193
Underworld 50–1, 60, 86, 159, 187; *see also* Hades
Unicorn Tapestries *1*, 48, 49, 60, *61*, 188, *188*, 189

V
Valentine's Day 92, 108
van Bruggen, Coosje, *Geometric Apple Core* 177, *177*
van der Goes, Hugo, altarpieces 94, 95, *95*, 121, 218

van Dyck, Sir Anthony 114; *Self-Portrait with a Sunflower* 114, 117
van Eyck, Jan, *The Arnolfini Portrait* 184, *185*
van Gogh, Vincent 104, 115, 116; *Almond Blossom* 76, 77; *Basket of Pansies* 150, *151*; *Garden with Weeping Willow* 83; *Giant Peacock Moth* 96, *97*; *Grapes, Lemons, Pears and Apples* 154, *155*; *Irises* 120, *120*, *121*; *Olive Trees* 66, *67*; *Portrait of Dr Gachet* 112, *112*, 113; *The Potato Eaters* 198–9, *198*; *The Starry Night* 51
van Houtte, Louis, *Nymphaea stellata* 133, *133*
van Huysum, J. 59, 129
van Oosterwyck, Maria, *Bouquet of Flowers in a Vase* 146, *147*
van Os, Maria Margaretha, *Still Life with Lemon and Cut Glass* 43, *43*
van Utrecht, Adriaen, *An amorous couple* 154, *155*
Vandamme, J., *Viola tricolor* 150, 151
vanitas paintings 93, 110, 146, 182, 184, 212, 224
Vayron, Lith, Baobab (*Adansonia digitata*) 32, *33*

Veneziano, Paolo, *Madonna of the Poppy* 140, 141
Venus (goddess) 65, *65*, 93, 98, 98–9
Vertumnus (god) 98
victory, symbols of 65, 66, 68, 159
Villafane, Ray 165
violet (*Viola*) 13, 70, 95, **148–9**, 150
Virgil 27; *Aeneid* 68; *Georgics* 138
virginity, symbols of 40, 41, 74, 90
Vreugdenhil, J., *Solanum tuberosum* 199, *199*

W
Walcott, Mary Vaux, Beaked Hazelnut 49
Walpole, Frederick A., *Aquilegia nikolicii* 94, *94*
Walpole, Horace, 4th Earl of Orford 166
Warhol, Andy, *Campbell's Soup Cans* 194, *195*
Waterhouse, John William, *The Awakening of Adonis* 92, 93, *93*
Watts, James, *Acacia oxycedrus* 28, *29*

weddings and marriage 28, 40–1, 91, 102, 110, 128, 184, *185*, 189
wheat (*Triticum*) 17, 53, 95, 138, 198, 199, 204, 208, **218–21**
Whitman, Walt, *Leaves of Grass* 208
Wilde, Oscar 114, 117
Wilkinson, Charles K. 69, 214, 219
willow (*Salix*) 11, **82–3**
Wilson, Matthew 132
wine 132, 174, 189, 212, 222
Withers, Augusta, Tree carnation *110*, 111
Wood, Grant: *Corn Cob Chandelier* 224, 225, *225*; *Corn Room* 225
Wordsworth, William 150
World Trees 24, 58, 78, 84, 174

Y
yew (*Taxus baccata*) 11, 24, **84–5**
Yonge, Charlotte M., *Triticum aestivum* 219, *219*

Z
Zephyrus (god) 118
Zeus (god) 42, 48, 54, 77, 78, 148–9, 174, 187, 212

Hope B. Werness is an Art Historian specializing in non-Western and modern European art. She has taught for over thirty years at California State University, Stanislaus. Her previous books include *The Continuum Encyclopedia of Native Art* (2000) and *The Encyclopedia of Animal Symbolism in World Art* (2006).

Front cover: Sandro Botticelli, *The Birth of Venus* (detail), c. 1495. Tempera on canvas, 172.5 × 278.5 cm (68 × 109 ¾ in). Uffizi Galleries, Florence (1890 n.878).

Spine: S. Watts after Mills, *Rosa gallica*, from Benjamin Maund's *The Botanic Garden*, Simkin & Marshall, 1825; Francis Sansom after Sydenham Edwards, *Robinia hispida, Rose acacia* from *The New Botanic Garden*, T. Bensley for John Stockdale, 1812; S. Watts after E.D. Smith, *Rosa centifolia*, from Benjamin Maund's *The Botanic Garden*, Simkin & Marshall, 1825.

First published in the United Kingdom in 2025 by Thames & Hudson Ltd, 6–24 Britannia Street, London WC1X 9JD

The Secret Language of Plants: Art, Nature & Symbolism © 2025 Thames & Hudson Ltd, London

Text © 2025 Hope B. Werness

All Rights Reserved. No part of this publication may be reproduced or transmitted in any form or by any means, electronic or mechanical, including photocopy, recording or any other information storage and retrieval system, without prior permission in writing from the publisher.

EU Authorized Representative: Interart S.A.R.L., 19 rue Charles Auray, 93500 Pantin, Paris, France
productsafety@thameshudson.co.uk
interart.fr

A CIP catalogue record for this book is available from the British Library

ISBN 978-0-500-02817-9
02

Printed and bound in Slovenia by DZS-Grafik d.o.o.

MIX
Paper | Supporting responsible forestry
FSC® C106600

Be the first to know about our new releases, exclusive content and author events by visiting
thamesandhudson.com
thamesandhudsonusa.com
thamesandhudson.com.au